NICARAGUA

NICAGUA

REVOLUTION IN
THE FAMILY

Shirley Christian

VINTAGE BOOKS
A DIVISION OF RANDOM HOUSE
NEW YORK

First Vintage Books Edition, June 1986

Copyright © 1985, 1986 by Shirley Christian

All rights reserved under International and Pan-American Copyright
Conventions. Published in the United States by Random House, Inc.,
New York, and simultaneously in Canada by Random House of
Canada Limited, Toronto. Originally published by
Random House, Inc., in 1985.

Library of Congress Cataloging-in-Publication Data

Christian, Shirley, 1938–
Nicaragua, revolution in the family.

Bibliography: p.
Includes index.
1. Nicaragua—History—1979–   2. Nicaragua—
History—Revolution, 1979. 3. Nicaragua—History—
1937–1979. I. Title.
F1528.C47 1986   972.85'053   85-40970
ISBN 0–394–74457–8 (pbk.)

Manufactured in the United States of America

Cover photograph by Keith Gunnar

CONTENTS

vi

MAJOR FIGURES

Many names figure in this book, and since most English-speaking people think that Spanish names are incredibly confusing, some explanation is in order. In fact, Spanish names are very logical and provide much more information about the person than do English names. It is customary to use both the father's and mother's last names, so the typical full name will appear as one given name and two surnames. But there are exceptions, most of which have to do with personal preference. Some people do not use their mother's name except on legal documents, and it is often dropped on second reference in newspapers and other printed material of general circulation. In addition, some people use both a first name and a middle name along with two last names; this makes four names. And some use both a first and a middle name, but only their paternal surname. Finally, when a woman marries she usually drops her mother's last name and adds her husband's last name, meaning the one he received from his father.

All of this can best be demonstrated with one family that figures prominently in this book. Pedro Joaquín Chamorro Cardenal, whose murder in 1978 unified Nicaraguans against the Somoza regime, was the publisher of the newspaper *La Prensa.* His "last name" in the English sense was Chamorro, his father's family name. Cardenal was his mother's family name. In addition, he was one of those Nicaraguans who use both a first and a middle name—Pedro Joaquín. His older son, Pedro Joaquín Chamorro Barrios, inherited his father's given names as well as his father's paternal surname and received his second surname, Barrios, from his mother. Her name is Violeta Barrios de Chamorro. She uses just one given name, Violeta; Barrios is her maiden name and Chamorro her married name.

The following list of major figures in the book, both Nicaraguans and other nationalities, should further help to clarify the name situation by presenting the "last name" in bold-faced letters. It does not pretend to include everyone of importance but rather to identify those who figure in the book over extended periods or those who should be recognized in order to follow the events.

Bayardo **Arce**   Member of the Sandinista National Directorate, influential in ideological and foreign affairs questions

Enrique **Bermúdez**   Former Nicaraguan National Guard colonel and prominent military member of the Nicaraguan Democratic Force (FDN), the largest anti-Sandinista guerrilla force

Tomás **Borge**   A founding *comandante* of the Sandinista Front of National Liberation (FSLN), member of its National Directorate, minister of interior

William P. **Bowdler**   Special U.S. envoy, directed 1978 mediation between Anastasio Somoza Debayle and opposition, Assistant Secretary of State for Inter-American Affairs 1980–1981

Adolfo **Calero** Portocarrero   Democratic Conservative Party leader and opponent of Somoza, later opposed Sandinistas, went into exile 1983, became military and political leader of the Honduran-based Nicaraguan Democratic Force (FDN)

Rodrigo **Carazo**   President of Costa Rica 1978–1982

Ernesto **Cardenal**   Priest who actively assisted Sandinista Front during its guerrilla days, Christian Marxist, minister of culture

Fernando **Cardenal**   Jesuit priest, brother of Ernesto, advocate of liberation theology, held various Sandinista government posts, including minister of education

José Francisco **Cardenal**   Building contractor and president of the Chamber of Construction, went into exile in 1980, one of the founders of the Nicaraguan Democratic Force (FDN)

Luis **Carrión** Cruz   Member of Sandinista National Directorate, vice-minister of interior

Alfredo **César**   Businessman who joined FSLN as combatant during insurrection, later president of the Central Bank, went into exile 1983

Pedro Joaquín **Chamorro** Cardenal   Publisher of *La Prensa*, murdered 1978

Carlos Fernando **Chamorro** Barrios   Younger son of Chamorro Cardenal; editor of Sandinista newspaper *Barricada*

Pedro Joaquín **Chamorro** Barrios   Older son of Chamorro Cardenal, co-editor of *La Prensa* until moving to Costa Rica at the end of 1984

Violeta Barrios de **Chamorro**   Widow of Pedro Joaquín Chamorro Cardenal, member of government junta 1979–1980

Xavier **Chamorro** Cardenal   A younger brother of Pedro Joaquín Chamorro Cardenal, publisher of *El Nuevo Diario*

Jaime **Chamorro** Cardenal   Another younger brother of Pedro Joaquín Chamorro Cardenal, business manager of *La Prensa*

Arturo José **Cruz**   Member of *Los Doce* (the Group of Twelve), later president of the Central Bank, member of the government junta, ambassador to the United States, led opposition coalition in the 1984 presidential campaign

Joaquín **Cuadra** Chamorro   Member of the Group of Twelve, later minister of finance

Joaquín **Cuadra** Lacayo   Son of Cuadra Chamorro, key leader in Sandinista internal front during insurrection, later chief of staff of Sandinista Popular Army

Miguel **d' Escoto**   Maryknoll priest, member of the Group of Twelve, later foreign minister

Enrique **Dreyfus**   President of the Superior Council of Private Enterprise (COSEP) 1979–1983

Juan José (Johnny) **Echeverría** Brealey   Minister of public security of Costa Rica 1978–1980

Thomas O. **Enders**   U.S. Assistant Secretary of State for Inter-American Affairs 1981–1983

Steadman Fagoth Müller   Miskito Indian leader, went into exile in Honduras 1981 and began to lead other exiled Miskitos in armed actions against Sandinista army in Atlantic Coast region

Carlos **Fonseca** Amador   Principal founder of the Sandinista Front of National Liberation (FSLN), killed by the National Guard 1976

José Esteban **González**   National coordinator of the Permanent Commission for Human Rights of Nicaragua, went into exile 1981

Luis **Herrera** Campíns   President of Venezuela 1979–1983

Colonel Federico **Mejía**   Nicaraguan National Guard director for a day and a half after the departure of Somoza Debayle on July 17, 1979

Uriel **Molina**   Parish priest who played a major role in the intellectual formation of guerrilla leaders for the FSLN during the Somoza years, later a leading exponent of liberation theology and director of the Valdivieso Center for Ecumenical Reflection

Carlos **Nuñez**   Member of Sandinista National Directorate, president of Council of State

Monsignor Miguel **Obando** y Bravo   Roman Catholic Archbishop of Managua, elevated to Cardinal in 1985

Daniel **Ortega** Saavedra   Member of Sandinista National Directorate, member of junta 1979–1984, elected president November 4, 1984

Humberto **Ortega** Saavedra   Member of Sandinista National Directorate, minister of defense and commander of the army

Luis **Pallais** Debayle   First cousin of Luis and Anastasio Somoza Debayle, key figure in Liberal Party affairs prior to fall of Somoza regime

Robert **Pastor**   Latin American specialist on the National Security Council during the Carter administration, 1976–1980

Edén **Pastora** Gómez   Sandinista *comandante* who captured the National Palace in August 1978, went into exile 1981, began armed actions against the FSLN in 1983 as military leader of the Democratic Revolutionary Alliance (ARDE)

Carlos Andrés **Pérez**   President of Venezuela 1975–1979, major figure in the Socialist International

Leonel **Poveda**   Prominent military figure in the Sandinista Southern Front during insurrection, later held various government posts, went into exile 1982

Lawrence **Pezzullo**   U.S. ambassador to Nicaragua 1979–1981

Sergio **Ramírez** Mercado   Civilian member of the FSLN, key strategist in political aspects of the insurrection, later member of the government junta, elected vice president 1984

Ismael **Reyes** President of the Red Cross and president of the Chamber of Industry, went into exile 1983 after government intervention in the Red Cross and confiscation of his factory and other property

Brooklyn **Rivera** Miskito Indian leader, went into exile 1981, later joined anti-Sandinista forces in Costa Rica led by Edén Pastora and Alfonso Robelo

Alfonso **Robelo** Callejas Business leader at the forefront of opposition to Somoza rule from 1974 onward, member of the government junta 1979–1980, went into exile 1982, became political leader of the Costa Rican-based Democratic Revolutionary Alliance (ARDE)

Henry **Ruiz** Member of Sandinista National Directorate, minister of planning

Jorge **Salazar** Arguello Private farm and business leader slain by state security agents in 1980

Augusto César **Sandino** Liberal general in the Liberal-Conservative wars of the 1920s, subsequently opposed U.S. Marine intervention, executed by National Guard firing squad in 1934

Mauricio **Solaun** U.S. ambassador to Nicaragua 1977–79

Anastasio (Tacho) **Somoza** García The first Somoza to rule Nicaragua, became National Guard director in 1933, assassinated 1956

Luis **Somoza** Debayle A son of Somoza García, succeeded his father as president, died 1967

Anastasio (Tachito, later Tacho) **Somoza** Debayle Youngest son of Somoza García, succeeded his brother and ruled Nicaragua until his overthrow in 1979, assassinated in Paraguay 1980

Anastasio (Tachito) **Somoza** Portocarrero Eldest son of Anastasio Somoza Debayle, National Guard officer during the 1978–1979 insurrection

Victor **Tirado** Mexican-born member of Sandinista National Directorate, prominent during insurrection but considered least influential of the nine *comandantes* once in power

General Omar **Torrijos** Panamanian strongman until his death in a plane crash in 1982

Carlos **Tünnermann** Bernheim Member of the Group of Twelve, later minister of education, then ambassador to Washington

Francisco **Urcuyo** Maliaño   President of Nicaragua for a day and a half after the departure of Somoza Debayle on July 17, 1979

Viron P. **Vaky**   U.S. Assistant Secretary of State for Inter-American Affairs 1978–1980

Jaime **Wheelock** Román   Member of Sandinista National Directorate, minister of agriculture

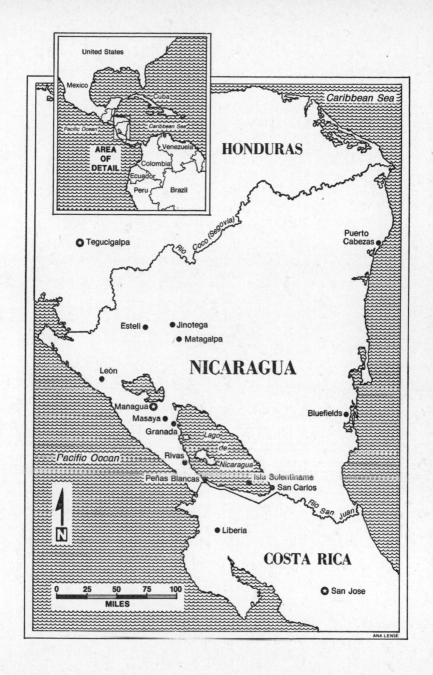

NICARAGUA

1

THE BAGGAGE OF
THE PAST

1821 to 1941

In his eighty-second year, the past almost caught up with Leopoldo Salazar Amador. As the rebel forces fighting under the banner of the Sandinista National Liberation Front moved into the Matagalpa region of north-central Nicaragua in February 1979, they ambushed and killed Federico Davidson Blanco, another of the original officers of the Nicaraguan National Guard and a participant in the killing of Augusto César Sandino in 1934. Shortly thereafter, Salazar decided to flee the country, partly out of fear that the Sandinistas planned to seek vengeance against all former Guardsmen and partly because, when Sandinista guerrillas set up camp on his farm, Salazar got into a scuffle with some of them and was slightly hurt.

In Costa Rica, just before Christmas 1983, I met Leo Salazar and was struck by the way his life—with relatively little design—had been caught up in the significant events of Nicaragua's twentieth-century history. The writing and rewriting of history has left us with confusion about cause, effect, and motivation in a past marked by almost continual warfare between and within political parties and by frequent foreign interventions, including the on and off presence of U.S. Marines over a twenty-four-year period. Salazar, while admittedly having his biases, offers a view of how many of the principals thought at a crucial time in Nicaraguan history. Although aware of the critical way people later came to view events of that period, he explains them mostly in the light of the past, not the present.

That is why I decided to use his story to help set the stage for this book, to blend the personal recollections of a still marvelously alert mind with the published accounts and interpretations of Nicaragua's yesterdays. Even those who may see in him the remnants of a misguided old order will find that his account unmasks many of the abstractions created by the passage of time.

Nicaragua is one of the least populous countries in Spanish America, with only about three million people in 1984. Most of them are clustered within a relatively small area on the Pacific side of the country. The vast department [province] of Zelaya on the Atlantic, or Caribbean, Coast, contains more than half of Nicaragua's land, but it is an almost unpenetrated region of timber and gold mines inhabited by fewer than three hundred thousand people. Once part of the Miskito Indian kingdom that was a British protectorate for two centuries, the region is inhabited primarily by Miskito Indians and descendants of black migrants or slaves from Caribbean islands. The people on the populous Pacific side are either whites, descended from Spaniards or other Europeans, or are *ladinos,* of mixed Spanish and Indian ancestry.

Nicaragua, then, is a small society and an inbred one, or really two such societies, one on the Pacific side, the other on the Atlantic. It seems you could easily count all of the last names in the country, though having the same last name does not automatically put two people on the same side of any issue. People who slander one another, conspire to destroy one another politically or economically, or threaten to shoot one another are often cousins, or married to cousins. Frequently, first cousins are married to each other. The justifications that are usually offered for such close marriages are that they keep landholdings in the family or that they protect descendants of the old Spanish families from marrying beneath themselves, although this doesn't explain why such marriages are common among the poor as well as the affluent. A blood or marital connection does sometimes cause people to temper their feuds before they become mortal. Making a disparaging remark about another person to almost anyone is dangerous because the person you are talking to could be his relative and childhood friend. On the other hand, saying something good about the third person may bring a detailed accounting of an indiscretion he committed twenty years earlier. At times the greater political and social questions seem irrelevant.

The nineteenth and early twentieth centuries in Nicaragua, beginning soon after independence from Spain in 1821, were marked by warfare between the two political parties that then dominated public life throughout Central America—the Liberals and the Conservatives. The main philosophical difference between them was their attitude toward the Roman Catholic Church, with the Conservatives, in general, believing the Church should have a lot of influence in government, and the Liberals thinking it ought to confine its interests to the soul. Sometimes the Liberals talked about social reform, but not a great deal. The Liberals were also identified more with the supposedly modernizing world of commerce while the Conservatives were identified more with big landholdings and feudalism, though there were Conservatives who were merchants and Liberals who owned large tracts of land.

The warfare was not generally related to these differences in philosophy. Rather, it was about power and the possibilities that power offered for enrichment. The two groups functioned more like tribes or armies than political parties, and those who aspired to public office needed the talents of a warlord more than those of a political thinker. The two parties had individual capitals, which each considered the national capital. León, the second largest city, was the Liberal stronghold, and Granada was the Conservative center, but the warfare between them ranged all over the country. Managua was eventually selected as the center of government in the hope that it might prove a neutral site. In large measure it was this inability to resolve Conservative-Liberal disputes peacefully that brought foreign intervention, either by governments or adventurers. In general, it cannot be said that the United States government found either the Liberals or the Conservatives more to its liking. Like the Nicaraguans themselves, it tended to find the personalities more compelling.

In 1855 the Liberals hired an American adventurer, William Walker, and his small mercenary army, to fight on their side against the Conservatives. Walker, a physician and lawyer from Tennessee who had earlier tried to conquer northern Mexico, landed on the Pacific Coast of Nicaragua with fifty-eight men and quickly took control of the Nicaraguan army and the entire country. He had himself elected president, made plans to institute slavery, and grabbed the railroad-steamship line that Cornelius Vanderbilt had built across Nicaragua to transport people from one ocean to the other, a route especially popular among people from the eastern United States who were going to California. This angered the other Central American nations as well as Vanderbilt and the British government, which was still exercising influence on the Atlantic Coast. Vanderbilt and the British provided guns to the Costa Rican government, which organized an 18,000-man army to invade Nicaragua. Walker and his army, grown to 1,200 men, were forced into exile on May 1, 1857. Subsequent attempts by Walker to return to Central America ended with his capture by the British navy and his demise before a Honduran firing squad on September 12, 1860.

For nearly forty years after the defeat of Walker there was relative peace in Nicaragua under a succession of Conservative presidents. Then, in 1893 a Liberal, José Santos Zelaya, became president and turned his regime into an unpleasant dictatorship. He also meddled in the affairs of other Central American nations and granted concessions to economic interests from various countries. When the United States bypassed Nicaragua in favor of Panama for the canal site, he tried to get other governments to build a canal across Nicaragua. And he executed a couple of American mercenaries captured while serving with rebel forces.

It was during the Zelaya era that Leo Salazar was born, in El Salvador, in 1897, of Nicaraguan parents.

"My father studied banking in England and France. The Medina family, who founded these English banks in Central America, they took my father to England and France and educated him as a banker. So my father was sent to El Salvador as the first manager of the Bank of London, and that is why I was born in Salvador, and my brother too. But after a few years of banking in El Salvador, my mother's mother was ill—she finally died of cancer—and my mother begged Dad to come back to Nicaragua before her mother died. So, they came back to Matagalpa.

"He bought this beautiful tract of Indian land, called, later on, Santa Emilia, for my sister, Emilia, and built himself this beautiful plantation. We had three thousand manzanas, which is [nearly] six thousand acres, of beautiful pasture, and we had at least three thousand head of cattle, a beautiful home. It was really a showplace . . . It was not bought from the Indians, but from the government. That particular place hadn't been given [deeded] to the Indians before by the king of Spain, so my Dad got hold of it. It was a showplace, I can tell you."

But the Salazars were of the then-opposition Conservative Party, and almost before he knew how to read, the boy had begun to learn first-hand about Nicaraguan politics.

"President Zelaya happened to make a visit to Matagalpa and he had already grabbed, down by the volcano Momotombo, [the farms] La California, El Diamante, and, in Chinandega, Campusano—a huge place, owned by Conservatives, aristocrats from Granada, and exiled them. He grabbed their properties. So these Liberals in Matagalpa, they told him, 'Look here, there's a beautiful property here, it belongs to Don Leopoldo. Why don't you get hold of that?' They kept at it, and he said, 'All right, I'll get hold of it. I'll get him out of the country . . .' But my mother's first cousin overheard the conversation —she was married to the leading Liberal of Matagalpa—so she told my mother what they were planning. So my mother told Dad, and Dad went to Mr. Spencer Richardson, the American consul, and said, 'Look here, I know you're looking for a place. Here's mine. I'll give it to you, whatever you want to pay, but I want to get out of Nicaragua.' So Mr. Richardson bought the place, paid my father eighty-seven thousand dollars, which was giving it away . . . but with the understanding that nobody would know it was sold to him, that the deed could not be registered until we left [the port of] Corinto. So, it began to circulate that the Salazar family was going to California to place the children in school . . . But as soon as we left Corinto—by boat in those days—the telegram, in code, went to Mr. Richardson from Corinto telling him to register the deed.

"And Zelaya, oh, he was furious. But he couldn't do anything because, fortunately, we had what you call the 'Big Stick' policy. That was the best policy that we have ever had in Nicaragua. This good, friendly, wishy-washy policy that we have later on has ruined us, and it ruined the American prestige in Nicaragua. Before, we used to respect Americans. They don't anymore. Because of this damned wishy-washy policy."

The Salazar family left Nicaragua in 1906. Leo was nine years old. The passenger-and-cargo ship on which they traveled, the *Pacific*

Mail, sailed slowly up the West Coast of Central America, then Mexico and California to San Francisco, at one point foundering for a week or longer with mechanical trouble while the food gave out. On April 18, 1906, the week before the *Pacific Mail* arrived in port, San Francisco suffered its most famous natural disaster.

"The earthquake was on a Wednesday, and we arrived there the following Monday. I walked over the hot, smoking ruins of San Francisco. A lot of buildings were still burning. We walked all the way from the wharves at Third and Townsend way up to Van Ness Avenue with bags and everything, and then we couldn't find a place to sleep. So, we finally came to a little dinky hotel, Hotel Hamlin, and they let us a room, and we all slept on the floor. What did we eat? Apples. That's what we had to eat. Then, Dad began looking for a place in Oakland.

"Oakland was full of refugees. So we finally landed in this little place called Fruitvale adjoining Oakland, which is now all Oakland. Fruitvale, then, was this beautiful Fruitvale Avenue with these mansions on each side of very rich people. And a Mrs. Darling, who had lost her husband and beautiful home in San Francisco, but they had this kind of like a country place to come and spend weekends at the farthest end of Fruitvale Avenue. My Dad went there and told her the sad story, that he didn't know what to do with his family, and she took us in as boarders, and that's how we came to live in Fruitvale. Later on, we rented a house. And when my mother died, she—Mrs. Darling —became our governess. She raised us . . . She was a wonderful woman."

The family was not to return to Nicaragua for sixteen years, by which time Leo was grown and educated. The normal turmoil had continued in Nicaragua during the family's absence. In 1909, opponents of President Zelaya within his own party joined Conservatives in a revolt that set off a new civil war and produced the first direct U.S. military intervention. Four hundred Marines landed briefly at Bluefields on the Atlantic Coast to help rebel forces control the town. Zelaya resigned, the presidency was negotiated for one of the dissident Liberal generals and the vice presidency for a Conservative, and the Marines went home at the end of the year. In 1912 a new rebellion brought the Marines back, and by October, Marine strength in Nicaragua had reached 2,700. The rebellion was suppressed, but when the Marines withdrew this time they left behind a hundred-man contingent, which supervised elections in 1924 and withdrew in August 1925. The elections brought Carlos Solórzano, a Conservative, into the presidency and Juan Bautista Sacasa, a Liberal, into the vice presidency.

Two and a half months after the Marines departed in 1925, General Emiliano Chamorro, the dominant Conservative personality of the time, seized power. Liberal uprisings against Chamorro followed, and Marines landed at Bluefields twice in 1926. Between the two Marine landings, Liberal General José María Moncada rallied his troops on the Atlantic Coast on behalf of the presidential claim of the former vice president, Juan Bautista Sacasa, who was in exile. Chamorro, unable to win U.S. backing, resigned the presidency on October 30, and Adolfo Díaz, a Conservative former president, who had invited the Marine landing of 1912, was named president. However, former Vice President Sacasa returned from Mexico with that country's backing for the presidency, including arms and ammunition, and set up a "constitutional" government in Puerto Cabezas under the protection of General Moncada. This time the ensuing warfare stretched out. The end of 1926 and beginning of 1927 saw a significant buildup in Marines, and also U.S. sailors, with landings on both coasts, though U.S. forces generally avoided fighting. The primary intentions of the United States were to protect foreign holdings, those of Americans and others, and keep the ports and customs houses open, but Washington was also nervous about Sacasa's ties to Mexico, which had recently taken a leftward turn under its revolutionary government.

During this period, two promising young generals appeared on the Liberal side of the struggle under the military leadership of Moncada. One, Anastasio Somoza García, showed more political shrewdness than military aptitude, while the other, Augusto César Sandino, demonstrated a degree of fortitude on the battlefields. Somoza García, several of whose ancestors had been flamboyant members of the Liberal armies of the nineteenth century, had turned to political warfare after failing at several business ventures. Sandino, the illegitimate but recognized son of an affluent landowner, had joined the Liberals after working as a mechanic in Honduras and Guatemala and in the office of an American oil company in Tampico, Mexico, where he read a great deal and was impressed by the growth of the Mexican labor movement.

President Calvin Coolidge sent Henry L. Stimson to Nicaragua in 1927 to try to resolve the latest crisis, and Somoza, who had attended business school in Philadelphia and spoke English, gave up fighting to become Stimson's interpreter. Stimson worked out an agreement whereby the Liberals, under General Moncada, would be given political control of six departments, or provinces, in return for laying down their arms, and the United States would supervise the 1928 elections. Another part of the peace plan was the decision to organize a non-political National Guard under American officers. The Conservatives, on the defensive militarily, accepted. The Liberal politicians, who thought they would win it all if their forces continued to fight, wanted to refuse. Their top general, Moncada, finally agreed after Stimson made it known that the Liberal troops would have to fight the United States if they persisted. There was also an offer of ten dollars for each weapon turned in, which Moncada feared would become an invitation for desertions if he held out. The agreement became known as the Peace of Tipitapa because Stimson and Moncada met under a black-thorn tree in the small town of Tipitapa, a few miles east of Managua. After several days of consideration, all but one of Moncada's generals signed a telegram of acceptance on May 12, 1927. The holdout was Sandino, to whom Moncada had offered the governorship of the department of Jinotega, adjacent to Matagalpa, and ten dollars a day for all the time he had spent in the Liberal army.

Over the next few days, Sandino, fearing that his own troops would be tempted by the money offer, headed up into the mountains through the departments of Matagalpa and Jinotega. At San Rafael del Norte, just above the city of Jinotega, he made public his decision to reject the peace accord, sending a telegram accusing Moncada of betraying the Liberal cause, and announced that he would continue to fight.

Fighting this time meant going against the Marines, but the U.S. military leaders were in no hurry to begin shooting. Numerous telegrams were exchanged with Sandino. On at least two occasions Sandino said he would lay down his arms if the U.S. military would take over the Nicaraguan government and run it until the next elections. What rankled him was that the government should continue in the hands of a Conservative, Adolfo Díaz, until the 1928 elections. In one telegram, Sandino said an American military government was the *sine qua non* for his disarming. U.S. authorities would not agree to his demands, so the Peace of Tipitapa brought no peace. For the next five and a half years Marine forces and the National Guardsmen trained by them chased Sandino around the mountains of Nueva Segovia, Jinotega, and Matagalpa, alternately trying to blast him off his isolated peak, El Chipote, and negotiate peace with him.

Leo Salazar found himself in the midst of this turmoil. After his family's return from California when he was twenty-five, the young

Salazar bought a farm of his own, at Santa María de Ostuma in Matagalpa, where much of the fighting between Sandino's forces and the Marines and government troops was taking place. But it was chance, in the form of a frightened Englishman, that got him more directly involved. Charles Potter owned a big coffee and cattle farm in Matagalpa called La Fundadora.

"Mr. Potter invited me to come and spend the weekend with him and to help him with his payroll on Saturday because his manager, Hans Frankel, a German, had been sent for vacation in Germany and the old man wanted someone to help him, so I went to help him. But one day we went to the corral to make an inventory of the cattle and the bandits fired two machine guns at us—one from this side and one from this side, brrrr, brrrr. I almost saw the bullets flying past, so I dropped to the ground and grabbed Mr. Potter by his seat and threw him down and that saved him. But then he said, 'Leo, I can't take this racket. You stay here and you take over. I'm going back to England.' That's how I came to manage his properties. He owned not only La Fundadora but other ranches around . . ."

After the Peace of Tipitapa, about forty Marines were stationed on La Fundadora, and Salazar became a useful friend to the Marine post in the town of Matagalpa, the capital of the department. He provided the Marines with information and, along with other Matagalpa Conservatives, tried without success to get them to move quickly and decisively against Sandino and his men. He explained why: "Sandino came up north to the little town of San Ramón, just outside Matagalpa. And then he raided the plantation of my uncle, Salvador Amador, and the beautiful house with beautiful furnishings and everything was completely destroyed by Sandino. They wrecked everything . . . They became bandits. They were really bandits. It was right after Moncada turned in his arms. Then all the leading citizens of Matagalpa rushed over to Captain [Gilbert] Hatfield, and we told him, 'Look, this fellow is going to go off into the hills and he's going to become a bandit, and this is going to ruin Nicaragua. Please, send your Marines and capture him there in San Ramón. He's there right now, raiding my uncle's place.' So Captain Hatfield said, 'All right. I'm willing, but I have to consult Managua.' So he calls us about half an hour later, and he says, 'Look, a telegram . . . It says to avoid all possible bloodshed.'

"So then Sandino left San Ramón and raided Jinotega, sacked the town, stole everything, and then he kept on going, and then he was up in the hills, in Wiwilí, in Chipote, and all around. When he left

Tipitapa he had four hundred men, maybe less. But later on he had a couple of thousand because he began getting more and more because, you see, they became bandits. They raped, they stole, they murdered, and they burned. And they said that they were against the Americans, but why did they come and burn my brother's ranch and my ranch? And why was he raiding and killing poor Nicaraguans up there? That's why up north we don't like Sandino . . .

"While I was at Mr. Potter's, running his place, one day I went around—the Marines were there, but I used to go around seeing all the coffee trees and everything . . . I was alone going through the forest and all of a sudden I was captured by these bandits. They pulled me off my mule and they got hold of me and they called me *machista* and began swearing at me. *Machista* because they used to call the Americans *machos*—for the light hair, like they do in Costa Rica.* So, then, this group over here, they threw me against that group over there, and then they pointed their bayonets like that and then I fell on them. And I was all pierced. I was so terrified that I lost my speech. I couldn't talk."

The attackers announced that they were going to perform a *corte de chaleco*—a vest cut—on him. It meant chopping off the head first, then the arms at the shoulders, then carving a design on the chest.

"But then this little dinky fellow—he was called Pablito Viegas—he was the one who was going to cut my throat. But then he couldn't wait. He said, 'I'm going to start now,' and he took his machete and cut here a little bit. See? As I say I couldn't talk, but when I felt this cut here—even now, when I shave, I can't stand this place. So when he began cutting here I grabbed his machete and pulled it down before he could slash my throat. Then my speech came back, and I said, 'Respect me. I'm a Nicaraguan like you are.' And then they threw me around and everything, but then I could talk. I said, 'Look here, furthermore, I have given you money. Which I can prove.' Because Mr. Potter had told me that whenever they wanted any money to give it to them. Give them anything. So, then, the head man—he was Colonel Alberto Gadea, chief communications officer of Sandino—we talked and talked and talked. That was at ten o'clock in the morning. By five o'clock in the afternoon my head was splitting, so I said, 'You'll have to let me go back because my [servant] boy, whom I sent

---

*A *machista* was someone who liked the Americans. This is a different use of the term *macho* from that in most Spanish-speaking countries.

to look at my potato patch, will go to La Fundadora and report that I'm lost, and then you'll have the Marines coming out here after me.' So they let me go home."

As Sandino withdrew into Nueva Segovia, then and now an isolated mountain fortress, the Marines sent an expedition force of fifty men to try to take control of the region. The troops left Managua on May 31, 1927, under Major Harold Clifton Pierce. They stopped in Matagalpa to outfit, then continued to climb into the mountains. At Ocotal they left Captain Hatfield and ten Marines to protect the town while Pierce and his troops climbed higher.

Hatfield received a telegram from Sandino on June 25, from San Fernando, a few miles to the northeast. A series of telegrams was then exchanged by the two men. At first there were taunts from Sandino, and Hatfield responded diplomatically with pleas for Sandino to come and talk with the Marines under a guarantee of safety. Hatfield said the Marines wanted only to bring peace and free elections to Nicaragua. Sandino invited Hatfield to come talk to him, but said to make his will first and closed by saying he wanted "to put you in a handsome tomb with beautiful bouquets of flowers." That brought a tough response from Hatfield. "If words were bullets and phrases were soldiers, you would be a field marshal instead of a mule thief," he wired, and called Sandino a "conceited maniac." In early July, Hatfield's command was beefed up with about thirty additional Marines and forty-eight Nicaraguan troops comprising the first company to be trained for the new National Guard, giving him about one hundred men total. At the end of June, Sandino seized the American-owned San Albino gold mine and from there proclaimed that he was on the march. On July 11, Hatfield sent him another telegram urging that he "surrender with honor" and play a meaningful role in the future of his country or be hunted down as a bandit with a price on his head. Hatfield said he expected Sandino in Ocotal by eight in the morning on July 14, 1927—to talk. Sandino replied that he would not give up, that he wanted a *patria libre o morir*—a free fatherland or die.

Hatfield was expecting what came next, in part because he noticed that Liberal families in Ocotal began hiding valuables and securing their homes. He assumed that they were Sandino sympathizers and had been forewarned. At about one in the morning on July 16, Sandino and his troops swooped down on Ocotal for their first battle with the Marines. Sandino had a core of about sixty officers and men, plus about six hundred peasants armed with machetes or other swords, who served mainly as a cheering squad and as pillagers. Both sides fought hard, with Sandino's auxiliaries taking time out to sack most of the Conservative homes in town and kill a few Conservative enemies.

What turned the tide of battle in favor of the Marines and the government troops was the appearance at midmorning of five De Havilland airplanes piloted by Marines. Each plane carried four bombs and twelve hundred pounds of machine gun ammunition. Locating rebel concentrations, they dived to as low as three hundred feet from the ground, firing their machine guns on the way down, then dropping their bombs. Neill Macaulay, in *The Sandino Affair*, perhaps the best researched study of the period, said it was the first organized dive-bombing attack in history. At the end of the day, the rebels withdrew. Sandino later claimed that had it not been for the planes, he would have wiped out the Marines at Ocotal. It was the first time warplanes had been seen in action in Nicaragua, and the noise, he said, was especially frightening to the Indians among his troops.

Hatfield counted the Marine losses at one dead and one wounded, while the National Guard had three wounded and four captured. He estimated Sandino's losses very high because of the bombings and noted that most of the Liberal families in town buried people in the days immediately after the battle. But Sandino was not deterred. He said later that the battle of Ocotal served as a combat school for him and his forces.

The battle of Ocotal was followed by several indecisive encounters. Then Sandino gathered his men on El Chipote, a nearly four-thousand-foot mountain in Nueva Segovia, and they signed the articles of incorporation for what he called the Defending Army of the National Sovereignty of Nicaragua. For a while the Marines had no idea that El Chipote existed as a Sandino hideaway and base of operations. After they heard rumors about it, aircraft began to patrol the area. On November 23, 1927, Marine planes spotted the camp on the heavily wooded mountaintop and began to bomb it almost daily. But the bombs had a small radius and caused relatively little damage in the wooded encampment. As the bombing and fighting continued, more than eleven hundred additional Marines were sent to Nicaragua at the beginning of 1928 to join the more than fourteen hundred already in the country. In the third week of January 1928, Sandino and most of his forces withdrew from El Chipote, leaving straw dummies behind, which confused the Marine aviators for a few days. When Marine ground forces reached the mountaintop on January 26, they found it deserted.

. . .

During his resistance, Sandino's political consciousness was developing as was his fame. From having opposed the Conservatives and criticized his fellow Liberals, he had now moved to opposing the "Yankee Imperialists." He had become a magnet for internationalists who represented a mix of worldwide revolutionary ideas and who contended for his mind. There were Communists, Socialists, members of Christian groups, and representatives of Peru's *Aprista* movement, which envisioned a combination of Marxism-Leninism and the continent's Indian traditions. Gabriela Mistral, the Chilean poetess, saw Sandino's movement as a "spectacular concept of a clash of races." For a while, the Communist International gave its support, though it does not appear that Sandino actively sought this. His secretary during that period was Agustin Farabundo Martí, the leading Communist from El Salvador.

Sandino became a darling of avant-garde political and social activists in New York, Mexico, and Europe, and they raised money for his cause. One such international group was the Anti-Imperialist League, a Communist front with branches in many countries of the Western Hemisphere. In Mexico, the exiled Venezuelan Communist Gustavo Machado organized a branch in collaboration with Sandino's people. Sandino's half brother, Sócrates Sandino, then living in Brooklyn, regularly addressed rallies organized by such groups in the United States.

Perhaps the most important foreign connection, though, was Froylán Turcios, a Honduran poet who edited a biweekly review in Tegucigalpa, the Honduran capital, and also distributed news dispatches that he received from Sandino's headquarters. The public's attention was due, in part, to a few sympathetic journalists who, with Turcios' help, got the story out to the world.

One of these journalists was Carleton Beals, an American who wrote for *The Nation*. While the Marines were bombing El Chipote in early 1928, Beals rode in from Honduras on horseback. But as he and his guide neared the camp, they learned that it had just been abandoned. They finally caught up with Sandino in San Rafael del Norte. Beal's articles depicted Sandino as an idealist and drew attention to his cause. Traveling around the villages of the north after his interview with Sandino, however, Beals reported a number of conversations with Liberals and Conservatives showing that the essence of the dispute for most of them was still the differences between the two parties, not the Marine presence. Liberals living in the area where Sandino operated identified with him because he was seen as the defender of the Liberal cause. What bothered them about the Marines was that they seemed to be helping a Conservative hold power. But Beals, overlooking the subtleties of the Liberal-Conservative conflict that came out even in his own reporting, drew this conclusion about Sandino: "He had fired the imagination of the humble people of Nicaragua. In every town Sandino had his Homer. He was of the constellation of Abdel-Krim, Robin Hood, [Pancho] Villa, the untamed outlaws who knew only daring and great deeds, imbued ever with the tireless persistence to overcome insurmountable odds and confront successfully overwhelming power. His epos will grow—in Nicaragua, in Latin America, the wide world over. For heroes grow ever more heroic with time."

After Sandino abandoned El Chipote the fighting spread out over a larger area, but was still concentrated in the north-central mountains. Sandino moved toward the bigger population centers of the region. His troops again occupied San Rafael del Norte, where his wife continued to live with her parents. El Chipote, he said later, was the place where his forces had "turned the tortilla over." He said they had used the siege time to organize and analyze for what would come next.

The Marines supervised the 1928 presidential elections, as planned, on November 4. There was a large turnout, and General Moncada, the Liberal candidate, won easily despite violence and anti-election propaganda by Sandino's forces. After the election, a new effort was made to convince Sandino to give up. His father, Gregorio Sandino, acted as intermediary and asked Sandino to send to the American commander his conditions for peace. Sandino replied that he was willing to deal with Moncada and give him a chance "to rectify his errors" but said there would be no peace until the Marines left Nicaragua. On New Year's Day 1929, he wrote Moncada proposing a meeting of just the two of them. Moncada spurned the offer.

In 1929, Sandino went to Mexico in search of arms and financial assistance, a trip made necessary in part by the decision of Froylán Turcios to accept a diplomatic post abroad with the Honduran government and break his ties to Sandino, an action that Sandino blamed on U.S. pressures and money. Sandino later characterized Turcios as an intellectual Judas and said he had "morally committed suicide" by making the break. Without Turcios, Sandino had to give more of his own attention to foreign relations.

Sandino left for Mexico at the beginning of June 1929, traveling via Honduras, El Salvador, and Guatemala, accompanied by various of his internationalist supporters, including Farabundo Martí from El Salvador. A Mexican aide, José Paredes, had supposedly laid the groundwork and found President Emilio Portes Gil willing to help Sandino. But instead of being allowed to go to Mexico City to see the president, Sandino and his party were directed to Mérida on the Yucatan Peninsula, where the Mexican government had a house ready. They arrived on July 11 and spent the rest of the year waiting to be summoned to the capital.

Unknown to Sandino at the time, two things had happened: First, Paredes had not actually met with Portes Gil, but, according to what Sandino claimed later, had simply passed along a request that Sandino be given asylum, and second, the U.S. ambassador to Mexico, Dwight Morrow, had reached an agreement with Portes Gil under which the Mexican would give Sandino asylum in Yucatan but would prevent his going to the capital or setting up a base of operations in Mexico. Sandino finally wrote a letter to Portes Gil setting out his needs and saying that if he was not to receive assistance, then he wanted to be allowed to return to Nicaragua. Portes Gil received him in Mexico City in early February 1930, and said he had understood that Sandino sought only asylum. He said he was unable to help him in other ways because he did not want to intervene internally in Nicaragua. Sandino returned to Mérida, and on April 24 he sailed for Veracruz, then took the train to Guatemala and was back in his mountains in the Segovias by early May, almost a year after he had left.

During the time in Mexico, squabbles over philosophy and tactics plagued Sandino's entourage. Sandino complained later that the press had made it look like a dog and cat fight, but he himself did not describe it much differently: "On the one hand, [there was] Farabundo Martí with the Communists; on the other [Esteban] Pavletich with the *Apristas*, and Paredes, who turned out to be a fool and a liar . . ." These disputes and the fact that he was otherwise idle focused Sandino's mind on what he really did want for Nicaragua and his movement, something that had not seriously occupied him before. From Mexico, Sandino wrote to a collaborator that he wanted a movement neither of the extreme left nor of the extreme right, but that the extreme left served a purpose in making him think in terms of social questions.

However, the Communists turned on him when he slipped out of Mexico to return to the battlefield, and Farabundo Martí left him.

Sandino said later that he had had to expel Martí because the Salvadoran wanted "to tangle me up, in Mexico, in a mess with the Communists that cost me a lot of headaches." The Mexican Communists claimed that Sandino had accepted money to make a worldwide tour against imperialism, then decided instead to resume what they disparagingly called his local fight alongside petit bourgeois groups, a reference to his rejection of the concept of class warfare. After returning home, Sandino said there was no need for the class struggle in Nicaragua, that the workers lived well there and struggled only against American intervention. Sandino told an interviewer three years later that he considered himself a Socialist but not a Communist. He also said his dispute with Martí was not specifically about ideology but the result of Martí's rebellious character and his refusal to understand the limitations of the mission to Mexico.

Martí returned to his homeland, where he died before a firing squad for his part in organizing El Salvador's 1932 peasant uprising. Just before his death, Martí said his break with Sandino had occurred because the Nicaraguan "did not want to embrace the Communist program for which I was fighting."

A few of Sandino's generals had kept the war with the Marines going in limited form while he was outside Nicaragua. After his return, fighting intensified and spread to the Atlantic Coast and Chontales, a south-central department some distance from the mountains of Segovia. About a month after his return from Mexico, Sandino was wounded in an air raid and apparently took no further part in military actions himself. He decreed the destruction of all United States-owned property, but his men also freely raided and pillaged other farms and especially those of the Conservatives. He later said that the size of his force reached two thousand men but that some were trainees as young as thirteen years old.

The organization and training of the National Guard had been under way since May 1927 under the direction of a retired Marine officer. During the Guard's formative years, all its officers were Marines, but those Marines serving with the Guard were not a part of the Marine brigade engaged in combat against Sandino. By the beginning of 1929 the National Guard had reached a strength of more than two thousand men. President Moncada was not happy with the idea of creating an apolitical force and regularly sought ways to control it and use it for political ends. For a while Moncada advanced the idea of a separate, volunteer Nicaraguan force to pursue Sandino with no holds barred. This was taken to mean shooting more of those captured. The Marine trainers, despite their efforts to make the National Guard nonpartisan, ended up accepting the concept of bipartisanship, with officers to be drawn equally from each party. The first young officers were commissioned in 1930 by the military academy, but it was soon decided that the senior officers should be slightly older men from prominent families.

In the United States, meanwhile, intervention in Nicaragua had become unpopular, and the public and Congress pressed to bring the Marines home. Anti-interventionists in the Senate almost succeeded in cutting off funds for the Marines in Nicaragua in February 1929, as the public and members of Congress began to complain of specific combat actions in which Marines died. Both the extreme left and the extreme right vocally opposed United States intervention; the left because it supported Sandino and the right because it feared that international activities, whether by business or government, would lead to the mixing of races and cultures. All of this opposition had convinced Herbert Hoover, even before his inauguration in March 1929, of the need to find a way to withdraw from Nicaragua. His administration decided in 1931 to reduce the size of the Marine force immediately and to bring all of the Marines home from Nicaragua after the 1932 elections there.

The U.S.-supervised elections of November 1932 resulted in victory for Juan Bautista Sacasa, the former Liberal vice president. One big question remained to be settled before the withdrawal of the Marines —the selection of a Nicaraguan to lead the National Guard. Anastasio Somoza García, who had moved into diplomacy after having given up Liberal warfare and had become foreign minister in the outgoing government, was chosen to be chief director of the new military force with the support of both the American minister, Matthew C. Hanna, and President-elect Sacasa, who was an uncle of Somoza's wife. United States officials had long been impressed by Somoza, in part because he spoke good English and was personally charming, but, more significantly, because during an earthquake that hit Managua in 1931 his had been the coolest head in the government. He was viewed as being very competent.

Leo Salazar found his way into the National Guard about the same time, under less auspicious circumstances. "President Sacasa, after he had been elected but not yet inaugurated—as he was a relative of mine and had known me since I was a little boy—called me one day to his office, and he said, 'Leo, I have made arrangements with the American government that we are going to form the *Guardia Nacional.* And I have to form it so that half of the officers are Conservatives and half are Liberals.' So, as I am of the old Conservative families, he said, 'You are my candidate.' I said, 'Oh, please, I don't want to join. No, no, no. I've been up in La Fundadora and I've seen what these *Guardias* do.' He says, 'You don't go out of this office until you say yes.' After two hours in his office I went to his secretary, who was my wife's godfather, Dr. Guerrero Montalban, a wonderful gentleman, and I said, 'Doctor, what shall I do? I have to leave.' He says, 'Go and tell him you'll join and then don't join, so you can get out.' So I went over and I said, 'Dr. Sacasa, I accept.'

"I returned to Matagalpa and one day, just right after, I was called to the Marine command . . . I went there and I saw Rigoberto Reyes standing in front of—he became General Reyes later on, chief of staff. Then, the commanding officer said, 'All right, stand there' and I stood there. He said, 'Lift your right hand.' And I said, '*Y para que?*' [Why?] '*Que la levante, le digo,*' he said. I thought, 'Why's he acting like this to me when we are such good friends?' So I lifted my right hand, and he swore me into the *Guardia* . . . I was appointed paymaster in Matagalpa as a captain. A few months later they transferred me to the north-central command in Jinotega, under General Reyes, the fellow who was sworn in with me. So I became the paymaster in Jinotega, keeping books and everything."

On January 1, 1933, President Sacasa was sworn into office. The Marines turned over command of the young National Guard to Somoza, and the next day the last of them went home.

The presence of the Marines had been prompted in large measure by the United States' desire to establish a constitutional system that would halt the warfare between the political parties. But behind that were a number of reasons for wanting to keep internal peace in Nicaragua. For one thing, there was concern about influence from Mexico, which was then emerging from its own revolutionary period and had been interested in controlling Central America since its independence from Spain. Also, there was some concern about the possible spread of Bolshevism. Probably of more immediate importance, however, was the need to collect customs duties in order to pay Nicaragua's debts to European bankers and, thereby, keep Europeans from intervening. Several European nations had earlier demonstrated a proclivity for sending gunboats to collect debts. What also cannot be ignored was that Nicaraguan politicians and warlords regularly sought outside help from the United States or European countries, to support their own cause. Those who complained about such interventions usually did so because the intervention of the moment happened to be working against them.

During the nineteenth century, U.S. interest in Nicaragua had been based on the fact that it was the most logical route for an interoceanic canal, cutting through the narrow strip of land between Lake Nicaragua and the Pacific and following the San Juan River between the lake and the Atlantic. But by the time of the first Marine landing in 1909 the canal was already well under way in Panama. A treaty was negotiated in 1914 between the United States and Nicaragua giving the United States the exclusive right to construct a canal across Nicaragua, but it occurred as part of a package deal in which a troubled Nicaraguan Conservative government was looking for financial aid from the United States to pay off some British creditors and wanted to offer something to make the arrangement attractive to the United States.

Leo Salazar insisted that I should not be misled by the various interpretations of Nicaraguan history that put the United States in a bad light. "I want to explain something that I wish you could stress," he said, "because these scoundrels, every time they can, they say, 'Nicaragua was attacked by the United States, Nicaragua was invaded by the United States.' It's not true. Every time the Marines came to Nicaragua it was because the Nicaraguan government asked them to come. They didn't come because they felt like it. They came on account of the Monroe Doctrine. You know, 'America for the Americans.' That is why we had forty American Marines guarding Mr. Potter's plantation, because the Nicaraguan government said it could not protect the lives and properties of foreigners . . . They were also guarding German properties and French properties and so forth."

Once the Marines had gone, President Sacasa, whose claim to the presidency was the original reason that Sandino had joined the Liberal ranks, quickly called a peace conference with the rebel general. Sandino's wife, Blanca Aráuz, and a Sacasa Cabinet minister handled the details of bringing the two together. On February 2, 1933, one month after the departure of the Marines, Sandino flew into Managua, and Somoza met him at the airport. The two embraced, then rode together to the palace. Sacasa and Sandino knew each other's positions and easily reached agreement. The accord, signed a few minutes after midnight of the same day, provided for Sandino and his men to turn in their arms in several stages in exchange for a large tract of land in the mountains along the Coco River on which Sandino intended to establish an immense agricultural cooperative. The largely virgin land covered 36,800 square kilometers and was one fourth of the national territory, though Sandino told an interviewer that it was at least half of Nicaragua. One fourth of the weapons were supposed to be turned in to the National Guard within twenty days and the remainder on a gradual basis. Sandino was allowed to keep a hundred men under arms.

On February 22, 1933, a large National Guard delegation met with Sandino in San Rafael del Norte for the official demobilization of his troops and to take possession of the arms that he handed over. About one thousand troops were involved, but the National Guard received only 361 weapons, mostly rifles of various makes. Among the witnesses was Leo Salazar, who fifty years later remembered Sandino this way: "He was a very nervous fellow, a little, dinky fellow, nothing to him. And he had this whip . . . he was always snapping the whip, and nervous. And always wearing the hat. And he talked—a funny way of talking. He was not brave, but he had what you call in the United States the gift of gab. He could stand on a tree stump and talk and talk and send his men off to fight."

Another of the witnesses to this ceremony was José Román, a young Nicaraguan journalist who had lived in New York for several years. Sandino invited Román to accompany him to his camps in the mountains, where Sandino gave Román long interviews over the next several weeks. Sandino decided to designate Román as the person to tell his story in depth to the Nicaraguan people. After recounting his versions of the fight against the Marines and his trip to Mexico, Sandino talked about his plans for the territory he felt he now controlled, predicting a "brilliant future" for the region. When Román expressed concern about Sandino's safety and asked why he didn't seek a diplomatic post abroad for a few years, Sandino said he had invitations to go to Paris, Buenos Aires, and Mexico but that such travels would only amount to "exhibiting myself like a movie actor, tango singer, politician, or showcase ambassador . . ."

At one point in the discussions, Sandino said he had frequently heard the Marines use an English expression that seemed to reflect their reaction to various things in Nicaragua—particularly the torrential rain, infernal heat, mudpits covered with wild growth, flies, and mosquitos. The expression he had heard, Sandino said, was "god-damned country." He wondered what it meant in Spanish. Román said he would translate it as *maldito país.* The phrase delighted Sandino. "Please," he said. "Put that title on your book. *Maldito País!*" So Román did.

Despite the peace accord, clashes continued between Sandino's people and National Guard patrols through 1933. In November of that year, Sandino went to Managua and met with Sacasa and Somoza separately. All parties displayed a conciliatory attitude. But a short time after the November meeting, one of Sandino's commanders went to Managua and said they needed additional arms for protection. Sacasa, by contrast, wanted to send a delegation to Sandino's area to collect the remainder of the weapons that Sandino then had. Part of the problem was that Sandino had begun to challenge the constitutionality of the National Guard and wanted Sacasa to recognize his—Sandino's—own force as the government authority in the northern mountains. Somoza was dismayed by Sandino's demands, and less patient than Sacasa. He was already experiencing difficulties in asserting his control over the National Guard, where some of the academy-trained younger officers were unhappy with the power given civilian appointees.

There was even more grumbling about Sandino among National Guard officers up in Matagalpa and Jinotega. Leo Salazar, who was one of those officers, explained how the issue was viewed among people in that region who were not Sandino supporters and how some of them proposed to deal with it.

"Sandino had made arrangements with Dr. Sacasa to receive control of all the northern departments, and Sacasa was so good that he had consented to let Sandino govern all the higher part of Nicaragua. So we were going to have two republics in one. He was going to take control of the whole mountain area. So we, as we are Segovianos—because we are of the old Spanish people who came from Segovia in Spain—we couldn't swallow that.

"So, without consulting Managua, we—the officers in Jinotega—decided we were going to bump him off. This nobody knows. This is the first time that I tell that. I have been very careful about telling anyone this . . . So then, one fine day, they notified us that Sandino was coming by plane with some of the politicians, who really ruined Sandino—the politicians ruined him—so we went to the landing field, which is now Lake Apanás—it used to be a valley, but now it's flooded, and it's a lake—and my mission was to save the American pilot. We dug some ditches and camouflaged the ditches with branches of trees and put men in there with machine guns, and as Sandino and these people came off the plane, these men were supposed to mow down Sandino, but I had to save the American pilot. When they landed there, I was supposed to go up to the pilot and say, 'Wait a minute, come over here, I want to show you something.' To get him away from there, see? Then, brrrrrrrrr—

"We saw the plane coming, and we were all nervous, waiting for the moment. Then, all of a sudden, the plane came over us, circled around three times, then went back to Managua. It didn't land. So he goes back to Managua. But as fate had decreed, he is invited by President Sacasa for dinner up at the palace, and coming down from dinner, he is killed. Can you beat that? [It was] the same day. We didn't know that they were planning to kill him in Managua. And they didn't know that we were planning to kill him in Jinotega."

The date was February 21, 1934. Sandino had been in Managua for several days discussing the problems with various government people. That night he had a pleasant dinner with President Sacasa, but as Sandino left the palace he and two of his generals were detained by National Guardsmen, driven to the airfield, and executed by a firing squad. Sandino's brother Sócrates was killed in a shootout with National Guardsmen who went to arrest him at the home of a Cabinet minister. Though Somoza was at a poetry reading that night, subsequent investigation established that earlier in the day he had presided, with fourteen of his officers, over the drafting of the plan for what was called The Death of Caesar.

Some accounts indicate that Somoza was the one who proposed killing Sandino, while other accounts suggest that Somoza wanted to act against Sandino but feared the consequences of going so far as killing him and that it was other officers who demanded Sandino's death. Somoza thought that Sandino and Sacasa were conspiring against him and the National Guard; and some accounts say that he claimed to have the support of the United States to take some kind of action. The historic accounts that appear most carefully researched indicate that the United States was not part of the plot. Arthur Bliss Lane, the American minister in Managua, discovered that something was afoot that night and made a frantic effort to stop it, but he mistakenly thought that it was a coup d'état against President Sacasa rather than the assassination of Sandino.

Salazar, who asked questions about the killing among officers who participated, said one of them told him that Somoza characterized their choice as being between the life of the National Guard and the life of Sandino. The concern was expressed that Sandino would not give up until he had taken control of all of Nicaragua. Despite these discussions, Salazar was told that once Sandino had been arrested, Somoza hesitated about proceeding to kill him but that other officers insisted.

It took Anastasio Somoza García two more years to gradually make the National Guard loyal only to him and to turn out the elected authorities. On June 6, 1936, he forced President Sacasa to resign, and in November of the same year he had himself elected president as the candidate of the Nationalist Liberal Party, which he founded as a Liberal offshoot. He also completely won over Leo Salazar, though Salazar was a Conservative and Somoza a Liberal.

"Somoza, when I was paymaster in Jinotega, made a visit to Jinotega, and there he met me . . . You know, the paymasters always had a lot of money left over and they used to pocket it, but I didn't. I used it for some improvements in the barracks and the office and everything . . . And he was delighted. And he says, 'Leo, you're coming with me down to Managua. You have to work by my side.' So I went to Managua—it was maybe 1935—and I became his personal secretary . . . and I used to manage his businesses.

"That's why I can tell you this: there's talk, you know, that he used to steal properties. He never stole any properties. The properties were sold to him, sometimes for nothing. For instance, when he bought Montelimar, this old German gentleman came to him and he said, 'Look here, I own Montelimar'—several thousand acres, beautiful. He says, 'But I have a thousand squatters there and if I try to take them out they will kill me, so here, you take the place,' and he sold it for a song. Of course, Somoza, with his National Guardsmen, he got everybody out and he became owner of Montelimar. Then, this beautiful place on the island of Ometepe [in Lake Nicaragua]. The owner came and said he had inherited this property and he didn't know how to run it, so why don't you buy it? So he bought that property. That's how he used to buy property. But he never really came and grabbed a place from the people, never. That's a big mistake [to say it]. I know because I was there with him, always, working with him. You see, his wife was my relative. Her grandfather was my grandfather's first cousin . . ."

Then there was the matter of La Fundadora, the beautiful farm that

Salazar had managed for Charles Potter. When Potter died in England, his heirs were willing to sell the farm cheaply to Salazar, but he could not raise the money, in part because the relatives from whom he sought financing thought it was too inaccessible. There were no good roads in the immediate area of the farm.

"When I saw that I wasn't going to buy it and that somebody else was going to get it, I had a dream—a highway—and that's why we [now] have a highway . . . up to Fundadora and clear on to Jinotega. Because I went to Somoza and I said, 'Look here, you buy this. This is a gift.' And he said, 'All right. I'll buy it.' "

And, as Salazar had expected, once Somoza owned the farm he had the government build the hard-surface road to the entrance, and beyond there to Jinotega.

Salazar continued as Somoza's secretary and as a National Guard captain until 1941, when he resigned to return to his own farm at Santa María de Ostuma, which his father was getting too old to manage. He left with only fond feelings for Somoza, as "a wonderful man . . . not mean or anything." Salazar and his wife, Esmeralda Argüello, raised a family of two daughters and a son. The son, Jorge, was born in 1939, two years before his father left Somoza's service. There is a story to tell about Jorge Salazar, too, but it is about another time, and for a later chapter.

2

THE YEARS
OF THE DYNASTY

From the overthrow of Sacasa in 1936 until July 17, 1979, Nicaragua belonged to Anastasio Somoza García and his sons and a circle of relatives and collaborators. He and his wife, Salvadora Debayle, had two sons and a daughter. The older boy, Luis, was groomed to take over the political life of Nicaragua, and Anastasio II, known as Tachito when he was young, was raised to run the National Guard. Both went to military preparatory school on Staten Island; then Luis went to Louisiana State University and Tachito to West Point. A daughter, Lilian, attended a girls' school in the United States, then married a Nicaraguan politician, Guillermo Sevilla Sacasa, and Somoza gave them the Washington Embassy as a wedding gift. Another son, José, who was born out of wedlock when Somoza García was only nineteen, went into the National Guard as an enlisted man and eventually rose to the rank of general.

Despite Leo Salazar's experience with Somoza García as "a wonderful man," many other Nicaraguans saw him in a different light after he had been in power a few years. At first, it was the natural Conservative opposition to having a Liberal in power, but it grew into wider dismay at his subverting of constitutional norms to retain power and the general absence of political liberty. Corruption became rampant. Besides acquiring wealth for himself through questionable means, he demanded kickbacks from other people whom he allowed to get rich, or from almost anyone who was simply trying to do business.

Somoza García also pioneered something that his sons would perfect: the manipulation of the U.S. government for the greater good of the Somozas. With the outbreak of World War II, Somoza strengthened his hand in Washington by firmly declaring Nicaragua on the Allied side. President Roosevelt had the war uppermost in his mind when he commented about Somoza: "He's a sonofabitch, but he's ours." Roosevelt found the same redeeming characteristic in Rafael Trujillo of the Dominican Republic. One of the things that Somoza did in behalf of the Allied war effort was to seize properties owned by German and Italian investors in Nicaragua and sell them at auction, where he bought the best holdings at bargain prices.

By the mid-1940s, Somoza was gradually developing a reputation for selective cruelty, but his was not viewed as a regime that used brutality on a wide scale. Somoza, in fact, bristled whenever he was lumped in the same category as Trujillo, whose methods, in his mind, tended to give a bad name to "strong executive rule." More typical of Somoza was that a few of those who demonstrated or plotted against him would be killed in confrontations with the National Guard, but most would live to serve an unpleasant year or so in jail, then go back to plotting. He terrorized some of his opponents in prison. With others he destroyed their self-respect or their businesses or personal reputations, or simply played dirty tricks on them. What mattered most to him was amassing and enjoying wealth, and Nicaraguans generally allowed him to do that.

When a poet named Rigoberto López Pérez, apparently acting alone, fatally shot Somoza García at a party in León in 1956, the family plan proved effective. Luis took over the presidency and Anastasio took over the National Guard. Luis, an easygoing man concerned about the image of the regime, took various steps to liberalize it and announced he would serve only one term. But his handpicked candidate, René Schick, ran in the next elections, in 1963, and Schick, naturally, won. Over the objections of Luis, Tacho II ran for president in 1967 and achieved an easy victory. But before the new president took office, Luis suffered a massive coronary attack and died at the age of forty-four. Thus, there were no restraints left on his brother.

Nicaragua under the Somoza brothers, as it had been throughout history, was a place where almost any problem could be straightened out by relatives, friendships, or money. Like their father, the sons constantly added to the family's wealth. Besides land, they acquired factories, a shipping company, an airline, and more. The government bureaucracy and National Guard interfered little in the lives of most Nicaraguans. As authoritarian regimes go, this one ceded to its political enemies and critics a relatively large amount of space to act in public life. By the 1970s the second Tacho liked to point out to skeptical journalists and diplomats that there could be no better proof of his tolerant nature than the fact that he allowed his chief political foe, Pedro Joaquín Chamorro Cardenal, to continue publishing *La Prensa,* the newspaper with the largest circulation in Nicaragua. The newspaper suffered occasional periods of censorship, but whenever the censorship was lifted, *La Prensa* came back with a vengeance.

What the Somozas would never entertain was the idea that they should permit the opposition, however moderate, to come to power. Nor would they even allow such opponents a share of power without extracting a piece of their soul in return. In the interests of legitimacy, the brothers continued to rule through the Nationalist Liberal Party that their father had created out of a portion of the old Liberal Party. Other Liberals formed what amounted to an opposition party. The question of participation in the Somoza governments and the Somoza-controlled congress also produced schisms in the Conservative Party, which over the years divided into four parties. Pedro Joaquín Chamorro labeled the first Conservative faction to go into the congress *la puta*—the whore—and the second group *la putita*—the little whore. Many other Nicaraguans called them *zancudo*—or parasite—parties.

Though Chamorro and his family fought a valiant and eloquent battle against the Somozas for press freedom, in many ways the conflict was rooted in the old Conservative-Liberal wars. While the Somozas were Liberals, Chamorro's ancestors, both on his father's side and the Cardenals on his mother's side, had been giants of the Conservative Party from Nicaragua's early days. The family had provided several presidents, the last being General Emiliano Chamorro during the period of the Marine interventions.

Pedro Joaquín Chamorro Zelaya, the father of Chamorro Cardenal, had acquired half the stock in *La Prensa* in 1930 and become full owner in 1932, the year before Somoza García was named director of the National Guard. The newspaper became the primary Chamorro vehicle for opposing Somoza rule, but not the only one. Young Pedro Joaquín, the eldest of five children, had grade-school fights with his classmate Tacho II and more serious clashes with the regime as a university student. In 1944 he was jailed for several weeks for taking part in demonstrations against Somoza García. At the same time, his father had encountered Somoza's wrath for articles in *La Prensa,* so when the son was released from prison he and his parents went into exile. The son went to Mexico and enrolled in law school, and the parents went to New York. But by 1948 everyone in the family was back in Nicaragua, and Pedro Joaquín joined his father at the newspaper. The elder Chamorro died in 1952, and the son became editor. His two younger brothers, Jaime and Xavier, later joined him at *La Prensa* on the business and technical sides.

Chamorro Cardenal also continued his political activities outside the newspaper, peaceful and otherwise. Though his family ties were to the Conservative Party, he was concerned with creating more broad-based political movements. His closest collaborators, however, were other Conservatives. In 1954 he took part in an unsuccessful attack on the regime and served a year in prison and another year of house arrest. Three months after Chamorro was freed, Somoza García was assassinated, and Chamorro, like many opposition figures, was accused of complicity. A military court found him not guilty of the murder but guilty of rebellion. He spent six months in prison, then was banished in early 1957 to the isolated community of San Carlos, on the far shore of Lake Nicaragua, less than ten miles from the Costa Rican border. From there, he and his wife Violeta (their four children were safe with relatives in Managua) fled to Costa Rica in a rowboat. They moved into a house in San José, where Chamorro wrote one of his many books, *Estirpe Sangrienta: Los Somoza (Bloody Stock: The Somozas).*

Fidel Castro came to power in Cuba on January 1, 1959, and within a few days Chamorro was in Havana with a delegation of Nicaraguan exiles. Like other people opposing dictators in Latin America, they were inspired by Castro's triumph and wanted his help. The group was received by Castro and also by Ernesto "Che" Guevara, but Chamorro wrote later that his request for assistance against the Somozas was refused "because our political line was different." However, another Nicaraguan who was in Cuba at the time told me that Guevara said he did not believe in Chamorro as a potential revolutionary but that if the group managed to establish a base inside Nicaragua, he would send arms. The group returned to Costa Rica, where Chamorro began organizing an invasion force. The only outside governmental help to reach him, Chamorro said, came from Venezuela, then in its first years of democracy under Rómulo Bétancourt.

Beginning in April 1959, more than a hundred young Nicaraguans, attracted to Chamorro's banner, underwent six weeks of military training on an isolated Costa Rican beach. On May 31 a C-46 transport plane picked up sixty of the would-be invaders and flew them into Nicaragua to a plains area known as Mollejones in the department of Chontales. The next day, the rest of the group was picked up and flown to an area straddling the departments of Matagalpa and Boaco. The plan was to initiate a series of attacks on the National Guard that would cause the citizenry to rise up and force the regime to relinquish power. There had already been various other such attempts to overthrow the Somozas, but this operation was bigger and better organized than others to that date. However, the invaders made mistakes and had some bad luck; after fifteen days they surrendered. A few died on both sides in the fighting, but 103 of the insurgents lived to stand trial. They were found guilty and sentenced to prison terms of up to eight years, but within a year Luis Somoza granted them amnesty.

Chamorro did not give up his anti-Somoza activities after the failed invasion, but with the coming of middle age he abandoned clandestine methods. He channeled his opposition through public political movements, the pages of *La Prensa,* business organizations, and international forums, such as the Inter American Press Association, where he became a major figure. Chamorro used all of these to fight the Somoza brothers through the 1960s and 1970s. In a sense, his activities were also useful to the Somozas because they helped to justify Tacho II's claim that there was considerable freedom in Nicaragua.

The Sandinista National Liberation Front was only an occasional inconvenience for the Somozas after its founding in Honduras in 1961 by three young men who had been active in leftist student movements during the 1950s. Their names were Carlos Fonseca, Tomás Borge, and Silvio Mayorga. All three of the founders of the FSLN—the Spanish acronym for the Sandinista Front—were under the influence of Marxism-Leninism, but they did not spell it out in their early plans. To reach power, the Sandinistas intended to use the methods of Castro and Guevara. However, Fonseca had studied and written about Augusto César Sandino, whom he interpreted as an advocate of proletarianism, and at his insistence the name of the new organization paid tribute to Sandino. Fonseca, the illegitimate son of the administrator of some of the Somoza agricultural properties, was the dominant political thinker and planner in the group. In 1953, as a seventeen-year-old, he had been briefly involved with one of the political movements that Pedro Joaquín Chamorro helped organize, but preferred what he saw as more revolutionary solutions for Nicaragua. He spent much of 1957 in the Soviet Union and East Germany and wrote a booklet, *A Nicaraguan in Moscow,* that depicted the Soviet system as a future model for Latin America. After Fidel Castro's triumph in 1959, Fonseca and Silvio Mayorga were among many Central Americans who went to Cuba. They found more political agreement with Castro and Guevara than had Chamorro and his group, but it is not known how much, if any, immediate help was given the FSLN by Cuba.

The Sandinistas launched their campaign in the jungles and mountains of Miskito territory along the Honduran border, not far from El Chipote, Sandino's old mountain hideout. But their first military action was such a failure that they appeared headed for the same end as the many other small bands that had tried to start insurgencies. After eighteen months of training at a jungle camp in Honduras, about sixty Sandinista recruits set out across the Coco River in late 1962 with the intention of occupying Wiwilí, the Miskito Indian settlement where the National Guard had found Sandino's arms cache after his death in 1934. The Sandinistas lost their way, attacked two other communities instead, then ran into a strong National Guard force, which destroyed about a third of the rebels. The rest fled back across the river, and most were captured by the Honduran military.

Through the mid-1960s, the group struggled against extinction, in large part trying to determine which sectors of Nicaraguan society were its natural allies. It made a brief attempt during that period at creating a proletarian base by infiltrating unions or organizing them where none existed, and by organizing the peasantry. Fonseca also speculated about the possibilities of making strategic alliances with the new Social Christian Party or even the Conservatives or dissident Liberals, but none of these projects bore fruit.

It was as part of this search for allies that the Sandinistas organized their next major undertaking, a full five years after their first combat experience. This time, they chose a mountain peak called Pancasan in Matagalpa, and the priority was peasant organization, not fighting the National Guard. The Sandinistas infiltrated thirty-five people into the region and, operating in three squads, tried to extend their political control over the rural zone while occasionally engaging Guard patrols in small battles. They began the operation in December 1966, but gave it up in August 1967, after the National Guard had killed twenty of the thirty-five rebels, including Silvio Mayorga. Most of the survivors fled to Cuba. Carlos Fonseca wrote later that the Pancasan operation failed because the Sandinistas encountered resistance from the peasants they sought to organize and because many of the peasants who did join the guerrillas soon deserted. After Pancasan, Anastasio Somoza Debayle declared that the Sandinistas no longer existed.

Pancasan, however, had captured the imagination of a group of Central Americans then studying at Patrice Lumumba Friendship of the Peoples University in the Soviet Union. The school, offering a full range of university courses for students from a hundred or more countries, was created in 1960 as part of Nikita Khrushchev's drive for Soviet influence in the Third World. The Central Americans there during the mid-1960s, including about a dozen Nicaraguans, were given scholarships arranged by various Marxist-Leninist groups in Central America and by the Cuban government. Outside the classroom, the Central Americans united in two cells, one named for Augusto César Sandino, in which they analyzed the situations in their own countries. They idolized Che Guevara, who was then trying to apply the Cuban insurgency method to Bolivia, but this conflicted with the Soviet policy of the time, which held that Marxist-Leninist groups in Latin America should operate as legal political parties. Guevara was captured and killed in Bolivia in October 1967, only a couple of months after Pancasan was written off as a failure, and the result in Moscow was increased differences between the pro-insurgency students and the authorities. They also came into disagreement subsequently over the Soviet occupation of Czechoslovakia in 1968 and the Soviet-Chinese border clashes, for which the Central American students publicly criticized the Soviet Union.

Toward the end of the 1960s, the Nicaraguans and some other Central Americans who favored insurrection began to abandon their studies in Moscow and return home. Some were expelled from the university, others left by their own choice. Some joined the remnants of the Sandinista Front in Matagalpa, determined to help the movement recover from Pancasan. At first, very little happened. Many of the Sandinista leaders began to spend most of their time outside

Nicaragua, particularly in Costa Rica, where they raised money through robberies and attempted to reorganize.

In 1969 the FSLN issued what it called its "Historic Program," the first significant statement of Sandinista aims. It concentrated on economic and social goals, saying, among other things, that once in power the FSLN would redistribute the land and wealth through a variety of measures, would expropriate many properties, would improve the status of women and minorities, and would provide health care and education. In political terms, it promised to respect human rights and individual freedoms, without stating them, and said it would govern through a "revolutionary structure."

The same year, 1969, Fonseca wrote a long article, "Nicaragua: Zero Hour," first published in Cuba, in which he analyzed Nicaraguan history around the theme that most of the country's problems were the result of United States aggression and imperialism. Then he analyzed Sandinista activities to date, such as the failure of Pancasan, and explained why the FSLN had not formally embraced Marxism. He said this stemmed from the fact that Marxism had heretofore been represented in Nicaragua by the Nicaraguan Socialist Party. It had been organized in 1944, while World War II was still under way, and had adopted the policy prevalent at the time that Marxist movements in the Western Hemisphere should work with the "capitalist class" and "North American imperialism" because the United States was then the Soviet Union's ally in the war. This meant they did not participate in armed struggle against Somoza or other U.S. allies. Being in disagreement with this policy of the Marxist political parties, Fonseca said, the FSLN "vacillated in putting forward a clearly Marxist-Leninist ideology." But he said it had been only a matter of time before the people of Nicaragua had begun to distinguish between "the false Marxists and the true Marxists." In general, however, Fonseca did not delve deeply into philosophical questions, for, while he was known as the intellectual among the Sandinista founders, even he did only limited writing and thinking. He found in Marxism an easy explanation for Nicaragua's shortcomings and contented himself to fitting the pieces of Nicaraguan history into that framework. Most of his writings concerned stragegy for reaching power.

During this period, various Sandinistas underwent military and political training in Cuba, and some also spent time in North Korea. In 1972 an effort was made to rejuvenate the front in the northern mountains with the people trained in Cuba, but the National Guard, which had undergone counterinsurgency training at United States bases in Panama, kept close on their heels. A number of significant Sandinista leaders were killed by the National Guard in that period and many others were captured. Again, much of the difficulty for the FSLN was that it could not win over the peasantry. Henry Ruiz, one of those who had come back from his studies at Patrice Lumumba to join the FSLN in the mountains, said years later that many of the peasants were Somoza supporters and others gave that impression, even if they did not feel that way in their hearts. Ruiz said peasants were part of the National Guard's informant network and would advise the local command post whenever they saw anyone walking in the area who was light-complexioned, as were most of the FSLN militants. And any peasant who did choose to work with the FSLN risked being killed by the National Guard.

However, these rural defeats served to attract new blood to the cause. This time it came from an unlikely source: a Roman Catholic church parish. One night in late 1971, about a dozen young Nicaraguans of university age, most of them from affluent families, went into spiritual retreat under the leadership of a priest named Uriel Molina. During the retreat they reflected on religion, but there was more talk of "political commitment," though without open references to the Sandinista Front. The group decided to form a commune and live together behind Father Molina's church in the Riguero neighborhood of Managua. The students remained in Riguero more than a year, attending a Bible lesson every morning, classes during the day at the university, then discussions in the evenings in which they applied Marxist analysis to the Nicaraguan condition. In late 1972 a Sandinista *comandante* moved into the parish for several days of meetings with the students, and a few months later, sometime in 1973, the students abandoned the parish for the underground movement.

Aside from *La Prensa,* however, the most serious opposition to Somoza at the beginning of the 1970s came, not from guerrillas, but from businessmen and industrialists, nudged along by a natural disaster. On December 23, 1972, a series of earthquakes rolled through Managua, destroying or damaging about 80 percent of the capital's structures, and killing 10,000 people. Hundreds of millions of dollars in relief and reconstruction money poured in from the United States and elsewhere, but many people soon began to grumble about the way Somoza was using it or distributing it.

The Nicaraguan economy was then controlled by three camps. One was dominated by Somoza and included his family and supporters and their individual and interlocking business and farming interests. The second was the Pellas group, made up of the many relatives and close associates of Alfredo Pellas, patriarch of the family that owned Nicaragua Sugar Estates Limited, the largest sugar mill in Central America, plus various businesses and a bank. The Pellases and their relatives bought the latest refining and distilling equipment and sent their offspring and managers to England and the United States for education, but otherwise they ran a tradition-bound, family enterprise. Incorporated in 1890 as an English firm—to discourage Nicaragua's warlords and politicians of that era from trying to grab it—Nicaragua Sugar Estates was kept closely held through the decades by marriages between cousins. While the Somoza clan was Liberal, the Pellases and their relatives were nominally Conservatives, but they gave money to both parties and generally stayed out of active politics. Thus, there were no problems between the Pellas group and the Somoza group. Whenever they ran into a question of business competition (Somoza was in sugar, too) they divided up the market rather than compete for it.

The third economic group in Nicaragua consisted of almost everybody else who was in business or owned farm land. They were Liberals and Conservatives, large, small, and medium-sized operators. Many owned factories that made light industrial goods for export to other Central American countries, a trade system fostered by the Alliance for Progress at the beginning of the 1960s. These people represented the degree of modern capitalism that existed in Nicaragua. While the Somoza and Pellas groups dealt with a union federation controlled by Somoza, many of the others dealt with independent trade union groups. Some of them studied at the Harvard-affiliated Central American Institute for Business Management, which attracted students from all over Central America to Managua and used the case study method in courses leading to an M.B.A. degree. The institute also had its roots in the Alliance for Progress era. Business and professional people from this economic group dominated and led the various chambers, such as industry and commerce, which were grouped in an umbrella organization called the Superior Council of Private Initiative. The council, known by its Spanish acronym COSIP, had grass-roots connections through two development programs that it operated—again stemming from the Alliance for Progress—to assist subsistence farmers and small business cooperatives.

It was these people who were most unhappy with the way Somoza ran the earthquake recovery program. Slightly more than a year after the earthquake, in March 1974, COSIP organized a large gathering of the private sector, from which emerged a statement accusing Somoza of corruption in the use of the funds. It was the first public break with Somoza by private enterprise. The business people accused him of not completing work on replacement housing for the poor, or doing nothing to replace the destroyed commercial center of Managua, and of favoring his supporters for business recovery loans while hitting others with high import taxes on materials and supplies needed to resume operations. They were not alone in this accusation. There were articles in some major U.S. media alleging the same, though the U.S. government officially found nothing out of order in the use of aid money. In addition to corruption, the businessmen felt that Somoza was using the reconstruction as an excuse to move into areas of the economy in which he and his cronies had not been involved previously, such as construction of housing for the affluent.

To most Nicaraguans, including the Somoza regime, the Sandinista Front was presumed to be dead or dying when, on December 27, 1974, a small band of Sandinistas carried out a spectacular raid that considerably altered that view and also replenished the guerrilla leadership ranks. Ten young men and three women crashed a party at the home of a wealthy businessman and took hostage the foreign minister and other Somoza associates, including his brother-in-law. They nearly captured Turner Shelton, the United States ambassador, in whose honor the party was held, but he had left a half hour earlier. Two and a half days of negotiations under the direction of Archbishop Miguel Obando y Bravo netted the Sandinistas the release of fourteen imprisoned colleagues, $1 million in cash, publication of a long communiqué attacking Somoza, and flight to Cuba, where training awaited for those who had not already been there.

The Christmas Party Raid, however, produced a bitter split within the Sandinista Front over strategy. It was blamed on Jaime Wheelock, a sometime Sandinista who had been studying and writing in West Germany for several years. He returned home in early 1975 and, according to several FSLN leaders, wrote a series of letters to his close collaborators criticizing the raid as a "petit bourgeois deviation." He said that it had caused a new wave of repression because of the martial law that Somoza declared the day after the raid and that more people had been arrested than freed as a result of the action. He also accused those who organized it of being "triumphalists and insurrectionalists," an allegation that they were not prepared to put in the years necessary for a true proletarian revolution. Wheelock, who had spent his years abroad in a more extensive analysis of Nicaragua and a deeper study of Marxism than Fonseca had, thought that if the Sandinistas wanted to be real Marxists, they had to devote themselves to building proletarian consciousness, regardless of how long it took to reach power by that route.

Eventually, those who agreed with Wheelock began to call themselves the Proletarian Faction, while those in the mountains embraced the Maoist strategy of prolonged peasant war, and those who had organized the Christmas Raid came to call themselves *terceristas* or third-way advocates, with the idea of reaching out to non-Marxists in the hope of producing a quick victory through mass insurrection. The antagonism toward Wheelock was so great among some Sandinistas that they sent a squad to kill him, but a priest gave Wheelock a hiding place.

The splintering of the FSLN, plus an ongoing feud between the Sandinista leaders inside Nicaragua and those outside Nicaragua over who had the right to give orders, led to the return in late 1975 of Carlos Fonseca, who had lived in Cuba since his release from a Costa Rican jail in 1970. Fonseca, who was looked to by the Sandinistas to arbitrate and instill order, held extensive meetings with various lieutenants, then wrote a long document that laid much of the blame for the FSLN's internal problems on Wheelock, who he said was unaware of Nicaraguan reality because of his years in Chile and Europe. He also critized others for staying outside too long, particularly a young man named Humberto Ortega, who was living a comfortable existence in Costa Rica, but who was demanding that those inside Nicaragua follow his orders.

Then, seeming to throw his weight to the side of the Prolonged War Faction in the internal struggle, Fonseca went up into the northern mountains to join the Sandinistas of that group. There, in the mountains, he was killed by the National Guard on November 8, 1976, one of numerous government successes at the time. When Fonseca's head was brought to him, Somoza was convinced he had finally eliminated the Sandinistas.

However, other events were taking place that November. For one thing, various groups, including the Roman Catholic bishops of Nicaragua, were adding up the toll in the war that Somoza had declared against the Sandinistas after the 1974 Christmas Party Raid. The bishops wrote a pastoral letter accusing the National Guard of killing more than two hundred peasants as part of the two-year campaign to wipe out the Sandinistas in the northern mountains. The bishops' estimate of the toll was the most conservative. It included only victims for whom identifications were established. American Capuchin priests serving in the Miskito region estimated the toll had been at least three hundred. The National Guard, not denying such killings, claimed the peasants had been collaborators of the guerrillas.

Another significant event for Nicaragua in November 1976 occurred outside the country. It was the election of Jimmy Carter as President of the United States.

3

THE
DYNASTY WEAKENED

JANUARY 1977 TO DECEMBER 1977

In late January 1977, shortly after Jimmy Carter was sworn in to the presidency, a group of academics from universities around the United States gathered in Washington at the behest of the State Department to present a Colloquium on Central America. The speakers and the discussions covered topics ranging from historical Central American dependency to U.S. options in dealing with military regimes and how to promote human rights. If a common thread ran through the two-day session, it was that nothing was about to occur in Central America to challenge U.S. interests or otherwise demand the urgent attention of policy makers. The discussions focused mainly on how the United States might reduce its involvement in Central America and the impact on the region of such a move.

Note was taken of the guerrilla groups in El Salvador, but that country's socioeconomic problems were judged more pressing. Note was also taken of the Sandinista guerrilla movement in Nicaragua, but it was written off as small and of little threat to the Somoza family, then entering its fifth decade of rule.

Hearing this bland assessment, the young Foreign Service officer assigned to the Nicaragua Desk of the State Department requested a transfer to another post, which he hoped would be more demanding and more likely to advance his career.

What these analysts could not have known was that the dynamics of the new government in Washington would become part of a coincidence of events and circumstances that thirty months later would allow the guerrilla band thought near extinction at the beginning of 1977 to come to power behind a broad shield of Nicaraguans indignant about Anastasio Somoza Debayle.

Even as the analysts in Washington were attempting to fathom events in Central America, the new Carter government was itself the subject of even more intensive analysis by Nicaraguans. From the moment of Carter's election, the perception had begun to spread among them that Somoza had lost one of the key underpinnings of his family's long reign: the support, real or imagined, of the United States. In many countries, even some others in Latin America, Washington's attitude would have meant little, but in Nicaragua the key to power over public policy was to give the appearance of having the support of the United States, whether the U.S. government was consciously giving this support or not.

A primary tactic of the Somozas in currying U.S. support or tolerance through the years had been to be as patriotically pro-American as anyone in the American Legion. This did not require the application of Jeffersonian principles in Nicaragua, but rather meant going along with whatever was the dominant foreign policy position in Washington at any given time. Nicaragua had been in the forefront of the anti-Axis countries during World War II, even responding to the plea to provide refuge to Jews fleeing Europe, then had embraced anti-Communism in the days of John Foster Dulles and had helped to mount the 1954 anti-Communist invasion of Guatemala and the 1961 Bay of Pigs action in Cuba. Nicaragua was always a sure vote for anything the United States was advocating at the United Nations. It also helped that the Somozas had learned to manipulate not only the executive branch but also Congress. Tacho II, in particular, had acquired friends on the Hill, just a few, but they were there when they were needed.

It was not that the Carter administration, when it took office, publicly declared it was out to get Somoza. Statements were made by the new President, for example, to the effect that the United States would no longer automatically tolerate right-wing dictatorships merely because they were friendly to the United States. It was not necessary to mention Nicaragua by name for this kind of statement to have an impact in Nicaragua.

Also, a few Americans who had past connections with Nicaragua, some of them career diplomats and some of them political appointees or people outside of government, thought there was now an administration in Washington that would see through the Somozas. From their Nicaraguan experiences had come a special animosity for Somoza, and at the same time a special affection for many other people in Nicaragua.

One such Nicaraguan was Adolfo Calero Portocarrero, a leader of one of the factions of the Conservative Party that did not participate in the government. From an office at the Coca-Cola bottling plant hung with wide-angle photographs of international conventions of Coca-Cola managers, Calero had long been a favorite dispenser of news, opinion, and gossip to diplomats and journalists. The tall Notre Dame graduate, then in his mid-forties, was easy to like, the kind of person who gave both friendship and information without concern for what he was going to get in return. He was a friend and tennis partner of Pedro Joaquín Chamorro, whose newspaper plant was just a few hundred yards away. And he was on speaking terms with Tacho II. Calero made frequent trips to the United States for business or personal reasons and took one in late 1976, between Carter's election and the inauguration. In Washington he made the rounds of people he knew who had once served in the U.S. Embassy in Managua, and he returned home with a sense of the new view of Somoza.

"I told Tacho, 'You're going to lose your best friends, the gringos. They are saying that they are going to make life impossible for you. They are going to try and get your ass.' He said, 'Aw, you think I have no friends in Washington. I can take care of Carter.' But the idea I had was not to warn him, but to convince him that the time had come to change," Calero recalled.

What Adolfo Calero knew was easily ascertained by almost anybody else in a nation as small as Nicaragua. In turn, if he and others in the democratic opposition could conclude that human rights advocacy in Washington would help to undermine the Somoza regime, so could the Sandinistas. Though Somoza thought he had defeated the Sandinistas in the two-year counterinsurgency campaign that followed the Christmas Party Raid, the *terceristas*—the faction primarily responsible for the raid—had saved themselves by their preference for living abroad.

Now, in the first months of 1977, the *terceristas* were making an analysis of their own possibilities that took into account not only the changing political climate in Washington but also the growing dissatisfaction of Nicaraguans from the landed, industrial, and professional classes, many of whom no longer found an adequate outlet in the traditional opposition parties. The *terceristas* decided on a bold step: to seek out the Nicaraguan Establishment as an ally. For some of the *terceristas,* this was an easy connection to make because they came from well-known bourgeois families. Their parents and grandparents were members of the Conservative Party who had been dreaming of a return to power during all the Somoza years.

The plan for the approach to the bourgeoisie grew out of discussions between Sergio Ramírez, a talented writer and academic who had joined the FSLN a few years earlier, and Humberto Ortega, the Sandinista so criticized by Fonseca for staying outside the country since 1968. Ramírez, then in his mid-thirties, had come to San José, Costa Rica, from West Berlin to work for a regional university organization and was not publicly known to be a member of the FSLN, but his essays and short stories focused on his distaste for the Somozas, the bourgeoisie, and gringos. Ortega, then thirty-one, was one of three brothers from a lower-middle-class family who had joined the FSLN while still in their teens. Their father had once been jailed for supporting Sandino and years later had collaborated with the Sandinista Front. However, the parents struggled to keep their sons in good schools, generally run by religious orders, until the clandestine life consumed them. Humberto came into the Sandinista Front by way of an organization called the Nicaraguan Patriotic Youth, founded by Carlos Fonseca the year before he founded the FSLN. In 1969 Ortega took part in an unsuccessful attempt to free Fonseca from prison in Costa Rica and, in a shootout with guards, suffered permanent damage to one arm. The would-be rescuers ended up in prison with Fonseca until they were freed the following year when another Sandinista squad hijacked an airplane.

Behind the decision to seek alliance with the bourgeoisie was a document dated May 4, 1977, called the "General Political-Military Platform of Struggle of the Sandinista Front for National Liberation." Written primarily by Humberto Ortega, it contained the basic insurrectional strategy, including (1) development of a program of government without leftist rhetoric; (2) creation of a broad anti-Somoza front with non-Marxist opposition groups; (3) creation of mass organizations to support the FSLN; (4) agitation to bring about the radicalization of the moderate opposition; (5) actions to undermine the integrity of the National Guard; and (6) unification of the three FSLN factions under a joint leadership. Though Ortega later claimed that he had drafted the rough outlines of this plan with Fonseca in 1975, it was basically a *tercerista* plan. Its success depended upon first getting the help of the non-Marxist opposition to Somoza, then winning over the other Sandinista factions.

As prescribed in the platform, Ortega and Ramírez produced what they called a "minimum plan" for a government based on three tenets: political pluralism, a "mixed" economy that would include both private and state enterprises, and international nonalignment. Then they set out to find adherents. Ernesto Castillo, a lawyer and bookstore owner who was secretly a member of the FSLN, went to San José for a discussion with his friend Ramírez and returned to Managua to spread the idea of forming a select network of men to lend political respectability to the Sandinistas. Castillo talked to another friend, Felipe Mántica, who with his brother owned a chain of supermarkets. Little by little, they reached out to others.

Joaquín Cuadra Chamorro, probably the leading corporate lawyer in Nicaragua, was brought into the group by a closer tie than friendship. His son, Joaquín Cuadra Lacayo,* then in his mid-twenties, was a seasoned guerrilla. He had left the family home several years earlier after becoming involved with a university study group led by a priest who advocated the mixing of Marxism and Christianity. The reason for the younger Cuadra's disappearance from home became clear when he appeared in the Sandinista band that carried out the 1974 Christmas Party Raid. After that, he underwent training in Cuba, then returned to Central America and began to make quiet contacts on behalf of the Sandinista Front in Managua's upper social and economic strata, beginning with his massive, silver-haired father. They met in Honduras in the first half of 1977 and the son invited the father to join the so-far unnamed group.

In late June, eight of these men gathered in San José to analyze the

*This is an example of the Spanish use of both the father's and mother's last names.

Nicaraguan situation with Humberto Ortega. He told them that the Sandinistas were willing to set aside their own Marxist-Leninist aspirations in favor of an alliance with outsiders, which would increase everybody's chances of ousting Somoza. Being a clandestine organization, he said, the Sandinista Front needed a separate group to make open political proposals. Should the Sandinistas reach power, he added, these generally older and more educated and experienced men would fill key positions in the government. Mántica recalled in an interview later that he had not been much concerned about ideological factors.

"I thought that the Somoza regime was an unjust regime that was drowning Nicaragua and it was necessary to take concrete steps to oust Somoza and establish a just regime. So the ideological part did not interest me so much, nor had I studied Marxism or worried much about it. I was motivated more by Christian considerations. I thought that Somoza, like all of the dictators in Latin America, was at fault in creating a situation that had carried us to an explosive revolution. [But] I thought that the solutions in Nicaragua would be pragmatic ones."

Mántica thought that the "minimum plan" presented to them by Ramírez and Ortega responded to his view and that what it promised was a degree of socialism, but within a pluralistic society. To him, however, the conversations bordered on daydreaming because he did not seriously believe that the undertaking in which they were engaged would go anywhere.

On July 25, however, they received a major assist from an unexpected source. Anastasio Somoza Debayle, fifty-two years old and weighing two hundred and sixty-seven pounds, was going through his morning shower and exercise ritual when he felt, first, the sensation that his throat was stopping up and then a deep burning heat across his chest. Somoza thought he was about to fall victim to the same kind of coronary that had killed his brother. Cardiologists ran tests, then a heart specialist flew in from Florida and decided that Somoza had to be transferred to the Miami Heart Institute. Before he was put aboard a converted DC9 of the U.S. Air Force, Somoza told his cousin, Luis Pallais Debayle, and his half brother, General José Somoza, that if he died in Miami, the two of them should seize power and form a government to hold office until elections could be held.

As Somoza underwent treatment in Miami, the group of men that had met with Humberto Ortega in San José in June held a second meeting, with several new recruits present, this time at the home of a Nicaraguan exile in Cuernavaca, Mexico. The tone of the discussions had become less hypothetical. The group was keenly aware of the impact of a heart attack on a government that emanated from one man, and there were now some who thought their planning was more than just dreaming. Also, the Sandinista representative present, José Benito Escobar, said the guerrillas were preparing to resume the military operations that had been largely halted after the death of Carlos Fonseca. In addition, Jimmy Carter's human rights policy was seen as encouraging political moderates in Nicaragua to be more open in opposing or criticizing Somoza. They still wanted to add to the group, and those present decided to send a delegation to Washington to talk to Arturo José Cruz, an official of the Inter-American Development Bank.

Cruz's attitude toward the Somoza family and his relations with it through the years were probably typical of those of many Nicaraguans from his social class. He and Tacho II were about the same age and had attended some of the same parties when they were young, but Cruz's family political ties were to the Conservative Party and he had been jailed several times during the same period for plotting against Somoza García, the father. One of his brothers-in-law was killed in one such attempt. Yet, Cruz did not feel himself in exile from, or persecuted by, the Somoza regime. He still visited Nicaragua regularly, and in one visit had run into Somoza Debayle at a dinner and accepted the president's invitation to stop by the house afterward. In the limousine, Somoza called Cruz "Arturito," and they talked about their children and joked about how they had both once been skinny. Inside the presidential house, Somoza embraced Cruz and remarked lightly that this time he was there as a guest, not a prisoner.

Despite this, Cruz was amenable to joining the group that came to see him after the Cuernavaca meeting. "It was not only [because of] corruption in the government, but the very fact that the republic, which I love, was being made a mockery of. I admit that the first time he [Somoza Debayle] was [elected] president he won cleanly. He got a blank check from all the people, but I despised the use of an army to perpetuate somebody in power. I believed that civilian power should prevail over military power, and that's why . . . I agreed to join."

Cruz also asked three questions of his visitors. First, in the event of an outright Sandinista victory, would there be a place in the economic structure for progressive and responsible private enterprise? Second, would there be honest elections for national and municipal authorities? Third, would the armed forces be depoliticized? All of the answers, as he remembered them, were positive.

Somoza came home from treatment in Miami on September 7 and settled into his Moorish-style mansion overlooking the Pacific Ocean at Montelimar, under doctor's orders to rest, exercise, lose weight, and take his medicine. He planned to run the country from there. Rumors soon circulated in Managua that Somoza was so weak and sick he could do very little. Many people worried that the country was without authority.

Two weeks after returning home, Somoza lifted the state of siege he had imposed at the end of 1974 as part of the National Guard campaign against the Sandinistas. He took this step, which reinstated constitutional guarantees, including freedom of the press, in response to pressure from Washington, which had been delaying decisions on military and economic aid to Nicaragua. Some of his critics immediately took advantage of the restoration of press freedom to publish a communiqué demanding Somoza's resignation and calling for the appointment of a National Guard officer not related to him as head of state.

Somoza's liberalization measures as well as the pressures on him from the political opposition worried Humberto Ortega, the Sandinista strategist in Costa Rica. He feared that the events in Managua, coupled with U.S. pressures, might produce a new regime or a commitment for an early change in government that would freeze out the Sandinistas or nip in the bud their alliance with political moderates. Believing that the Sandinistas would become irrelevant unless they did something dramatic, he decided to speed up plans to try to set off an insurrection.

On October 6 several Sandinistas operating out of Costa Rica moved onto a farm called Las Brisas, which straddles the Nicaraguan-Costa Rican border, and began preparations for an assault on the National Guard post at San Carlos, just inside Nicaragua. It was supposed to be one of a series of simultaneous attacks around the country that the Sandinistas hoped would spark the beginning of a mass uprising. As they went about the work of cleaning weapons and selecting ammunition, they were visited by Fernando Cardenal, a Jesuit priest. Cardenal, a member of one of the prominent old families of Granada, the nineteenth century Conservative Party stronghold, was part of the group of wise men that Humberto Ortega and Sergio Ramírez had been organizing. He was effusive in his praise of the preparations and the battle spirit of the guerrillas.

On the night of the tenth, they crossed the river in a launch and stayed at a farm called La Loma, three kilometers from San Carlos. The next day, the rank and file was supposed to arrive, but only two came. On the twelfth, the others straggled in very tired, having come from Solentiname, an island in Lake Nicaragua, where Fernando Cardenal's brother Ernesto, also a priest, ran a peasant and artist commune. After seeing off the guerrilla force, Ernesto Cardenal had left for San José. There were now twenty-eight gathered at La Loma ready for the assault, planned for the next day. They were armed with a variety of rifles, including M-3s, FALs, Garands, and M-1s. There were 240 rounds of ammunition for each fighter and twenty-six grenades among all of them.

Late that night, the command leaders received instructions by radio to postpone the attack because units in the rest of the country were not ready. In the early morning hours another call came with instructions to proceed as planned. They got out of bed, rode into town in the back of trucks, and began firing on the command post before daylight. José Valdivia, the top Sandinista commander in the attack, was wounded in the first burst of shooting and had to be evacuated. The shooting continued for an hour, when Plutarco Hernández, another of the Sandinista commanders, learned from his radio that the planned attacks at eight other National Guard posts around the country had, in fact, not occurred. Hernández's prior instructions had been to capture the barracks at San Carlos and then go to the nearby town of Cárdenas to join up with other units. When he learned the other attacks had not come off as planned, he decided to order a retreat. The rebels began to flee any way they could. Some got on to river launches, others ran on foot, and a few surrendered to Costa Rican border guards. Four Sandinistas died as a result of the action as did an unknown number of National Guardsmen. All in all, it did not seem to add up to a momentous event, but the Sandinistas would later write it into their history as a watershed, an action that marked the beginning of the mass appeal of their cause.

Five days later, a smaller Sandinista band made a suicidal attack on the National Guard post in the town of Masaya, just twenty miles from Managua, in a jeep and a truck stolen from a moving man. Six of the dozen attackers lost their lives, but like many previous Sandinista actions with no military significance, this one impressed people with the fearlessness of the guerrillas.

Meanwhile, the Sandinistas' group of establishment backers, now numbering twelve, had gathered again in San José. Had the San Carlos and Masaya attacks set off the mass uprising as hoped, they would have announced themselves as the next government. Instead, on October 18 they issued a statement praising the "political maturity" of the Sandinista Front and saying it must be part of any solution to the country's problems. However, the close nature of the alliance between the Sandinistas and the signers of the communiqué, as well as the way they had been brought together, was not made public. Among the signers were priests, businessmen, lawyers, other professionals, and intellectuals. Four of them, including both priests, were already affiliated with the Sandinista Front, but some of the others did not yet know it. When the statement reached the newspapers in Nicaragua, someone counted the names and dubbed them the Group of Twelve, which was soon shortened to *Los Doce* in Spanish.

From that beginning, *Los Doce* went on to what would be their primary function for the Sandinista Front in the coming months: diplomacy in the Western Hemisphere and, to a lesser extent, Western Europe. They did not so much set out to sell Marxist-Leninist revolutionaries to people of other political persuasions as they went about trying to convince the world that the Somoza regime was repressive, corrupt, and undemocratic.

"The FSLN [Sandinista Front], being involved in an armed, clandestine fight, had no one to campaign in its favor internationally, to make the situation in the country known to the world," recalled Carlos Tünnermann, a member of the group who had formerly been rector of the national university. "So, the Group of Twelve undertook the international work, to visit governments and international organizations, to make known that the boys of the [Sandinista] Front were not terrorists, that they had taken up arms because it was necessary and that the terrorist was the government and the *somocista* system."

They visited General Omar Torrijos, the Panamanian strongman, and President José López Portillo of Mexico, explaining that if the Sandinista Front won, it would install a "pluralistic" government. Miguel d'Escoto, a Maryknoll priest who belonged to *Los Doce,* went to Washington and made the rounds with the head of the Washington Office on Latin America, an organization financed by Protestant churches. They went to the White House to see Robert Pastor, the member of the National Security Council responsible for Latin

American matters, and one of the things that d'Escoto told Pastor was that the group he represented was not Marxist. Joaquín Cuadra Chamorro, during his travels, dropped in on the man who was then U.S. ambassador to Venezuela, Viron P. Vaky, and, with tears in his eyes, made clear that love for his son had brought him into the group.

Felipe Mántica, the supermarket owner, also went to Venezuela, to talk to President Carlos Andrés Pérez. Venezuela was then approaching two decades of vibrant political democracy after throwing off a long tradition of authoritarian rule. That, coupled with the clout of its oil wealth, had turned Venezuela into something of a mecca for people from around the region who dreamed of change in their own countries. President Pérez believed in playing to the hilt his country's growing international role. Mántica was selected for the mission to Pérez because an uncle of his, General Carlos Pasos, for a time the archenemy of the first President Somoza, had developed a close friendship with Pérez more than twenty years earlier while both were in political exile in Costa Rica.

Pérez received the visitor amicably and listened with interest to what he had to say. Then Pérez began to talk about another old friend of his in Nicaragua, Pedro Joaquín Chamorro, the publisher of *La Prensa*. Theirs was a friendship also forged during exile in Costa Rica, and they were still close. When Pérez was inaugurated president in 1974, he had invited the Nicaraguan publisher to come to Caracas to share the moment of glory. Pérez told Mántica that he wondered what Pedro Joaquín Chamorro thought of the present situation in Nicaragua. The meeting ended with Pérez committing himself to nothing but sympathetic understanding.

Almost at the same time that *Los Doce* began to function, Archbishop Miguel Obando y Bravo called another group of Nicaraguans together in his offices in Managua, and they agreed to seek a way to eliminate "the cause" of violence in their country. This meeting was a reaction to the attempted Sandinista insurrection as well as the barrage of communiqués and manifestoes against Somoza that had appeared from nonviolent groups since the restoration of freedom of the press. Some of these people were Somoza opponents while others, at that moment, fit into the milder category of critics of the regime. They created what was called the Committee of National Dialogue. The intention was to negotiate a solution with Somoza that would satisfy most people and reduce the tension. Besides the archbishop, the committee included a lawyer who was a sort of stand-in for Pedro Joaquín

Chamorro and Alfonso Robelo Callejas, a Rensselaer graduate who had achieved considerable success in industry when young and now, at thirty-eight, was president of the Superior Council of Private Initiative—COSIP—the umbrella organization for most of organized private business.

The immediate catalyst for getting private enterprise involved in the undertaking had been a survey of retail stores showing that sales dropped substantially after any guerrilla action, even when it did not hit the town or area of a particular store. But private enterprise in Nicaragua still felt antagonism toward Somoza as a result of the earthquake reconstruction dispute just four years earlier. Alfonso Robelo, the COSIP president in 1977, had been a leader of the group that formulated the earthquake-related complaints in 1974.

Although the Dialogue Committee did not adopt a detailed position, those who supported it were people who wanted, or were willing to accept, a phased change that would not disrupt the economy and other aspects of Nicaraguan life. They talked about reaching some kind of agreement with Somoza whereby he would agree not to run again when his term as president ended in 1981 or would step aside sooner in favor of someone else from his party or the National Guard, with a guarantee of free elections at the end of 1980. They also wanted removal of General José Somoza, the president's half brother, from his post as director of the National Guard. In December, the Dialogue Committee met with Somoza. Robelo told him that the country would be swept into civil war if the government did not make some changes. Somoza agreed to proceed to a "dialogue" with them but said it would have to wait until after the municipal elections scheduled two months hence, in February 1978.

One of the keenest observers of these events was Mauricio Solaun, who arrived in Managua in August 1977 as the new U.S. ambassador. The Cuban-born Solaun was teaching sociology at the University of Illinois when Carter tapped him to go to Nicaragua. For the previous several decades, the job into which he stepped had been held primarily by men who thought it their first obligation to keep happy whichever Somoza was ruling at the time. Among other things, this had meant paying very little attention to Somoza's critics or opponents, no matter how moderate, reasonable, or nonviolent they might be. This attitude had been especially notable during the years the embassy was presided over by Turner Shelton, the appointee of the Nixon administration. After a spate of U.S. press criticism of Shelton, the Ford

White House accepted his resignation and named James D. Theberge, a Latin American expert at Georgetown University, to replace him. While not setting out overtly to rock the boat when he arrived in Managua in mid-1975, Theberge had begun to open up the embassy's range of contacts. He had, for example, taken up what Somoza viewed as the inconsiderate habit of talking to Pedro Joaquín Chamorro of *La Prensa.*

Now came Solaun, and he and his staff went far beyond Theberge's tentative beginning, aggressively making contacts with Nicaraguans all across the political and economic spectrum, with the exception of the clandestine Sandinistas, whom the CIA had judged to number fewer than two hundred when Solaun went to Managua.

What Solaun saw and heard from Nicaraguans and the embassy professional staff in the last months of 1977 grew into a proposal that the United States should begin working with the Nationalist Liberal Party and the nonviolent opposition to ease the Somoza family out of power, at least by the time his current term ended in early 1981. Solaun felt that it was impossible to create a political center in Nicaragua without retaining part of the large Somoza political apparatus in public life, but he thought it was possible to remove Somoza and his closest family members and associates. He acknowledged that it would be *somocismo sin Somoza*—the same system, but without Somoza—at least for a transitional period.

Toward the end of 1977, Solaun went to Washington to push his idea of using U.S. pressure to open up the system in Nicaragua. However, the man whose personal background and analytical skills had allowed him to see what was happening in Nicaragua was naïve about the ways of Washington, ignorant of who held the strings of the administration power structure and how to pull them. He had a hearing before the cool and impersonal Warren Christopher, Deputy Secretary of State. Solaun was nervous and ineffective, and most of his listeners from outside the Latin American Bureau of the department thought this was a problem not worthy of their attention. A State Department official who was in basic agreement with Solaun later recalled thinking that Solaun's position might have had more impact if offered by someone else.

Unknown to Solaun, the Latin American specialists in the State Department were already dividing up over the Somoza question. Terence Todman, the assistant secretary in charge of Latin American relations, was arguing internally that Somoza would survive his problems and the United States should do nothing to undermine him, while some lower-ranking officials were beginning to argue that Somoza could not last and the United States should facilitate his departure. At the same time, Todman was giving most of his attention to his battle with the political appointees in the Human Rights Bureau over how to deal with the big military regimes of South America, a feud that would eventually cost him his job. As a result, the plea from Managua found neither understanding at the top nor support from the specialists.

4

THE CATALYSTS

JANUARY 1978 TO SEPTEMBER 1978

In Managua, on the morning of Tuesday, January 10, 1978, Pedro Joaquín Chamorro began the usual drive from his home facing Las Palmas Park to the offices of *La Prensa* in the industrial district on the North Highway. Shortly after eight o'clock, as he passed through the overgrown ruins of what had been the downtown area before the 1972 earthquake, his Saab was intercepted by a Toyota pickup carrying three armed men. They forced his car to stop, jumped out and fired on him through the windshield, then fled. Chamorro was hit about twenty times in the face, chest, arms, and throat. He died in an ambulance on the way to a hospital.

As soon as word spread of the shooting, businesses began to close throughout Managua, and tens of thousands of people followed Chamorro's body home from the hospital for the wake. It was the beginning of a mass outpouring of frustration and anti-Somoza rage. When Chamorro was buried two days later, about 10,000 people took part in the funeral procession, and as many as 50,000 roamed the streets, burning buses and trucks, attacking banks and factories. Some carried the black and red colors of the FSLN, though Chamorro had taken the view that the Sandinistas were brave but politically misguided.

From the funeral, the leaders of the Chamber of Construction and the construction workers union went to the offices of the Chamber and decided to call a national strike. It began on January 23 with the walkout of 4,000 construction workers. The next day, COSIP urged all its members to join the strike. A strike committee came together under Alfonso Robelo, the business leader who had been a member of the Dialogue Committee, and operated out of a nerve center in *La Prensa*. It was effectively a lockout, with employers paying their employees while they did not work, though some labor federations supported it.

Somoza, still living at his seaside estate thirty-five miles from Managua, derided the action as a "capitalists' strike" and predicted that the naturally competitive nature of businessmen would soon end it. He also said he was surprised and sorry about the death of Chamorro, and not responsible for the killing. He promised to find those who were responsible. Within a few days five men were arrested, and one of them said he had been paid $15,000 by a Cuban-American physician to organize the killing. The physician, Dr. Pedro Ramos, lived in Miami but owned a blood-plasma exporting company in Managua that had recently been the subject of critical investigative reporting in *La Prensa*. Ramos had filed a libel suit against Chamorro and had left Managua the day before the shooting. About two weeks after the killing, Ramos and the five Nicaraguans were charged with murder and association to commit a crime.*

At first, no one who liked Chamorro wanted to accept the possibility that Somoza had not been responsible for his death. The family —Pedro's widow, Violeta, and their four grown children—concluded after the funeral that the explanation lay somewhere in the aggressive

---

*The accused had not been brought to trial when the Somoza government fell in July 1979. The new government re-charged all six men, but as of the beginning of 1985 the State Department said it had no record of extradition proceedings having been initiated against Ramos by the Nicaraguan government. Ramos denied, in various interviews with media in Miami, any involvement in the crime.

reporting on corruption that *La Prensa* had been doing recently, rather than Pedro Joaquín's own political views, but they did not specifically accept that it was linked to the Ramos articles. Many of the investigative pieces, after all, had touched situations linked to Somoza himself. When emotions cooled, many of Chamorro's friends and supporters came to accept that Somoza may not have ordered or approved the killing, but they argued that he was still indirectly responsible because he had remained in office after he was too weak to prevent such things. Eventually, there were allegations linking Somoza's eldest son, Anastasio III, to the Ramos group, and it was generally held that the heart attack had loosened Somoza's grip on decision-making and perhaps encouraged those around him to branch out on their own. Even among those who hated him most, Somoza was viewed as politically astute enough to understand that the death of Chamorro would do him more harm than good. Which it did.

Chamorro's death also handicapped the middle-of-the-road opposition, the broad spectrum of political, business, and labor groups that had looked to him as unofficial leader. Pablo Antonio Cuadra, a poet who was Chamorro's co-editor at *La Prensa,* said a few days after the killing that Chamorro's death would have the effect of strengthening the unity of the opposition as well as its conviction that the Somoza regime must end, but that at the same time, it left the opposition without its most significant leader, the most obvious alternative to Somoza. "He was the figure that at a given moment could catalyze a great opposition party," Cuadra said.

Conscious that Somoza's regime was in crisis because of his heart attack and U.S. policies, Chamorro and his friend Adolfo Calero and other Conservative representatives had begun talks for the reunification of their party just days before his death. The murder interrupted these talks, and the Conservative unification did not come about until the following year.

The death of Chamorro also had the effect of canceling the dialogue planned for February between Somoza and the committee led by Archbishop Obando y Bravo. Chamorro's representatives pulled out of the Dialogue Committee almost immediately after the murder, saying they no longer wanted to sit down and talk to Somoza. There was a general feeling that more drastic action was called for now.

The groups that had been issuing communiqués demanding gradual change now began to call for Somoza's immediate resignation, and those that had already been demanding his resignation turned to acts of petty sabotage, such as throwing nails on the highway in the path of his car.

In addition to their outrage, a strong sense of fear swept businessmen, politicians, and trade unionists as they realized that what had happened to Chamorro could happen to them. They had always known, or suspected, that the National Guard treated the poor in a repressive manner, especially in isolated settlements where most detainees were not considered important enough to bring into the capital for questioning, but they had felt themselves reasonably secure to carry out peaceful opposition. They had known they could be thrown into jail for a few weeks but had never expected to be killed. It was part of the unwritten agreement covering the political and economic space that Somoza had long allowed them. But Pedro Joaquín Chamorro was not a peasant. He had been one of them, the most outstanding among them, a descendant of presidents and generals, the one whose international reputation should have protected him. His death changed things for all of them. Whether Somoza was responsible or not, it still meant that he could no longer guarantee their right to peaceful protest. Even those who were politically ambivalent now thought that Somoza should go because he could no longer provide the one thing that made strongmen attractive: public order.

In the early days of the strike, leaders said that 80 percent of the stores and factories in major towns had shut down, and when the strike went into its second week they were still claiming 75 percent success. It went into a third week and then gradually petered out as some COSIP leaders argued that they should hold out until Somoza resigned, while others said they had made their point and should end the strike for now. Above all, they now hoped the United States would step in and play its traditional role as arbiter of power struggles in Nicaragua.

But the Carter administration still took the view that Nicaragua was to be dealt with basically as a human rights problem, through withholding aid and other pressures to achieve specific goals, such as freeing prisoners and lifting constitutional restrictions. While some of the Latin specialists in the State Department disagreed, the official view was that it was not a situation calling for political reorganization of the government, nor a military problem.

The Nicaraguan opposition, however, was putting out the word to the embassy and to journalists that there was a limit to how much good the human rights policy would do without some decisive direction. The businessmen and politicians said that they, like the Sandinistas, had been encouraged by the human rights policy to be more open in their opposition and now there was a need for U.S. help to prevent chaos. Most of the moderates had long distrusted the Sandinista Front, which had heretofore been considered too small to matter, but now the businessmen and politicians saw the guerrillas in a position to move into the growing void. Some, thinking nothing more could be accomplished with strikes and communiqués, were already tempted to join forces with the Sandinistas.

As the strike was ending, one ad hoc businessmen's group sent its leader, Leonel Poveda, to San José, Costa Rica, to make contact with the Sandinista Front. Poveda, then thirty-seven, had spent much of his youth in Southern California, where he had been drafted into the U.S. Army and trained as a heavy artillery specialist during eighteen months in West Germany. After service, he returned to California, earned a degree at UCLA at night and worked for the Bank of America. When he was twenty-eight he came home to Nicaragua, got a job in a bank, and began to look critically at his country's politics. What particularly struck him was the realization that Nicaraguans of his generation had never had the opportunity to vote in honest elections. Without a specific plan, he began to buy ammunition and store it. Now, the death of Chamorro seemed to demand action.

"I asked the FSLN's help in getting war matériel—rifles, dynamite, bullets and the like. I told them we were forty professionals disposed to do whatever necessary to get rid of Somoza," Poveda recalled. "The FSLN said yes, that they would help us. They told me they were going to contact me in Managua."

So Poveda returned to Managua, where his group had recently broken up into small cells. Poveda became the leader—the Zero in Sandinista terms—of a cell that included five other men, basically middle-management types, green at both politics and warfare. Members of his cell submitted humbly to Sandinista direction, Poveda said, because they hated Somoza so much that they thought there was no alternative. The ideology of the Sandinistas did not concern them much because they thought the *tercerista* faction, with which they were dealing, was being taken over by people like themselves.

Within a short time Poveda's cell was contacted by the high command of the *terceristas'* "Internal Front"—four young men who had recently moved into guerrilla safe houses in Managua and were trying to organize sympathizers in order to put the FSLN at the head of the growing opposition to Somoza. The military leader of the Internal

Front was Joaquín Cuadra Lacayo, the corporate lawyer's son who the year before had convinced his father to join *Los Doce*. Working with Cuadra in the Internal Front were Raúl Venerio, Walter Ferretti, and Oscar Pérez Cassar.* Poveda's cell members were assigned a series of small actions and duties in the coming weeks, but mostly they were told to be available; they were also asked to get in shape and give up cigarettes and liquor.

In early February, a month after the death of Chamorro, Mauricio Solaun, the U.S. ambassador, made one of his regular visits to Somoza, who asked what he had to do to satisfy the United States. Solaun, still lacking instructions from Washington, told him that a stated promise to get out of politics in 1981, when Somoza's six-year term would end, might satisfy Washington. Despite the growing radicalization of his contacts in the moderate opposition, Solaun continued to believe that some kind of middle way was preferable to the abrupt ending of the regime. Somoza said he was willing to make such a commitment. The Nicaraguan leader had always been convinced that if he had a problem, it was with the people in Washington, not with Nicaraguans. So the important thing was to do whatever was necessary to survive the political thinking of the moment in the U.S. capital. Now, if Washington wanted him to say he was giving up power in 1981, he would do it—that is, he could at least say he was going to do it. Jimmy Carter had to face elections before that, anyway.

Somoza said it on February 27 in the midst of a show of both his continuing power and his vulnerability. His party and government turned out tens of thousands of people for the occasion, held in an open field bounded by Somoza's headquarters in a military post on one side and the Inter-Continental Hotel on another. The turnout may have been 150,000 as Somoza estimated or it may have been fewer, but there was no doubt that the crowd cheered him fervently. He announced he was going to step aside in 1981, after presidential elections in late 1980, but he had to deliver the promise from inside a bulletproof glass booth for fear of assassination.

By then, Somoza's announcement satisfied almost no one. It was received by opponents not so much as a promise to step aside as the determination to stay three more years, time in which to arrange a

---

*Except for Pérez Cassar, who died in the war, all of these men would eventually assume high-level military or security positions in the Sandinista government.

succession to his liking. Many did not believe he would do what he promised. After all, it was by constantly changing the written rules of electoral politics that the Somozas had stayed in power more than forty years under a constitutional façade. The speech set off antigovernment protests and clashes with police in which at least ten people died.

A separate uprising was already under way in Monimbó, an Indian artisan community in the city of Masaya, just twenty miles southeast of Managua. It began on February 21, as a group of people left a mass commemorating the forty days since the death of Pedro Joaquín Chamorro. The National Guard, trying to break up the crowd, attacked with tear gas and rifle butts, and the entire neighborhood rose in rebellion. Determined to keep the Guardsmen out of their community, the Indians resisted with the few weapons they had. Though the uprising was not planned by the Sandinistas, they infiltrated a few people into Monimbó in an unsuccessful attempt to manage it once it was under way, and one of them, Camilo Ortega, younger brother of Humberto, died there. The Monimbó fighting was heavy for days, then continued sporadically for months, and the Indian community became a symbol of heroic resistance to the National Guard. The number of deaths was put at anywhere from several dozen to two hundred.

At the end of February the unrest spread to several other towns, with clashes between the National Guard and youths in León, Chinandega, and Managua. These actions were at least in part directed by small numbers of Sandinistas who moved into these and other towns after the beginning of the uprising in Monimbó. Humberto Ortega, the Sandinista strategist, said later that after seeing what happened in Monimbó the Sandinista Front concluded that it had to create a group quickly that could work to arouse the population and then take over leadership of such uprisings once they began. A forty-man column was created for this purpose, and its members dispersed among the main population centers, especially in crowded, poor neighborhoods.

Meanwhile, in neighboring Costa Rica, the Sandinistas had quietly begun to establish small training camps in the hills and mountains surrounding San José, the capital. By April 1978, four such schools were operating, with a few dozen trainees at each. One camp was devoted almost entirely to training "internationalists"—sympathizers from other countries, primarily Latin American, who wanted to fight for the Sandinista cause. On occasion, light planes loaded with arms and ammunition landed at some of the nearly one hundred private airstrips and dozens of wide, empty beaches in the department of Guanacaste, a region bordering Nicaragua on the Pacific. This was made possible by friendships and other ties that the Sandinistas were establishing with local farmers. Guanacaste's valleys, so broad they seem like immense prairies, are filled with cotton, rice, and cattle farms. Most of the cotton farms have their own landing strips for fumigation planes, to which aviation authorities almost never direct their attention.

As the only fully functioning political democracy in Central America, Costa Rica had long provided sympathy and refuge to Nicaraguans wanting to overthrow the Somozas. The Sandinistas were no exception. But in May 1978, Costa Ricans inaugurated a new president whose policies would gradually, but dramatically, increase the freedom of movement of the Sandinistas. Three weeks after Rodrigo Carazo, the candidate of a coalition of several small centrist parties, was sworn in as president, he pardoned an imprisoned Sandinista named Plutarco Hernández, who had been picked up two months earlier while transporting arms and held on old charges pending against him. A Costa Rican descended from the illegitimate branch of a prominent family, Hernández had joined the Sandinista Front as a student at Moscow's Patrice Lumumba University in the 1960s and had been one of the commanders of the October 1977 attack on the National Guard post at San Carlos, just inside Nicaragua.

According to Hernández, soon after his release from prison he happened to see President Carazo at a restaurant outside San José and approached him with a plea on behalf of the Sandinistas. The way he put it was that there was a need for Costa Rica to do something to help Nicaraguans in their struggle against Somoza. He recalled that Carazo told him the Costa Rican government could not provide direct help but that it could "tolerate" certain activities of the Sandinistas. The president recommended that Hernández discuss the specifics with the minister of public security, Juan José (Johnny) Echeverría Brealey. Carazo later told me he did not recall the chance encounter with Hernández in a restaurant, but he acknowledged that a policy of tolerance of Sandinista activities was established early in his administration. Echeverría used the same word, tolerance, to describe the policy and said Hernández did come to see him about that time to discuss the expected arrival of an arms shipment from Panama.

. . .

At the same time, Carlos Andrés Pérez, the president of Venezuela, motivated by the death of his friend Chamorro, abandoned his uncommitted stance. Somoza had dispatched a vice minister soon after the murder to assure Pérez that the killers had been captured and would be tried, but the Venezuelan leader was more interested in the political impact of the killing. He saw the death of Chamorro as the spark that ignited in Nicaraguans their unanimous repudiation of Somoza. Pérez was a Social Democrat who had come of age politically under the aegis of the major figures of the so-called "Democratic Left" around the Caribbean Basin, men such as José Figueres in Costa Rica, who had helped both Chamorro and Pérez in exile, and Rómulo Bétancourt, the father of Venezuelan democracy. After the 1948 civil war in Costa Rica, these men and their political friends had sworn to devote their energies to helping rid the region of dictators, specifically Trujillo in the Dominican Republic, Batista in Cuba, Pérez Jiménez in Venezuela, and Somoza García in Nicaragua. In one way or another these dictators fell, except in Nicaragua, where the Somozas had evolved from a one-man dictatorship to a reigning dynasty. Now, Pérez, who considered himself the heir to the mantle of the Democratic Left, faced the tempting prospect of toppling the man who had inherited the Somoza mantle. He went to work behind the scenes with government leaders.

When President Carter visited Pérez in Caracas on March 28, 1978, Nicaragua was on the agenda. Pérez told Carter that strong intervention was needed to force Somoza to step aside, but that he was not advocating the Sandinistas' cause as such at that time, for he feared that to back them would lead to unpredictable consequences. What Pérez then envisioned, if Carter would force out Somoza, was an interim government along the *somocismo- sin-Somoza* lines that would retain part of Somoza's Nationalist Liberal Party and the National Guard. Pérez thought he had won Carter over to this idea and could count on him to bring it about. Pérez also made his unhappiness with Somoza known to General Omar Torrijos, the leader of Panama, who played host to Carter on June 17 for the signing of the Panama Canal treaties.

Torrijos' own feelings about Somoza were relatively ambivalent. For one thing, his ruling style had more in common with Somoza's than that of Pérez or Carter. In fact, in many ways, Torrijos ran Panama in a more authoritarian manner than Somoza ran Nicaragua. Torrijos, for instance, did not allow the kind of press criticism that Somoza had usually tolerated from Chamorro, and Torrijos was given to shipping political opponents out of the country. He did appear to have a stronger desire for social justice than Somoza, though it was difficult to judge how much of that was rhetoric and how much was real. Through the years, the two strongmen had been useful to each other. Torrijos had had some help from Somoza when he and two other National Guard officers ousted an elected civilian president, Arnulfo Arias, in late 1968. During his early years in power, Torrijos had looked to Somoza with respect, as a sort of model for himself. He had acted timidly around Somoza and called him *jefe* (boss). Torrijos, a small man, was impressed by Somoza's large size, commenting once in awe that the Nicaraguan had the bearing and manner of a king. Both had proven reputations for drinking and womanizing, though Somoza liked to wear a suit and tie while Torrijos appeared more freewheeling with his hip pistol and broad-brimmed fatigue hat.

In later years the friendship between Somoza and Torrijos soured. People close to the two men thought that their differences began in February 1972, when Somoza went to Panama on behalf of the Nixon administration to try to convince Torrijos to be more reasonable in his demands for new treaties governing ownership of the Panama Canal. Big issues and little marred the meetings, which were held at the Contadora Island beach home of Gabriel Lewis, a Panamanian businessman. The problems began even before Somoza arrived in Panama, when he advised the Panamanians how many people would be traveling with him. There were too many in the view of the Panamanians, who were paying the bills, and they threatened to cancel the invitation until Somoza agreed to reduce his delegation. Whatever was said in the meetings themselves, the assessment of Lewis and of Luis Pallais Debayle, Somoza's cousin, who had helped to arrange the sessions, was that everything had gone wrong. It may have been because Somoza's security people tore into the walls of Lewis' house looking for listening and recording devices, which led Torrijos to think Somoza did not trust him. It may also have been because Somoza lectured Torrijos about becoming too friendly with Communists, or it may have been because Somoza said or did something that struck Torrijos as arrogant.

Some months later, Somoza telephoned Lewis, whom he had known before the Contadora meeting, and invited him to Nicaragua for lunch. Somoza began offering advice to pass along to Torrijos. "He was telling me, 'Look, tell Torrijos that if he wants a treaty, I can get him a treaty with my senator,* my very dear friend. I have a lot of

---

*Lewis said he had no idea which senator Somoza referred to.

influence in the Senate.' I don't know whether he wanted to be nasty or what. Torrijos didn't even answer him."

People close to the two men believe their differences evolved into a sort of competition for the role of Washington's man in the Caribbean, or, rather, Torrijos' attempt to take the play away from Somoza. To be sure, what separated the two was not domestic political style but the way each related to the world outside. They were nearly the same age chronologically, but intellectually they were two decades apart.

Somoza, like his brother and father before him, thought the important thing was to be outwardly and vocally loyal to the United States, something he regularly expressed in the 1950s American slang that so fit his views. Torrijos thought the United States no longer expected this kind of overt allegiance. True, Torrijos had some Communists in his inner circle, as he also had conservative businessmen such as Gabriel Lewis. He thought it broadened his knowledge, knowledge that the Yankees could use to their benefit if they would only listen to him from time to time. While Somoza found friends and business partners among Cuban-American exiles, a fact that angered many Nicaraguan businessmen, Torrijos enjoyed inviting Gabriel García Marquez, the famous Colombian novelist who moved in leftist circles, to Contadora for long weekends. It was part of Torrijos' flirtation with Cuba, with Fidel Castro and the global network of Marxist-Leninist internationalism. Torrijos had seen the rise of Third World antagonism toward Washington and had concluded that one of the necessities for staying in power was to keep up the proper rhetoric internationally—leftist rhetoric, or rhetoric that at least pleased the left. Torrijos had a reading of U.S. public opinion rooted in the 1970s, not the 1950s, and it found that the U.S. public was no longer impressed by foreign rulers who offered nothing but anti-Communism, that public opinion even worked the other way.

In mid-1978, fresh from contacts with Carlos Andrés Pérez and Carter, Torrijos had a message for Somoza, so he called Luis Pallais Debayle, who in addition to being Somoza's cousin was vice president of the Nicaraguan Chamber of Deputies, and asked him to come to Panama. Torrijos and Pallais were old friends. It was Pallais personally who had gone to Panama in 1968 and helped Torrijos bring off the coup that put him in power, carrying money to pay off Panamanian National Guardsmen, and arranging exile in Nicaragua for a vice president whom Torrijos found extraneous. Their friendship had survived the break between Torrijos and Somoza after the 1972

Contadora meeting. Pallais recalled of the meeting in mid-1978: "Omar told me Tacho should resign. In part, he was passing on this idea from Carlos Andrés Pérez. Omar said Carter was after Somoza's ass, that in Carter's view people like him [Torrijos] and Somoza were no longer appropriate to rule in the region and that they should, therefore, look for a way to step aside. He said Tacho should not believe so much in the United States. Omar said he felt he had a responsibility to tell Somoza this because Tacho had helped him. But he said he could not help Somoza stay in power because he had a greater responsibility to Panama. He said Somoza should be smart, that he could save his party, his prestige, his capital [wealth] and the National Guard, that he could get exile in a convenient place, but that he should form a national unity government and leave."

Torrijos also pointed out to Pallais that he himself was taking steps to withdraw from active control of Panama, that he was moving Aristides Royo into the presidency, creating a political party, and planning eventual elections. If Somoza failed to take this advice, Torrijos warned, he should not ask him for anything again.

When Pallais returned to Managua, Somoza reacted angrily to the message and would have nothing to do with such a suggestion. Somoza still thought he could work his old magic and turn the United States in his favor. Deciding to respond to the pressures from the Carter administration, he announced a series of liberalization measures on June 19, 1978. They included amnesty for some prisoners, allowing the members of the Group of Twelve to return home, promised reform of the electoral system, and an invitation for the OAS Human Rights Commission to make an inspection trip to Nicaragua.

Then Somoza left for the United States, in search of people with good Democratic connections. He went to New York, Washington, Miami, and New Mexico, talking to various people. In New York, Somoza asked Clark Clifford, a former Secretary of Defense, to intercede on his behalf with Carter. According to Somoza, Clifford said the effort would be futile.

A few days later, he checked into the Four Seasons Hotel in Albuquerque, New Mexico, then called on Governor Jerry Apodaca at his office in Santa Fe. Apodaca had never met Somoza and when he learned the Nicaraguan president was coming to New Mexico he had tried, without success, to get guidance from the White House or State Department on how to treat him. So Apodaca planned a reception in Somoza's honor at the end of the five-day visit, and on the day of his arrival called the press in to meet him. Somoza told reporters he was there to learn something about energy and also implied he had some business interests in New Mexico. In private, he made clear to Apodaca that his mission was very different. Apodaca recalled it this way: "He had been led to believe I was very close to President Carter. I don't know who ever is really close to a President, but he determined that I could probably try to influence Carter's position . . . I think he was looking for as much political support as he could get, anything I could provide. I could not . . . There are certain situations where you instinctively know there is little you could do about it. There was no one in the White House I could talk to, principally because I didn't feel it was up to me to interfere. Also, human rights had been Carter's strong, or weak, point, depending on your view, and Somoza was one guy they didn't like. Did I call anyone? The answer is no."

Whether anyone called or not, somebody at the White House decided it would be a good idea to give Somoza a pat on the back for his efforts. Robert Pastor, who was the Latin American adviser on the National Security Council, received instructions to draft a letter to Somoza. He was worried about whether Somoza could be trusted and decided to use the letter to pin him down to his promises, to remind him that the United States was looking forward to their being carried out. He sent the draft to the State Department for the comments of both the Human Rights bureau and the Latin American bureau. The human rights people were adamantly opposed to sending the letter. The career diplomats in the Latin bureau, who in general wanted a more activist policy, whether it was to remove Somoza or work out a gradual change, also disliked it. However, the Latin bureau was virtually rudderless at that point and had no one to argue its case effectively at the top. Assistant Secretary Terence Todman, after losing his struggles with the Human Rights bureau over other issues, was being sent to Spain as ambassador, and his successor, Viron P. Vaky, was still involved in making the move up from Caracas. Opponents of the letter found no support in Secretary of State Cyrus Vance; it fit in with his preference for putting things on paper. One critic of the letter told me that while many people in the administration had misgivings about sending it, no one was willing to go to the President and tell him it was a bad idea. Eventually, the internal State Department criticism was reduced to a plea to delay sending the letter for a week or two because of delicate negotiations then under way for the entry of the Inter-American Human Rights Commission. Carter agreed and then sent it. The letter, dated June 30, 1978, said this:

Dear Mr. President:

I read your statements to the press on June 19 with great interest and appreciation. The steps toward respecting human rights that you are considering are important and heartening signs; and, as they are translated into actions, will mark a major advance for your nation in answering some of the criticisms recently aimed at the Nicaraguan government.

I am pleased to learn of your willingness to cooperate with the Inter-American Commission on Human Rights. I believe that multilateral institutions can be a most appropriate and effective means of protecting human rights and alleviating concerns expressed about them. I sincerely hope that your government can rapidly reach agreement with the Commission on a date for their visit.

The Commission will be favorably impressed by your decision to allow the members of the so-called "Group of Twelve" to return to peaceful lives in Nicaragua. The freedoms of movement and of expression that are at stake in this case are among the central human rights that the Commission seeks to protect.

You have spoken about a possible amnesty for Nicaraguans being held in jail for political reasons. I urge you to take the promising steps you have suggested; they would serve to improve the image abroad of the human rights situation in Nicaragua.

I was also encouraged to hear your suggestions for a reform of the electoral system in order to ensure fair and free elections in which all political parties could compete fairly. This step is essential to the functioning of a democracy.

I would also like to take this opportunity to encourage you to sign and ratify the American Convention of Human Rights. I have signed this agreement and am working hard to have my country ratify the Convention.

I look forward to hearing of the implementation of your decisions and appreciate very much your announcement of these constructive actions. I hope that you will continue to communicate fully with my Ambassador, Mauricio Solaun, who enjoys my complete confidence.

Sincerely,
Jimmy Carter

Before the letter itself reached the embassy in Managua, its contents arrived in a cable. Solaun sat on the matter for a while, then called a meeting of the Country Team—the heads of the embassy sections, the CIA station chief, and the deputy chief of mission. They thought that if the letter were leaked to the press, it would be detrimental to their efforts to get Somoza to open up the political system, and they concluded that it was certain to be leaked. Solaun decided to convey the contents to Somoza verbally, so he went to see Somoza and read it to him. Then he cabled Washington saying he had read it to the president. A few days later, however, the letter itself arrived, preceded by a cable ordering Solaun to deliver it, which he did. Solaun told Somoza the contents were not supposed to be made public.

Somoza, without giving the letter a close reading, was elated, but thought it would do him very little good unless he could make it public. Then he decided that the letter might be used to influence Carlos Andrés Pérez. It was something on paper from Carter to throw back at the Venezuelan president as proof that the United States, in fact, did not want him to resign. Somoza sent an aide to Caracas to meet with Pérez, who reluctantly issued an invitation for Somoza to make an unpublicized trip to Venezuela. They met secretly in late July on the island of Orchila, off the Venezuelan coast in the Caribbean.

Somoza, in his account of the meeting, said he spent three hours explaining Nicaragua's domestic situation to Pérez, stressing details about the Sandinistas and their ties to Cuba. He told Pérez that Communists were trying to take over Nicaragua and that much more was at stake than the political future of Anastasio Somoza. Pérez, however, insisted that Somoza had to abandon power. "I warned him of the high price in blood and human lives that his permanence in power would mean," Pérez recalled. "Repression could lengthen the life of a dictatorship, but in the end it would not achieve anything. The dynamic of violence was going to create more and more opposition, terminating by binding all of the people together against him. All of that I told him with the greatest frankness, speaking plainly." Regardless of this, Somoza thought he had won a pledge from Pérez to talk to some of the Nicaraguan internal opposition leaders and try to convince them to open negotiations with the government.

At one point, Somoza claimed he had proof that at least some of the things he was doing were pleasing to the White House, but he apparently did not say specifically that he had received a letter. Pérez said Somoza told him he had reached an understanding with Carter. Pérez said it was not until several days later, when information on the letter was leaked to the Washington *Post,* that he realized what Somoza was talking about. Pérez, who said he had advised Carter of his plans to meet with Somoza and had thought that he and Carter understood each other on how to deal with the question of Nicaragua, was furious over the letter. A short time later, when he saw Viron Vaky, the new Assistant Secretary of State, at a gathering in Colombia, Pérez said he told him: "If I had known of that letter from the President of the United States to Somoza I would not have bothered to spend that bad time meeting with the dictator."

Somoza, on his plane returning home, reread the letter more carefully and concluded that it had not been as complimentary as he had earlier thought. Instead, he decided that it was a "ruse and ploy," a duplicitous act on Carter's part. "When the letter was written," he thought, "it was anticipated that, as a result of the friendly tone, I would cooperate with those forces which were determined to destroy me and the government of Nicaragua."

Before Somoza's trip to Venezuela, *Los Doce* had been allowed to return to Nicaragua in accordance with one of Somoza's promises. Tens of thousands of people lined the streets when they drove in from the airport on July 5. By this time, however, the Group of Twelve was only eleven. Felipe Mántica, the supermarket owner who had been one of those most active in seeking out members for the group, had withdrawn under the pressure of family members who had close ties to some of the Somozas. He had come home earlier and resumed management of his business.

During July and August 1978, with sporadic protests and small clashes occurring around the country, the opposition political parties, two labor confederations, and *Los Doce* gradually came together under the name Broad Opposition Front, which became known by its Spanish acronym, FAO. The U.S. Embassy strongly encouraged the union by regularly telling such opposition leaders as Adolfo Calero and Alfonso Robelo that the only hope for the moderates was to diminish their differences. Organized private enterprise, through COSIP or its various chambers, was not among the sixteen groups in the FAO, but it did have indirect representation through Robelo. He had just completed his term as president of COSIP and was an active member of FAO through the Nicaraguan Democratic Movement, the social democratic political party he had organized six months earlier.

The differences among the various elements in the FAO related to how strong their demand should be for Somoza's immediate resignation and how far they should go in negotiating with him. *Los Doce* took the toughest line against Somoza, and Calero thought that

Robelo was too susceptible to the influence of *Los Doce*. While they were trying to work out the differences, *Los Doce* called a news conference and charged that certain unnamed capitalists were trying to get the church and *La Prensa* to seek a solution in collaboration with Somoza, something that would have as its priority not hurting business. The next day, Archbishop Obando y Bravo said he did not know anything about any "capitalist plan," but said he was willing to discuss solutions to the country's problems with anyone. A few days later, he and other members of the bishops' conference issued a communiqué calling on Somoza to resign and for the National Guard to be reorganized as an apolitical force. On August 21, apparently overcoming at least some of its differences, the FAO released a sixteen-point plan calling for Somoza's departure, organization of a national unity government to succeed him, and the transfer of control of the National Guard to officers not related to Somoza. The FAO also said it would call another general strike at any moment.

But in the suburban hills on the south side of Managua an operation was taking shape that would grab the momentum from the talkers, strikers, and negotiators and dramatically change the image and the fortunes of the Sandinista National Liberation Front. It was timed with that in mind. Again, Humberto Ortega, the Sandinista strategist, feared losing out to the growing momentum and power of the nonviolent opposition.

At the beginning of August, Oscar Pérez Cassar, the political leader of the *terceristas'* Internal Front, had appeared at the home of Leonel Poveda, one of the businessmen who had offered their services to the Sandinistas early in the year. Pérez had a stranger at his side and asked Poveda to take him in. Poveda and his wife, Auxiliadora, gave the man a room and meals and had the maid do his laundry. They did not ask his name, though he knew theirs. The stranger spent most of his time in his room but joined the family occasionally to watch television. The Povedas took a liking to him. He was stocky, with thick black hair, intense and friendly, and given to quick, strong embraces of both men and women. About two weeks into his stay, the stranger asked Poveda if he would find one of his high school classmates from the Colegio Centroamerica—a Jesuit-run boys preparatory school—and bring him to the house for a talk. The man he wanted to see was Alfonso Robelo, the business leader then involved in organizing the FAO. Poveda did as he was asked, and when Robelo came, he and the stranger embraced and talked alone, and Poveda learned that his guest was Edén Pastora.

Though not yet widely known, Pastora, then forty-one, had been fighting the Somoza family off and on for nearly twenty years, first with a short-lived band called the Sandino Revolutionary Front, later as a member of the Sandinista Front. Unlike most of the longtime Sandinista activists, who approached the struggle from a Marxist ideological perspective, Pastora had been motivated by the death of his father in a land feud that he blamed on members of the National Guard. Early in the 1970s he had abandoned the Sandinista group in the northern mountains and had moved to a village on Costa Rica's Caribbean coast, where he made his living as a shark fisherman and by operating a small electric generating plant. In late 1976 or early 1977 he established contact with the Sandinistas in Costa Rica and returned to guerrilla warfare in time to take part in the unsuccessful uprising in October 1977. Since his days in the northern mountains Pastora had carried a wild idea in his head about the way to bring the Somoza regime to its knees: capture the National Palace.

A week after Robelo's visit, Pastora told the Povedas he had to leave for the mountains. They outfitted him with a first aid kit, mosquito repellant, and the like, and he left, again in the company of Oscar Pérez Cassar.

A few days later, on the morning of August 22, Pérez Cassar reappeared at Poveda's door, this time with Raúl Venerio, another of the Internal Front leaders. They told Poveda to get his gun, that they were going on a mission. The three of them got into Poveda's car, had the gas tank filled up, and took the South Highway to the isolated house of Dionisio Marenco, another member of Poveda's cell of businessmen. Suddenly Poveda saw about a dozen National Guardsmen wearing the distinctive black berets of graduates of the elite Basic Infantry Training School. He thought he had driven into an ambush, but then Joaquín Cuadra Lacayo appeared and told him it was a transcendent moment, that they were going to take the National Palace. The National Guardsmen were really Sandinistas, who had been practicing for the past three days to act like Guardsmen.

They went inside and Poveda saw his friend Pastora, resplendent in the uniform of a National Guard officer, standing in front of a layout of the palace on the wall. Everybody embraced. With the help of Dora María Téllez, a twenty-two-year-old woman who was to be one of his two lieutenants, Pastora explained what the operation would be. Two truckloads of Sandinistas dressed as National Guardsmen were going to capture the palace. One truck was sitting outside; the other would come from a safe house north of the city. Poveda, in civilian clothes, was to drive one of the escort vehicles for this truck.

It was common practice for plainclothesmen to accompany the National Guard.

"This is an operation *patria o muerte*—fatherland or death," Cuadra told Poveda. "The objective is achieved, or we all die. You have to see to it that that truck reaches the palace. It does not matter whether you make it or not. What we want is for that truck to get there."

Nicaragua's National Palace is a half-century-old building covering a square block that looks across a plaza to Lake Managua. Most of the surrounding buildings were laid waste in the 1972 earthquake, but the palace survived. Diagonally across the plaza from the palace is the weed-infested shell of the National Cathedral, which was not so lucky. The palace, however, did not serve as the presidential office for Anastasio Somoza. He preferred to operate out of a command center that everyone called the "Bunker," though it was above ground, in a military post about a mile to the south. The palace housed the Congress and the ministries of finance and interior.

On the morning of August 22, 1978, Congress was in session, and many other people were working in offices there or wandering about the building on one mission or another, a total of more than 1,500 people. Luis Pallais Debayle, Somoza's cousin, was sitting in as acting president of the Chamber of Deputies. The government had earlier picked up intelligence reports about a guerrilla plan to attack the palace or some other major government installation, and since then, a sixty-man National Guard detail had been showing up daily to guard the Congress, but on this day, the Guardsmen had not appeared. Only four or five regular palace guards were there. At about ten o'clock, Pallais called General José Somoza to complain, and the general promised to send some men. Pallais was still worried. He noticed the Peruvian ambassador in the chamber and suggested that he ought to leave because of the absence of security.

At the house out on the South Highway, seven miles from the palace, the Sandinistas were boarding their troop truck. Pastora and Dora María Téllez were among them. Another group, under the command of a guerrilla named Hugo Torres, was doing the same at Tipitapa on the North Highway. At ten-thirty the group from the south departed. Poveda led the way in a Mercedes-Benz, a common National Guard plainclothes vehicle. Accompanying him in the car were Raúl Venerio and Oscar Pérez Cassar. Joaquín Cuadra was in the escort car for the truck coming from the north. The two groups met, as planned, in front of a shopping center. The timing was near-perfect. When the group from the south arrived, the caravan from the north was in sight just two blocks away. They continued together, and as they passed near Asososca Lagoon, two small National Guard antiterrorist patrols known as BECATs appeared, and Poveda's heart leaped into his throat. He had previously proved himself adept at acting the irate National Guard officer, and he thought he was going to have to do it again. But, apparently unsuspicious, one BECAT jeep positioned itself ahead of the caravan and the other behind, and they escorted the Sandinistas for a distance. At the Montoya statue, a Managua landmark, the Sandinista group turned east and the BECATs went in another direction.

The caravan reached the palace without incident. Pastora's group entered through the main entrance and those under Torres went in through the back door. In all, there were twenty-five Sandinistas in uniform. The palace guards were caught between the two arriving groups, but apparently suspected nothing at first. One asked what was happening, and Pastora shouted, "The chief is coming. Keep quiet." And he kept moving. Pastora had given orders not to open fire until they reached the Chamber of Deputies. He climbed the stairs with his troops behind him, but at the doors to the chamber two guards waited with guns ready. The Sandinistas killed one and disarmed the other.

Then they burst through the doors of the chamber and paused. Everyone inside turned to look. Pastora began firing in the air and shouting that no one was to move. Instead, everyone dived under the tables. Luis Pallais, who was sitting at the president's desk talking by telephone to the U.S. ambassador, was grazed in the head by one of the flying bullets. When Hugo Torres and his troops burst in a few minutes later, none of the fifty or so congressmen was to be seen, except Pallais, who was still at his desk.

Pastora told Pallais the invaders were the "Army of the People, the Sandinista National Liberation Front." He said they were going to see how much Somoza valued the lives of these people who were his loyal servants. Unless Somoza met their demands, he said, everybody would die. Pallid faces stared back at him. Pastora later admitted being afraid himself in those early moments, but he also experienced the exhilarating feeling that, at long last, he had in his grasp "the bird, with the nest and everything."

In a matter of minutes a group of National Guard commandos led by Michael Echanis, an American mercenary and Vietnam veteran who had been hired to train a counterinsurgent force, raced to the palace in several trucks. The Sandinistas opened fire from inside and killed a captain in the first truck. One of the Sandinistas from down-stairs went up to the chamber and told Pastora about the shooting. He went to the door and threw a grenade, then the Sandinistas closed and locked all the doors. Back upstairs, Pastora said his forces would begin killing hostages unless the shooting stopped, and Pallais passed the threat to Somoza by telephone. Echanis, in communication with the Bunker by radio, wanted to assault the palace before the guerrillas could get organized, but he was ordered to pull back.

Those in the Sandinista escort vehicles had waited until they heard the shooting, as expected, from the second floor, then they drove to Poveda's house like normal people. Poveda became concerned that some of his neighbors might suspect his involvement in the raid when news of it came out, so he decided to make himself visible in the neighborhood. He drove to McDonald's and bought hamburgers for all the people gathered at his house. When he returned, Joaquín Cuadra and Oscar Pérez were trying to figure out a way to make contact with those inside the palace. No one had thought to get the direct telephone number to the desk of the president of the chamber.

Poveda had an idea. His brother-in-law, René Sandino, leader of a faction of the Conservative Party that participated in the government, was one of the hostages. The two couples had not been on good terms since Poveda had written a letter to *La Prensa* criticizing Sandino's Conservatives for "playing into Somoza's hands" and asking why they did not break with him. Now, he suggested to his wife that this might be the time to reestablish contact with her sister. She called, but in the excitement of the moment her attempt to console her sister became a bit confused. Some friends of theirs had taken the palace, Auxiliadora de Poveda told her sister, but she should not worry because they had promised that if it became necessary to begin shoot-ing hostages to win their demands, René would be the last to die. However, she managed to get the telephone number they needed.

When Oscar Pérez dialed the number, Pastora picked up the tele-phone and boomed out, *"Patria libre o morir"*—free fatherland or die —a welcome response to those at Poveda's house. Pastora later es-timated it had taken his forces two and a half or three minutes to capture the Chamber of Deputies and twenty minutes to bring the entire palace under control.

Besides Pallais and the other congressmen, the hostages included the minister of the interior and José Somoza Abrego, son of the general and nephew of the president. Archbishop Obando y Bravo was asked to come to the palace to receive the Sandinistas' list of demands for delivery to Somoza. When reporters began calling into the palace, Pastora told the world his name was *Comandante Cero,* that he was a good Catholic and not a Communist and that the raiders were not controlled by Cuba. Hugo Torres was identified as *Comandante Uno* and Dora María Téllez as *Comandante Dos.*

The Sandinistas demanded release of eighty-three prisoners, publication of a series of FSLN communiqués, and $10 million in cash. While the archbishop shuttled back and forth to present the positions of each side, Pallais talked frequently with Somoza by telephone from the small mezzanine office where the Sandinistas held him. Pallais was convinced he was going to die before it was over. One or another of the guerrilla commanders regularly told him he would be the first to be shot.

Pallais had known Pastora slightly before and had recognized him soon after he realized the attackers were not National Guardsmen. He also knew who Dora María Téllez was after hearing her name. In the Nicaraguan sense they were related—"Her mother, I think, is a sister of the wife of one of my first cousins on the Pallais side." He and she had long political discussions during the siege, conversations that angered the tougher-talking Hugo Torres.

As the takeover went into its second day, the guerrillas released about three hundred people, mostly women and children, from among those who had been in the palace on business at the time of the capture. They still held more than 1,200.

At Somoza's headquarters, Echanis and General José Ivan Alegrett, one of the National Guard commanders, argued in favor of storming the palace with a dozen or so elite troops. Echanis, in an interview about ten days later with Associated Press correspondent Tom Fenton, said he drew up a plan under which he could take the palace in eighteen minutes. "I figured maybe two hundred to three hundred would be killed," Echanis told Fenton. "The plan was to shock the building with tank fire and blow the doors with recoilless rifles. I was going to helicopter in with my commandos and drop down through the roof hatches. The old man [President Somoza] wouldn't buy it and the only reason was they held Papa Chepe's son." Papa Chepe was General José Somoza. President Somoza, in his book, said he thought the guerrillas would begin shooting congressmen if an attack occurred and that in twenty minutes the entire Congress would be dead. It was the image of grieving families, he said, that made him decide to

negotiate. Alegrett and Echanis stormed out of his office in anger.*
Negotiations eventually led to an agreement for the release of about
fifty prisoners—the others on the Sandinistas' list were not in jail,
Somoza said—plus payment of half a million dollars, which was all
Somoza said was available in the Central Bank at the time, and
publication of the communiqués.

The communiqués filled six pages in *Novedades,* the Somoza-owned
newspaper. The most interesting was one that attacked the political
parties and private enterprise for being slow to join the fight against
Somoza and particularly for being willing to accept the continued
existence of the National Guard as part of any agreement for
Somoza's departure. Such groups, it said, had the right to join the
opposition to Somoza but they did not have the right to dictate the
terms of his departure. It said the Sandinistas could accept nothing
less than the formation of a new army along with Somoza's departure.
This and other political communiqués published at the time were
signed by Humberto Ortega, the Sandinista strategist in Costa Rica,
plus his brother Daniel, and Victor Tirado, a Mexican who had been
one of the early members of the FSLN. All three were part of the
tercerista faction.

The siege ended on the morning of August 24, almost forty-eight
hours after it began. The governments of Venezuela and Panama sent
planes to Managua to pick up the freed prisoners and the guerrillas.
Thousands of people lined the streets and cheered as Pastora and his
raiders left the palace on buses accompanied by the archbishop, Pallais, and a few other congressmen. The crowds chanted, "Down with
Somoza!" and "Somoza to the Gallows" as the buses went to the
airport, where jubilant people broke through security lines to see the
two planes take off. Pastora, waving his G3 rifle in one hand, a
grenade hanging from his shirt, was the man of the moment. He also
had a personal memento of the occasion: a gold Rolex wristwatch he
had taken from José Somoza Abrego, the president's nephew. Almost
unnoticed amidst the appreciation for Pastora was the presence of
Tomás Borge, the surviving founder of the FSLN and one of those
freed from prison.

The palace raiders and the former prisoners flew off to glory in
Panama and Venezuela, and about half of them continued on to Cuba

---

*Both Alegrett and Echanis were to die less than three weeks later in an
airplane accident.

to be trained and returned to Central America in good health. Pastora and Dora María Téllez were among those who rested a few days in Panama as the guests of General Torrijos. Apparently meeting Pastora for the first time, Torrijos took an immediate liking to him. Torrijos had a tendency to view people in his inner circle in a paternalistic way, often saying that so-and-so was the kind of son he wished he had. Pastora, though only about ten years younger than Torrijos, received that kind of affection. During the same period, Pastora also went to Venezuela and met President Pérez, who was equally taken with the Nicaraguan guerrilla. The close ties that Pastora established with those two leaders after his triumph were to prove fateful for both the Sandinista Front and Somoza.

From Panama, Pastora returned to Costa Rica and applied his efforts to organizing what Sandinista forces were there. In Guanacaste, the region on the Nicaraguan border that was becoming the Sandinistas' operations center, he struck up a friendship and business relationship with Elio Espinar, a tall, handsome rice farmer in his thirties who liked guns and basketball. Espinar quickly became known in Costa Rica as the Sandinistas' "purchasing agent," and his house on the Pan American Highway just south of Liberia, the departmental capital, was the stopover for Sandinista leaders traveling from San José to the border. Espinar's private landing strip on one of his farms—Hacienda Pájaro Rojo—was also useful to the Sandinistas.

In Managua, the day after the palace siege ended, the Broad Opposition Front (FAO) called its previously announced general strike, but it began slowly, lacking the support of the Chamber of Commerce or COSIP. The drama and excitement of the palace takeover had stolen the momentum from nonviolent groups, just as the FSLN had hoped. Fighting also broke out between youths and the National Guard in Matagalpa, the capital of the coffee-growing region to the north of Managua. This appeared to be a spontaneous action by boys in the town, not a planned operation of the FSLN, but it continued for days, with each side taking control of various zones of the city until the National Guard retook the entire city after five days of fighting. Two days after the general strike began, the Chamber of Commerce voted to join, and its effectiveness soon spread. In early September the government arrested about sixty leaders of the strike and heads of political parties, including Adolfo Calero, one of the Conservative leaders, plus several hundred youths and others seen as troublemakers.

The Sandinistas' Internal Front—Joaquín Cuadra, Oscar Pérez Cassar, Poveda, and others—busied themselves with new plans from their comfortable spots in the suburban hills. They laid plans for insurrections in about a half dozen key cities and at first planned for them to occur on September 7. The date was changed to the eighth, then delayed until the ninth because the organizers were waiting for an arms shipment, which had to be transported to León. In midafternoon of the eighth, the armaments arrived at Poveda's house in Managua. He assumed that the shipment, a collection of old M-1s, a few FALs, and a lot of ammunition, came from Costa Rica. How it got to Costa Rica, or from where, was beyond his concern. Everything that had arrived was immediately driven to León in a pickup truck, with Poveda following in his car. On the ninth, a Saturday, Poveda's squad of five businessmen gathered again at the house of Dionisio Marenco on the South Highway. Their assignment was to attack a National Guard command on the highway just a third of a mile away.

"It got to be two P.M. and I began to give instructions about how we were going to attack. I told them we were going to make a commando attack and I could not guarantee that any of us would survive. I said the people of Nicaragua were desperate and we had to do it. 'If any of you doesn't feel the valor to do this, you are not a coward,' I said, 'because what we are doing is suicide. The possibilities of beating the National Guard are few.' "

Poveda gave them gum and cigarettes to calm their nerves, something he had learned in the U.S. Army, and he gave precise, simple instructions—who would go in which vehicle, who would lead, who would carry the only submachine gun. It would be a quick raid. They would go in firing, disarm the Guardsmen, and recover as many weapons as possible. At five o'clock, a jeep drove up and four volunteers got out, saying they had come to help. One of them was Alfredo César, the young general manager of Nicaragua Sugar Estates. César and Joaquín Cuadra, the military leader of the Internal Front, had been friends and neighbors during childhood. Earlier that year, when Cuadra returned secretly to Nicaragua, he had sought out César and convinced him to join the struggle. Poveda told the new arrivals it was too late to incorporate them into the attack plan but that they could be useful by stopping traffic on the highway at the hour of the attack —six o'clock.

At five minutes to six, they got into a truck and a car and drove by the command post, then turned around and went back, parked, got out and began firing on the four Guardsmen at the front. All four Guardsmen, so surprised they did not return a shot, were killed or wounded almost immediately. The attackers gathered up a few weapons and returned to their vehicles, but as they were getting in, they saw an armored vehicle filled with National Guardsmen approaching. So Poveda's squad and those who had helped them by stopping traffic ran to a nearby house and took refuge behind a low stone wall. The Guardsmen surrounded the house and the two groups exchanged fire until dark, when the rebels began slipping away individually and in pairs.

Attacks were launched simultaneously on National Guard posts at other locations around Managua and in four other cities—León, Estelí, Masaya, and Chinandega. The assaults in Managua produced relatively little reaction from sympathetic citizens and few ongoing exchanges between rebels and Guardsmen, but in the other cities local youths and other residents picked up after the rebels withdrew and kept the fighting and sniping going for several days. The most serious fighting was in Estelí, where the National Guard used air attacks to subdue the uprising and assaulted several schools where participants had holed up. The Sandinistas said they had suffered sixty-six deaths in the fighting around the country, and Somoza said the National Guard lost thirty men, but civilian deaths were much higher. The Red Cross estimated that three hundred died in Estelí, a figure that may have included some of those counted as Sandinista casualties. Somoza also said that a fifty-man guerrilla column had tried to enter from Costa Rica but had been turned back by the National Guard. Costa Rica complained that the National Guard had dropped a bomb inside its territory in the action.

As the fighting died down, most of those who had initiated the action sought asylum in various Latin American embassies, taking advantage of the tradition of granting political asylum even in cases involving violence. One of those was Leonel Poveda, who, after fleeing the shootout on the South Highway, walked around in the suburban hills all night with two members of his squadron looking for the safe house to which they had been instructed to go. After twenty-four hours they stumbled into a house occupied by a sympathetic French couple who gave them pitchers of ice water and then drove them to the safe house.

Poveda did not stay long at the first safe house and spent the next two weeks on the run, moving from the house of one friend or collaborator to another, all in the Managua area, until he received a message from Joaquín Cuadra on September 23 telling him to seek asylum in the Colombian Embassy. About two hundred rebels in all turned to the Colombians for protection, while a few dozen went to

other embassies. Diplomats and others analyzing the attempted insurrection concluded that those who showed up at the embassies probably represented almost the sum total of all the combatants the
Sandinista Front then had. A note that Poveda received from Joaquín
Cuadra after arriving at the embassy indicated the thinness of the
ranks had been very much on the Sandinistas' minds in planning the
September action.

"The card said we were stronger than ever, that he [Cuadra] wanted
to congratulate us for our action, that we had been patriotic and had
achieved the objective and so forth, that the nation was grateful and
that the number of combatants had multiplied by three. What it
amounted to was that the middle class, when it realized that we were
participating with the [Sandinista] Front, decided that this must be
good. So the whole world began to support the Front—capitalists,
noncapitalists, peasants."

5

THE MEDIATION

SEPTEMBER 1978 TO JANUARY 1979

The bloodshed of September finally drew the attention of the White House to Nicaragua, which was no longer something that the Carter administration thought it could handle within the general framework of human rights policy. Nicaragua had now become an issue in its own right. As the Sandinistas were trying to get their insurrection off the ground, President Carter was preparing to go to Camp David for a Mideast summit with Anwar Sadat and Menachem Begin. The day before the summit began, various aides told Carter about the developments in Nicaragua, and he told them to meet and come up with recommendations, then left for Camp David. White House staffers and others sent him reports on Nicaragua throughout the summit.

"He [Carter] basically decided we were not going to do it alone, that the age of U.S. unilateralism was past . . . [Carter said] 'Let's go out there and consult, let's get everybody's views.' He said to send a letter to Carlos Andrés Pérez, to Torrijos, and to Carazo, and to several other people and get their views," according to Robert Pastor, the Latin American specialist on the National Security Council.

On September 13, Viron P. Vaky, the Assistant Secretary of State for Inter-American Affairs, went before an executive session of the Senate Foreign Relations Committee to talk about the unrest in Nicaragua. Vaky himself was already convinced that Somoza could not survive politically, but this view was not widely shared in the higher reaches of the State Department, where there was still a feeling that Nicaragua was a small, containable problem. Several of the senators, swayed by Vaky's argument, were disturbed at the possibility that the United States might soon be faced with having to choose between accepting the Marxist-dominated Sandinistas and propping up Somoza. Pushed by Senator Jacob Javits, the committee told Vaky it wanted a U.S. policy aimed at creating a moderate succession to Somoza. Vaky understood that to be backing for what he wanted the United States to do: to actively work with the politically moderate opponents of Somoza in the interest of getting some of them into power.

The State Department issued a plea for Somoza to accept mediation by the Organization of American States, and the Venezuelan government called for a meeting of foreign ministers of OAS nations. William J. Jorden, who had just retired as ambassador to Panama, was called to Washington on September 12 and dispatched on a swing around Central America and the northern rim of South America in search of support for an OAS-backed mediation. For two weeks, from a base in Panama, Jorden left almost daily at six in the morning for a different country, then returned after dark to write his day's report and prepare for the next day's trip.

His mission was three-fold: to find other OAS members willing to participate in the mediation, to convince Somoza to accept mediation, and to ask President Pérez in Venezuela and General Torrijos in Panama to cool their support for the insurgency in order to give mediation a chance. Though those two national leaders had previously pressured merely for Somoza to step aside, after meeting Edén Pastora at the end of August, they had begun to assist the guerrilla movement, believing that it was then dominated by Pastora. There was, for example, evidence linking the ammunition used in the September uprising to Pérez. When Jorden called on Pérez, the Venezuelan president expressed great animosity toward Somoza in very emotional terms, but he agreed to a period of restraint. Among other things, he ordered home some fighter and transport planes that he had sent to Costa Rica for unspecified purposes.

In Managua, meanwhile, the FAO named a three-man committee to speak for its sixteen organizations: Alfonso Robelo, the recent past president of COSIP and strike leader, who now had his own political party; Sergio Ramírez, the Sandinista writer who played a key role in forming *Los Doce;* and Rafael Córdova Rivas, a longtime political associate of Pedro Joaquín Chamorro. It was understood the three were to act as the opposition link to any mediation effort.

The OAS foreign ministers gathered in Washington on September 21, and the United States proposed a resolution calling for OAS mediation, which encountered resistance from some, primarily military regimes, on grounds that it violated the principle of nonintervention. On September 23 a compromise was passed "to take note that . . . Nicaragua has stated that it is willing in principle to accept the friendly cooperation and conciliatory efforts that several member States of the Organization may offer . . ." While that wording was vague, it could still be turned into mediation if all parties agreed.

Ambassador Jorden met five times with Somoza between September 23 and September 29. In the first conversation, Jorden told Somoza the United States thought the Nicaraguan situation had become "dangerously polarized," not only in the obvious sense between the Sandinista guerrillas and the regime, but also between Somoza and the moderate political parties, the church, and business. Jorden told him the United States was "terribly concerned that everything you have built up, and your brother before you, is in danger of being destroyed. And that means the political structure, institutions." He pointed out that commercial activity had come to a halt and capital was fleeing the country. If the opposition came only from the Sandinistas, Jorden told him, the situation would be manageable, but it was much bigger than that; it was something that could fall into chaos, that played into the hands of Communists and Castro, who were hoping to use the Nicaraguan situation to "establish a base in the mainland and go from there."

Jorden said he had to be honest and say, "The possibility of your departure from office before 1981 is one of the possibilities that has to be considered. I am not saying it has to be done, I am saying it has to be considered."

Somoza did not respond directly to the question of his resignation, and Jorden broached the possibility of power being passed to some kind of junta composed of people from Somoza's Nationalist Liberal Party and the opposition parties. Somoza responded by saying there was no other real leader in his party and that while the National Guard had potential leaders he had proved himself the military leader of the moment by putting down the latest uprising.

In the end Somoza agreed to accept "the friendly cooperation" of the United States, the expression that had been invented by the OAS to avoid the implication of intervention. Somoza did not tell Jorden he was willing to resign, bragging at times that he had more friends in the U.S. Congress than Carter and that they were backing him. But Jorden thought there was a tone of desperation in his arguments and that if the United States handled the situation with firmness, he could be brought around.

The Sandinistas and *Los Doce* had not wanted the United States to participate in the mediation, but it quickly became clear that there would be no mediation without the United States at least unofficially directing it. At the other extreme, Somoza did not want the participation of governments that were friendly to the opposition—Venezuela, Mexico, Panama, and Costa Rica. In the last days of September, agreement was finally reached that one political democracy—the Dominican Republic—and one military regime—Guatemala—would join the United States in forming the International Commission of Friendly Cooperation and Conciliation. William P. Bowdler, a career diplomat who was then director of the Bureau of Intelligence and Research and had extensive experience in Central America, was named to represent the United States. The Dominican Republic named its foreign minister, Admiral Ramon Emilio Jiménez, and Guatemala appointed a former Cabinet minister, Alfredo Obiols Gomez.

Meanwhile, the Sandinistas were not sitting by idly, even though *Los Doce* had joined the FAO and given their backing to the idea of mediation. As the mediation began, the United States was apprehensive that the Sandinistas in Costa Rica, their numbers growing since the palace raid and the September insurrection, were preparing a major assault in the border region, which would interfere with the negotiations. In addition to Jorden's entreaties to President Pérez in Venezuela, the United States asked the Costa Rican government to intervene with the insurgents. President Carazo in Costa Rica turned to his minister of public security, Johnny Echeverría, who had earlier established contacts with the Sandinistas. Echeverría met with Pastora and recalled: "We sort of made an agreement with them. We said, 'We are going to let you stay here. We're not going to deport you, but you don't operate against Nicaragua during these months.' Which they did. They did not operate during those months."

The fact was that although guerrilla military activity may have been minimal, the Costa Rican authorities had to capture and deport a number of Sandinistas to Panama during October and November 1978 as part of their agreement to support the mediation. Most of the Sandinista camps in Costa Rica continued to function and were busy training the hundreds of recruits who had shown up after the September fighting. Pastora received a few journalists at one camp and worked on a promotional film that was shown before the end of the year in New York and other major cities. The journalists and the film makers left with the impression that he was the most important Sandinista.

The OAS mediators met in Guatemala on October 3 and 4 to define their goals and methods, then flew to Managua. Somoza, despite the strong words he had heard from Jorden just two weeks earlier, announced that he expected the mediation panel to set up a framework for the 1981 elections, not to establish an interim government, but he said he was willing to offer Cabinet posts to some members of the opposition. The FAO, on the other hand, felt the need to reassure the Nicaraguan people that its participation in the mediation did not mean it intended to make a pact with *somocismo* and said that any solution had to be based on the removal of Somoza and his family from all positions of power.

The members of the FAO, given the demonstrated strength of the opposition to Somoza since the death of Pedro Joaquín Chamorro and the fact that they had been brought together under U.S. auspices, assumed that Bowdler and the rest of the team were there for the purpose of finding a face-saving way for Somoza to leave. They also assumed that they would be given the opportunity to form the new government. The mediators themselves concluded within days of their arrival that opposition to the regime was so widespread that the only way to reach a peaceful solution was for Somoza to resign and pave the way for an agreement between the FAO and Somoza's Nationalist Liberal Party on the country's future. Conversing individually with various Nicaraguans, both Bowdler and his deputy, James Cheek, used the analogy that Somoza was a sick man who needed oxygen and that the United States controlled all the valves. The only question, they implied, was arranging an acceptable succession before closing the valves.

However, while Bowdler's immediate superiors in the Latin bureau of the State Department agreed with that view, he carried no such instructions from the White House and the upper reaches of the State Department, where the only consensus was on the method of proceeding. Nor was it entirely appreciated among many of the FAO members, who were surprised at being asked to negotiate with Somoza's political party. They thought that was the same as making a pact with *somocismo*, which most of them had historically avoided doing.

After considerable internal debate and pressure from the mediators, the FAO came up with its formal negotiating position on October 25. Essentially a revised version of the sixteen points the FAO had put together in August, it called for Somoza to resign and leave power to a "government of national unity" composed of a council of state and a three-man junta. The council would be made up of two representatives of each of the sixteen groups in the FAO and also two from the Nationalist Liberal Party. The council, once constituted, would name a three-man junta to govern the country and a constitutional assembly to lay plans for elections to be held in December 1981. Reorganization of the National Guard and the justice system was also part of the plan.

Simultaneously with this proposal, however, came a major crack in the FAO. *Los Doce* withdrew their representative, Sergio Ramírez, from the FAO political commission, and he and the six other members of *Los Doce* who were in the country at the time sought refuge in the Mexican Embassy. The stated reason for their withdrawal was the decision of other groups in the FAO to accept continuation of the National Guard, even in reorganized form, and to include Somoza's Nationalist Liberal Party among the groups that would have representation in the proposed council of state. The United States was accused of forcing the FAO into that position.

"The United States, in place of taking away once and for all the support that it gives to Somoza, has chosen to raise the hopes of the opposition for the doubtful prospect of the early departure of Somoza from power, but on the condition that there must first be agreement on a 'viable solution,' in the preparation of which the mediation commission makes 'suggestions' that signify leaving practically intact the corrupt structures of the *somocista* apparatus. 'Suggestions' that imply, in addition, a dialogue with *somocista* representatives," *Los Doce* said in a statement.

The withdrawal was viewed with great concern by the mediators and all the other parties to the mediation. Although the extent of *Los Doce*'s connections to the FSLN was not fully known at the time, it was accepted that they were the channel to the Sandinistas. Without them in the mediation, it seemed likely that the Sandinistas would quickly resume violent activities. Somoza picked up on this possibility in the coming weeks. He frequently alluded to the fact that the opposition with which he was negotiating no longer had any influence over armed rebels and he, therefore, wondered what value there would be in an agreement reached with the FAO.

At least one member of *Los Doce* disagreed with the decision to quit the mediation. Arturo Cruz, who lived in Washington and had given the others permission to use his name without consulting him in every instance, had no advance knowledge of the withdrawal. When he heard about it he was so dismayed that for a while he considered writing a letter of protest to *La Prensa*. Cruz, who had continued to identify himself as a member of the Conservative Party, thought the action and public statements of *Los Doce* had damaged and discredited the Conservatives and the rest of the democratic opposition. Later, as he learned more about the direct ties to the Sandinista Front of Ramírez and several other members of *Los Doce,* Cruz concluded that they were opposed to any kind of political solution that would not assure ascendancy for the FSLN. A successful mediation at that time would have produced a middle-of-the-road government in which the Sandinistas would have had only minority participation.

Within a few weeks after *Los Doce* left the FAO, they and the FSLN were calling on Nicaraguans to give their loyalty to two new groups —the United People's Movement, which was organizing residents of poor neighborhoods to help the FSLN, and the Patriotic Front, an umbrella group for political and labor groups that were not in the FAO or that quit the FAO. Most of the groups that joined the Patriotic Front were more leftist politically and smaller in size than most of those in the FAO.

With *Los Doce* gone, the mediators presented to Somoza the FAO demand that he resign and leave the country, and the Carter administration at the same time convinced the International Monetary Fund to postpone a decision on a $20 million line of credit to which the Nicaraguan government had a right under IMF rules. The IMF postponement, which was expected to influence other international creditors, was a shock to Somoza, and he appeared to be seriously considering for a few days whether he could resist such pressures. But on November 6 the Nationalist Liberal Party issued a statement saying Somoza would serve out his term—until 1981—but proposing a sort of plebiscite to test the relative electoral strength of each of the opposition political groups. The strongest among them would be allowed to join the Somoza government until the next elections.

The three mediators, disappointed in this position, went to see Somoza and asked whether he was "disposed to consider his constitutional separation from the presidency of the republic" prior to 1981. They told him that during their time in the country they had observed "that the departure of Your Excellency from the presidency of the republic reflects a widespread sentiment of the people of Nicaragua." Somoza said no.

Alfonso Robelo, speaking for the FAO, said Somoza's plebiscite proposal was "completely absurd" and that the FAO had set a deadline of November 21 by which the mediation had to show results, or the entire FAO would withdraw and fighting would resume. Robelo could speak with a degree of authority on the question of fighting because, while lacking formal alliance with the Sandinistas, he had had more contacts with them than most of the moderate opposition. For one thing, he had access to his old high school classmate, Pastora. In addition, he had traveled to Costa Rica earlier in the year to meet with Humberto Ortega. Other founders of his political party, the Nicaraguan Democratic Movement (MDN), had been in frequent contact with other members of the *tercerista* faction of the Sandinistas in recent months. Robelo's party was thought to have some arms caches of its own, and many of the Nicaraguans arriving in Costa Rica to offer themselves as combatants were affiliated with the MDN. The distinction between *terceristas* and MDN was growing fuzzy.

The mediators flew home on November 12 to talk to their respective governments. When William Bowdler arrived in Washington the debate that ensued was almost as heated as the one he had left behind in Managua. The Latin American specialists of the State Department were on one side of the argument and Secretary of State Cyrus Vance and most of the White House were on the other.

Bowdler and Viron Vaky, the assistant secretary, dismissed Somoza's plebiscite idea as a "tar baby," something the United States would be unable to put down once it had been taken up. They distrusted Somoza's motives. The plebiscite proposal struck them as typical of the ploys the Somoza family had been using for nearly half a century. They thought the United States should force him to step aside as soon as possible in order to create a new government before the tenuous opposition coalition fell apart and the Sandinistas picked up the pieces. The departure of *Los Doce* had already been followed by the departure of a non-Communist labor federation with no known ties to the Sandinistas, and Bowdler was worried that others would follow suit.

Going through Vaky's mind was something Henry Kissinger used to say when Vaky was serving as his Latin American expert on the National Security Council a decade earlier: The great agony of foreign policy is that you often have to act on the basis of a premise you cannot prove at the time.

Vaky thought Somoza could be made to go by additional pressure tactics, such as cutting Nicaragua's beef export quota to the United States, threatening to deny Somoza exile in the United States, and seeking the help of the congressional leadership to isolate Somoza's backers on the Hill. United States' intentions must be made clear, with no wavering. If the king was to be touched, he must be killed—symbolically—and quickly.

Robert Pastor of the National Security Council agreed with Bowdler and Vaky that if the United States did nothing, Somoza would stay, the moderate opposition would lose influence, and the Sandinistas would eventually win it all. But he strongly disagreed with them about what the United States should be prepared to do to prevent that happening. Pastor recalled later: "Pete [Vaky] felt that we could and should force out Somoza in the fall of '78, and I felt that we couldn't and shouldn't. I sensed that he [Somoza] was probably taping our demarches, which later proved to be true, and that if we had someone say, 'You have to go or else,' then we would be hearing it on the CBS News that night, and then we would have to answer the question the next day, 'Are you trying to overthrow this man?' . . . I felt that Carter should not overthrow a government. I felt that we were in the business too long and it was time to get out of that business, regardless of what the circumstances were."

Pastor's position coincided with that of a number of foreign policy people who had resigned from government during the Vietnam era in disagreement with Southeast Asian policies, but who had returned to government under Carter. These people generally had no knowledge of Central America, nor understanding of what it meant when a *caudillo* such as Somoza was weakened. Their positions were shaped by the Vietnam experience, which had left them unwilling to use United States influence to effect change. One of these people was Anthony Lake, who had quit Kissinger's National Security staff in 1970 because of the Cambodian invasion and was now the State Department's director of policy planning. In discussions about Nicaragua in late 1978, Lake strongly argued against using United States power to force out Somoza, and his view had considerable influence on Secretary Vance.

Vaky's view was that Somoza had been disingenuous with the plebiscite proposal, and the United States was getting itself into knots trying to figure out how to respond to a tactic instead of concentrating on an objective—getting Somoza out. He thought an error was being made out of ignorance of Nicaraguan dynamics, as he thought had been done with the letter that Carter had written Somoza in June. The letter, he felt, had already sent Somoza the wrong signal, making him think the United States wanted him to stay in power.

Pastor, along with Vance and Deputy Secretary Warren Christopher, thought that the United States should not dismiss out of hand Somoza's idea of a referendum or plebiscite. Did not the United States believe in self-determination? How could it oppose an election? They told Bowdler and Vaky that, given American political philosphy and congressional and public opinion, the possibility had to be explored. They proposed that, instead of allowing the referendum or plebiscite to be used to keep Somoza in power, it should be organized in a way that would work against him.

While in Washington, Bowdler met with President Carter and discussed the problems confronting the OAS mission. Although Bowdler declined to be interviewed for this book, a source close to him at the time said he explained to the President that the Somoza regime was crumbling and that if something were not done to get Somoza out of the way in order to bring in the moderate opposition, then the crumbling would create a vacuum in which the radicals would take control. Carter understood Bowdler's point, but he also understood that it meant the United States would be telling another country what kind of government it ought to have, or that he would be telling another sitting president that he had to leave.

"Mr. Ambassador," Carter asked at one point, "is Somoza a moral man?"

"In no way, Mr. President," Bowdler replied.

Back in Managua, the embassy staff was also divided over the plebiscite issue. Some, not fully aware of the policy dispute in Washington, thought Bowdler was being too soft on Somoza. They thought the only way to pursue the mediation was to tell Somoza bluntly that its purpose was to find a face-saving way for him to leave, then proceed to find and use the leverage necessary to make him cooperate. Ambassador Solaun was less inclined to the ultimatum idea than some of his staff, but he was also dismayed at the way Washington was dealing with the situation. In his view, the Carter administration had gone abruptly from having no plan for dealing with Nicaragua to one in which Somoza had to leave immediately, but for which the United States was not prepared to exert the necessary pressure. Solaun thought the White House was too wrapped up in its own ideals to compehend Nicaraguan reality. Gradually, however, the entire embassy staff, including Solaun, was cut out of the mediation process, and Bowdler and James Cheek, his deputy, handled virtually everything.

After returning to Managua, the mediators tried to fashion a voting plan that could be used against Somoza. On November 21 they issued a proposal for people to vote not, as Somoza had suggested, on the relative strength of the opposition, but on whether Somoza should stay or go. The voting would be carried out within sixty days under the supervision of 2,000 international representatives named by the OAS. If Somoza won, the mediators said, the government would be restructured as proposed by his Nationalist Liberal Party in its earlier position paper. If Somoza lost, a new government would be organized in conformity with the sixteen-point plan of the FAO.

Both sides were suspicious of the proposal. Robelo and other FAO leaders, under pressure from *Los Doce* and the FSLN, which continued to verbally snipe at them for allegedly giving in to the *somocistas,* told the mediators it was impossible to have an honest election with Somoza in the country and his relatives running the National Guard. The Nationalist Liberal Party complained that the vote plan would violate the constitution and then went into a historical analysis of the use of the plebiscite in ancient Rome and the referendum in eighteenth-century France. Somoza himself told Bowdler that the trouble with the proposal was that he could not win an election like that, but the FAO was also worried that it might not be able to win.

On November 30, Somoza called a news conference and said he would accept the plebiscite idea in principle, but would not agree to leave the country during the campaigning or after he lost—if he lost —and that the alternative offered to the voters would be to call a constitutional convention, not a government created by the FAO.

Exchanges and clarifications followed among the three parties to the mediation, and then the Nationalist Liberal Party and the FAO agreed to hold their first face-to-face talks to work out details of what the mediators had now begun to call a "popular consultation" in deference to the criticism of terminology voiced by the Liberals. The first of six meetings was held on December 8 at the Dominican Embassy. To meet a condition of the FAO for these direct talks, Somoza lifted martial law and announced an amnesty for political prisoners. Snags developed almost as soon as the Liberals and the opposition went into the same room. The Liberals insisted that if Somoza won the "consultation," then the FAO must end its opposition and join his government, and Alfonso Robelo replied that under no circumstances would the FAO agree to go into a government with Somoza. The Liberal representatives also said their side could not accept the proposition that Somoza and his family would have to leave the country if he lost.

While the debate dragged on in Nicaragua and Washington, other interested parties were getting itchy. President Pérez of Venezuela, who already suspected a failure of will on the part of the Carter administration, was now disturbed at the reluctance of the United States to get tough in the mediation, from which he had expected quick results. Pérez espoused noninterventionist theory with great flourish in international forums, but in the back-room politics of the tropics he believed in using presidential power to its limits. As long as he agreed with the policy, he expected U.S. chief executives to act with their traditional resolve. Deciding now that the United States could not be trusted to manage the situation, Pérez opened informal negotiations with Somoza's cousin, Luis Pallais Debayle. At the instigation of their mutual Panamanian friend, General Torrijos, Pallais flew to Caracas in late November for the first of many hours of conversations with Pérez over the next two months.

Pallais recalled their first conversation: ". . . Carlos Andrés told me . . . that Tacho was a liar, that he did not fulfill his promises to him, that Tacho had promised him to make a public announcement that he was going to resign and that a national unity government would be formed. I told him, 'But Tacho said you promised him you were going to talk to the opposition, and you haven't done that.' Well, we talked . . . about how to solve things in Nicaragua, many things, and I went back to Managua and convinced Tacho that if I could convince Carlos Andrés Pérez to stop the war and convince the FAO to form a national unity government [with Somoza's party], then he should resign. Carlos Andrés told me that he didn't believe Tacho, that he would never resign, that he was just playing for time."

The Sandinistas in Costa Rica were grateful for the time, and they were using it well. The friendship that Edén Pastora had struck up with Torrijos in September proved beneficial. Torrijos decided to help the passionately pro-freedom and anti-Somoza Nicaraguan, but the Panamanian leader had relatively little military hardware to spare. However, he had a friend in Cuba who had access to an almost limitless supply. Torrijos dispatched one of his chief deputies, Colonel Manuel Noriega, on a series of visits to Cuba to work out something with Fidel Castro. A former member of the Panamanian Communist Party named Marcel Salamín also was sent to talk to the Cubans. It was typical of Torrijos' style to open two or more independent channels through people of vastly different political orientations. He often did not let one person know what he had the other doing.

Also beneficial to Pastora and the Sandinistas was his new friendship with President Pérez in Venezuela. Pérez found that he and the personable guerrilla shared similar social-democratic political views and, while he was aware of the Marxist politics of some of the Sandinista leadership, he thought he could influence the movement through Pastora, or that his help would enable Pastora to wield more power in the FSLN. The constraints imposed by Venezuelan political democracy—an inquisitive congress and press—meant that Pérez had less freedom of movement than Torrijos in assisting Pastora. However, it was perfectly legitimate for the Venezuelan government to provide military aid to the democratic government of Costa Rica, whose Civil Guard was poorly equipped to confront the Nicaraguan National Guard patrols that were entering Costa Rica with increasing frequency in pursuit of Sandinistas camped near the border. According to the official version given in both Costa Rica and Venezuela, Pérez promised to send a thousand M-14 rifles and ammunition to the Costa Rican government, with the understanding that some of this would go to Pastora.

The result of these contacts in Venezuela and Cuba was that the trickle of weapons that had been coming into Costa Rica for the Sandinistas on light planes grew quickly into a heavy flow. It was accomplished with the active, though then publicly unacknowledged, assistance of President Carazo and Johnny Echeverría, his public security minister. The trips to Havana by members of Torrijos' inner circle had produced an agreement for arms and ammunition from

Cuba to be flown into the provincial town of David in western Panama near the Costa Rican border, then transferred to Panamanian planes and flown to Costa Rica. At first, most of the planes on which the supplies arrived in Costa Rica were registered to the Panamanian Air Force, which helped to deflect any curiosity in Costa Rica.

Echeverría said in an interview that, according to his recollection, the Cuban arms began to arrive in either December 1978 or January 1979, but the CIA reported that arms from Cuba were already being flown into Panama as early as September 1978 for transshipment to Costa Rica. The CIA report, prepared in May 1979 on the basis of information from a high-level informant in Panama, said eight crates of weapons, including .50-caliber machine guns, came from Cuba in September and that three additional flights came into Panama from Cuba during the week of November 5 to 11 and were flown to Costa Rica later the same month.

The proof of these shipments soon showed up in Nicaragua, where the National Guard captured several hundred Belgian-made FALs, which had been the rifle of Marxist guerrilla groups around Latin America since Fidel Castro came to power in Cuba on January 1, 1959. Castro's forces inherited thousands of nearly new FALs from the Fulgencio Batista regime, but after the new Cuban army began to receive Soviet equipment the FALs were available for other uses. The first place they were detected in guerrilla hands was in Venezuela, where the fledgling democracy fought off an insurgency in the late 1950s and early 1960s.

The Sandinistas also acquired arms from commercial sources in late 1978. According to the subsequent testimony of a Costa Rican pilot, a Boeing 707 flew into San José's international airport from West Germany in December with 60,000 pounds of supplies for the FSLN, and a DC8 landed from Portugal carrying 90,000 pounds of matériel.

By December 1978 the Costa Rican government had made the decision to go all out in support of the Sandinistas. Carazo and Echeverría both told me the motivation had been fear of an invasion by Nicaragua. The best way to protect Costa Rica, they claimed, was to make the Sandinistas the primary line of defense. That meant providing the means for the Sandinistas to face the Nicaraguan National Guard. The growing sympathy of the Costa Rican public for the Sandinistas in their midst also provided justification for the actions of Echeverría and Carazo. Later, after the Sandinistas had taken power and the affection for them had soured in Costa Rica, there would be allegations of payoffs, either in money or in boxes of weapons, to various officials of the Carazo administration, but no charges were brought in court. An investigation into gun running by the Costa Rican National Assembly in 1980–1981 did not delve into payoffs, but it raised the possibility that they had occurred.

In late 1978 a few Cubans established a command center in a house in San José to oversee the distribution and use of weapons and other matériel, and to recruit people for training in Cuba. The U.S. Embassy learned of the existence of the command center, and Ambassador Marvin Weissman complained to the Costa Rican government. Johnny Echeverría went personally to the house and told the Cubans there was a problem, so they moved their headquarters to the Cuban consulate. Echeverría told me he recalled having contacts with five Cubans, two of them regular members of the consulate staff and three of them having come from Havana to help the Sandinistas.

Among the Nicaraguans arriving in Costa Rica to offer themselves as combatants in those days was Leonel Poveda, who came from Bogotá, Colombia, to which he had received safe passage after taking asylum in the Colombian Embassy in Managua. Another who arrived in Costa Rica toward the end of 1978 was Alfredo César, the sugar mill executive who had joined Poveda's unit in the attack on the National Guard post in September. César had been captured by the National Guard within hours of the assault, but he was freed in the political amnesty that Somoza declared in early December. César was assigned by the Sandinistas in Costa Rica to work on a committee that was drafting plans for a future government. Poveda, whose exploits inside Nicaragua had earned him considerable military stature, went to work at Pastora's side. He was known as "El Comanche," a name that Pastora gave him when some of the other Sandinista leaders complained about Poveda being addressed as *comandante*. It was also suggested by the others that Poveda go to Cuba for training. He declined, but many of those gathering in Costa Rica during the early months of 1979 did go to Cuba, primarily for artillery training.

The stalemate in the negotiations in Managua continued for nearly two weeks, until on December 20 the mediators presented their own revised plan that took into consideration some of the complaints of the two sides. It essentially accepted the FAO position on the future government, saying if Somoza won, he could reorganize the government as he saw fit and the FAO would remain in "peaceful opposition." If Somoza lost, he would resign and leave, the Congress would elect an interim president, then pass some constitutional reforms by April 15, 1979, and by May 1 elect a president as proposed by the FAO. The new president would serve until May 1, 1981, when a popularly elected president would be inaugurated for a full term. At that time, Somoza also would be allowed to return to Nicaragua if he desired. It did not call on Somoza to leave during the campaigning and voting, which was to occur on February 25, 1979, without prior registration.

The day after the mediators put forward this proposal, Lieutenant General Dennis McAuliffe, commander of the U.S. Southern Command in Panama, flew into Managua, and he and Bowdler went to see Somoza. Bowdler told Somoza that he was throwing up a major roadblock in the negotiations by insisting that the FAO agree to join the government if he won the plebiscite. Somoza, for his part, expressed concern about Communists taking over and said he wanted a consolidation of democratic forces against the left. Bowdler replied that the moderate opposition did not want to team up with the Left but did not want to join Somoza either. ". . . the main issue here, in all candor, is your presence in the government," Bowdler said.

McAuliffe told Somoza he had come because the Joint Chiefs of Staff were concerned about the instability and potential for violence and that they supported the plebiscite idea as a means of bringing peace to Nicaragua. But he said U.S. military leaders felt that Somoza was not cooperating with the mediation team. "Speaking very frankly, Mr. President," said the general, "it is our view that peace will not come to Nicaragua until you have removed yourself from the presidency and the scene."

Somoza responded that he was laying himself wide open by proposing a free election but that the mediators were imposing restrictions unacceptable anywhere in the world. Bowdler told him that because of Nicaragua's electoral history, the FAO could have no confidence in an election unless it was actively supervised by outsiders, that mere observation on the part of foreigners would not be enough.

McAuliffe said the United States had no intention of permitting a settlement that would lead to the destruction of the National Guard. If Somoza followed the plan suggested by the United States, McAuliffe said, "the leftists and Communists will not take over and we will have a moderate government. What I'm saying, Mr. President, is that we [will] have a moderate government that does not have the name Somoza."

That same day, the FAO, after initial hesitation, accepted the mediators' revised electoral plan. Somoza's party said he was rejecting it, but that a counterproposal would be made in a few days. The day after Christmas, Bowdler, McAuliffe, and Ambassador Solaun were called to Washington to discuss Somoza's position.

On the day the Americans went to Washington, Cuban radio announced that the three factions of the Sandinista Front—Prolonged War, Proletarian, and *tercerista*—had agreed to merge their forces both politically and militarily. The agreement presumably ended the bitter dispute over strategy and tactics that had divided the Sandinistas in the aftermath of the 1974 Christmas Party Raid. That it was not easy was evident in a remark that Fidel Castro made to Gabriel García Marquez, the Colombian novelist. García Marquez told a friend that Castro had warned him against being as close as he was to the Sandinistas because it was impossible to know when one of the leaders was going to knife another in the back. Though details of Castro's role in the unification discussion are unknown, various would-be Sandinista combatants who had come into Costa Rica during late 1978 and early 1979 said it was widely understood that Cuba had made military assistance conditional on this unification. The brief unification announcement on December 26, 1978, did not name the leaders, except to say that Tomás Borge, the surviving FSLN founder, was the coordinator of the unified group.

William Bowdler returned to Managua on December 27 and went to see Somoza, who gave him a counterproposal that essentially put in writing some of the things Somoza had been proposing verbally for the plebiscite. It included creation of a national, rather than international, authority to oversee the voting, registration for four Sundays before the voting (instead of no registration), and creation of a constitutional assembly to replace Somoza if he lost the voting. The three mediators met again in the Dominican Republic to consider the latest Somoza proposal. They returned to Managua on January 13 and said they would be willing to recommend creation of the national plebiscite authority but that they stood by the rest of their proposal. The Nationalist Liberal Party, speaking for Somoza's side, said its last proposal also stood. The mediators, convinced that Somoza intended to drag the thing out forever over one detail or another, concluded there were no more negotiation channels to pursue. They abandoned the plebiscite idea and went home.

Bowdler wrote a report for Vance on the unsuccessful mediation in which he concluded by expressing the fear that without a negotiated solution the escalating violence in Nicaragua would "transcend the limits of an internal conflict and affect the peace and tranquility of the whole of Central America."

As the OAS mediators were giving up their effort, Luis Pallais made the last of his trips to Caracas to talk to Carlos Andrés Pérez, who had privately made clear all along that he had little faith in any solution arranged under the OAS banner. He wanted something tough and direct. The Venezuelan president now felt a greater sense of urgency. Presidential elections had been held in Venezuela on December 3, and Pérez's party—he was not eligible for reelection— had lost to the Social Christian candidate, Luis Herrera Campíns. Pérez would leave office in March. When he arrived, Pallais recalled, Pérez offered him a drink, the first time in their talks that he had done that. "I said okay, so he had a drink, too, and he was quiet for a while and then he said, 'Look, we have a solution, but it has to be done immediately.' And I said, 'Okay, what?' He said, 'You are going to organize a coup d'état.' 'Me?' 'Yes, you are going to stage a coup, in agreement with Tacho. Talk to him. You are [then] going to form a national unity government. We have the approval,' he told me, 'of the United States, the Andean Pact countries, Panama, Costa Rica, and Zero [Edén Pastora].' And I said, 'Look, Mr. President. You are putting me in a very difficult situation. What would Somoza think— that during all these four or five meetings with you I have been coming to this? I cannot carry this message.' "

Pallais knew that Somoza, in his heart, had all along been looking for a way to stay in power and had never been convinced that the circumstances might require his departure. The key to staying in power, Somoza had often told Pallais, was "riding the waves" of U.S. policy until it changed. When he talked that way it was as if, in his mind, the Sandinistas and the strikers and demonstrators did not exist, and as if his heart attack and the murder of Pedro Joaquín Chamorro had never happened. One of the reasons he had temporized so long on the details of the plebiscite was that he was looking for a way to force the United States to back him once more in the fight against Communism. Winning the plebiscite vote would conceivably have done that, though it certainly was not contemplated within U.S. strategy.

Pallais, like the other confidants, had always tried to straddle the fence on the issue of Somoza's permanence in power, although he had put forward some mild suggestions after the heart attack that Somoza ought to consider resigning. Pallais' acquiescence reflected something about Nicaragua and Somoza that was unusual in Latin America: the refusal or inability of those around the ruler to plot against him. While there was some occasional disgruntlement from within the National Guard, it was relatively minor and usually came from men who lacked a following. Most of the Guardsmen looked to Somoza as their personal patron and morale booster. Somoza's half brother, José, was director of the National Guard; his eldest son, Harvard-educated Anastasio Somoza Portocarrero, who had inherited his father's old nickname, Tachito, was head of the military training school. Those two, in turn, were part of Tacho's inner circle, along with Pallais, plus an uncle, and a very few politicians from the Nationalist Liberal Party. But in one way or another, Somoza had seduced all of these people. Those who may have had political ambitions of their own had lost them in the process of personal wealth-building that he encouraged. As for Tachito, all he had to do was bide his time until it was appropriate to move ahead. Pallais, who was related through the socially superior Debayle side of Somoza's family, had originally been close to Luis, Tacho's older brother and the one viewed as more likely to have modernized the nation's politics. After Luis' death, Tacho turned to Pallais for political counsel. It was thought that Somoza would listen to him if anyone. But for the cousin with the pleasant manner and unquestioned loyalty, it was impossible to contemplate trying to convince Somoza to cooperate in what amounted to a self-coup.

Pérez told Pallais he should promise Somoza to save his properties and other interests, and tell him to leave the country for temporary exile with certain members of his government and the National Guard. Then, backed by the remaining National Guard leadership, Pallais would form a government in cooperation with the FAO. If Pallais could not give this message to Somoza, Pérez said, then he himself would do it. He called Managua. Five times, as Pallais remembered it. But Somoza did not pick up the telephone when aides put the call through to him. Pérez finally said it was up to Pallais to decide whether he wanted to propose it to Somoza.

Back on his plane, Pallais began writing a memorandum to Somoza about the conversation. When the plane stopped in Panama to refuel and drop off two aides to Torrijos who had traveled with Pallais to Caracas, a Panamanian National Guard officer was waiting with a helicopter. Torrijos wanted to see Pallais. "So I got in the helicopter and went to a house. It was about one-thirty in the morning. Torrijos was there, and he got me a drink and he says, 'Louie, you don't want to be president of Nicaragua? You don't want to solve the problem of your country?' I said, 'I'm not saying I don't want to—I'm all for it—but the truth is that I cannot go and say this to Tacho.' Then he says, 'Louie, Louie, we are backing you up. We are backing Somoza. We are backing everything up. This is the solution for Nicaragua. The Communists will go to hell. You will have Zero [Pastora] there, the [Sandinista] faction of Zero, which is not a Communist faction. He likes you. He accepted. I have talked to him personally. We'll have opposition from the Sandinistas,' he says, 'of course. But those guys without our help cannot even get twenty FALs,' he told me . . . And I said, 'Omar, that's all fine, but, I cannot talk to Tacho.' "

Like Pérez, Torrijos began trying to telephone Somoza, who again did not pick up the phone. "Okay," Torrijos told Pallais, "I have my ways of making it known."

Pallais reached Managua at four in the morning, but Somoza was waiting for him in the Bunker. Torrijos had leaked to his friends in the Panama office of the Spanish news agency, ACAN-EFE, a story to the effect that Pallais was replacing Somoza. Somoza had the cables in hand. He was furious. Pallais told Somoza about the events of the long night and asked what he wanted him to do. Somoza told him to call a news conference the next day at which Pallais would deny the story Torrijos had leaked.

6

THE INSURRECTION
BEGINS

JANUARY 1979 TO JUNE 1979

The failure of the mediation left the moderate opposition forces in
Nicaragua—political parties, the church leadership, and private enterprise groups—dangling in the wind without desirable options.
Their choice now lay between throwing their lot in with the Sandinistas or making peace with Somoza. Most were shocked at what had
seemed to them a display of impotence on the part of the United
States.

Alfonso Robelo, one of the leaders of that group, was dismayed that
the United States had had no contingency planning for the possibility
that Somoza might resist efforts to remove him. He told me several
years later: "When the United States put it to Somoza that they
wanted him out, they didn't expect him to say no. But what pressure
did they use? They used no pressures. If, at that moment, in October,

November, December of 1978, they had been ready to put pressures on Somoza, like saying, 'Okay, forget it, you're not going to have a sanctuary in the States' . . . things of this nature or other things they can do, Somoza would have stepped down and a different thing would have happened. We lost the best opportunity we had at that time . . . After that the Broad Opposition Front was left with nothing and the only people who had initiative were those in the violent mode, the FSLN . . ."

President Pérez of Venezuela also criticized the Carter administration. In his state of the union address, delivered on March 7, 1979, just a few days before finishing his term, Pérez said that while he had felt encouraged when the Carter administration took office because of the prospects for a new kind of relationship between the United States and Latin American nations, he felt "profoundly frustrated today at the wavering and contradictions with which our cordial appeals to adopt common stands on human rights regarding the drama in Nicaragua have been answered."

After the collapse of the OAS mediation, the United States was left with no policy toward Nicaragua. As the mediation was coming to an unsuccessful close in January, the Carter administration issued threats about "reassessing" its relations with Somoza and his government, but another issue was intruding on the Carter administration's maneuverability on the question of Nicaragua and restricting its ability to create a new policy, if that policy were to be based on the replacement of Somoza. That issue was the Panama Canal.

Jimmy Carter had come into office with a promise to do two specific things in Latin America: promote respect for human rights and reach agreement on new treaties governing ownership and operation of the Panama Canal, which Carter viewed as the right of the Panamanian people. The Senate had ratified the two treaties with just one vote to spare in March and April 1978, after one of its more heated debates. General Torrijos took a warm view of Carter as a result of the President's commitment to the treaties. At the beginning of 1979, however, Carter still needed companion legislation passed by both houses of Congress to implement the treaties. That legislation had to be drafted by the House Merchant Marine and Fisheries Committee, which had jurisdiction in canal matters, and whose chairman was John Murphy of New York, one of Somoza's closest friends since youth. Murphy was dropping hints to the Carter administration that he might bottle up the crucial implementing legislation if Carter persisted in forcing Somoza out of office. Although he is not known to have said this publicly in Washington, Murphy was asked by journalists during a trip to Panama whether he would link the implementing legislation to the Somoza affair, and he said that he would.

Another Somoza friend, Representative Charles Wilson of Texas, put fear into the heart of the administration over its entire foreign aid program. Wilson was a member of the Appropriations Committee and was considered the swing vote on the Foreign Aid Bill.

On January 19, 1979, Murphy had lunch with Carter. Both sides said later the other had asked for the meeting. White House staff members concerned with foreign relations were strongly opposed to such a meeting, but those responsible for congressional relations, who needed Murphy's help on several bills in addition to the canal legislation, convinced Carter to invite Murphy. Robert Pastor of the National Security Council staff said Murphy tried to connect the two issues—Somoza's permanence in power and the canal legislation—but Carter refused the proposal. Murphy himself told me he did not make the connection between Somoza and the canal but that he did tell Carter the canal bill drafted by the State Department could not pass the House but that his version could pass. Murphy also told Carter that Somoza was dismayed that the mediation had been terminated when he still had a counterproposal to make.

Whether or not a tradeoff deal—Somoza's permanence in power for the canal treaties—was struck at the luncheon, the one thing that clearly emerged was Murphy's willingness to proceed to draft and sponsor the canal legislation during the next few months, though it was not the bill that the White House or the State Department wanted. At the same time, the Carter administration seemed to forget that Nicaragua and Somoza existed.

After talking tough in January about how it would treat Somoza in the aftermath of the failed mediation, the administration settled on a middle way, deciding in February to formally end the military aid program, suspended since September anyway, and to call home more than half of the embassy personnel. Ambassador Solaun came home, too, resigned, and returned to teaching. The immediate reason for Solaun's decision to leave was concern for his safety—the CIA had uncovered evidence of a Sandinista plan to kill him—but it also extricated him from a situation in which he expected to be increasingly at odds with Washington decisions.

For the Sandinistas, the several months following the Christmas 1978 unification announcement were devoted, in large measure, to working out differences over who would form the leadership. The biggest and most recurring issue was what to do about Edén Pastora, whose audacious command of the Palace Raid, coupled with his personal charm and non-Marxist views, had made him the favorite of the Western world.

First, according to information from several people close to the debate, there was an effort by one of Pastora's closest collaborators to expand the three-man *tercerista* directorate, then made up of the Ortega brothers—Humberto and Daniel—and Victor Tirado, so as to include Pastora. But it was protested by some other top *terceristas,* particularly Oscar Pérez Cassar, one of the Internal Front leaders. Pérez argued that except for the Palace Raid nobody had heard of Pastora and that other comrades had a longer, more consistent trajectory of revolutionary struggle. Pastora was also criticized, anonymously, by others in the faction as "a bourgeois, committed Christian who is not ideologically consistent," and as one whose strong sense of his own personality created problems for the movement. Pastora's backers countered with a proposal to expand the directorate so as to include not only Pastora but also Pérez Cassar and Joaquín Cuadra, the military leader of the Internal Front. Cuadra said he had no such ambitions, and the expansion idea was dropped.

The Ortegas then offered to make Pastora supreme military commander of the unified Sandinista Front. Since the Ortegas were not known as big Pastora backers, the move was presumably linked to the desire to retain the assistance of General Torrijos and outgoing President Pérez, both of whom wanted Pastora to be the dominant figure in the FSLN. That, too, encountered opposition. Humberto Ortega traveled to Cuba during this time, and when he returned to Costa Rica, he and his brother announced that Pastora was military commander of the Southern Front, the name used for the military theater coming together in Costa Rica, but excluding anything organized from within Nicaragua or from across the northern border in Honduras.

Sometime in March 1979 representatives of the three factions were brought together in Havana and a nine-man directorate emerged made up of the three top men from each faction. From the Prolonged War group, they were surviving FSLN founder Tomás Borge, Moscow-educated Henry Ruiz, and Bayardo Arce, a former *La Prensa* reporter. From the *terceristas,* they were the Ortegas and Victor Tirado. From the Proletarians, they were Jaime Wheelock, the writer and academic whose criticism of the 1974 Christmas raid had led to the division of the FSLN, Luis Carrión Cruz, the U.S.-educated son of a wealthy businessman, and Carlos Nuñez. Only Bayardo Arce, who spent virtually all of the war months inside Nicaragua, was not present in Cuba for the signing of the agreement for what was called the National Directorate.

Havana Radio distributed the announcement of the unified directorate at the end of March with a statement by Borge acknowledging the past internal differences. "There have been political and strategic differences. There were differences regarding political alliances. We had differences regarding the manner of waging war. We differed regarding the time to launch certain types of military actions." But through all of these disputes, he said, the Sandinistas had always been united ideologically. Now it was important to reunify in all ways because the divisions had opened the doors to political maneuvers among the Sandinistas by "Yankee imperialism," "*Somocista* tyranny," and "domestic reactionaries." "If division provided a broad field of opportunities for the enemy to fight us, unity means restricting the enemy's field of activity."

One of the immediate effects of the change of presidents in Venezuela was that that country stopped shipping rifles and ammunition into Costa Rica. While not backing Somoza and not formally rejecting the commitment Pérez had made to Costa Rica, the government of President Luis Herrera Campíns simply did not find its way clear to processing the matter. Johnny Echeverría, the Costa Rican public security minister, said a total of five hundred M-14 rifles and more than a million rounds of ammunition arrived from Venezuela in February 1979, some of which was turned over to the Sandinistas. This was just half of what had been promised.

Despite this, the rebels' supply line was growing and becoming more efficient. From December 1978 to July 1979 there were at least sixty flights into Costa Rica with arms, ammunition, and other war supplies. This was confirmed both by Echeverría, who oversaw the operation from the Costa Rican end, and by the subsequent investigation conducted by the Costa Rican National Assembly. Except for the flights that brought the Venezuelan offering and one carrying items supplied by Panama, Echeverría said, all the flights carried matériel supplied by Cuba, though initially transshipped via the town of David in Panama.

During late 1978 and early 1979, the planes that brought the supplies to Costa Rica landed at the international airport in San José. They were unloaded, and, according to testimony taken by the National

Assembly investigators, an unknown percentage of the boxes went to various Costa Ricans during the unloading, while the rest of the boxes were turned over to the Sandinistas, who trucked them to Guanacaste, their operations area. The Costa Rican officials kept no inventory of the matériel that had originated in Cuba, so the National Assembly investigators never learned how much remained in Costa Rican hands and what happened to it.

In April 1979 the flights began to bypass San José and fly directly to Liberia, the provincial capital of Guanacaste. Alfredo Sánchez Rodríguez, then the administrator of the Liberia airport, told investigators two years later that one of the top deputies of Johnny Echeverría and several national security agents drove into the airport shortly before the arrival of the first flight, a DC3 without a visible matriculation number, on Good Friday—April 13—and told him the flight and its cargo were a matter of state secrecy. The next day, he said, another DC3, also without matriculation, arrived and was not unloaded until dark.

Other planes followed, mainly Aztecs with Panamanian registrations, usually coming several at a time over various weeks. One of the small Aztecs could not carry more than 1,200 or 1,300 pounds of supplies, Sánchez said. There was also a "Sky Van" that he learned was registered to the Panamanian Air Force. The cargo, Sánchez gradually learned, was being hidden up in the mountains near the border for the day of a big offensive. Any time a flight was expected, at least one senior aide to Johnny Echeverría would appear at the airport. At first, the planes were unloaded after midnight and often took off again before daylight, but later they would be unloaded in the middle of the day. Sometimes the smaller planes took off again with part of their cargo and headed north, presumably to leave it at a landing strip inside Nicaragua or in Honduras.

Only occasional public allegations were being made during these months—late 1978 and early 1979—about Cuban assistance to the guerrillas. The United States, which had suspicions but very little concrete information, tried quiet pressures on those it thought were involved. What public charges there were came from Somoza, who had a credibility problem. In December 1978 a Cuban diplomat in Mexico denied that Cuba was providing arms. In mid-March, about the time of the unity talks in Havana, the underground Sandinista radio station said the FSLN "has never received arms from Socialist countries. Our arms come from the sacrifice of honest Nicaraguan people, and they are bought with money 'recovered' by our squadrons and commandos throughout the country and the unselfish cooperation of true Nicaraguans." Pastora told a Panamanian journalist that he had gone to Castro to ask for help and had been told: "The best help I can give you is not to help you at all."

In addition to the preparations in Costa Rica, a smaller number of Sandinistas was organizing and arming in Honduras in early 1979 to push into Nicaragua from the north. Much less is known about how that operation was organized. It was run by the secretive Prolonged War Faction and directed by Henry Ruiz, a retiring former student of Moscow's Patrice Lumumba University known primarily at that time for his tenacity in surviving in the northern mountains during the National Guard counterinsurgency campaigns of the early and mid-1970s. Several groups of a few dozen Sandinistas were deported to Panama from Honduras in late 1978 and early 1979, but they were usually back in Honduras in a matter of days. Some were also detained for several weeks at a time, until Honduran sympathizers of the Sandinistas could stir up enough fuss for them to be released. Honduran authorities, like the Costa Ricans, knew that keeping Sandinistas in jail would only expose their government to the possibility of kidnap-ransom actions. In general, Honduran authorities and the Honduran public were not as sympathetic to the Sandinistas as people in Costa Rica. The Sandinistas in Honduras, who comprised the top ranks of what became the Northern Front, also had an arms supply operation, but it was less extensive than that in Costa Rica, and at least part of it involved supplies and planes that had come through Costa Rica. A Sandinista supporter who worked for an international organization in Tegucigalpa, the Honduran capital, kept an account to pay pilots and buy cooperation from Honduran military officers when necessary.

During the early months of 1979, Somoza's own arms situation suffered surprisingly little damage from the cutoff of U.S. military assistance. The National Guard had a substantial stockpile of automatic weapons, including 5,000 M-16s ordered from Colt before Carter took office that arrived after he was in office. The National Guard's primary ongoing need was for ammunition for both light and heavy weapons.

Even before the official termination of U.S. supplies, Somoza had turned to Israel, which was filling the gap. He also bought on the black market through South Africa, Argentina, and the Bahamas. Diplomats who were involved in the mediation believed that one reason Somoza was so cocky in resisting pressures to resign was the knowledge that Israel, which had a full-time arms salesman working the countries of the Caribbean Basin, could and would supply whatever the National Guard needed. Lieutenant Colonel James L. McCoy, who was defense attaché of the U.S. Embassy in Managua during that time, said Israel initially provided Somoza with some three-quarter-ton trucks and Galil rifles, then ammunition on a continuing basis. A few months later, however, in about April 1979, after a number of complaints from the Sandinistas and their supporters, the United States put pressure on Israel to cease selling to Somoza. A ship, the *Liberian Star,* loaded with ammunition from Israel turned back as it approached Central American waters.

Then Somoza turned to his fellow Central American military rulers, whose promise of support he had obtained in a meeting at the end of December 1978. Most of the gap left by Israel's withdrawal was filled by Guatemala, with smaller amounts of help from Honduras and El Salvador. McCoy, who was in almost daily contact with Somoza's son and other top National Guard officers during this time, said the Guatemalan defense minister "took stock from the Guatemalan arsenal and put it on C47s and flew it to Nicaragua at night, then replenished his own stocks on the world market. This was kept secret. There was a regular series of flights. Some nights you would hear there had been two, other times just one." Most of what Guatemala supplied was ammunition, but it also provided some aviation fuel.

When Somoza realized he would have to look elsewhere than the United States for his munitions, he also concluded it was time to upgrade and expand the National Guard. Son Tachito, back home at the age of twenty-eight after being educated at Harvard and the U.S. Army Command and General Staff College at Fort Leavenworth, took over and updated the Basic Infantry Training School in late 1977. The name was a misnomer because the school, while it did train recruits, concentrated especially now on creating elite units and training staff officers. In late 1978, when the rebel side was attracting hundreds of volunteers in reaction to the Sandinistas' September uprising, the National Guard launched its own highly successful recruiting drive. In October and November, after the call went out, young men mobbed recruiting offices in hopes of being selected for what was one of the few ways for the poor in Nicaragua to improve their lot.

Despite the frequent claims made by Sandinista leaders in Costa Rica that they were going to undertake a new offensive toward the end of the mediation, such an offensive did not occur. Instead, there was a series of frequent but small actions around the country during the first three months of 1979 that involved little guerrilla manpower. Some of them were not mounted by the Sandinistas as such but were clashes between the National Guard and students, perhaps guided by Sandinistas. At other times, there were quick attacks on National Guard posts by Sandinistas who fired from moving vehicles. People continued to die, however. And it did not require a lot of manpower to set off a hundred bombs in Managua over several days, but they served to keep the population jittery.

April brought this relative hiatus to an explosive end. On Saturday night, April 7, 1979, between two hundred and three hundred Sandinistas came down from the mountains and moved into Estelí, a city of an estimated 35,000 people about fifty miles below the Honduran border. They occupied public offices empty for the weekend and claimed control of the city. This occurred about the same time as actions in various smaller northern towns—Ocotal, El Sauce, Condega—and was followed quickly by rebel attacks in the western cities of León and Chinandega.

The National Guard post in Estelí did little at first. The civilian population, fearful of being trapped in the same kind of fighting as had occurred in September, began to flee the city in cars flying white flags. The next day the Guard flew in reinforcements from Managua, set up an operations center a short distance outside town, and cut the water and power supply. The troops surrounded the city and then began to retake it block by block with apparent high casualties, though each side challenged the other's figures. The Sandinistas set up barricades in neighborhoods they held and fired on advancing Guardsmen. As the fighting intensified, the Guard force in Estelí grew to about a thousand men. They had a Sherman tank, two armored personnel carriers, and mortars, plus air support. On April 14 the National Guard called a truce of several hours to allow the Red Cross to evacuate the remaining civilians. But that night, the guerrillas slipped through the military circle and withdrew into the hills.

The guerrillas called it a strategic retreat, but in fact they had scored a nonmilitary victory because the National Guard bombardments to retake Estelí turned many of the civilians there against the government and further damaged Somoza's image outside Nicaragua.

The guerrilla occupation of Estelí and the other actions during April in the north and west revealed that the unification of the three FSLN factions and formation of the National Directorate had not eliminated the differences among them. While the occupation of Estelí was under way, a guerrilla commander there issued an appeal for Pastora's Southern Front to jump into the fight and alleged that the combatants in Costa Rica were not doing their part. However, a representative of the Southern Front told Los Angeles *Times* correspondent David Belknap shortly after the Estelí action ended that it had violated the battle strategy agreed upon in March when the three factions unified. The battle plan, he said, was to conduct only hit-and-run attacks through April and then in mid-May to occupy eight principal cities simultaneously. The Southern Front, with much larger manpower, was not yet ready, he said. While this may have represented a misunderstanding between the Northern and Southern Fronts over strategy, it just as likely indicated a race for Managua— and power—among various Sandinista leaders. From the time of the Estelí attack in early April until the end of June there was almost continual fighting in a number of large and small towns of the north and west. They were taken, retaken, abandoned by both sides until several were a mass of ruins, weak and ripe to fall.

The U.S. Embassy had, throughout the early months of 1979, been issuing assessments that Somoza probably could survive the Sandinista attacks, though after the April actions in Estelí and elsewhere in the north, Colonel McCoy sent to Washington a scenario under which Somoza could lose, based more on what McCoy saw as the repudiation of Somoza by the entire population than on the military capabilities of the Sandinistas. The importance of public sentiment was becoming so obvious to McCoy that he once asked Tachito Somoza why he couldn't see this himself and convince his father to resign and permit an orderly transition. Tachito asked McCoy which Nicaraguans he had been talking to. "My gardener and my barber, for starters," said McCoy. Tachito suggested that he get a new gardener and change barbers.

After McCoy sent his pessimistic assessment of Somoza's possibilities to Washington, the Joint Chiefs of Staff asked him, on a contingency basis, what the Nicaraguan National Guard would need from the United States. McCoy talked to Somoza's son and advised Washington that the primary needs would be .50-caliber ammunition and small arms. None came, however.

. . .

Throughout the first months of 1979, the FSLN and its front organizations issued numerous appeals to the groups remaining in the FAO —the Broad Opposition Front—to join forces, saying the Sandinistas were anti-imperialist but not anticapitalist and were willing to include all political persuasions in a future government. In late April, unification talks were opened in Managua between the FSLN's National Patriotic Front and the FAO. At the end of April, two FAO leaders, Alfonso Robelo and Rafael Córdova Rivas, were jailed. The government said it was for investigation of arms trafficking, but Robelo understood that the real reason was the fear that they were working with the unions to organize a new strike for May 1. When they were freed in mid-May, Robelo issued a call for opposition groups to unite and form a provisional government. Then he went to Florida to visit his family and continued to Costa Rica, where he got in touch with leaders of the *tercerista* faction.

About this time the insurgents received a major diplomatic assist. The Mexican government broke diplomatic relations with the Somoza government on May 20 and urged other Latin American nations to follow suit. It also pleaded with the Carter administration to resist the pressures of Somoza's friends in Congress and take a tough line against the Nicaraguan ruler. Mexican President José López Portillo announced the rupture after back-to-back visits by Fidel Castro and President Carazo of Costa Rica. The Costa Rican government had broken relations with Somoza at the end of 1978 because of the border disputes, but Mexico's break was much more significant because of the possibility that other countries of the region—influenced by Mexico's emerging oil power—would follow suit. The importance of the decision to the Sandinistas was obvious. The FSLN National Directorate issued a statement expressing "revolutionary joy" at the Mexican action, and eight of the eleven members of *Los Doce* immediately traveled to Mexico to thank López Portillo. The United States began pleading with General Torrijos in Panama and countries on the northern rim of South America not to do as Mexico had done.

In Costa Rica, an estimated 1,500 men and women were preparing for an all-out invasion of their homeland. Lacking the mountain cover of the northern guerrillas and with immense Lake Nicaragua in their path, they faced the prospect of forcing their way up the relatively flat strip of land between the lake and the Pacific, an area which, at places, was less than ten miles wide. The objective was to capture Rivas, a departmental capital twenty-five miles northwest of the frontier, and establish it as the seat of a liberated zone.

As the time of the southern offensive, planned for late May, grew close, it was decided to eliminate the Panamanian town of David as the transshipment point for weapons and ammunition. Instead, everything would be flown direct from Cuba to Costa Rica, right into Liberia, just fifty miles from the Nicaraguan border on a good highway. Johnny Echeverría said the change was made because it was a waste of time and energy to come through David. The planes being used had relatively small liftloads, he explained, and just one antiaircraft battery with 20,000 rounds of ammunition would take up the entire capacity.

However, it was also convenient to General Torrijos to remove Panama from the route. The United States had recently confirmed its suspicions about the use of David as the transit point—in part, because Colonel Noriega, the Panamanian officer who had dealt with the Cubans in establishing the route, had one day taken some information out of his file on the operation and handed it to the CIA. Since Noriega was a firm Torrijos loyalist, it was probable that the action was done with the encouragement or knowledge of Torrijos. To understand why would be to have understood Torrijos.

As a result, the Carter administration had stepped up pressure on Torrijos to halt the arms trafficking, arguing that publicity about such activity would do no good in the battle for implementing legislation for the canal treaties. Ambler H. Moss, Jr., then the U.S. ambassador to Panama, was given instructions "at least a dozen times to go in and make demarches to Torrijos in the sense that Washington certainly hopes that nobody in this area is fueling this war and we wouldn't want to see guns going through Panama and there are rumors that guns may be passing through Panama. And, of course, Torrijos, with an absolutely straight face, would swear up and down that there weren't any guns going through Panama and [that] he would know if there were. On one occasion he even snatched a piece of paper . . . and wrote down, 'If anybody is caught running guns, I'll have him put in jail.' He gave it to me and said, 'Here, take that to Washington.' "

To make the flights direct from Cuba to Costa Rica, Edén Pastora struck a deal with a Costa Rican who owned a private flying service called EXACO, which had a fleet of DC6s, most of them in bad shape.

In late May or early June they began to make runs between Havana and Liberia. Sánchez Rodríguez, the airport manager in Liberia, calculated that there were twenty-three flights to and from Cuba by EXACO planes between then and the end of the war in mid-July. In addition, the Sandinistas had a DC6 of their own that made a number of flights. Sánchez said officials of Johnny Echeverría's Public Security Ministry told him never to say that the flights came from Cuba, and, if asked, to say they came from Panama. Costa Rican National Assembly investigators later estimated that at least one million pounds of war matériel entered Costa Rica from Cuba during that period of six to eight weeks, a figure that did not include what had been shipped earlier via David. The shipments were primarily rifles and ammunition, but also mortars, rocket launchers, bazookas, and antiaircraft weaponry.

Various Sandinistas came regularly to the Liberia Airport to receive the supplies, particularly Victor Tirado, the Mexican who was a member of the National Directorate. Elio Espinar, the rice farmer who was working with Pastora, also showed up frequently. There were occasional disputes among the Sandinistas and Costa Rican security officials and those connected to the flying service over how the arriving goods were to be divided. One day, Sánchez saw Tirado "crying like a child" during such a dispute. Tirado said his people were being killed and had no ammunition while the Costa Ricans were trying to keep what should go to the Sandinistas.

Some of the clandestine flights brought foreign passengers into Liberia instead of supplies, and the passengers simply got off and disappeared into Guanacaste's open spaces without passing through immigration. At times, Sandinistas or Costa Ricans involved in the flights would get on one of the planes leaving Liberia and go to Havana, returning a few days later. There were always many foreigners, other than Nicaraguans, hanging around the soda bar in the airport. Many of them were Panamanians and Venezuelans, and there was also a group identified to Sánchez as Spaniards, whom he did not hear speak for eight or ten days. One day, he overheard them talking on the telephone and realized they were Cubans.

In late May, Victor Tirado called Leonel Poveda to Liberia from San José and apologized for having left him largely unoccupied for several months. They were going to give him a column to attack Peñas Blancas, the border control post just inside Nicaragua. Poveda asked when. Day after tomorrow. They gave him thirty men, of whom ten were Panamanians, and two mortars, one 81 millimeter and the other 60 millimeter.

At eight in the morning on May 24, Poveda's forces took up a position three hundred yards from Peñas Blancas and opened fire with the mortars. He considered it the first shots in the southern war. After firing ten rounds from each mortar, they stopped, then resumed firing at noon. The idea was to distract the National Guard and make it think the Sandinistas were entering Nicaragua through Peñas Blancas. In reality, the main force was going to try to enter through El Naranjo, another border point. Poveda's troops spent five days bombarding the National Guard in Peñas Blancas, then joined the main force at El Naranjo. But an incredible downpour erupted and the Sandinistas spent the next seven days in the rain in foxholes full of water. When the rain stopped, the entire force—about four hundred people—retreated to a farm on the Costa Rican side to repair weapons and heal the funguses that covered everybody's feet.

In the first days of June, the reorganized force returned to Peñas Blancas and opened fire before dawn one day. When Poveda reached the firing line, he found total confusion. "Nobody could tell where to shoot or who was shooting at whom. They [the Sandinistas] had put their artillery up front, and I said, 'How can that be? It ought to be behind us.' The National Guard almost took the artillery away from us. I arrived just as the National Guard was about to circle the artillery. Some of the *compas* [Sandinistas] had already given up to the National Guard. That's how the sad things began. We were there through June and into July."

Somoza sent his best troops, in large numbers, to face the Sandinistas in the south and complained to the OAS that he was being invaded. On June 9 the National Guard claimed victory in the south, saying it had killed at least 136 rebels and chased the others back into Costa Rica during twelve days of fighting. Major Pablo Emilio Salazar, Somoza's star combat leader, led journalists into the region and showed off about a hundred captured rifles, half of them FALs, plus Chinese rockets, .50-caliber machine guns, and thousands of rounds of ammunition for heavy weapons. With a sense of elation he said it was probably the first victory the National Guard had ever won in conventional warfare.

But his war was not over.

7

DEFEAT
AND TRIUMPH

JUNE AND JULY 1979

Sometime before the end of May 1979, General Torrijos in Panama
had begun to have second thoughts about the trend of Nicaraguan
events and to fear that he was losing to Fidel Castro in a high-stakes
game. His involvement with the Sandinistas had been like buying a
volatile stock—risky, but with great potential return. It was time to
cut his losses and try to help his friend Carter. According to Torrijos'
friend Gabriel Lewis, the general had come to feel "that Jimmy Carter
was sort of a priest, with high moral standards and very courageous."
In his heart, Torrijos wanted to be that good, but his approach was
different. Ambler Moss remembered: "Torrijos always wanted Carter
to be a partner in an enterprise to get rid of Somoza and put some sort
of nice, left-of-center social democratic government in, and he
thought: 'If only these gringos had the good sense to rely on my

judgment and listen to me I could work this out for them, but they are dumb people and don't do what I say. I only want to be used.' That sort of thing."

At the beginning of June, Torrijos asked Gabriel Lewis to get a message to Carter that Torrijos had important information for him about Nicaragua. Lewis called a friend on the White House staff in the middle of the night, timed intentionally to impress the White House with the urgency of the matter. The next morning, Carter told Robert Pastor of the National Security Council to rush to Panama and find out what Torrijos had to say. Pastor went to tell Zbigniew Brzezinski where he was going, and they decided it was a good opportunity to press Torrijos on the arms issue.

Pastor and Moss, who happened to be in Washington that day, left together. They reached Panama that night and used a U.S. military helicopter to go to Lewis' house on Contadora, where Torrijos received them. Pastor and Torrijos talked through the night of June 4 and June 5. Various other people came and went.

"Essentially, I tried to convince him that we had gone a long road together on the Panama Canal treaties and we had just gotten to the last stage and he was about to throw it all out the window," Pastor recalled. "And he said to me, 'Don't talk to me about the canal treaties. That's over. We're on to something new now.' I said, 'General, you have this good relationship with Carter, and what are you doing? You're trying to covertly overthrow a neighboring government.' I said, 'What's the Panama Canal treaty all about? It's nonintervention.' And he says, 'I'm not doing anything.' "

Pastor also argued that it was foolish to anger Somoza because U.S. intelligence indicated that Somoza could survive the present Sandinista offensive and probably hang on to power for some time to come. This raised the point for which Torrijos had wanted Pastor to come. He had his own information on Nicaragua, and he wanted the gringos to hear it. Colonel Noriega, who served as chief of intelligence for the Panamanian National Guard, was there, as were Marcel Salamín, the former Communist who was Torrijos' liaison with the Sandinistas in Costa Rica, and a National Guard major who was the Panamanian military attaché in Nicaragua and very pro-Somoza. Each gave his view of the situation, what Moss called "sort of triangulation, people talking from different perspectives." They provided a lot of battle data and differed sharply with the Washington view of Somoza's ability to hold out.

Torrijos finally agreed that both he and Aristides Royo, whom he had installed as president the year before, would sign letters to Carter assuring him that Panama was not intervening in Nicaraguan affairs. At three or four in the morning, Pastor flew to Panama City and began working out the wording of the letters with other Panamanian officials. When Pastor got on a plane back to Washington in mid-afternoon, he was carrying both letters. Royo's letter, which was made public in Panama, said that "Panama is not intervening and will not intervene in the internal affairs of any country . . ." Pastor said Torrijos' letter was only slightly different. By that time, the letters were probably technically true because the town of David was no longer being used as the transshipment point for arms and ammunition going to the Sandinistas.

In Managua, on June 11, amidst heavy fighting in the industrial district along the North Highway, National Guard tanks pulled up in front of *La Prensa* and opened fire, destroying a large part of the complex and leaving the press a smoldering ruin. The newspaper—now directed by Pedro Joaquín's brother Xavier—had ceased publication the week before when Somoza reimposed censorship, so few employees were present. All survived.

Violeta Barrios de Chamorro, the widow of Pedro Joaquín, had left in late May for Costa Rica to accompany one of her daughters, Claudia, whose husband had disappeared from home and was thought to be among those preparing for combat on the Southern Front. The women rented a house in San José to wait out the war with Claudia's two small children. On the evening of the attack on *La Prensa*, the house filled up with Nicaraguans, journalists, and sympathizers, including two members of *Los Doce*—Sergio Ramírez, the writer, and Miguel d'Escoto, the Maryknoll priest. Unable to get a quiet moment with Mrs. Chamorro, they told Claudia that they were forming a "group" in which her mother would be "the appropriate person" to represent her late husband and *La Prensa*. When Claudia told her mother about the proposal, Mrs. Chamorro protested that she was not a politician, that politics was repulsive to her, but said she would do it for the love of her country. "I said I didn't want a cent for it. I wanted this all to get over with rapidly for Nicaragua, I wanted free elections and press liberty, things we had never had, and to make an example for the world."

Alfonso Robelo, who had arrived in San José from Florida, was approached by Dionisio Marenco, the man whose house in the suburbs of Managua had served as takeoff point for the Palace Raid.

They discussed formation of a provisional government junta. Marenco by then was a fullfledged member of the *tercerista* faction and was speaking for the Sandinista National Directorate. Robelo later recalled: "He said, 'Look, this war will have to end in a political negotiation.' They [the FSLN] never expected a total military victory. This was something that they made clear. They never expected it. So they say, 'In a negotiation'—this was in the back of their minds, they didn't actually say it—'we need a junta that we can sell.' They thought that the junta would win a lot of international support for them, that it would isolate the *somocistas,* and that it would reassure a lot of countries within Latin America and even people in the United States."

Initially, Robelo said, he was told that the junta of National Reconstruction would be made up of only four people—himself, Mrs. Chamorro, Sergio Ramírez, and an unidentified representative of the United People's Movement, the group that had organized support for the Sandinistas in poor neighborhoods. Once they had accepted, he said, the FSLN decided to include a member of its own National Directorate, Daniel Ortega Saavedra, the older brother of Humberto. Then thirty-three, Daniel Ortega had been imprisoned in Nicaragua in 1967 and freed as a result of the 1974 Christmas Party Raid. Until he was named to the junta, he was known to most Nicaraguans only for a poem he wrote in prison—"I Never Saw Managua when Miniskirts Were in Fashion."

The timing of the creation of the junta appeared linked to the Mexican rupture with the Somoza regime and with Mexican pressures on other countries to do the same. On June 10 the Sandinista Directorate complained that the United States was trying to convince the five member countries of the Andean Pact—Colombia, Venezuela, Peru, Ecuador, and Bolivia—to undertake a new mediation effort, which the Sandinistas said was just another ploy by the "geniuses" of the State Department to prevent the establishment of "true democracy" in Nicaragua. A few days later, however, the chiefs of state of the Andean countries met and decided that the Nicaraguan fighting constituted a "true state of belligerency" and the rebels should be entitled to the prerogatives and obligations that international law imposes on "legitimate combatants." It was a backhanded recognition of the rebels, but, perhaps in deference to the United States, the Andean governments did not go so far as to break with Somoza's government.

Nevertheless, on June 17, the day after the Andean Pact declaration, the names of the five junta members were announced in San José. The fifth member—in addition to Daniel Ortega, Robelo, Chamorro, and

Ramírez—was Moisés Hassan, a university dean with a doctorate in mathematics from the University of North Carolina. Though identified as a founder of the United People's Movement, he, like Ramírez, later turned out to be a member of the FSLN. It was suggested by various rebel sources that the junta would be installed in Rivas as the government of Nicaragua as soon as the Sandinistas took the town. Pastora told Costa Rican journalists, who found him at the battlefield just inside Nicaragua, that he expected to accomplish that within seventy-two hours.

Shortly before noon the next day in Washington, the new U.S. ambassador to Nicaragua, Lawrence Pezzullo, called on Luis Pallais Debayle at the Guest Quarters Hotel with a message that indicated the United States was abandoning its noninterventionist posture. Pezzullo, a career Foreign Service officer, had arrived in Washington from Uruguay less than three weeks earlier and had been rushed through confirmation hearings. Then, instead of going to Nicaragua, he remained in Washington to take part in what had suddenly become a frantic search for a Nicaraguan policy. Top officials of the State and Defense Departments, the CIA, the National Security Council, and sometimes Carter himself, were meeting at least twice a week at the White House. Now, Pezzullo was about to convey to Pallais part of what was emerging from those talks.

Taking notes as Pezzullo spoke in a calm tone, Pallais wrote that the United States wanted Somoza to resign in a "statesmanlike" manner after helping to arrange for a national reconstruction government that would include representation from the Nationalist Liberal Party, the Conservatives, other members of the FAO, and the FSLN. Individuals mentioned, according to Pallais, included Alfonso Robelo; Adolfo Calero; Archbishop Obando y Bravo; and Edén Pastora—but none of the more radical Sandinistas. This government would organize elections within a "prudential" time with the help of the OAS. The National Guard would be maintained under a new leadership. If Somoza cooperated in all of these things, Pezzullo said, his residency in the United States would be assured. If not, according to Pallais' notes, Pezzullo predicted "chaos for Nicaragua, isolation and sanctions, and Nicaragua would fall and all of Central America would be condemned to more bloodshed and destruction."

The State Department wanted a definite reply from Somoza by three in the afternoon the next day—June 19—as to whether he would resign and cooperate.

Pallais flew to Managua that afternoon and met through the night with Somoza, Tachito, General José Somoza, the Cabinet, and party leaders. At two o'clock on June 19, Somoza told Pallais he had made up his mind. Pallais took a sheet of paper out of a stenographer's notebook lying in Somoza's office and took down the following: (1) Resents the ultimatum; (2) If the circumstances are created for an orderly transition under OAS auspices, he will resign; (3) No extradition [from exile] of him or his family; (4) Exile visas [to live in the United States] for him and his family. Then Pallais called the U.S. Embassy to relay what Somoza had said.

With Somoza's reply in hand, the United States had to put together the rest of the package. It required first catching up with, and then getting some control over, political events in Costa Rica, while hoping for a stalemate on the battle fronts. At this point, all of the elements except the Sandinista Front were looking to the United States to pull the situation out of the fire. General Torrijos was turning meek, Carlos Andrés Pérez was out of office in Venezuela, and the new Christian Democratic government was more willing to follow the United States' lead. Even the Carazo government in Costa Rica was beginning to rethink what it was doing. But the moderate forces in Nicaragua had been politically defeated or divided, and while the National Guard was not losing battles as such, the all-important perception had been created in Nicaragua and abroad that the FSLN was on the ascendancy. State Department officials dealing with the issue knew a lot about the background of the Sandinista leaders and were under no delusions that the FSLN had a democratic future in mind for Nicaragua, but the United States' freedom of action was still hampered by the old fears and bugaboos about intervention in the region.

In San José, on the day that Somoza was responding to the United States' ultimatum, the junta broadcast a proclamation giving what it said would be the bases of its government. The plan was almost identical to one announced a week earlier by the FSLN itself, but its preparation had also involved the ideas of many opposition groups still inside Nicaragua, such as the labor federations and private enterprise. It promised a socioeconomic reconstruction program, a nonaligned foreign policy, and confiscation of Somoza property. It did not specify elections, but it promised political pluralism and liberties of speech and religion. Also, Nicaragua would honor its foreign debt obligations, and a new national army would be formed in which men who immediately abandoned the National Guard could find a place.

. . .

The United States requested an OAS foreign ministers' meeting, but before it opened on June 21, the Carter administration went through an internal debate about what it was seeking. Vaky and Pezzullo wanted to propose a resolution condemning Somoza and saying the OAS would play an active role in finding a solution, vague wording that would provide cover for a broad range of U.S. actions in working out the successor government. Zbigniew Brzezinski, who until now had shown only sporadic interest in the Nicaragua issue, thought the State Department people were too sanguine in assuming that "some middle-of-the-road regime would somehow or other miraculously emerge in the wake of Somoza." He argued for creation of an OAS peace or police force to move into Nicaragua when Somoza left. Vaky and Pezzullo said such a move would arouse the hostility of Latin American governments on the intervention principle. The speech for the OAS, which Secretary Vance was to deliver, was written by the State Department without reference to a peacekeeping force, but when it went to the White House, Brzezinski again pushed for it. Finally, Vance told Vaky that the President wanted it included.

When the OAS meeting opened in Washington the next day, Vance proposed that the ministers call for a cease-fire in Nicaragua, the end to arms shipments to all factions, and the replacement of Somoza by a "transitional government," and that the OAS put together a multinational military force to restore order. As predicted, the peace force idea was opposed by most Latin American governments. A large group of them countered with a resolution containing everything Vance asked for except the peace force. It said the solution to the Nicaraguan crisis lay in the immediate replacement of the Somoza regime with a democratic government and in the calling of elections very soon. The ministers adopted the resolution 17 to 2 with 5 abstentions on June 23. However, it contained no provision on responsibility for carrying out the things it called for except a vague reference to OAS countries doing what they could to "facilitate" peace.

In Nicaragua, towns and cities in the north and west were falling to the Sandinista forces that had been moving in and out of them for several months. That they felt ready to stay this time was evident in the fact that they began to organize municipal governments. The most significant takeover was León, the second largest city in the country. They held most neighborhoods of the city from early June, then on June 17 the National Guard abandoned its barracks to the rebels and moved into a nearby prison for safety. On June 24 the rebels claimed

Masaya, just twenty miles southeast of Managua, where Indian artisans had set off the country's first mass uprising in February 1978. Nearby Diriamba also fell to the rebels, but it was accomplished not by organized Sandinistas but by local teenagers who put their own lives on the line to force Guardsmen out of their neighborhoods. Increasingly, this was the pattern of action. Another general strike was under way as well, and planeloads of foreigners were evacuated in anticipation of a battle for Managua. But there was still no clear pattern of victory and defeat on the ground. For example, the National Guard was pounding rebel concentrations in eastern neighborhoods of Managua so hard that in late June the rebels organized a mass retreat to Masaya of insurgents and civilian sympathizers. Rebel leaders in the area called the Red Cross with a request to pick up the wounded after they had departed. When Red Cross volunteers arrived in the Bello Horizonte neighborhood they found sixty-eight badly wounded people, some of them missing arms and legs.

Somoza, once he had agreed privately to resign, seemed to ease up his pressures on the National Guard to retake towns after the Sandinistas or local youths had captured them. The Guard, now at its maximum size of about 10,000 uniformed troops, including those in routine police assignments, was hard-pressed to respond when action erupted in several towns at once. With Guatemala the only significant remaining supply source, ammunition was also beginning to run low, but Colonel McCoy of the U.S. Embassy thought this was not decisive in any Guard decision against retaking a town.

Overwhelmingly, however, the National Guard remained loyal to Somoza and most of the men stayed at their posts. Although desertions became more frequent after the April fighting, few of the deserters responded to Sandinista radio appeals to join them. The Guard leadership was so loyal that when McCoy approached a few of the top field commanders in June with the suggestion that they ought to prepare themselves for Somoza's probable departure in the near future, they went to Somoza and told him what McCoy had said. Somoza called Washington and complained to the Army chief of staff, General E. C. Meyer, that McCoy was plotting a coup.

The one place where the National Guard was still enjoying unquestioned military success was in the south. But Carlos Nuñez, a member of the Sandinista National Directorate from the Proletarian Faction, told French journalist Claude Urraca, who found him at a safe house in the El Dorado neighborhood of Managua, that the Southern Front was essentially a diversionary tactic on the part of the Sandinistas. He said Pastora's forces were not supposed to advance but were supposed to tie down the largest possible number of government troops a few miles from the border in order to weaken the National Guard on other fronts.

This would not have been pleasing news to those in the Southern Front, who were suffering the heaviest casualties among Sandinista combatants in the entire war as they repeatedly threw themselves against the National Guard's most effective troops. While, in mid-June, Joaquín Cuadra Lacayo could report that in the Managua area only four rebels had been lost to date but "unfortunately many innocent civilians," in the south the story was very different. Leonel Poveda, who kept what records there were for the Southern Front, estimated that about three hundred Nicaraguan rebels died in the many battles for Peñas Blancas, and a hundred others trying to fight their way beyond there to Rivas. This was more than a fourth of all those who had poured into Costa Rica to volunteer. Poveda said the commanders had tried to keep six hundred in the trenches firing at all times and the others resting, but as the end approached there were no longer people in the camps to replace those who died.

Pastora, during this period, sent a message to the United States through former Costa Rican President José Figueres that if it wanted to prevent a victory by radicals, it should convince Somoza to pull the National Guard back from the south and give him a chance to get to Managua with his troops. Pastora realized that because of his popularity and fame the FSLN would be forced to concede him more power in the new regime if he got there first. The message went through, all the way to the White House, but the United States was hoping for a military stalemate that would give it more leverage in putting together the kind of government it wanted, one not dominated by the FSLN. Stopping Pastora in the south was part of the equation.

One June 26, Ambassador Pezzullo flew to Nicaragua and the next day held the first of many meetings with Somoza. Also there when Pezzullo arrived were Luis Pallais, Foreign Minister Quintana, and, sitting on the corner of Somoza's desk, Congressman John Murphy, the New York Democrat who had long argued Somoza's case in Washington. The friendship between Murphy and Somoza and their brothers had begun in the seventh grade at a military academy on Staten Island. The congressman and the strongman had grown into lifetime barracks buddies. That is why Murphy had a tendency to plop himself down on the president's desk, that and the fact that—according to a former aide to Murphy—they had both been impressed by old Jimmy Cagney movies. Murphy had flown to Managua this time because Somoza wanted help in convincing his son to give up the fight, but in the meeting with Pezzullo he functioned as a key adviser to Somoza. As in his meetings with other U.S. envoys, Somoza taped the conversations with Pezzullo.

Pezzullo told Somoza the United States wanted to see him depart in dignity. Somoza responded that he wanted guarantees that Nicaragua would not be taken over by Communists. He also raised the question of the future of the National Guard, saying that the way to preserve it was for the United States to resume military sales and assistance. Dodging that point, Pezzullo talked about the need to find a way to prevent the National Guard from breaking up and going when Somoza went—because of its strong loyalty to him—and on the other hand a way to present the Guard with a new face, new leadership, that would convince the population it was not just Somoza in disguise.

Somoza kept reminding Pezzullo about how he had helped the United States to overthrow Jacobo Arbenz in Guatemala in 1954 and had offered to "bomb the hell" out of installations in Cuba during the Bay of Pigs invasion. Then he talked about convening Congress the next day or so to resign and turn over power in line with the constitutional succession. Pezzullo said a more significant break from the past was needed, which the United States was trying to put together, and cautioned Somoza against a hasty resignation before something else had been arranged. He suggested that whatever leverage the United States had in working out the successor government came from its ability to deliver Somoza's resignation and that this should not be played wrong.

On that same day, in Panama, President Aristides Royo sent a plane to Costa Rica to pick up three members of the junta—Violeta Chamorro, Alfonso Robelo, and Sergio Ramírez—for a round of meetings and a news conference. That evening the three slipped into Gabriel Lewis' house on 50th Street in Panama City and were joined by Daniel Ortega for a meeting with Special U.S. Envoy Bowdler and Ambassador Moss. The meeting, arranged by Torrijos and Lewis, was the first between a U.S. government representative and a member of the Sandinista Directorate.

In the next few days, various proposals moved between Managua, San José, and Panama to create a transitional government made up only of the non-Marxist members of the San José junta, plus some people still in Nicaragua, such as Conservative leader Adolfo Calero, Red Cross President Ismael Reyes, or others for whom Bowdler had developed respect during the 1978 mediation. Such ideas angered the Sandinistas. Miguel d'Escoto and Sergio Ramírez, speaking for the junta in San José, criticized the United States for trying to convince business leaders in Managua and what remained of the FAO to support its proposal instead of the junta as it then existed. The business groups and the FAO, in turn, were confused and felt pulled both ways.

In the midst of these negotiations, President Carter decided to invite General Torrijos to Washington to take part in policy discussions. The Carter White House had learned that Torrijos was nothing if not duplicitous, but it also felt that Torrijos' end goals were not contrary to U.S. interests. Carter could not feel that same confidence in all of the Caribbean leaders involved in the Nicaraguan question. Furthermore, the general was closer to the Sandinistas than any other friend of the United States.

The Torrijos party landed secretly at Andrews Air Force Base on July 2. At the White House, Carter first invited Torrijos into the Oval Office for a private meeting of fifteen to twenty minutes. Torrijos expected to be chastised for helping the Sandinistas. Instead, as he recounted it later to Moss: "Like a schoolteacher, he told me to sit down. Then, he spoke to me very amicably, as if I had not done anything."

A series of meetings on Nicaragua followed that day and the next involving the top people in the government, plus those dealing with Latin America, and, in at least some of them, the Panamanian strongman. The discussions revolved around two key questions: expansion of the junta and saving the National Guard in some form. By that point, however, the United States appeared to have concluded that the National Guard was more important than who was on the junta.

Zbigniew Brzezinski, who presided over some of the meetings, was still unhappy with the failure of his peacekeeping force proposal. His research had convinced him that only polarization resulted from revolutionary situations and that preventing this required strong action. He thought Vance and Vaky had not made their best effort to sell the idea to Latin American governments—because they did not like it themselves. Now, the State Department was offering a plan to save at least part of the National Guard. Torrijos, too, had become convinced of the need to save the Guard and use it as a balance to the Soviet- and Cuban-trained elements among the Sandinistas. Despite his distaste for Somoza, he was a loyal member of the Central American military fraternity. While the National Guard was getting a bad press on human rights grounds, most of these people in their behind-the-scenes discussions viewed that as a problem of leadership, not of the institution. Torrijos, whose own officers knew many of those in Nicaragua, brought to the White House meetings a list of Nicaraguan Guard officers who might be elevated to leadership.

Later that day or the next, the group met with President Carter in the Cabinet Room. Brzezinski continued to press for putting together a peacekeeping force. Another participant remembered his using the term "third force," though Brzezinski said he could not recall using that particular term. Defense Secretary Harold Brown said the Defense Department assessment was that the Sandinistas were dominated by Marxist-Leninists. Carter asked some of the others present whether they agreed with that, and at least some of them said they did. Regardless, what emerged was a decision to give up the peacekeeping force idea. It was decided to make another attempt to expand the junta, but to put the greatest effort into a campaign to save part of the National Guard. This required the help of other governments.

When the White House meetings ended, Vaky left on a military plane for Venezuela and was to continue to Colombia and the Dominican Republic. Pezzullo, Bowdler, and Moss left together on another military plane. The three spent the night of July 3 in Guatemala, where Bowdler met with a retired Nicaraguan National Guard officer, who resisted efforts to involve him in the plan. They continued to Nicaragua the next day. Because of fighting on the North Highway not far from the Managua airport, the pilot of the small Air Force plane came in high over Lake Managua, then dropped almost straight down before leveling out. As he did, he asked Pezzullo if he would mind if one engine were kept running while he got out. Bowdler continued to Costa Rica and Moss went to Panama.

Over the next few days, Bowdler raised the question of an expanded version of the junta—accepting the five members already announced but adding a couple of people still in Nicaragua, such as Adolfo Calero. Miguel d'Escoto, speaking for the junta, dismissed the expansion proposal as blackmail. However, Robelo said in an interview later that the Sandinistas had decided to agree to expansion, without specifying names, after both Torrijos and Castro told Tomás Borge and Daniel Ortega to do so. Paradoxically, it was blocked by Mrs. Chamorro, who said it was unwarranted intervention in Nicaraguan affairs and threatened to resign. Carlos Andrés Pérez, the former Venezuelan president, called and tried to convince her to change her mind, but she broke into tears and said if she was a hurdle for all the presidents and their plans, then she would withdraw, but she would not agree to the changes.

After some testing of the waters, Larry Pezzullo was bringing together the pieces of a complicated changeover in which he envisioned that the five-member junta as constituted in San José would become the new government of Nicaragua, while the new military force of the nation would be a combination of the National Guard and the Sandinistas, under leadership acceptable to the United States. The change was to begin with Somoza's resignation and departure. As Pezzullo had it planned, the Congress would elect a stand-in president—Urcuyo—who would await the arrival of the junta, which would fly in from San José. The junta's plane would be preceded by a plane carrying Archbishop Obando y Bravo and eight or nine Latin American foreign ministers, whose presence would hopefully assure that everybody behaved in a civilized way. Urcuyo would call for a cease-fire, the new National Guard director and the Sandinista commanders would discuss what Pezzullo called the "amalgamation" of forces, and the process would begin for passing power from the stand-in president to the junta. There would be no outright winner and no outright loser. Somoza would go and the new power structure would emerge from everybody not closely aligned with him. National Guardsmen trained in counterinsurgency by the United States and Sandinistas trained in insurgency by Cuba would shake hands and move into the same barracks. All of this was expected to require two or three days once the principals were in Managua.

Pezzullo and Somoza talked daily, discussing National Guard officers who might be capable of holding the institution together while still giving it a new image. Somoza continued to make the point that the United States had the obligation to prevent a Communist takeover. Somoza revealed publicly on July 6 that he was willing to resign, but said the timing was up to the United States.

Pezzullo's game plan seemed in a constant state of flux. On about July 10 or 11, he sent for Ismael Reyes, then a heroic figure in Nicaragua as president of the Red Cross and also a respected industrialist, and asked if he would be willing to assume the presidency on an interim basis. "I asked him two questions," Reyes recalled later. "Nicaragua was in a disastrous situation, so I said that in order to begin to reactivate we needed at least a billion dollars. 'Will that be available?' I asked. And he said yes. So my head began to swim with that possibility. I saw the industry working, the people getting good wages and so forth. Then I asked if a peacekeeping force was going to come to Nicaragua—I didn't want the Marines but a peacekeeping force—and would there be a show of military force in the Atlantic to prevent Castro from bothering us? But he said no, that the people knew we took out Somoza and the people would be with us. So I said to the ambassador, 'No, the people are not with you. One has to put his feet squarely on the ground.' So he gave me 250 million córdobas for the Red Cross and said to think about it. But I said that I had already replied."

On July 11, Bowdler met all day in San José with four of the five junta members—the fifth, Moisés Hassan, was inside Nicaragua—and they debated the issue of the National Guard. At the end of the day, the junta said that those members of the National Guard who agreed to an immediate cease-fire and a return to barracks when Somoza departed would be incorporated into a new Nicaraguan army. This did not go as far in preserving the Guard as Pezzullo was suggesting in his conversations with Somoza, but it was well beyond anything the rebels had committed themselves to previously. It appeared to satisfy the United States.

The next day, Bowdler and Marvin Weissman, the U.S. ambassador to Costa Rica, called on President Carazo at his beach house at Puntarenas on the Pacific. Bowdler told Carazo that Somoza would be gone in less than a week. When they left, a larger group gathered that included Carlos Andrés Pérez, Torrijos, former Costa Rican President José Figueres, four members of the junta, Tomás Borge, and Edén Pastora. The main topic was whether the Nicaraguans were willing to make a commitment to call elections, which had not been stated in any of the rebel government plans released to date. Nudged along by the foreign leaders present, they said they would do it. Then everybody had lunch.

After the meeting at the beach house, the junta wrote a letter to the OAS essentially accepting the resolution adopted by the foreign ministers on June 23 and announcing the intention "to convoke the Nicaraguans to the first free elections they will have in this century, so that they can elect their municipal officials and a constituent assembly, and, later, the supreme authorities of the country."

In Managua that night—it was July 12—Somoza called Francisco Urcuyo Maliaño, speaker of the lower house of the Nicaraguan Congress, to the Bunker and told him that presidential authority would soon pass to him. Somoza and Pallais had been talking for several days about who that person should be and had decided on Urcuyo. While not viewed as a strong personality, Urcuyo was known as a decent man, even among the opposition. A physician then in his sixties, he had been an opponent of Somoza Garcia during his youth but had later been drawn into the government by a favorite cousin, who married Luis Somoza.

The next day, July 13, Somoza left Managua unannounced in his plane and rumors spread that he had resigned. In fact, he went to Guatemala to meet again with the military leaders of Guatemala, Honduras, and El Salvador. Luis Pallais, who went on the trip, said Somoza wanted the other generals to make a public statement committing themselves to back up the remaining National Guard force during the one- or two-day period after Somoza's departure, during which he expected that a national unity government would be negotiated between his constitutional successor and the junta. Pallais said Somoza was not seeking an occupation force, but he wanted them to have planes loaded with supplies ready to fly into Nicaragua as a sign of support. The Guatemalan leader, General Romeo Lucas García, protested that he had already provided a great deal of assistance, and in general there was little enthusiasm.

On July 14, in San José, the junta announced the names of twelve members of a planned eighteen-person Cabinet, including only one man publicly known to be a Sandinista—Tomás Borge, the surviving FSLN founder, who was seen by the United States as the hardest of the hardliners. He was named interior minister, with responsibility for the police and state security. However, the other key post, defense, was given to Bernardino Larios, a National Guard colonel who had defected the year before. Alfonso Robelo said the original FSLN plan had been to put Humberto Ortega in that job but that it was changed because of U.S. pressures.* Other Cabinet members included four of *Los Doce:* Miguel d'Escoto as foreign minister, Arturo Cruz as Central Bank president, Joaquín Cuadra Chamorro as finance minister,

---

*Humberto Ortega, in fact, took over the post five months later, and Larios was imprisoned.

and Carlos Tünnermann as minister of education. The makeup of the Cabinet quieted some of the United States' fears about the future government, and on July 15 Bowdler gave the junta the United States' blessing.

However, one significant opposition group was being left out of these plans and negotiations: the remnants of the FAO still inside Nicaragua. This included the Social Christian and Conservative parties, some of the trade unions, the Roman Catholic church leadership, and the big private enterprise umbrella organization, which had recently made a slight change in its name to Superior Council of Private Enterprise—COSEP. Some of the FAO elements, such as Alfonso Robelo, had moved temporarily to Costa Rica, but most of those on whom the United States had once pinned its hopes for a moderate succession were now cut off from contacts with the U.S. government and the negotiations occurring outside of Nicaragua. Since the departure of Ambassador Solaun early in the year, these people had felt ignored.

While the United States was moving toward acceptance of the FSLN-named government, they were becoming nervous about what was going to follow Somoza. Because of this concern, some of the FAO groups were hesitant to support the June strike called by the FSLN. Adolfo Calero went to San José in early July to try to find out what was happening, then returned to Managua and argued against accepting everything the FSLN was proposing. COSEP then asked for a clear statement in the Plan of Government about elections, and the letter the junta wrote the OAS from Costa Rica calmed that concern. Some of the other FAO members still wanted an expanded junta in which non-Marxists would be the majority. From Costa Rica, Robelo convinced the COSEP leaders in Managua to accept the junta of five members, but others sought the help of the new Venezuelan president, Luis Herrera Campíns. He sent a plane to pick up a group that included Archbishop Obando y Bravo, Ismael Reyes of the Red Cross, and the national coordinator of the Permanent Commission for Human Rights, José Esteban González. When they reached Caracas on July 15, former President Pérez met with one group and told the Nicaraguans the junta question had already been decided in San José. President Herrera received the archbishop and Ismael Reyes and left the impression that he was still seeking expansion of the junta. He also asked the two of them, as leaders of the Church and the Red Cross, to fly from there to Costa Rica to meet with the junta.

. . .

During Pezzullo's visits to the Bunker in early July he had told Somoza he had the right to decide the new leadership of the National Guard. However, the names Somoza suggested were unacceptable in Washington, so on July 15—the day Bowdler was extending tacit U.S. approval to the junta—Pezzullo appeared with a list of six names that he said had been approved by the White House and State Department. From that list Somoza selected Colonel Federico Mejía, a National Guard engineer in his early forties. Mejía was elevated to general and named to two posts—National Guard director and chief of staff. The reason, according to Pallais, was that Mejía was going to offer one of the posts to Edén Pastora in the negotiations that were expected to follow Somoza's departure. That same day an order was signed retiring all National Guard officers with thirty or more years of service, a total of nearly a hundred men, including all active-duty generals and most colonels and lieutenant colonels.

While Pezzullo's succession plan may have been fully understood by all the U.S. officials involved as well as such other key players as President Carazo in Costa Rica and General Torrijos in Panama, the same could not be said for the Nicaraguans. On both sides—Somoza's and the rebels'—there were telltale signs that they were headed for collision rather than agreement over a plan that seemed to ignore their yesterdays and to pretend there would be no tomorrow in which the pieces would, somehow, have to work. The Somoza people acted, throughout, as if the United States were going to pull out of its hat a new government that would bear no similarity to the one taking form in full public view in San José. On the other hand, the rebels were proceeding as if they had no inkling that they were supposed to share power with several thousand military men trained by the old order.

Over the next few days after Somoza advised Urcuyo of his decision, there were various meetings in Managua involving Urcuyo, Pezzullo, other embassy officers, at times Somoza and Pallais, and, after his selection, General Mejía. Transition details were supposedly worked out, but almost everybody involved would subsequently disagree on what was said.

The Congress was called into session about one in the morning on July 17 in the Rubén Darío salon of the Hotel Inter-Continental. In order to get a quorum, Pallais had gone to Miami and rounded up some of those who had already fled for security reasons. Somoza's letter of resignation was read, then Urcuyo was elected, and he gave a speech calling on the "irregular forces" to put down their arms and for all "national democratic organizations" to join him in a dialogue to create a new government. Urcuyo's speech shocked Pezzullo. Like the press and many others, Pezzullo interpreted it to mean Urcuyo had no intention of resigning soon, that he planned, in fact, to serve out Somoza's term.

Pallais and Urcuyo crossed the street to the Bunker after the session and found Somoza meeting with the new high command of the National Guard while waiting for Pallais to be ready to leave. It was about four in the morning. The telephone rang, and it was Pezzullo calling for Urcuyo. Pallais remembered that when Urcuyo hung up, Somoza asked him what had happened. "Chico [Urcuyo] said, 'Pezzullo wants me to go and have the meeting with the Sandinistas and the high command and make my speech in the Hotel Las Mercedes [near the airport] and that he wanted the junta from Costa Rica to be present. I said, No.' So I said, 'Chico, don't be silly.' Tacho was quiet. 'This is your great opportunity. It is the day of national reconciliation . . . What better occasion do you want? This is your chance to get in.' "

Then Somoza left, with Tachito and his half brother, José, plus Pallais, members of Congress, and the recently retired top military officers—about one hundred men who had formed the heart of *somocismo*. Shortly after five their two planes took off for Homestead Air Force Base in Florida, where Somoza got into a waiting Cadillac limousine and rode to his house on an island in Biscayne Bay beneath the Miami skyline.

In Managua, after daylight, Pezzullo, Colonel McCoy, and other embassy people went to the residence above the Bunker and woke up Urcuyo. Pezzullo said he had to resign in favor of the archbishop, who would, in turn, pass power to the junta. Urcuyo, in his book *Solos*, published in Guatemala, said he told Pezzullo it would be unconstitutional to turn over power to anyone who was not a member of Congress, and that he planned to propose adoption of a "constitutional process" to transfer power to a "true pluralistic junta and not a Communist junta . . ." Each man was outraged at the other. As McCoy remembered the scene: "Pezzullo said, 'You have to go,' and Urcuyo said, 'Like hell.' Pezzullo said, 'There was an agreement that you are to step down,' and Urcuyo said, 'The hell there is.' Pezzullo stormed back to the embassy. He said we might have to close it, but then he talked to Washington, and they said to keep trying."

. . .

Ismael Reyes, after meeting during the predawn hours with the junta in San José, flew into Managua at seven in the morning on a Red Cross food flight and encountered pandemonium at the airport. National Guardsmen were trying to commandeer arriving flights, and wounded men were grabbing medicine out of Red Cross supplies. It shocked him to see the National Guard, which had been the unchallenged force in Nicaragua for most of his sixty-four years, in a state of panic and terror. "This is the end," Reyes thought. The National Guard had neither ammunition nor Somoza. It was a family army and now it was lost.

In San José, a red carpet had been laid from the VIP lounge at the airport to a waiting BAC-III of the Costa Rican national airline for the expected gala departure of the junta and Cabinet at ten o'clock. The hour came and went. Word came from Managua that things were not going as expected. Sergio Ramírez told journalists that the junta had no intention of having any talks with Urcuyo. In the early afternoon, the junta met and decided to delay travel plans a day. Meanwhile, Ortega, Borge and other Sandinista leaders had taken off for rebel-held León.

The rebels were advancing on Managua from León in the northwest and the Masaya-Diriamba-Jinotepe triangle area to the southeast, moving toward Managua on two of the three main highways into the capital. Small Sandinista forces were supplemented by ragtag volunteers, many barely teenagers, who joined them as they fought their way to Managua. The National Guard ranks, like the men Reyes had encountered at the airport, were confused about what was happening, unsure whether they should continue fighting or lay down their arms. Estelí, now barely a ruin because of previous battles, had fallen to the rebels on July 16, and the local National Guard commander died defending his post. But in the south, the National Guard launched a new counteroffensive against Pastora's beleaguered troops.

Pezzullo and embassy staff members spent the day of July 17 trying to put the pieces back together, to convince Urcuyo and explain to Mejía about the cease-fire plan. Pezzullo went to see Mejía and asked what he had understood. "I asked if he had been told to meet the Sandinista [military] leadership, and he said no. It was clear some dirty work was afoot. I explained it to him, and it was news to him."

Between meetings with Pezzullo and Mejía, Urcuyo appointed Cabinet officers as if he planned to stay in office for a while. That evening,

Urcuyo met with the new high command of the National Guard and told the officers about Pezzullo's request that Mejía meet with the Sandinista commanders to plan a cease-fire and unification of forces. Later, the officers discussed their situation among themselves, particularly assessing their supplies. About eight in the evening Lieutenant Colonel Alberto Smith called Colonel McCoy and asked whether any military assistance would be forthcoming. Somoza had told Urcuyo there was only a three weeks' supply of ammunition left but that the United States had promised to resume supplying Nicaragua once he was gone. McCoy remembered telling Smith that he did not think the Carter administration was willing to do that. "But I gave them Ambassador Pezzullo's bedside number. They called and were told to hang tough but that there would be no support." McCoy had earlier suggested to Pezzullo that U.S. military planes fly low over Nicaragua and that the United States ship in some supplies as a means of bolstering the Guard's morale and holding it together. "I had tried to bring Pezzullo along [on the issue of helping the Guard], but it conflicted," McCoy told me. "He wanted to bring in the Sandinistas and get off on the right foot with them. We [the embassy staff] all felt a little betrayed and frustrated because that's not the way we had been looking at it."

At one in the morning on July 18, General Mejía called Urcuyo to another meeting with the high command. The officers told him the National Guard had no more ammunition for its 105-millimeter artillery or its armored units and was out of fuel. Further, they said the Sandinistas controlled Puerto Somoza, the Guard's main supply port.

By then, part of the future government was flying out over the Pacific in two Piper Navajos to slip into León before daylight. When the plans for the ceremonial arrival in Managua went awry, Costa Rican President Rodrigo Carazo had become fearful that the result would be a total military victory and power for the hardest line Marxist-Leninists, with the carefully constructed junta falling apart. The only chance now of preventing a radical victory, he concluded, was to get the civilian junta members into Nicaragua. Just after midnight on the eighteenth, the first plane took off carrying Robelo and Ramírez, and the second followed shortly with Mrs. Chamorro. Fearing that the National Guard might send planes to intercept them, they turned toward the Pacific before reaching the Nicaraguan border, coming back over land just as they approached rebel territory, where they landed safely.

. . .

About two-thirty in the morning, Colonel McCoy received another telephone call at his home in Managua. "They said that the National Guard commanders had decided it was all over without U.S. support, that they were getting on planes to Honduras and so forth. I called the ambassador and said, 'The National Guard is disintegrating now.' " Pezzullo told him to try to confirm they were actually leaving. About six o'clock McCoy got an assistant into the air force headquarters at the airport, and he reported back that there was no one left there but a woman burning documents. McCoy went to the embassy and advised Washington that the National Guard no longer existed.

Later that morning, as Pezzullo and most of the embassy staff flew out of Managua in an attempt to show that the United States was not a party to the aborting of Pezzullo's plan, Deputy Secretary of State Warren Christopher telephoned Somoza in Florida and told him to convince Urcuyo to resign. Otherwise, Christopher said, Somoza would face the loss of his right to residence in the United States. "So Tacho called Urcuyo—I heard the conversation," Luis Pallais said. "And Chico said to him, 'I have never said that I would stay until 1981 . . . The only thing,' he says, 'is that this Pezzullo . . . wants me to resign and give power to the Sandinistas, and I will never do that. I'd rather die than give this government to the Communists.' So Tacho said, 'Chico, you are ruining me. They will deny me political asylum here if you don't do this.' Chico said, 'I'll never give it to the Communists, so what can we do?' 'Why don't you give it to the National Guard?' Tacho said."

In Managua, Mejía negotiated by telephone with Humberto Ortega in Costa Rica over the terms of what Mejía expected to be a cease-fire in place. But their talks reached a stalemate when the Sandinistas broke the understanding and demanded unconditional surrender. Ortega said this was because Urcuyo had already violated the understanding. At three in the afternoon, Urcuyo called President Lucas García in Guatemala and asked him to send planes to evacuate him and his government. Before the planes arrived, Urcuyo met with the National Guard high command to formally turn over presidential power, but in the midst of drafting the declaration Mejía told him to carry constitutional authority into exile with him in the hope of someday bringing it back. At eight o'clock, with the airport under Sandinista fire, three Guatemalan air force planes landed and picked up Urcuyo, his family, and other civilian officials. General Mejía, unwilling to make an unconditional surrender, left before dawn the next morning on the last departing National Guard flight.

Pezzullo said later the plan fell apart either because Somoza had intentionally told Urcuyo something different from what he and Somoza had discussed or because Urcuyo had ambitions of his own at the end. However, Pallais said there was never any understanding to turn over power directly to the junta, that Urcuyo planned to resign all along—once he had overseen the organization of a non-Communist government—and that the wording in his speech to the Congress implying that he intended to serve out Somoza's term was a matter of constitutional nicety. Pallais acknowledged, however, that both he and Somoza encouraged Urcuyo to think he might negotiate himself a place in the new government. Urcuyo said Pezzullo had never once, during their planning meetings, told him that he was expected to give up power to the junta coming from San José, though he said two other embassy staff members asked him on July 14 if he would be "disposed to enter into conversations with a democratic junta" once he had occupied the presidency. To Urcuyo, that did not mean the San José group. Later that same night, Urcuyo said, Somoza told him not to entertain any suggestion from Pezzullo that would imply giving power to that group. Urcuyo said Somoza suggested that he invite people from the "democratic opposition" to join him in the government and suggested some people by name, primarily from the Conservative Party.

On July 19, disorganized rebel groups poured into Managua from all directions. Lieutenant Colonel Fulgencio Largaespada, the head of the traffic police, continued to negotiate with the Sandinistas and in the evening read over radio the surrender that they had demanded. He called on National Guardsmen to cease firing immediately, to deposit their weapons with the Red Cross, in churches or embassies, and to fly white flags to indicate unconditional surrender.

When Ismael Reyes learned that the Red Cross was to accept the surrenders, he raced around to the various military and police posts in Managua, including the hospital and the academy, and declared them Red Cross territory, then he began rounding up officers and herding them into the Venezuelan Embassy and its ample grounds. At many of the military locations, he had to brave a line of Sandinistas or their armed supporters outside. He was the Red Cross, he kept saying. Everyone should keep calm. At the police headquarters he found a shoot-out under way between Guardsmen who wanted to surrender and others who refused to believe that Largaespada had ordered a surrender. Reyes threw himself on the floor until the shooting stopped, then took a group of them out to the airport to confirm the surrender. After that, he had to talk his way through a Sandinista blockade to get the panicky Guardsmen to safety at the military hospital.

At the airport, the vice president of the Red Cross, Wilfred Cross, was unable to find a way to transport the surrendering Guardsmen across town to the embassy area, so he convinced the Swiss representative of the International Red Cross to declare the free trade zone near the airport a protected refuge for several thousand Guardsmen.

About 2,000 National Guardsmen reached Honduras, some in planes, most in vehicles or on foot from Guard posts in northern and western Nicaragua. Those on the Southern Front, numbering about a thousand, made their way to the port of San Juan del Sur, took over the fishing and pleasure boats in the harbor, and sailed for El Salvador.

Although nobody kept records on how many people died in the war, the Red Cross estimated that 10,000 Nicaraguan lives were lost during the period from September 1978 to July 19, 1979.* At least 90 percent of them were civilians.

On July 20, 1979, the junta and the top Sandinistas drove into Managua in triumph, standing up in a fire engine for the last five miles of the trip from León. In the newly named Plaza of the Revolution—

---

*The question of how many people died in the insurrection has been tremendously manipulated and twisted in the years since 1979. Although roughly 10,000 was the estimate used by relief workers in the last month of the insurrection, just a month or two later the Sandinista Front began to raise the toll. It first claimed that 30,000 had died, later saying 35,000, then 40,000, then 50,000, sometimes more. The figures were repeated by other organizations and governments and took on the aura of credibility. In fact, there is nothing to substantiate them. I tried to establish a ballpark figure by talking to people who appeared knowledgeable about casualties from the three groups: Sandinistas, National Guardsmen, and civilians. The Sandinista deaths, according to a man who kept what statistics were kept on the Southern Front, were at least 300 and not more than 600. A well-placed official of the Smoza Government said National Guard deaths were likewise no more than a "few hundred," though he said the records were left behind in the Bunker. Had there been more, he said, much more recruitment would have been required than was actually done. Finally, Ismael Reyes, the Red Cross leader, thought civilian deaths fell into the 7,000 range, possibly fewer. This means that the total could not have exceeded 10,000.

in front of the National Palace—the new government was presented to an ecstatic crowd of about 50,000 people. Pastora received the most applause and gave the shortest speech. In about a hundred words, he promised to "remain vigilant at all times so that this revolution is not betrayed or changed."

On that same day in Miami, Anastasio Somoza Debayle, worried that the mixup over Urcuyo's resignation might lead the United States to expel him, packed up and sailed to the Bahamas on two hired yachts. Several of his children and his longtime companion, Dinorah Sampson, went with him. So did his half brother, José, who piled automatic rifles on one of the beds. Somoza paid the yacht captains in cash from suitcases filled with big bills, and he directed the expedition as if it were a naval exercise, using a gold bullhorn.

On July 25, a sixty-member Cuban medical brigade landed at the Managua airport, and a Sandinista commander greeted them with a prediction that "these ties of revolutionary friendship and brotherhood will be expanded more and more in the struggles of oppressed people against Yankee imperialism."

On July 26, Alfonso Robelo and Humberto Ortega traveled together to Cuba, where they were warmly received by Fidel Castro and treated as honored guests at the annual celebration of the beginning of his march to power.

On July 28, Lawrence Pezzullo returned to Nicaragua on a U.S. military transport loaded with food and medicine. Tomás Borge met him at the airport and escorted him to the embassy, where they sat down and had a cup of coffee together.

A few days after his trip to Cuba, Robelo went to Venezuela, where he had a private meeting with President Herrera Campíns. There were already disturbing signs of Sandinista intentions, Robelo told Herrera, and he had his doubts that this thing was going to work.

But all of that was to be played out later. For now, everybody who had remained in Nicaragua embraced and cheered and set out together.

8

THE TROUBLED HONEYMOON

JULY 1979 TO JANUARY 1980

In the months following July 1979, power in Nicaragua seemed to reside in a confusing array of *comandantes* in fatigues and civilians in shirt sleeves who shouted from podiums in dusty plazas hung with red and black banners, then took off in caravans of cream-colored Mercedes-Benzes confiscated from the old order. Talk masked the absence of government and political consensus. An intricate dance began among all the elements that sought power, influence, and voice. Authority seemed up for grabs, available to whoever dared pronounce himself on a topic. After nearly five decades in which power rested in one last name, there was now no understanding about who had a mandate to do what.

At times the new government was difficult to find, spread out as it was all over Managua in buildings that in the recent past had been the home or business of someone who had fled. The four-story building that formerly housed the Central Bank became the Casa de Gobierno—Government House—headquarters of the junta. Opposite it stood the gleaming white tower that had been the headquarters of the Banco de America, now also housing government offices. The two modern structures stood as lonely survivors in the center of the weed-grown ruins of what had been downtown Managua before the 1972 earthquake. A few blocks to the north, facing Lake Managua, the Finance Ministry operated in the former National Palace, another earthquake survivor. Other ministries and *comandantes* were setting up operations in buildings on the highways and bypasses circling the city.

In public, those in the government, as well as the leadership of the Sandinista Front, were generally polite to one another and presented a surprisingly united face, with almost a collegial quality to their behavior. But while junta members, Cabinet officers, and Sandinista *comandantes* did not contradict one another publicly, they often talked around each other, leaving subtle signs of the differences to those who read or listened carefully between the lines. Alfonso Robelo, when asked about the inherent differences among those in the government, would say they had put ideological matters aside for the time being because of the need to rebuild the country. But the nine *comandantes* of the National Directorate of the Sandinista Front talked ideology and political rhetoric all the time. No one knew just where the *comandantes* fit into things. They themselves were testing the waters. Except for Tomás Borge as Interior Minister, and Daniel Ortega on the junta, they had no official role in the government, but they were omnipresent. The unclear nature of power aided the FSLN, which, in the uncertainty and vacuum, began assuming for itself the right to determine and define power. The Sandinista leaders confused the FSLN with the state and made little effort to separate the two.

Daniel Ortega, during a series of televised broadcasts at the end of July, raised the question that was troubling nearly everyone. He also gave a strong indication of FSLN intentions. "There are many people asking who is the government of Nicaragua, the Sandinista National Liberation Front or the Junta of National Reconstruction. It was wrong to think that the Sandinista Front was only a military organization. It was, is, and will continue to be a political organization . . . We are going to stay until our program is fully accomplished."

About six weeks after the fall of Somoza I asked Tomás Borge, just back from celebrating his fiftieth birthday with Fidel Castro, for his views on the emerging issues. He was presiding over the Ministry of Interior from a windowless office with carpeted walls on the third floor of a modern building that had formerly housed a finance company. It was beyond the old downtown area, a few hundred yards east of where a statue of Luis Somoza had recently stood but where now there was only a base lacking anybody's likeness. Downstairs, people waited in long lines for permission to go upstairs and inquire about missing relatives. A Sandinista in battle dress was seated at a small desk beside the elevators, surrounded by a dozen or so handguns collected from those going up on the elevator. Borge, a small man wearing large shell-rimmed glasses, had already become the most active of the *comandantes* in carrying ideological issues into the rallies and other public forums. He was talking constantly about the problems of the remnants of *somocismo* as well as what he termed the ultra-left. The solution to all, he was insisting, was *sandinismo,* an uncertain philosophy. Instead of defining it, he told me what it would not be.

"Anti-Communism is a *somocista* philosophy," he said. "Anti-Communism in Nicaragua has been the banner of Somoza. A Sandinista revolution is not going to fall into the trap of anti-Communism, because it is a dirty banner, repugnant, that has served to assassinate thousands and thousands of Nicaraguans." He claimed there were also problems with what he termed the far left. "The Nicaraguan revolution is directed by the Sandinista National Liberation Front, and there are some who want us to jump over stages. They want us to decree Socialism right now. Socialism cannot be decreed. We have our own political project. The Nicaraguan Revolution will do what the circumstances demand at each moment." Borge said the FSLN was building its political organization throughout the country under a system in which people would have to be selected for militancy, the highest level of membership, on the basis of their revolutionary commitment and general good character. He denied, however, that the Sandinistas were building an official party in the style of any other country. "We don't copy. We are a revolutionary organization that has its own identity. There will be other parties to contest for power, as long as they have support. Political pluralism exists here. I want to make that clear."

To Alfonso Robelo, however, there were already disturbing signs that the FSLN intended to do the opposite of what Borge claimed, though he did not yet say it publicly. "The old Somoza newspaper *Novedades,* instead of becoming the official government newspaper, the newspaper of the revolution in the broad sense, had become the FSLN official newspaper, *Barricada,*" he recalled later. "And they gave the whole Casa del Obrero—Worker's House—to the Sandinista labor federation. In other words, instead of being a national house for all unions, to be used for their gatherings and meetings, it became only for the use of the FSLN."

These things "were never discussed. They just happened. The old mansion of Luis Somoza was taken as the headquarters for the [Sandinista] party. I was shocked by that, and I expressed concern and I didn't agree with it. Even worse, with money from the government, [the Sandinista Front] bought the house where the National Directorate Secretariat is, in front of my house, and I opposed that. That house was a law firm, and the firm sold the house to the FSLN, which purchased it with government money—one million and some córdobas."

On a day-to-day basis, government ministries—except for Borge's Interior Ministry, which was an empire in itself—seemed in the first few months to work basically for the junta. This was aided by the fact that many posts at the level of vice minister, department or agency head, and other senior professional and technical jobs were filled by people who identified with Robelo's political party, the Nicaraguan Democratic Movement (MDN). Despite this, the Sandinista *comandantes* made clear that they would insert themselves into Cabinet matters when they considered it necessary.

Arturo Cruz, the Group of Twelve member who had come home from Washington to become president of the Central Bank in the new government, was called to Government House a few weeks after the victory to discuss problems related to withdrawing large bills from circulation. "For the first time, next to Sergio and Violeta and Alfonso and Daniel Ortega and Moisés Hassan, I saw some guys in uniform, fancy uniforms." Among them was his nephew, Luis Carrión Cruz, whom he had not seen much in recent years. The nephew had left home after joining the commune run by Father Uriel Molina at his church in the Riguero neighborhood. Another was Henry Ruiz, whom Cruz had sometimes seen on the streets of their mutual hometown, Jinotepe, before Ruiz left to study in Moscow. "It had not dawned on me until then that the National Directorate was going to run the country," Cruz remembered, "and that created havoc and chaos because it undermined the authority of all the ministers of the government."

. . .

The FSLN decided there were three priorities for Nicaragua: economic reconstruction, mass organizing, and creation of the army. The FSLN said the last two were reserved for itself and the first was the task of the junta.

The Sandinistas gave their most serious attention to the matter of the army. The guerrilla force that had fought the National Guard had been relatively small, and several hundred were foreigners, including some Panamanian National Guardsmen. The foreigners went, or were sent, home within a short time. Many other guerrilla combatants had been middle-class people who were given desk jobs in the new government or returned to their own businesses.

Bernardino Larios, the former National Guard colonel who had been named defense minister to help satisfy U.S. demands for a moderate government, was a man with a job in name only. On July 26 he spoke of creating a new army with elements of both the Sandinista Front and the National Guard, but he said he had not yet met with any FSLN military leaders to discuss this plan. Larios said some former National Guard officers had contacted him about their desire to be incorporated into the new army.

But two days later, on July 28, the Sandinista Directorate held a news conference at which Larios was not present, and announced creation of a three-man "general command" made up of three members of the Directorate: Borge, Humberto Ortega and Luis Carrión Cruz. There was also to be a general staff led by Joaquín Cuadra Lacayo, who had directed the Internal Front during the insurrection. Asked why Larios was not present, one of the nine said they had called the conference to discuss matters of concern only to the FSLN. The Sandinista leaders did not say how large an army they planned to build but said they wanted mandatory draft authority to use as necessary. They said they also planned to develop a separate militia force, using as a base the young people who had assisted them in the last days of the war. A couple of days later army training began for a thousand youths. On August 18 the name of the commander-in-chief of the new Sandinista Popular Army was announced: Humberto Ortega.

Larios, Robelo, and the other non-Sandinistas in the government uttered no public criticism of the FSLN's takeover of all things military. Probably the only person who could have expressed effective discontent at that point was Edén Pastora. His former Southern Front army was still partly intact. Three hundred men remained under the command of Leonel Poveda, who was intensely loyal to Pastora, at Peñas Blancas, the southern border post. But Pastora had become the tenth man in a country run by nine. He was named deputy interior minister and set up in an office at the opposite end of the building housing Borge. The FSLN kept him busy appearing at rallies to please the crowds. There were some rumblings from people close to Pastora about his relatively low status in the new government, but at that point there was apparently little communication, if any, between Pastora and other moderate elements inside or outside the government. There were some suggestions from Pastora's supporters, even in those early days of the new regime, that he was naïve, that from his vantage point he could quickly see that hardliners were taking over the process in Nicaragua, but chose to ignore it.

Leonel Poveda had been less than happy that when the others were celebrating in Managua, people under his command were still fighting the National Guard around Rivas for several days. He quickly concluded that people assuming top positions in Managua were those who had not done much fighting, while he had to contend with reopening the frontier at Peñas Blancas and establishing rules for the thousands of Nicaraguans waiting to return from refuge in Costa Rica. One night, about eleven o'clock, an aide came to him and said Luis Carrión Cruz was outside, and Poveda asked, "Who is Luis Carrión?" The aide said, "He says he's a member of the [Sandinista] National Directorate." So the two men talked, and Poveda vented some of his frustrations, telling Carrión that while those in Managua had been celebrating a victory, he had captured a hundred National Guardsmen and sent them to Pastora on a bus.

In late August a representative of Borge showed up at Peñas Blancas and told Poveda he was to turn over command to him. Unhappy and inclined to resume fighting if necessary, Poveda went to Managua and asked Pastora if he wanted him to hand over command. "I said, 'Comandante, I'm going to ask you three times if you are sure you want me to do this,' and he said yes every time." Poveda gave up the command and returned home to Managua to take a civilian post in the government.

In addition to the army, the FSLN created a network of "mass organizations," entities emanating from itself on Leninist concepts. Most important were the Sandinista Defense Committees, which were the outgrowth of the United People's Movement that had been created in poor neighborhoods during the last months of the insurrection. The

FSLN also organized new labor, women's, peasant, and youth groups as part of its structure for "mass" participation. The FSLN declared that it intended to be "the political organization, the spokesman, and recipient for the people's concerns."

The Defense Committees, known by their Spanish acronym CDS, were organized from the block level through neighborhood councils, districts, and regions to the national level, though the initiative to organize came from above, not the grass roots. They were to be the "eyes, ears, and voice" of the revolution, as well as the hands of reconstruction. They were to coordinate communal work such as vaccination campaigns and food supplies. They would denounce any counterrevolutionary activity, "internal enemies," and "imperialism." The refusal to join was to make one suspected of being opposed to the revolution. The FSLN said the CDS's would be the roots of "popular power."

The first assignment of the CDS's was to sweep aside and weed out remnants of something called *somocismo*. This presumably meant any attitude sympathetic to the old regime, though it quickly became apparent that it could be used against anyone else who happened to express doubts about Sandinista wisdom. "*Somocistas* are also those parties who pretend to shelter themselves in the flag of the revolution for their own benefit, and these people are also going to be cleaned out with this campaign," declared the national CDS organization in an early statement. Critics said all of this bore some of the elements of the less-organized Somoza system of *orejas,* or neighborhood informers. In fact, some of the same people who had performed this function under Somoza soon became active in the CDS's and went about rooting out *somocismo.*

The FSLN said the media had to be organized in the "service of the revolution"—meaning specifically the Sandinista plan for the country. Bayardo Arce, a former journalism professor who was one of the nine *comandantes* on the Sandinista Directorate, said, "We support freedom of the press, but, of course, the freedom of the press we support will be a freedom of the press that supports the revolution." The FSLN leaders and journalists who supported them began to distinguish between "market-place journalism" and "revolutionary journalism." Nicaragua had three daily newspapers. In addition to *Barricada,* the newspaper created by the FSLN, there was a newspaper published by a Maoist group, *El Pueblo,* and *La Prensa,* which resumed publication on August 16. The Chamorro family newspaper, which had to take its news material to León every evening to be printed because its press had been destroyed by the National Guard bombardment in June, promised a "free, critical, and independent journalism."

The new Education Ministry organized a series of "national consciousness-raising programs" on radio and television intended to set teachers and the general public on the proper political path and overcome the years of Somoza influence. Education was to be focused on creation of "a new man," a term usually associated with Marx and Lenin, though Carlos Tünnermann, a Roman Catholic who became minister of education, said it also came from Saint Paul. Crash courses in political education were set up at the university and taught by "internationalist" academics who poured into Nicaragua from Cuba, other Latin American nations, and Europe. It was pointed out that Nicaraguans had previously been denied the chance to study Marxism, so there was now a lot of enthusiasm for it. On the other hand, seventeen professors at the national university were fired in the first few weeks for "systematic opposition" to change, including Adán Fletes, the head of the Social Christian Party.

One of the early decisions of the new government was to postpone until May 4, 1980, the creation of the Council of State, the thirty-three-member, quasi-legislative body contemplated in the Plan of Government that had been drawn up in San José in June. The postponement met with criticism from several non-Sandinista political parties and from COSEP, the private sector umbrella organization that had played a leading role in the nonviolent opposition to Somoza. The Council of State was supposed to have the power to approve or reject junta actions. Alfonso Robelo apparently agreed to the postponement; at any rate, he announced it. At the same time, the CDS's and other organizations being created by the FSLN began to demand revisions in the planned makeup of the Council of State to include the new Sandinista-linked groups. As then envisioned, the Sandinista Front did not have an automatic majority in the council.

All the holdings of the Somoza family and those of other *somocistas* were expropriated. These included about one fourth of the cultivated land, some 130 businesses and industries, and hundreds and hundreds of houses and vehicles. Also, included was La Fundadora, the immense farm that Leo Salazar had managed during the days of Sandino and the Marines and that was later acquired by Somoza García. Officials claimed that La Fundadora now covered 50,000 manzanas (90,000 acres). A new agrarian reform agency took over the land, another state agency took the businesses, and the new Sandinista Popular Army took control of the houses and vehicles. By October, Wheelock claimed to have gained control of 1,250 farms covering a million manzanas (1.8 million acres).

Within a week after taking power, the new government nationalized banking and foreign trade. The nationalization of foreign trade meant agricultural producers would sell their coffee, sugar, cotton to the government for resale abroad, giving the government more control over hard currency. In October and November insurance and mining companies were nationalized. Otherwise, there was a promise of full respect for private property, but there was an element of chaos in the whole question of property ownership and business management, whether the person had *somocista* connections or not. An estimated 20 to 30 percent of business owners left the country just before or after the change of government, many because they had connections to Somoza and expected to be, or were, confiscated; but others left out of a general unease. The leading banker in the country, Eduardo Montealegre, had left for Miami before the war ended because he felt that he was viewed by the Sandinista leaders as "the symbol of capitalism."

The confiscations added to the nervousness that had already been created among businessmen, non-Marxist political parties, and trade union federations by Sandinista rhetoric and the activities of the new mass organizations. Anyone in uniform might simply commandeer a vehicle or house when he thought he needed it. There were also many land takeovers by groups acting on their own or at the instigation of mass organizations or the new agrarian reform institute.

In addition, the newly organized Sandinista labor federation (CST) took over many factories. It would send small groups into a business armed with an M-16, a pistol, and a fragmentation grenade and declare it taken. CST leaders later acknowledged they had permitted a degree of anarchy to erupt. Some small labor groups emerged advocating Trotskyite principles and claimed ownership of the factories in the name of individual groups of workers, saying they were trying to bring about a worker-peasant government. Some of the most enthusiastic Trotskyites were "internationalists," especially those who had served in the Simon Bolivar Brigade during the insurrection. There was confusion within the FSLN about how far to allow the takeovers to go, but they were slowed down after the CST leadership declared that all takeovers had to be carried out by the state, not the workers, and foreign groups were expelled.

One of the non-Marxist labor federations, the Confederation of Trade Union Unity, known as CUS, whose former secretary-general, Luis Medrano Flores, had been killed on January 9, 1979, opposing Somoza, complained that CST organizers and other FSLN types were using force against CUS organizers. The Sandinista labor activists were armed and were accusing CUS of being "counterrevolutionaries, thieves and imperialists."

Retail business, which suffered damage from bombardments and looting during the war, was nervous about reopening and reinvesting in stock or raw materials. A few weeks into the new regime, I went to Rivas, the departmental capital in the south that Pastora's Southern Front forces had fought in vain to capture, and found about half the houses gutted and much of the downtown reduced to rubble. A pharmacist who lost most of his stock in the looting but whose combination home and shop still stood, said, "Everybody robbed and everybody was robbed." His counter held a disorganized mound of medicine bottles and a jar of sugar cookies. "People are afraid to invest in new stock now," he explained. "There is no confidence in what will come. Many people want Communism. It's best to keep my mouth shut."

Business and private farm leaders, through their organization, COSEP, began to express some concerns within a few days, not only about economic matters, such as respect for private initiative and property, but also press freedom, separation of the government from the FSLN political aparatus, and freedom of movement. These non-Marxists defended their turf on the grounds that the victory over Somoza was as much theirs as the Sandinistas'. COSEP sent representatives to meet with several members of the Sandinista Directorate on July 30, just eleven days after the victory, and complained that things were being done that were contrary to the Plan of Government. Expressing fear that the framework was being created for a one-party dictatorship, COSEP asked for immediate corrective measures. It said the FSLN and junta would have to eliminate uncertainty and motivate people to reactivate the economy.

Other groups were complaining about some of the same issues. The Roman Catholic bishops called the CDS activities an "indoctrination process." The Democratic Conservative Party said the CDS's threatened to become the instruments of a form of neighborhood and workplace espionage. Among other things, the party said, the CDS's were assuming the right to approve applications for permission to travel abroad and for automobile license plates.

The *comandantes* promised privately to halt the illegal takeovers, but in public they increased their tough talk. They appeared before crowds of people and lectured on politics and socioeconomic matters, using the rhetoric and logic learned only by careful study of Marx and Lenin.

Bourgeoisie was one of the words that received a thorough workout, usually accompanied by some adjective, such as "traitorous." A process began of charactizing as bourgeois whatever the Sandinistas did not like. Sometimes the term was used in a socioeconomic sense to describe middle-class and wealthy people and at other times in a political sense to refer to those who expected Nicaragua to develop a traditional Western political system, with its accompanying rights and liberties. Any political ideas or demands the Sandinistas did not like might be dismissed as bourgeois notions, even if they came from dark-skinned trade union members. This allowed the Sandinistas to place the demands of their critics in a pejorative, elitist framework. By telling a group of peasants or laborers, for example, that a particular political concern was bourgeois, the Sandinistas were able to imply that it was something of interest only to an elite.

Humberto Ortega declared that the Sandinistas could wipe out the bourgeoisie immediately if they so desired, but he said they did not plan to do so. He refused to define the term, saying that "rigid concepts lack importance in a revolutionary process . . ." At one point, to restrain the new Sandinista mass organizations' zeal for confiscations, Tomás Borge felt obliged to give a limited explanation of the word. Merely owning a house and a car did not make one bourgeois, he said, and besides, there were some enlightened bourgeoisie, such as Alfonso Robelo.

Aside from such occasional references to bourgeoisie who were in the government, though not Sandinistas, the *comandantes* tended to ignore one obvious contradiction in their attempt to square themselves off against the bourgeoisie. It was that some of those within the upper ranks of the Sandinista Front itself were from affluent families, and if the term were taken in its broader sense, including the entire middle class and people with access to education, then the majority of the Sandinista Front was overwhelmingly bourgeois in economic origin, if not in political outlook.

Pedro Joaquín Chamorro, the late publisher of *La Prensa,* had foreseen this debate in the last editorial he wrote. Published January 6, 1978, four days before his death, it took note of criticism, even then, of the "bourgeois opposition" by Sandinista factions and offered these thoughts: "To begin with, a big percentage of the Nicaraguan population belongs to the bourgeoisie, large, medium, or small, such as those who have a corner store, the artisans, small manufacturers, grain vendors, the people with stalls in the markets, the lawyers who defend [those accused of subversion], the medium-sized farmer, and even the small farmer, who is part of what we could call the rural bourgeoisie, with his hoe, his few cows, and his harvest of coffee, sugar cane, beans, corn that he sells in the towns and cities. Those are bourgeoisie, not proletarians.

"True that the majority of our population is made up of peasants and workers, but the small and medium bourgeoisie, people who make their living from the sweat of their brow and whose contribution to the national production is considerable, cannot be pushed aside and, much less, underestimated, as pretend certain people who use a 'proletarianizing' vocabulary, which has no relation to the lifestyle of those who use it . . ."

Members of the Sandinista Directorate regularly declared that they did not plan a "Communist" government. They claimed they had never said they were Marxists and could not define the new government's ideological line. But they did not say they were not Marxists. It was unclear how much agreement existed among the Nine about how to govern the country. Some had not met until March 1979, or later. But the differences among them that had produced the split into three FSLN factions in 1975 had to do with strategies for reaching power, not philosophy of government. Once in power, some of the Nine showed a tendency toward modifying Marxism to Nicaraguan tradition while others tended more toward modifying Nicaraguan character to fit the new mold. Among FSLN leaders below the level of the National Directorate, some believed there could be Marxism without Leninism, and some believed there could be Marxism-Leninism without it becoming Stalinism.

Most of the differences within the National Directorate seemed linked to how far each *comandante* was willing to deviate from Marxism-Leninism in order to honor the written commitment made in San José to establish a system of political pluralism with such traditional Western liberties as freedom of press and religion, and to permit the continuation of private enterprise. This commitment to do one thing, coupled with the natural political inclinations of the Sandinistas in another direction, produced a power structure that in the first months often seemed to suffer an advanced case of schizophrenia.

Some indications of whatever FSLN consensus existed emerged from a three-day meeting of Sandinista militants that began on September 21 and ended on September 23. The gathering gave birth to the Sandinista Assembly, a group of eighty-one top Sandinistas (27 from each faction) that was supposed to become the ultimate authority within the FSLN. The meeting was secret, but a thirty-six-page written report on it was circulated privately under the title, "Analysis of the Situation and Tasks of the Sandinista People's Revolution."

The report claimed the victory over Somoza was totally the work of the FSLN, which had "thwarted the imperialists . . . the international effort to salvage what it [the United States] could, and the attempts to preserve a bourgeois democracy." The report said the FSLN action in joining forces with non-Marxist opposition figures had constituted an "alliance of convenience" that had been necessary to bring down Somoza and that this alliance had to be maintained now to avoid U.S. intervention and obtain Western financial assistance. Key events in the development of this alliance of convenience, it said, were creation of the Group of Twelve *(Los Doce)* in 1977 and formation of the junta and Cabinet with the help of many non-Marxists, and the writing of the Plan of Government promising political and economic pluralism. It was acknowledged that the Plan of Government was not especially to FSLN liking, but this problem was supposed to be resolved by the presence of several Sandinistas in the junta and Cabinet. It also said the FSLN should not move too quickly or too radically in making revolutionary changes because of the need to maintain a certain political posture internationally to prevent intervention or destabilization. Another part of this "defensive posture" on international questions was the need to maintain relations with the bourgeoisie and non-Marxist political parties. In order to consolidate itself and be able eventually to make those changes it desired, the FSLN had to create "an army politicized to an unprecedented degree . . ."

In the document, the FSLN spoke of the need to "appear reasonable during this 'intermediate' period" in order to encourage good relations with the left-of-center non-Marxist political parties, such as Robelo's MDN and the Social Christians, and keep those groups from falling in with the bourgeoisie. Again, the Sandinistas did not spell out exactly what they meant by the term, but in this case bourgeoisie presumably meant the landowners and Conservative Party people who had not been compromised with Somoza but who were lukewarm toward the FSLN. One such group identified was large coffee growers, whom it called reactionary bourgeoisie. But non-Marxist labor federations were also characterized as potential allies of the bourgeoisie and counterrevolutionaries. The activities of these labor federations were to be carefully watched.

The report warned against a resumption of the old dispute that had led to the division of the FSLN into three factions, saying it was crucial for the Sandinistas to remain unified. It said the FSLN must be "flexible" in getting through this period in which the bourgeoisie, political parties, imperialists, and other non-Marxist elements could still wield influence. During this time the FSLN had to convince the people that it was "the legitimate leader of the revolutionary process" if it were to reach the long-term goal of retaining "revolutionary power." A separate document, drafted within the Sandinista Police political commission about the same time, gave instructions for organizing a party on Leninist lines.

The report of what became known as the 72-hour Meeting did not cause the anguish outside the FSLN that might have been expected. Since it was not presented immediately as a policy announcement, but gradually found its way into the hands of non-Marxists and the U.S. Embassy, it seemed just one more in a long line of issues developing. Some non-Marxists within the government at the time did not panic when they read it because they still viewed the situation as unclarified. They thought that the "Analysis of the Situation and Tasks" merely represented the goals of the FSLN, and that implementation of such plans might be prevented if non-Marxists remained in the country and the government.

Adolfo Calero, one of the leaders of the Democratic Conservative Party, the name under which three of the four factions of the Conservative Party had united in March, was at first shocked by the document. "But, then, we decided it was what they had said all along—the pronouncement they made in Chema Castillo's house [in the 1974 Christmas Party Raid], and the one they made in August 1978, when they took over the palace. So this was the same, we thought."

Nevertheless, Calero and several other Conservative leaders wanted to make their general unhappiness known to the Sandinista Front. They invited Bayardo Arce, one of the nine *comandantes* from the

National Directorate, to Calero's house for dinner. The mood was congenial, the tone friendly. Arce accepted a gin and tonic before dinner and noted Calero's well-stocked bar.

"You bourgeoisie still have a variety of stuff," he said.

"Yes," Calero said, "and we hope to keep on having it."

Then the Conservatives began to tell Arce what they thought. They said they were already totally disenchanted, that their party had pronounced itself in favor of the Plan of Government, but the plan was not being kept. Arce responded that the government and FSLN were just beginning and had a lot of problems. Before they sat down to dinner, Calero told Arce the 72-hour Document indicated that the goals of the FSLN were not as innocent as Arce was claiming. Arce seemed surprised that the document had found its way to people outside the FSLN.

Arbitrary confiscations and other abuses continued, and on November 14 COSEP addressed to the junta and the FSLN a document repeating, in stronger terms, many of the complaints made on July 30. With this, the two sides became caught up in a self-perpetuating cycle that would govern their relations for the coming years, and out of which neither seemed willing to break: the private sector saying it needed guarantees against confiscations and a general improvement in the investment climate if it was to produce, and the Sandinista Front saying private enterprise, including agriculture, had to prove itself by producing before it could demand anything of the regime. Despite the name-calling and feuding, the two sides were willing to talk to each other.

Four months into the new government, William Báez, a frequent spokesman for the organized private sector as executive director of the Nicaraguan Development Institute (INDE), told me: "As long as the government is receptive to dialogue, there is hope for the private sector to play an important role . . . In order to reactivate the economy we want the rules settled. We understand there has been a revolution, not just a change in name. We have to give up some things, but we will never give up the freedom to educate our children as we want, freedom of movement and thought, and the existence of the private sector. Those things we cherish. We believe in the revolution and have decided to stay. The more private sector people who stay, the better chance we can swing it." Entrepreneurs, he said, were 30 percent of the work force, a fact that gave private enterprise considerable leverage.

Alfonso Robelo, from his vantage point on the junta, was reaching conclusions about the path of the new regime that were not to his liking but which, since he was keenly aware of who held the guns, he did not publicly oppose. Instead, he told his former business and political colleagues, in a neutral tone, what he saw developing. Going to a meeting of the directors of the Chamber of Industry in the first weeks of the new government, he angered the industrialists by beginning his remarks: *"Se acabó la piñata"* ("The party's over"). A month after the victory, he said in a speech at a government rally: "We should all understand clearly that our revolution is socialist, but socialist with freedom, and that there is room for each and every true Nicaraguan who wants to fight for this new Nicaragua." In a meeting with his own MDN a hundred days into the new government, he predicted that all production assets in Nicaragua would eventually pass into state hands. He said the speed with which that would occur would depend upon the ability of the new order to absorb and learn to manage things. People in business groups and non-Sandinista political parties began to feel he was aligning himself with the FSLN. This isolated him from those with whom he had shared goals and interests. Larry Pezzullo, the U.S. ambassador, was also at times dismayed, preferring that Robelo be more forthright in his own views and less accepting of those of the Sandinistas.

Non-Sandinista political parties began to test the degree of political freedom in the early months of the new order, with mixed results. The Democratic Conservatives were holding small gatherings around the country. The Social Christian Party, which had had a considerable base among university students during Somoza's time, began to expand its organization with the help of the international Christian Democratic movement. Robelo's MDN was also organizing. Smaller parties to the left of these tended to subordinate their interests to those of the Sandinista Front in the early days of the new regime.

A group of former Conservative youth formed a new party that wanted to call itself the Sandinista Social Democratic Party, claiming that Sandino's legacy belonged to all Nicaraguans who had opposed Somoza. But the Sandinista Front reacted by announcing that only it had the right to apportion use of the term Sandinista. It accused the fledgling party of tarnishing "the political and military image of *Sandinismo*." Declared the FSLN: "*Sandinismo* in our country has a political expression. It carries out a political project that is classist in nature and which we are going to maintain because *Sandinismo* intends to become the expression of the popular [people's] interests and to defend the popular conquests . . . None . . . of those who pretend to be part of that party, the Sandinista Social Democratic Party, have participated in the struggle which the Sandinistas have in particular waged." The junta followed the lead of the FSLN and adopted a decree saying only the FSLN and groups receiving political guidance from it could use the word Sandinista.

The FSLN repeatedly said it did not plan to take reprisals against former National Guardsmen and others identified with the old order, but the headquarters of the Permanent Commission for Human Rights, a nongovernmental organization founded in 1977 that had previously publicized the rights abuses of the Somoza regime, was soon jammed with people concerned about jailed or missing relatives. When accusations of such began to emerge, Borge and others said human rights violations were not government policy, that the number of reported executions was exaggerated, or that some things could not be controlled because so many people had been given weapons in the last offensive of the war and had not turned them in. They did not deny all abuses and generally got high marks and sympathy internationally for good intentions on human rights. However, a subsequent report by the Permanent Commission for Human Rights said executions and disappearances of people had occurred in significant numbers from the victory through October 1979. It said at least forty-three people were killed by military or security forces in those early months and that people had come to the commission offices to inform it of the disappearances of more than six hundred people during the first year, mostly peasants and laborers from outside the capital. At least some of them had been seen in jails or were known to have been in the hands of authorities before they disappeared. A few were thought to have been imprisoned during the Somoza era and not accounted for subsequently.

The most significant case of killings occurred among prisoners at La Polvora, a jail in Granada, where Sandinistas imprisoned a number of people picked up during the first few days after the triumph. It was not clear why they were detained. Very few had obvious National Guard connections, though some were alleged to have been Guard collaborators. The Human Rights Commission was advised of the disappearances only after relatives spent many futile weeks trying to find out on their own why the men and boys had disappeared from jail. On October 3, 1979, acting on information gathered by the wife of one of the missing men, the Human Rights Commission sent a delegation to a hilly area outside Granada, where it dug up human remains, among which the woman recognized her husband's trousers. Another common grave was later found. The rights group concluded that at least thirty prisoners from La Polvora had been killed, though some of the family members claimed the number of victims had to be higher, based on the number of people captured. The human rights group ran into opposition from the Interior Ministry, which refused to exhume the bodies and hand them over to the families. The commission also discovered that the Interior Ministry was establishing in Granada unofficial detention centers and a network of people with security authority but no recognizable title.

The thousands of National Guardsmen who had jammed the Free Trade Zone near the airport under Red Cross protection at the end of the fighting were soon declared prisoners of the new regime, over the objections of Ismael Reyes. Others declared prisoners included many teenaged boys who had taken refuge with their National Guard fathers, and also an assortment of collaborators. Other National Guardsmen, who had thought they had nothing to fear of the new regime and had stayed in their homes, were also arrested. Borge and others in the FSLN first estimated that detainees totaled as many as 7,500, about half of them former National Guardsmen. Later, official figures put the number of imprisoned National Guardsmen and collaborators at 6,310. Some were people captured on the accusations of CDS leaders. *La Prensa*, noting the zeal of the new informers and collaborators, warned that unjust arrests were occurring, and people often had no idea who had accused them, or why.

In October, when José Esteban González, the national coordinator of the Permanent Commission for Human Rights, began to total up and release the figures on the prisoners, the disappeared and the dead, as well as to complain about conditions in the prisons run by Borge, the FSLN turned on the bearer of the unpleasant message. In so doing, it chose to forget that during the Somoza era the Human Rights Commission had frequently aided jailed Sandinistas, including Borge, who received legal and moral help when he went on a hunger strike while in prison.

Now, Sandinista groups organized several protests in front of the commission headquarters, accusing it of defending *somocistas*. Sandinista leaders launched verbal assaults on the commission and especially González, citing his affiliation with the Social Christian Party as indication of a conspiracy against the new order. The Social Christian Party had been among those criticizing the decision to postpone creation of the Council of State. Daniel Ortega also accused González of having been part of an effort in July 1979 to head off an FSLN victory, pointing out that he had traveled to Caracas with the archbishop to meet with officials of Venezuela's new Christian Democratic government as Somoza was preparing to flee Nicaragua.

FSLN leaders soon concluded that the Human Rights Commission was incompatible with the "revolutionary process," that it had counterrevolutionary ideas and, furthermore, was unnecessary on the grounds that the new government was sufficiently guaranteeing human rights. Two priests on the commission's board who now served in the government—Edgard Parrales and Fernando Cardenal—demanded that González resign because of his activities as a member of his political party, finding no conflict in their own political roles for the FSLN. González refused, and Cardenal, Parrales, and various other people involved with the government soon resigned from the commission.

In December, trials began for former National Guardsmen and collaborators. Their cases were handled by nine special tribunals of three people each, which operated outside the judicial system but used the existing punishment code calling for a maximum of thirty years in prison, with no death penalty. Each of the "tribunals of conscience" was made up of one lawyer or law student and two "honest, respected, morally solvent" lay people selected by the government. The trials brought subdued criticism from international human rights groups, which found that the tribunals were not impartial because some of the members of the courts had suffered under Somoza, that the tribunals abandoned normal legal processes, and that they were using political criteria to pass judgment. Some of the Guardsmen were accused of specific crimes, but most were accused of guilt by association and convicted on the basis of belonging to an institution that was judged repressive, or of being known to have been present in a town where killings occurred.

The end of 1979 also brought a major realignment in Cabinet posts that made official what had been growing clear since July 19: that the FSLN National Directorate, not the junta, was going to run the country. Many Nicaraguans viewed the December 1979 shifts as a purge. The most significant single change was that Bernardino Larios, the former National Guard officer, was fired as defense minister,* and Humberto Ortega, who was already army commander, replaced him. The FSLN had wanted to make Ortega defense minister at the beginning, when the government was created in San José, but it had agreed to put Larios in the job to help reduce United States opposition. His appointment had been an element in the U.S. decision to accept the junta as the next government. But there was no public complaint from Washington about the December change. It represented no real change in the way things were done because Larios had been an extra wheel in the military structure from the beginning and had been ignored in its decisions. Those who analyzed the distribution of power saw that three key *comandantes* now controlled what were probably the three key areas of the power structure. Borge had police and internal security; Humberto Ortega had the military, and his brother Daniel, as the dominant member of the junta, controlled the bureaucracy and was the public face of the government.

But there was more. Henry Ruiz, of the Prolonged War faction of the FSLN, was named minister of planning, replacing a civilian economist. Ruiz, the *comandante* with the most visible ties to the Soviet Union, soon had a team of a dozen or more Bulgarian economic advisers in the ministry. Jaime Wheelock, the leader of the Proletarian Faction, was named minister of agriculture in addition to the post he already held as head of agrarian reform. Although there were other ministerial posts dealing with the economy, these two assured the FSLN virtual control or a veto over all decisions and actions. In addition, Luis Carrión Cruz, also a member of the Proletarian Faction, was named vice minister of defense.

The Cabinet changes meant six of the nine members of the National Directorate, two from each faction, now held key government jobs. A government that had been put together to look civilian, moderate, and pluralistic just six months earlier in San José now looked far less that way.

---

*About eight months after his departure from the Cabinet, on September 9, 1980, Larios was jailed on accusations of plotting to kidnap the nine members of the National Directorate. He was found guilty, sentenced to seven years in prison, but freed in April 1984 after the Supreme Court overturned the conviction and ordered a new trial, in which he was acquitted. After his release, Larios denied the accusation and said what he had done was to send a letter to Tomás Borge declaring himself in open opposition to the Sandinistas and saying, "You know that I am not a Marxist-Leninist, and I know that you are." He was arrested the same day.

9

CUBANS, GRINGOS, PANAMANIANS, AND "REVOLUTIONARY INTERNATIONALISM"

JULY 1979 TO EARLY 1980

While praising the help they had received from Costa Rica, Panama, Venezuela, and Mexico, *comandantes* and others in the new regime gave priority to contacts with Cuba and, to a lesser extent, other countries of the Soviet bloc. Hundreds of Cuban doctors, nurses, and teachers soon followed the first contingent, which had arrived on July 25, just eight days after Somoza fled. Although it was not said publicly at the time, the first Cuban military and security advisers also arrived. By November the State Department estimated there were about two hundred Cubans performing military and security functions in Nicaragua, and Panamanian military information substantiated that.

The same *Cubana de Aviacion* plane that brought in the first medical brigades took a large Nicaraguan delegation—Alfonso Robelo, Humberto Ortega, Bayardo Arce, and others—to Cuba on the return flight for the 26th of July celebration, the anniversary of the beginning of Fidel Castro's movement. Castro compared the guerrilla war in Nicaragua with that of Cuba twenty years earlier, but said the political structure that emerged in Nicaragua would probably be very different from the one in Cuba. He noted that in order to reach power the FSLN had made some concessions to people of other political persuasions. He said this was acceptable under the circumstances and called the Sandinistas realists, implying that this had been necessary to keep the United States from intervening. "The Sandinistas have said, 'If an election is needed, we do not mind if one is held.' " Then he added, "Regardless of the many resources that may be given to the reactionary groups and all that, any election held in Nicaragua would be won by the Sandinistas by a very wide margin."

The next day, July 27, diplomatic relations between Nicaragua and Cuba were renewed, and in a matter of weeks relations were established with various other Soviet bloc countries. Henry Ruiz traveled to Moscow, Bulgaria, Libya, and Algeria during the first days of August. When Ruiz returned, he said he had concluded technical aid agreements. In mid-August, Borge went to Cuba on a visit with little public attention, and many others followed. At first, relatively few went to the Soviet Union, primarily Ruiz and others from the Prolonged War Faction of the FSLN, those viewed as the most antagonistic toward reaching accommodation with non-Marxists in Nicaragua. These travels were not given great attention in the Sandinista press. Cuba was the real magnet; there seemed to be a public fever among many Nicaraguans to travel to Cuba.

There were soon daily flights between Havana and Managua. They carried Cuban teachers, medical personnel, supplies and advisers to Nicaragua, and the return flights to Cuba carried Nicaraguan students. By the end of August, Nicaraguan children of secondary school age were leaving regularly in groups of a hundred or more to study on the Isle of Youth, where Cuban authorities created two schools for 1,200 Nicaraguan students. By November 1979, seven hundred were in residence. When Bayardo Arce visited they complained about being unable to get letters to relatives at home, and so he took back 3,000 letters. They also complained about Cuban food, and he solved that by telling the small group of Nicaraguan teachers with the students to do the cooking. When some parents expressed concern that the students were being coerced into going to Cuba, the government offered to send some parents to Cuba to confirm that the children were there of their free will.

Cubans took a leading role in re-organizing the educational system in Nicaragua. Top Cuban education officials came to Managua in August, promoted their methods and textbooks, and offered forty full scholarships in Havana for university or technical education. Within three months a thousand Cuban teachers were in Nicaragua at elementary and secondary levels, most to serve in rural areas that were short of, or lacked, teachers. Cuba also provided "technical aid" to FSLN radio and television and the national university, but most of the aid consisted of personnel—professors, scriptwriters, programming experts, and others—though there was also some broadcast equipment involved. Cuban officials made a point of saying they had more people than money to offer.

Panama also sent a delegation of security and military advisers to Nicaragua within days of the victory, but the Panamanians, while warmly received at first, soon were having a very different experience from the Cubans. Torrijos had played a major role in assisting the Sandinistas in the insurrection, but his actions had been rife with ambiguities and contradictions that could not have gone unnoticed by the FSLN. Even before the insurrection ended, Torrijos had become doubtful about the kind of government the Sandinistas would permit and also how they would fit into the Western Hemisphere. He had been unsuccessful in his efforts during the final months of the war, first, to put Pastora in a position of power and then to salvage part of the National Guard. Torrijos had also protected some of his *somocista* friends and contacts in the last days of Somoza, getting the U.S. Southern Command to bring out a load of these people on one of its C130 evacuation flights. The U.S. Embassy in Panama was told that they were stranded Panamanians.

But in the ways of Torrijos, and to the convenience of the FSLN and its desire to maintain the appearance of Western support, none of these things was discussed in public once the Sandinistas had marched into Managua. Both sides were full of praise for, and confidence in, each other.

On July 30, just eleven days after the new regime took power, fifteen Panamanian National Guard officers flew into Managua, led by Colonels Rubén Darío Paredes and Manuel Antonio Noriega, Torrijos' top two deputies in the National Guard. Under the direction of Paredes, the Panamanians were to organize a series of thirty-day training programs for the new police force. Torrijos also sent Marcel Salamín, the former Communist who had helped arrange the arms shipments out of Cuba during the insurrection, to be his ambassador to Managua. Noriega soon returned to Panama, but Paredes and Salamín and lower-ranking officers remained, providing an effective information channel for Torrijos from inside the Sandinista structure. Paredes and Salamín were at philosophical odds in their views of what was occurring in Nicaragua, and Paredes was more inclined to discuss what he was seeing with Larry Pezzullo at the U.S. Embassy than with his own ambassador. But together they provided Torrijos with a well-rounded view. Ambler Moss, the U.S. ambassador in Panama, with whom Torrijos shared some of his information, found Torrijos' way of running an intelligence service to be intriguing and entertaining, if unorthodox.

"Most people in the world run an intelligence service by recruiting people who think the same way they do, training them, and sending them out to report. Torrijos would recruit people who thought in vastly different ways. He used to call me over to [his house on] Fiftieth Street sometimes right after July 19 to hear how things were developing [in Nicaragua]. He'd say, 'Ambler, listen to this.' He was a non-reader basically. He had oral presentations, usually cassettes recorded from telephone conversations. First, there would be Salamín: 'My general. The revolution is going beautifully,' and this is happening, *et cetera,* glowing terms. Then, clunk. Stops his tape. 'Now listen to this.' Puts in a recording from a major in Noriega's G-2 outfit who was up there. *'Mi general. Hay Cubanos por todos lados. Se han instalado en el Bunker'* (There are Cubans everywhere. They have installed themselves in the Bunker). Then the third report might be from a Spanish priest out in the countryside with a totally different version. Triangulation from biased sources, but you knew what their bias was. Therefore, you could read them."

Torrijos did not like what he was hearing, but he covered it up publicly when he visited Nicaragua in August for the new government's observance of its first month in power. In a celebration honoring his help to them, the Sandinistas presented Torrijos with a Galil rifle captured from the National Guard. They had also presented a Galil to Fidel Castro a month earlier in Havana and had accompanied that presentation with a verbal attack on Israel for supplying the Somoza National Guard with weapons and ammunition. Mindful of the Panamanian military's close ties with Israel, the rifle was described to Torrijos only as a symbol of the defeat of the Somoza dynasty.

A military cooperation agreement was to have been signed between the two countries during that visit, but it did not occur, and Torrijos explained it in perfect ambiguities: "Since relations are so good, so fluid, so effective and so full of love, the convention is rather redundant . . . Since the agreement is understood to exist as a fact of life, there is no reason to sign it." The Sandinistas also used the occasion of his visit to announce the appointment of Humberto Ortega as commander of the new army, a fact that probably did not sit well with Torrijos, given his friendship with Pastora and his past efforts on behalf of the defunct National Guard.

A month later, after the first class of Sandinista police had been graduated by the Panamanian trainers, the Panamanian team returned home without fanfare, and Torrijos told Ambassador Moss and others that it was because of interference from the growing number of Cubans in military and security functions in Managua. Even if there had been no outright differences between the Cubans and Panamanians, the Panamanians could have been easily overwhelmed by the Cubans, who represented a military and security apparatus many times larger and better equipped than that of the Panamanians. Forty-seven Panamanians, some of them National Guardsmen, who had fought on the side of the Sandinistas during the insurrection also returned home about the same time, and Torrijos implied that it was because he believed that the Nicaraguans should be free of excessive foreign influence. But in late November, Ambassador Salamín was replaced, and *La Prensa* speculated that this represented a downgrading in Nicaragua's relations with Panama and wondered why Panama had ended up playing such an insignificant role in police and military matters in Nicaragua, contrary to expectations.

In early December, an FSLN-junta group—Robelo, Borge, Pastora, Arce—traveled to Panama for meetings. Though Aristides Royo, Torrijos' handpicked president, acted as if relations were normal, Torrijos gave a rare interview to Panamanian television during the visit that revealed his dissatisfaction with the situation in Nicaragua. It boiled down to one word: Cubans. But Torrijos used much more polite and convoluted terms to say this than the ones Anastasio Somoza had once used in warning him against getting too chummy with Communists.

Torrijos began by acknowledging that there were differences of opinion between him and the Sandinista Front and said they may have arisen because he was "overly caring" toward the Sandinistas. He pointed out that Nicaragua, because of its geography, "slept with" the military regimes of El Salvador, Honduras, and Guatemala and went on to suggest that it was necessary to understand the problems and viewpoint of those with whom one "slept." The military leaders of those three countries, he said, had zealous anti-Cuban attitudes. Without mentioning the Cuban military presence in Nicaragua, not yet acknowledged by the Sandinistas or Cuba, he said, "For me, it is not at all significant that there are one thousand or two thousand or five thousand Cuban teachers because the alphabet has never overthrown anyone, has never destabilized anyone in the civilized world . . . In reality, Nicaragua was built with blood by a tyrant and it was punished with blood." But he then said the Sandinistas must come to understand their neighbors' concerns if they were to live at peace with the other countries of the region.

As for relations between the United States and Nicaragua, Ambassador Pezzullo began his work with the new regime with a positive attitude. "We had made a decision right at the beginning that you didn't have many options in dealing with a situation like this," he said later. "A regime had fallen, a new government was coming in. The country was in an economic state of chaos, exhaustion . . . You either took a positive position of trying to be helpful and trying to build a new relationship or you'd be sitting around wringing your hands forever." The ambassador gradually developed good personal relations with most of the National Directorate—except for Borge and Tirado, who he thought were too old to change their views. He operated on the theory that the others still had maturing to do and that as they distanced themselves from their old clandestine lives, they might moderate. If they showed any such inclination, Pezzullo, a one-time high school social studies teacher, intended to be there to offer some guidance. Pezzullo became closest to Jaime Wheelock, the leader of the Proletarian Faction within the FSLN, with whom he was soon having lunch every couple of weeks. He made a conscious decision not to put excessive emphasis on relations with moderates in the new government, such as Robelo and Arturo Cruz, believing he had an understanding of their attitudes and that it was the *comandantes* who were the challenge.

The policy required a lot of turning the other cheek on the part of the U.S. Embassy because, in a country where anti-Americanism and xenophobia had previously been almost nonexistent, the Sandinista *comandantes* and their propaganda organs were suddenly making the United States the main culprit for everything that they found wrong with the world. This outbreak of gringo-baiting after the insurrection surprised U.S. officials because they had previously judged leaders of the Sandinista Front not to be inherently anti-Yankee.

As early as July 22, Daniel Ortega was warning about U.S. intentions. "We must realize that there are powerful enemies watching this process. There are reactionary forces and groups in the United States that are opposed to this victory," he said when the junta attended a rally in Monimbó. On August 5, when Senator Edward Zorinsky, a Nebraska Democrat who was chairman of the Western Hemisphere Subcommittee of the Senate Foreign Relations Committee, arrived in Managua, Borge greeted him with a statement that the Sandinistas could be "excellent friends" or "excellent enemies" of the United States.

It fell to Pezzullo to educate congressmen, staff members, and private sector visitors on his theories of how the United States might influence the path of things in Nicaragua. He also set out to educate the FSLN and other Nicaraguans about the mysteries and powers of the U.S. Congress, a knowledge gained during his time as deputy assistant Secretary of State for congressional relations.

The new Nicaragua, despite the anti-Yankee talk of the *comandantes,* clearly looked to the United States for help, as it did to Western Europe and the relatively affluent Latin American nations. The Sandinistas viewed U.S. economic assistance as something of a birthright, a sort of payoff for the past sins of the United States. The moderates saw U.S. aid as a tool to give them leverage within the regime. The need for large-scale economic assistance was pressing. When the new government took office there was only $3.5 million in the foreign exchange account. There were foreign debts of more than $1.5 billion, $662 million due by the end of 1979. Physical damage from the war was estimated at $600 million and capital flight over the previous two years at more than a half-billion dollars. This economic necessity produced some fancy verbal footwork by the Sandinista leaders. While declaring the independence of the new government and criticizing the historic U.S. role in Nicaragua, they hinted that theirs was a government for sale, seeming to invite the forces of East and West to enter into a bidding competition.

A Nicaraguan aid proposal was drafted in August, the month after the new government took office, by Lawrence E. Harrison, the new director of the U.S. Agency for International Development, and by Sidney Weintraub, a deputy assistant Secretary of State, who came down from Washington. They talked to Cabinet ministers about programs and needs and studied the country's finances. They also traveled around the country. One day while driving toward León, Harrison said to Weintraub, "What do you think of the figure seventy-five million?" Weintraub said it was just what he had in mind. Harrison said he thought it would be a good idea to designate 60 percent for reactivation of the private sector and other nongovernmental uses and 40 percent for the public sector. Weintraub thought that was a good idea. Both the amount and the distribution reflected their attempt to balance Nicaraguan needs with the opposition they knew the proposal would encounter in Congress. They cabled the proposal to the State Department at the end of August.

However, a variety of U.S. aid was already going into Nicaragua. It had begun on July 28, when Pezzullo arrived on a transport plane loaded with food and medicine. Other such flights followed. Financial help also came in the early days, some of it reprogrammed from aid designated for countries not using it, some as an emergency grant, and some resurrected from funds that had been approved, but not used, during the Somoza era. Getting these funds for Nicaragua was a tribute to the abilities of Pezzullo to milk the U.S. bureaucracy and Congress. When Arturo Cruz, for example, took over the Central Bank and found only $3.5 million on hand in hard currency, Pezzullo came up with about $8 million in reprogrammed funds in a matter of weeks, for which Cruz was long grateful. But, in many ways, Pezzullo, who wanted a substantial aid program to give him leverage, felt frustrated by U.S. red tape at a time when it seemed the Cuban ambassador could just call Havana and get a planeload of anything he needed.

The Sandinistas themselves were doing nothing to help their own cause with the U.S. Congress. Daniel Ortega went to Havana for the summit of "nonaligned" nations the first week of September and gave a speech citing every misstep he thought the United States had made in Nicaragua from 1855 to the present, peppering his comments with Marxist rhetoric. He had been saying similar things in Nicaragua, but his remarks in Havana attracted more outside attention. Three weeks later, after being received by President Carter at the White House, Ortega went to the United Nations General Assembly in New York and delivered a plea for international aid to rebuild Nicaragua; but he coupled it with a series of pronouncements on international issues that were anti-United States, anti-Chinese, and pro-Soviet. Aid proponents in the U.S. Embassy in Managua and in Washington were thrown into a state of dismay by all of this, out of concern for how it was being received on Capitol Hill.

It was not until November 27 that the State Department made the formal request to Congress for $75 million in supplemental funds for Nicaragua. Assistant Secretary of State Viron P. Vaky told the House Foreign Affairs Committee that the administration proposed giving Nicaragua a grant of $5 million and a loan of $70 million on concessionary terms. Most of the grant would go to nongovernmental voluntary service agencies, and 60 percent of the loan would, as Harrison and Weintraub had proposed, be used to provide imports for reactivation of the private sector.

Vaky acknowledged that there was a sort of East-West competition to help Nicaragua and that the United States wanted to undercut Soviet bloc countries. "Nicaragua's future course, and certainly its relations with other nations, will be largely determined by the relevance of those nations to Nicaragua's problems. This critical fact is made abundantly clear by the energy and speed with which Cuba has provided teachers, doctors, technicians, and military advisers. It is borne out by the significant contributions other countries—Mexico, Germany, the Andean Pact, Spain—have made in both people and money."

Vaky and others in the administration argued that the aid was justified by the need to strengthen and support moderates in the government, as well as to give the private sector and other nongovernmental groups a chance to survive. The Sandinistas, he said, were in strong positions and many of them wanted to organize Nicaragua on a Cuban model as a single-party, Marxist-Leninist state, but there were restraints on them as the result of the way they came to power. Pezzullo told Congress all of the FSLN leadership came out of a "Marxist-Leninist training base." But in October 1979 and February 1980 he brought leaders of the private-sector organizations in COSEP to Washington to make the rounds of Capitol Hill and argue that it might still be possible to avoid a totalitarian regime in Nicaragua. The U.S. aid, they said, would help in this regard.

The point made by the administration and the supporters of aid in Congress was that not to provide assistance would be to give up the field before the game was decided. It was abundantly clear that while there was human need in Nicaragua, the intent of the aid was as much political as humanitarian. It was, as some of the congressmen said bluntly, an investment to try to prevent Nicaragua from "going Communist," though many thought the chances of preventing that were few.

When Congress debated the aid proposal, opponents argued that

Nicaragua was already Marxist and under the domination of Cuba. Therefore, U.S. aid would be wasted. Proponents claimed there was still a chance for pluralism to emerge, but that the Cubans and Soviets would dominate things if the United States did not respond with help. In the Senate, supporters had to beat back an attempt by Senator Jesse Helms to attach the Bill of Rights to the bill as a condition the Nicaraguan government would have to comply with to receive the money. When finally approved, after many months of haggling, the bill did contain a series of restrictions and conditions, including the right of the President to terminate assistance and call in the loans for immediate repayment if he determined that Nicaragua was supporting terrorism or violence in other countries, such as assisting guerrillas in El Salvador.

What did not come from the United States was military assistance, although the Sandinista *comandantes* made a number of pleas in the early days of the new regime about the need for, and right to, such help. Starting the day Pezzullo arrived, various of them told him of the "pressing" need to acquire weapons for the new army. Later, they talked publicly about buying weapons wherever they could. If the United States would not provide weapons, Tomás Borge said, they would turn to Europe, and, if Europe refused, to the Socialist countries. He said the armaments would have to be free and without conditions.

Pezzullo made a strong pitch in Washington that the United States should provide military assistance of some kind, but there were problems on both sides. When Nicaragua, for example, said it needed medical teams for remote areas, the United States offered military medical teams, which the Sandinistas turned down out of concern that they would staffed by CIA operatives. The United States also offered to resume military training programs for Nicaraguans at U.S. bases in the former Panama Canal Zone, made possible by some credits left over from the Somoza period. The Sandinistas, however, were more interested in weapons than in training or advice, but aside from the obvious obstacles in Congress, there was a question in Pezzullo's mind about how much military equipment Nicaragua needed if it intended to remain at peace with its neighbors. Among other things, the new army had inherited at least 5,000 never-used M-16s from the National Guard.

In November 1979, Joaquín Cuadra Lacayo, the mastermind of the FSLN Internal Front during the war and now chief of staff of the new army, visited the United States at the invitation of the U.S. Army. He toured military bases, and the mood was friendly on both sides. But after Cuadra's return home, Humberto Ortega, the army commander, said Nicaragua would not spend a cent on weapons, although if the United States wanted to donate some, they would be accepted. Ortega himself was supposed to visit the United States in early 1980, but he canceled the trip just two or three days before it was to begin, reportedly because he felt he was not going to be received by military officers of sufficiently high rank in the United States. That virtually ended communications between the Sandinista Popular Army and the small military liaison office at the U.S. Embassy.

If the new regime presented a schizophrenic side to Nicaraguans, it also had several positions on a question that kept the U.S. government in a state of quiet panic: whether the regime intended to help Marxist guerrilla movements elsewhere in Central America and beyond. As the first great insurrectionary success in Latin America since Cuba twenty years earlier, the Sandinistas had attracted the attention and admiration of most of the hemisphere's struggling and exiled extreme leftist leaders. The question troubling the United States and Nicaragua's neighbors was whether the FSLN would follow the dictate of Lenin, and feel an obligation to these other movements.

Many representatives of clandestine groups were in Managua within days of the fall of Somoza. Among them was Mario Firmenich, the Argentine Montonero leader, who said he came to study the strategy used for the victory. Large numbers of "internationalists" from around the region, many but not all representing Marxist groups, fought in the last offensive against the National Guard, so they were also present for the beginnings of the new government. But the Sandinista Front became concerned about Trotskyite influence and soon began deporting some of them.

Delegations from the Palestine Liberation Organization and radical Arab regimes became regular visitors to Nicaragua in the first few weeks. The FSLN returned the visits, and there were frequent joint solidarity declarations. In late August 1979, just five weeks after coming to power, the FSLN conducted a ceremony of homage at the tomb of a Nicaraguan named Patricio Argüello who had been killed in 1971 while helping Palestinian extremists in the hijacking of an El-Al airplane.

The Sandinista leaders usually skirted the frequent questions about whether they intended to support violent movements elsewhere, saying reactionaries would try to pin responsibility on them for other insurrections. But they did not deny their interest. They said Nicaragua and the FSLN could not help it if they inspired others but that they had not created the circumstances in other countries that made insurrections possible. When Plutarco Hernández, the Costa Rican who had been among the FSLN senior people since the late 1960s, said at the end of July that he was organizing volunteer brigades to fight elsewhere, Daniel Ortega said Hernández had no authority to make such statements. In a month or so, Hernández returned to Costa Rica and went back to helping his father in the shoe business. Nevertheless, there were reports of a few former FSLN combatants leaving for El Salvador. The National Directorate did not deny them but said if it was occurring, then people were doing it on their own, not as part of any organized FSLN effort.

In early August, Borge told one interviewer: "Revolutions are the result of each people's effort. They cannot be exported. We believe we have helped these people enough by carrying out our own revolution, by showing that it is possible to fight and win. But we will not send any of our own fighters. We will not send one single weapon to those fighting in Guatemala, El Salvador, Paraguay, and Chile. No. We will not send men or weapons. We can only give our political and moral solidarity."

In other interviews, especially with media from Socialist countries, he spoke of having a duty or moral obligation to other struggles but suggested the best way to fulfill it was by first consolidating FSLN power in Nicaragua. "Perhaps this will be . . . a spark that will illuminate to a certain extent the political strategy in this continent," he said in another interview, "consequently, how alliances in the revolution can be created, maintained, and expanded . . ." In another, he explained that Cuba had been a stimulus in the sense of encouraging guerrilla wars in all of Latin America, but that Nicaragua went beyond that because it showed guerrillas how to forge alliances with other "social forces"—non-Marxists or nonviolent groups—and other governments of the region.

In reference to the issue of help for other guerrilla movements, the document issued after the 72-hour Meeting, in September 1979, said the FSLN's foreign policy would embrace both national independence and Lenin's principle of revolutionary internationalism. One of the Sandinista Front's tasks, it said, was to contribute to and help push "the struggle of the people of Latin America against fascist dictatorships and for democracy and national liberation."

10

THE RUPTURE

APRIL AND MAY 1980

It took nine months for the tensions over the future course of Nicaragua to erupt into public discord and end the honeymoon between the Sandinista Front and the great majority of non-Marxists who had remained in the country. During a three-day period in April 1980, Alfonso Robelo and Violeta Chamorro resigned from the junta, and *La Prensa* was closed by an internal dispute over the attitude the newspaper should take toward the policies imposed by the FSLN. The immediate issue for Robelo was the Sandinistas' effort to expand the size of the Council of State then being formed and give themselves a clear majority. Violeta Chamorro diplomatically cited a lame leg as her reason for resigning three days before Robelo, but she had joined him in opposing the expansion and reapportionment of the Council of State. For both, the issues went deeper and wider.

The junta had decided back in October to postpone organization of the Council of State until May 4, which was the anniversary of Sandino's decision in 1927 to resist the U.S. Marines and the National Guard. Robelo's political party, the Nicaraguan Democratic Movement (MDN), had agreed to the postponement, but some non-Sandinista parties outside the government, particularly the Democratic Conservatives and the Social Christians, had criticized it. According to the Plan of Government drawn up in San José in June 1979, the Council of State was to have been made up of thirty-three members, all representing groups that had opposed Somoza, ranging from the FSLN and most political parties, to six private sector organizations, labor federations, and miscellaneous others. One third of the seats, as then allotted, would have been controlled directly by the FSLN, and various others were assigned to groups closely aligned with the FSLN at that time. This meant the FSLN would have had the upper hand, but would not have automatically controlled the outcome of most votes, especially if some of the fence-straddling groups were to go into opposition, as eventually happened.

As the time approached for creation of the Council, distrust and antagonism were growing between Robelo and the FSLN. On March 16, at the anniversary celebration of the founding of the MDN, Robelo had made a speech containing strong allegations about noncompliance on the part of the FSLN with the Plan of Government. He argued that social change should be accomplished in a climate of political liberty, including elections. He also complained that the soon-to-begin Literacy Crusade for adults was being organized in such a way as to manipulate the poor and the ignorant for ideological or partisan political ends. This, he said, was immoral.

The FSLN responded in an internal memorandum to its militants charging that the MDN was being used by "reactionary forces" and "Yankee imperialism." Nevertheless, the FSLN said it had to proceed with care in the matter because the junta was still trying to renegotiate the foreign debt and wanted to avoid economic reprisals by the Carter administration or international agencies.

On April 16, four of the five junta members met (Daniel Ortega was out of the country) and a proposal was introduced on behalf of the FSLN to increase the size of the Council to forty-seven and reapportion the seats in the FSLN's favor. The FSLN, which just a month earlier had signed an agreement in Moscow for party-to-party relations with the Soviet Communist Party, openly admitted that it wanted an absolute, assured majority in the Council. It was going to give itself additional seats and give most of the other new seats to groups of its creation, primarily the CDS's (the Sandinista Defense Committees), which were allotted nine places, and the Sandinista labor federation, which was given three, while the other labor federations received one or two. Robelo and Chamorro voted against it, and Sergio Ramírez and Moisés Hassan voted in favor, theoretically meaning a tie and no decision under the junta's rules.

Three days later, before the dispute became public, the MDN wrote a letter to the FSLN proposing that the Council be kept at thirty-three seats, but with a slight realignment that would give representation to the new groups and at the same time increase the FSLN's sure vote while still not guaranteeing the FSLN a majority.

Mrs. Chamorro resigned on April 19, the Saturday after the meeting, without mentioning the dispute. She was given the treatment of a retiring revolutionary heroine. Sandinista chieftains crowded her home on Las Palmas Park that afternoon to pay her tribute as she hobbled about on crutches.

But on April 21 the junta secretary sent for publication in *La Gaceta,* the legal newspaper, a decree embodying the Council of State changes. At the end of the decree appeared the names of all five junta members. The next morning, Robelo called a news conference and announced his resignation. In a letter to the junta, Robelo said he was quitting because "essential parts of the unity that was the determining factor in our triumph over the dictatorship have been broken, substantive changes have been imposed in our Plan of Government without the indispensable consensus, and steps have been taken that deviate from the aims of our revolution . . ." Robelo was followed out of the government by several dozen members of his political party who had filled senior management posts in government ministries and agencies and nationalized business enterprises. However, there was no party-wide decision to withdraw, and various MDN members remained in the government.

The next day three of the nine *comandantes* on the National Directorate—one from each faction—held a news conference and said, among other things, that Robelo had resigned because he was unable to identify with a revolutionary process. They accused him of choosing a politically propitious moment for a resignation that he had long intended to make. This was an apparent reference to the crisis over *La Prensa* and the delicate international financial situation (President Carter was almost ready to sign the $75 million aid package). Bayardo Arce, one of the *comandantes,* said the problem came from the fact that Robelo "did not succeed in identifying himself with a political program that limits indiscriminate enrichment and benefits the dispossessed majority of the country." All three *comandantes* claimed there was no real crisis in Nicaragua but that Robelo was trying to make it appear that there was one.

From the news conference I went to talk to Robelo at the small suburban house that the MDN used as its headquarters. He winced when I told him what Arce had said about enrichment. There were other rich people still in Nicaragua, but Robelo was the most visible. Now forty years old, he was proud of having made most of his wealth on his own, and it offended him when people suggested that he was less sensitive to human suffering than the *comandantes*. One of them had been born rich and several had received good educations but had chosen to use them in radical politics and guerrilla warfare at a time when Robelo was using his to build a business empire. The first time I had interviewed him, about eight months earlier, I began by asking whether it was true that he was a millionaire, and he asked if I had something against millionaires. Now, he chose not to argue with the *comandantes* about wealth. Nor did he challenge their assertion that he was trying to create a crisis. That was exactly what he had in mind.

"To continue in the junta was impossible for me," he said. "It was becoming a situation where I was not doing anything. To continue there would just have been to lend my presence to the appearance of a pluralism that was not listening to our point of view. So we opted to withdraw because we believe it makes it possible to provoke—as it has provoked—a strong blow that will make the FSLN reflect on what it is doing. We hope they will reconsider."

In addition to the dispute over the Council of State, Robelo repeated some of his complaints about other issues. He had been trying to get the junta and the Sandinista Front to set a date for the first round of elections, but they were refusing. To back up his point about the obligation to hold elections, he gave me a copy of the letter that had been written to the Organization of American States by the members of the junta from San José in July 1979, just before the end of the Somoza regime, promising to convene elections. The existence of the letter had not been widely known before.

He had also been complaining that the FSLN controlled both television channels and denied access to other political parties. The MDN had proposed to buy one hour's time each week for political programs and had been refused on the grounds that not all groups could afford to buy time and that space would end up being controlled by those with money if political time were sold. The FSLN found no contradiction in the fact its own control of television was based on having the guns. It chose to depict itself as being above partisan politics, as being the conscience and protector of the people, though it carried many of its own partisan or propaganda programs on what was called the Sandinista Television System.

Robelo was soon being vilified by Sandinista *comandantes* at outdoor rallies. They repeated the usual charges: that he was disloyal, that he was trying to destroy national unity, and that he was unable to adapt himself to a political system that did not want people to get rich. Worse yet, he was equated to Somoza, now in exile in Paraguay. Jaime Wheelock of the Sandinista Directorate declared that "Robelo's friend is in Paraguay," and someone in the crowd responded, "Robelo and Somoza are the same thing."

Sergio Ramírez, one of the remaining junta members, wondered during a conversation with a small group of journalists why it had taken Robelo "nine months to feel the pain of birth," meaning the realization that the Sandinista Front and not the junta was in charge. Responding to Robelo's desire for an electoral timetable, Ramírez told us, "I must point out that in Nicaragua we don't have an electoral system. The dictatorship took great care not to establish it . . . The literacy campaign is a priority. The improvement of the health system is a priority. Housing is a priority. Organizing an electoral system is not a priority of the government."

The other half of this rupture in the Marxist-bourgeois alliance was being played out in the dusty grounds and makeshift buildings that were the headquarters of *La Prensa*. When I arrived there with another journalist a couple of days after the shutdown began, a hand-lettered sign had been tacked to the side of the building housing the newsroom. FOR THE MEMORY OF P.J.C.C. WITH XAVIER TO THE END, it read. P.J.C.C. was Pedro Joaquín Chamorro Cardenal, the martyred publisher. Xavier, one of Pedro Joaquín's two younger brothers, had taken charge of *La Prensa* after Pedro's assassination in 1978. The first person we found to talk with us was Luis Hernández, the newspaper's economics editor of the past ten years. It was not a takeover, he said, but a strike by the employees in support of Xavier, whom the rest of the Chamorro family had decided to fire as editor and publisher. The FSLN, he said, had nothing to do with the shutdown, but he did say there had been a number of disputes in the newsroom about which stories to report.

Gradually, talking to others, I concluded that the dispute was part family, part political. On one side were Xavier, his wife, Sonia, and the news editor of *La Prensa,* Danilo Aguirre, all with a rising revolutionary consciousness. On the other was young Pedro Joaquín Chamorro Barrios, at twenty-eight the eldest of four children of the late publisher, who wanted to take a more critical attitude toward the Sandinistas and who had won the backing of the other members of the all-family board of directors.

Shortly after the new government came to power, Xavier had told me that *La Prensa* would maintain a position of "critical support." He said it planned to be independent, but would point out the errors of the new government. While management looked for technicians and foreign loans to resurrect the press from the damage of the National Guard bombardment, reporters and editors filled the twelve daily pages with stories on the new government, the reconstruction effort, and the most recent discoveries of excesses on the part of the Somoza regime. At the same time, they published complaints of disappearances or mistreatment of people at the hands of the new regime. There were also stories about the political, labor, and private sector organizations that gradually began to express unhappiness with the way things were going. *La Prensa* questioned the takeover of some farms outside a legal framework, expressed worries about the zeal of the Sandinista Defense Committees, and campaigned against the red tape involved in getting exit visas.

But on the editorial page, where a wide variety of people expressed opinions, it became obvious that a philosophical gap about both journalism and politics was growing within the staff. Though Xavier was theoretically editor, he came from the technical side of the paper, so the news and editorial side was led by the strongly pro-Sandinista Danilo Aguirre and the abrasive, self-confident Pedro Joaquín, Jr., with the result being a monumental clash of wills. Perhaps responding to criticism of his youth and background, Pedro Joaquín had written an editorial in November declaring himself a "social democrat" and a "progressive bourgeois," saying he believed in Socialism, in liberty, and in a mixed economy; and that he feared totalitarianism but not democracy. These views, which carried over into his ideas of what constituted news stories, did not sit well with Danilo and some others of the staff. On the other hand, Pedro Jr. was incensed when men in the composing room added a political comment of their own at the bottom of a story with a foreign dateline by a Western news agency, a tactic used in Cuba in the early days of the Castro regime.

Within the family, various Chamorros began to attack Xavier, claiming that he was not independent enough of the FSLN. Xavier argued that the revolution was part of the Chamorro family and that *La Prensa* should support it as much as possible. He offered his resignation several times. Finally, in mid-April his relatives accepted it, but before the resignation was announced, the FSLN leadership heard about it and asked Xavier to delay things. The *comandantes* knew that Violeta's departure from the junta was imminent and feared that the two events coming together would set off a national crisis. But on April 20 the family majority decided to act. Almost on deadline for the next day's paper, Jaime Chamorro, the other brother of Pedro Sr., telephoned the composing room with instructions to save front-page space for an important anouncement. The workers, knowing what was coming, walked off the job, demanding that Xavier be retained as editor. That edition of the paper did not appear. The last edition, published on April 20, had devoted the front page to Violeta's resignation from the junta, with photographs of *comandantes* and others at her house the day of the announcement.

A few days after the stoppage began, I returned to the newspaper plant and found most of the two hundred *La Prensa* employees standing around the grounds listening to Danilo Aguirre. He was telling them that the problem had been that Pedro Jr. was always wanting to do such things as shorten or leave out stories on the Literacy Crusade to make space for stories about the private enterprise organizations and other dissident segments. The result usually came out to be one for the FSLN and two for conservative interests, Aguirre said, suggesting that was an unfair balance.

The problem, in Pedro Jr.'s view, was that Xavier had taken out certain stories and told him they were counterrevolutionary, and that Xavier, who was nearly blind, was allowing Danilo to make decisions and often did not know what Danilo was putting in the paper. Danilo, according to Pedro Jr., had been extremely well paid by Nicaraguan journalistic standards and at the same time had been ingratiating himself with the FSLN by running the Nicaraguan Journalists' Union, an organization the Sandinistas had set up in the hope that it would become an accrediting organ for all journalists.

A number of the striking employees told me that Pedro Jr. had no delicacy in dealing with people, politics aside, and that they feared Xavier's departure would mean they would have to work for him. Everyone agreed that Xavier was a nice man. The employees tended to think his easygoing nature allowed him to be done in by the family.

The family tended to think the same characteristic allowed him to be taken in by Danilo.

Cristiana, one of Pedro Jr.'s two sisters and a sometime newsroom worker herself, wanted to fence-sit in the dispute. On the one hand, Cristiana told me, she didn't want to be identified with what she considered a somewhat reactionary position by her older brother and her Uncle Jaime. On the other, she felt that her uncle Xavier was allowing himself to be unduly influenced by Danilo and the Sandinista journalists' organization.

Her mother, Violeta, tried to be diplomatic in the matter, but she had made her position clear when she gave Pedro Jr. the power to vote her shares. "In my house there is liberty of thought," she said when I called on her with three other journalists. She sat in what had been her husband's den, the walls lined with books and photographs of a life in journalism and politics. Her right foot, in a cast below the knee, was propped on a bench, and she twisted uncomfortably as she talked about newspaper and family. It was not the first dispute over journalistic integrity within the family. Carlos Fernando, her other son, and at twenty-four the youngest of the four children, had actively worked with the Sandinistas during the war and was now the editor of the FSLN newspaper *Barricada,* which was learning the anti-imperialist, class-struggle line. Carlos Fernando's attitudes were dismissed by Violeta with an exasperated, upward roll of her eyes, a gesture she often used to imply something without having to fear being quoted as having actually said it. Also, there was a strong hint that rivalry between two male siblings was as much at play here as politics. But she loved them both. Carlos Fernando, like Cristiana, still lived under her roof. All four children still sat down at her table on occasion.

Yes, she acknowledged, she had sided with Alfonso Robelo over various issues in the junta, particularly in opposing the Sandinista-packing of the Council of State, but she wanted to avoid talking about things that might anger the *comandantes* now. Also, she wanted to avoid contributing to a bad image for Nicaragua outside the country. She was worried about U.S. aid and the debt situation, fearful the country would end up without enough food. But her most immediate concern was saving *La Prensa.* She did not want to be involved in its demise after fifty-three years of Chamorro stewardship. "It has been closed many times," she recalled. "My father-in-law was sent into exile. We also went into exile. The paper was burned by the dictatorship. It is certain that *La Prensa* has been firm in its support of the people of Nicaragua. No one helped us and we tried to help everybody."

But the unity that went without question when it was the Chamorros and *La Prensa* against the Somozas was now torn by more complicated factors. Into the world of personalities that was Nicaragua now had intruded the geopolitical issues of the modern world. Still, the inclination was to deal with things in the old personal style. She saw the stoppage as a *toma* (a takeover), and as soon as she heard what had happened she assumed some or all of the *comandantes* were behind it. She had called one of the nine on Sunday morning, less than twenty-four hours after they had left her house in a congenial mood, and pleaded with them to allow the reopening of the newspaper. They denied responsibility, claiming it was nothing but a family problem, though it was acknowledged that some of them had been talking to Xavier in the days before the shutdown.

Maybe, said Pedro Jr., there would have to be some separations within the family and the newspaper in order for all to survive. That was fine with Danilo, who told the employees that he and Xavier were going to organize another newspaper, a cooperative venture with the workers. Within two to four months, he predicted, the Nicaraguan people would close down *La Prensa*. The two camps began regular meetings to see who was definitively with whom. Pedro Jr. admitted that he would get only a small minority of the staff, a fourth or less, but he counted on a few key news and technical people. On one of his more pugnacious days, Pedro told me Xavier was going to do him the favor of taking the "garbage." Offers of volunteer help were pouring in from among his supporters outside the paper.

Xavier, Danilo, and most of the employees held their meetings at the newspaper plant, which they promised to turn over to the other side once financial arrangements for the split had been made. The other side held its meetings among the hammocks and wicker chairs in the shaded garden at the home of Margarita Cardenal de Chamorro, the eighty-year-old mother of Xavier and grandmother of Pedro Jr. She had had her own say just four days before *La Prensa* closed. Dismayed by the adulation that many Nicaraguans, including her son Xavier, were expressing for Cuba at a time when Cubans were stampeding to leave their island on the Mariel boatlift, she wrote a three-paragraph editorial whose operative sentences said: "Those who have gone to Cuba lately have come back telling of the marvels there. What do they say now in the face of the massive flight of Cubans to the Peruvian Embassy?" Then she took to her bed with what Pedro Jr. claimed was a Xavier-induced illness. Xavier said he had seen his mother at the beach house over Easter weekend and she had looked fine to him.

Despite their inflammatory rhetoric over the resignation of Robelo, the *comandantes* responded in a manner that was much more conciliatory in private than in public. It was helped along by the determined hand of Larry Pezzullo, who postponed a scheduled vacation to help deal with what he saw as a watershed crisis. Senator Zorinsky, chairman of the Western Hemisphere Subcommittee of the Senate Foreign Relations Committee, had been on the telephone to the embassy, especially unhappy over the closing of *La Prensa*. Without Zorinsky's continuing help, Pezzullo knew the aid battle could still be lost when it came up for appropriations. Moisés Hassan, one of the remaining junta members, called Zorinsky to try to convince him that nothing of significance had changed in Nicaragua.

Pezzullo also saw in the public eruption a potentially useful shakedown that could help clarify the rules of Nicaragua's internal politics. Just hours after Robelo's resignation, Pezzullo and Jaime Wheelock met for one of their regular lunches at the ambassador's residence, and as soon as it was over Pezzullo called the headquarters of COSEP, the umbrella organization of private business and agriculture, and said the *comandantes* wanted to open talks. The COSEP leaders were surprised but delighted. Pezzullo led them to believe Wheelock had proposed the talks, but they later concluded that Pezzullo had put the bug in Wheelock's ear. Since the fall of Somoza, COSEP had constituted the strongest and most unified non-Marxist group, though some of its active members were also affiliated with political groups. The Broad Opposition Front, or FAO, which had spoken for most of the non-Marxist opposition groups in 1978 and early 1979, had come apart in the last months of the Somoza regime, with some, such as Robelo and his party, joining the new government and others keeping their distance.

Enrique Dreyfus, the president of COSEP, and junta member Sergio Ramírez talked several times by telephone. Then there was a number of meetings between the COSEP leadership on one side (Dreyfus and presidents of the five private enterprise groups making up the council) and Ramírez and three members of the FSLN Directorate on the other.

COSEP put forward a list of written demands that covered its previous complaints—an end to illegal confiscations, revoking the state-of-emergency law, a decree guaranteeing the right of private property, unrestricted freedom of press and speech—and some new demands: a formal commitment from the FSLN to permit elections, separation of state and party (the FSLN); conservation of the original size and apportionment of the Council of State; and replacement of Robelo and Chamorro on the junta with two other non-Marxists. But COSEP was not going to give its assistance in selecting two other non-Marxists for the junta, and convincing them to accept what many viewed as a thankless job, unless agreement could be worked out on the other demands.

The FSLN, on its side, also wanted two other non-Marxists to join the junta, and it wanted the opposition to take its seats in the Council of State when it opened on May 4. These things were necessary in the FSLN's eyes to prevent the spread of mass dissatisfaction and to keep the U.S. Congress and the Carter administration in a mood to disperse the $75 million. Larry Pezzullo had bluntly told them the money would not come through unless the junta was put back together in acceptable form.

The Sandinistas' style and tone ranged from threatening to "break heads" to reassuring the COSEP leaders of their intention to maintain private ownership and political pluralism. They tried to separate the matter of Robelo's resignation from treatment of private enterprise as a whole. Bayardo Arce, known for one of the sharpest tongues on the National Directorate, declared in one meeting with the business leaders that the Sandinistas would do nothing that might lead to their giving up power, even if it meant that Nicaraguans had to eat grass.

At first, the FSLN said only that it was willing for the issues the COSEP leaders had raised to be taken up by the Council of State after it was convened on May 4. On May 1 the COSEP leadership told the Sandinistas that their organizations would not take part in the Council of State unless some of the demands were met beforehand, including the question of returning the Council of State to its original size. The threat to boycott the Council of State angered not only the Sandinistas but also Larry Pezzullo, who thought some of the COSEP leaders were too confrontational, too unwilling to negotiate and compromise.

Meanwhile, the FSLN opened contacts with some private sector and opposition figures not closely identified with COSEP, apparently in an effort to undercut the demands of the COSEP leaders. A businessman privy to both sets of talks later told me the FSLN move to broaden the negotiations to "more than one front" had resulted from another of Pezzullo's suggestions. Carlos Pellas, scion of the family that owned Nicaragua Sugar Estates Limited, the largest private enterprise operation in Nicaragua, met with two of the *comandantes*—Humberto Ortega and Bayardo Arce—at his home into the early hours one morning, and Ortega asked Pellas to join the junta. Pellas, a Stanford graduate in his early thirties, was affiliated with COSEP through the Chamber of Industry, but he was inactive and not vocal in criticizing the Sandinistas. His philosophy, like the one his father had followed under the Somozas, was to protect the business by getting along with the FSLN. However, Pellas turned down the offer to join the junta, not wanting to undercut the organized group and, in general, agreeing with its demands.

The FSLN also opened a third "front," this one with Arturo J. Cruz, the former member of *Los Doce* who had been named president of the Central Bank in the new government. Just before Robelo's resignation from the junta, Cruz had handed in his resignation and made plans to return to his family and his old job with the Inter-American Development Bank in Washington. But he had not yet left town. Pezzullo had developed an early respect for the conscientious and reliable Cruz. He was on the fringes of all the conversations between the Sandinistas and the opposition, protesting all the time, that all he wanted was to leave. Pezzullo, on the other hand, wanted him to help work things out. So did Robelo, who urged Cruz to stay, saying maybe he himself had been too abrupt and things should be patched up.

Late on Friday afternoon, May 2, Pezzullo and his chief deputy met with the COSEP directors at their headquarters and argued against their threat to stay out of the Council of State. Also, Sergio Ramírez of the junta called and asked for a meeting with the business leaders. The archbishop was already expecting a visit from the COSEP leadership, so three of the six top leaders—José Francisco Cardenal, president of the Chamber of Construction; Ismael Reyes, president of the Chamber of Industry; and Gilberto Cuadra, head of the organization of professionals—went to keep that appointment. The other three went to the meeting with the Sandinistas, who were represented by Humberto Ortega, Jaime Wheelock, Bayardo Arce, and Ramírez. Arturo Cruz, who had by then privately agreed to join the junta, was also present. Enrique Dreyfus, president of COSEP, led the opposition group in that meeting. Another member was Reinaldo Hernández, head of the Chamber of Commerce. The third was Jorge

Salazar, president of the Union of Nicaraguan Agricultural Producers, the private farmers' association known by its acronym UPANIC.

The meeting that night of the business leaders and the *comandantes* was tense and angry. The Sandinistas wanted an assurance that the business groups would take their seats in the Council of State at the ceremonial opening less than forty-eight hours away. There was more at stake than just the six seats of the business groups. There was the probability that some or all of the non-Marxist political parties and trade union federations would follow COSEP's lead. The Sandinista Front well understood the negative impact of staging a ceremony before foreign diplomats and the media in which only its loyalists took part, an impact that could be counted in lost foreign aid. Progress had been made in earlier exchanges on some of the issues at stake, such as repeal of the state-of-emergency law and a commitment to end illegal property confiscations. But the Sandinistas adamantly refused to budge on the COSEP demand that the size of the Council of State be returned to the original thirty-three members, and the COSEP people were determined not to allow the Council to become the same rubber-stamp body for the Sandinistas that the Congress had been for Somoza. They also wanted a timetable for elections.

Salazar jumped to his feet at one point and said, "We're tired of threats. If you're going to confiscate, do it. We're not afraid." He pointed out that it was almost cotton-planting time and implied that if there were no satisfactory agreement, then the cotton farmers would not plant that year. Cotton alternates with coffee as Nicaragua's biggest dollar earner. It is a relatively expensive and technologically complicated crop to grow, and Salazar said cotton planters had to feel confidence in the government if they were to make the necessary investments of time and money.

Eventually, there was a trade-off. The COSEP leaders conceded on the issue of the size of the Council of State, taking into account the argument Pezzullo had made to them that it was only an interim body anyway, and the Sandinistas agreed to announce by July 19—the first anniversary of the revolution—a timetable for elections. The timetable was to include a first round for municipal officials and a constituent assembly and a subsequent election for president. Salazar said later the election timetable promise had been won from the Sandinistas at one-thirty in the morning. The COSEP people wanted it in writing, so it was put in writing, but Humberto Ortega asked that it remain "deposited" with the FSLN and insisted that the contents be kept secret. The other side agreed and left without a copy.

Back at the COSEP headquarters, the three men who had gone to meet with the archbishop had been waiting since about eleven o'clock. When the other three arrived and revealed that they had made a secret agreement with the Sandinistas, there were protestations that too much had been given away or that they had not received enough in return. Particularly unhappy was José Francisco Cardenal. He had not expected the others to make an agreement without consulting the full COSEP leadership. They argued until about three in the morning, and Cardenal demanded a meeting of all COSEP directors later in the day.

Cardenal was viewed by some in COSEP as overly hawkish and too quick to anger, but he had been equally hawkish in his opposition to the Somoza regime. Cardenal, now forty and overweight, looked like the successful contractor that he was, but when Fidel Castro came to power in Cuba at the beginning of 1959, he was an idealistic eighteen-year-old student at Catholic University in Washington, D.C. Swept up in the euphoria and hope that Castro's victory meant to many Latin Americans wanting democracy for their countries, he was on a plane bound for Havana in early February 1959. In Havana, Cardenal joined the crowd of would-be revolutionaries, all of whom wanted help. He also made contact with other Nicaraguans, including his distant cousin Pedro Joaquín Chamorro of *La Prensa,* who had flown in from exile in Costa Rica. After Chamorro and the other leaders of his group were unable to reach an agreement with Che Guevara, they had returned to Costa Rica in April to plan their own invasion, and Cardenal was one of the young combatants who joined them. After training in Costa Rica, he took part in the airborne invasion of Nicaragua, and, like the others, was captured. Cardenal served seven months in prison, then returned to his studies in Washington. After graduation, he returned to Nicaragua and eventually created his own construction company. But being a businessman did not make him complacent. In 1978, as president of the Chamber of Construction, he had tried to convince other business leaders to push harder in the strike that followed Chamorro's killing. He thought they could force Somoza out of power then. It had frustrated him that the others wanted to let up and make a try at negotiations.

Now, in the negotiations with the Sandinistas, Cardenal again thought that people who wanted democratic pluralism in Nicaragua were being too timid, that they were backing down. However, when the COSEP directors met on Saturday afternoon, the others wanted to accept the agreement and go into the Council of State. Cardenal's organization had agreed to honor the decision of the majority. The word on the decision was passed to the various political parties and labor groups that planned to follow the decision of COSEP. Among those people there was also some unhappiness with the decision, but they generally accepted it.

The next morning, Sunday, May 4, the members of the new Council gathered for a preparatory session. José Francisco Cardenal showed up a bit late after two other directors of the Chamber of Construction rejected his plea to represent their organization. Bayardo Arce of the Sandinista Directorate was elected president of the Council to cheers and applause. Then several vice presidents were elected. The last, nominated by Arce himself, was Cardenal. Not informed in advance that he was to be nominated, Cardenal sat stoically as he was elected by acclamation. He was feeling equally outraged toward the Sandinistas and his COSEP colleagues.

That night, everybody gathered at the modern Rubén Darío Theater on the shore of Lake Managua in a quietly festive mood for the formal opening. The Council members sat on the stage, and the audience was filled with *comandantes,* government officials, bishops, diplomats, representatives of Latin American legislative bodies, and journalists. Sergio Ramírez read a two-hour state of the union speech that went into excruciating detail about such things as the number of pounds of fish caught and the price of cheese. It largely ignored political matters, except for a brief statement at the end saying the government planned to keep the pre-victory commitment to hold elections for municipal officials, a national assembly, and president. He did not say when that would be.

After the ceremony, Cardenal went home and told his wife he thought they should leave Nicaragua. She agreed, but they had to find a logical excuse that would not arouse suspicions. On Tuesday, May 6, there was a COSEP meeting, and Cardenal complained about what he saw as the complicity of other business leaders in his election to a vice presidency of the Council. He felt tainted by the office. It was the same as the *zancudismo* (parasitism) of old, when the opposition members of Congress accepted the plums handed out by Somoza. At the COSEP meeting, Cardenal also found the way out of Nicaragua for which he was secretly searching. There was to be a conference the coming weekend in San José, Costa Rica, of private enterprise organizations from all of the Central American countries. Cardenal said he wanted to be one of the representatives from Nicaragua.

He and his wife and two other COSEP representatives flew to San

José the following Sunday, and the next day Cardenal announced to all of the delegates at the conference that he was resigning and going into exile. Costa Rican President Rodrigo Carazo heard of Cardenal's announcement and asked all three Nicaraguan representatives to come meet with him that same day. They spent two hours with the president, who tried to convince Cardenal he should remain in Nicaragua. He had no success, nor did his vice president, who invited the Nicaraguans to dine that evening. The next day, May 13, Cardenal flew to Miami and two days later to Washington, where he began to search for the means to overthrow the Sandinistas.

On May 18, two new members were named to the junta, replacing Violeta Chamorro and Robelo. One was Arturo Cruz, the former Central Bank president. The other was Rafael Córdova Rivas, a former justice of the Supreme Court who had been a close political collaborator of the late Pedro Joaquín Chamorro Cardenal. Both were members of the Democratic Conservative Party. The COSEP leaders found both men acceptable, but they sensed that Larry Pezzullo's candidates, not theirs, had been selected.

As for the newspapers, the agreement that was eventually worked out included a financial settlement for the employees who were leaving *La Prensa* and the purchase of Xavier Chamorro's stock by the other directors. *La Prensa* also agreed to provide newsprint and ink for starting up *El Nuevo Diario,* a newspaper that Xavier said would speak to the new Nicaraguan man and woman. It set up shop in a former hardware store a couple of blocks from *La Prensa* on the North Highway, and *La Prensa* went about rebuilding its depleted staff. On the day the departing staff members gave up the plant, Cristiana Chamorro stood at the door of the newsroom and kissed and hugged everyone. Newspaper journalism in Nicaragua was still a Chamorro family monopoly. In mid-May, the first issue of *El Nuevo Diario* was published, and Danilo Aguirre said it had sold 73,000 copies. A week later, *La Prensa* resumed publication with a skeleton staff, and the first issue was a best seller. Reporting the first day sales in headlines in the second day's paper, the editors borrowed a line frequently used by the Sandinista Front and declared: THE PEOPLE ALREADY VOTED: 123,000 COPIES!

11

THE FIRST ANNIVERSARY

JULY 1980

On the evening of July 17, 1980, as the Sandinistas prepared to receive Fidel Castro and other honored guests for the celebration of their first anniversary in power, two other American journalists and I had dinner at a Managua restaurant with Adolfo Calero, one of the leaders of the Democratic Conservative Party, and his wife, María Lacayo de Calero. A year earlier on the same date, Anastasio Somoza had boarded a plane and flown to Miami, never to return. The restaurant, La Terraza, which consisted of a series of small, air-conditioned dining rooms around an open-air patio with a bar and bamboo lounge chairs, reflected the changes that had occurred in Nicaragua in the year just past. Previously a private dining club owned by such people as the Caleros, it had become the property of the employees after the members decided private clubs were not in keeping with the egalitarian mood of the new Nicaragua. It was now open to the public, but the quality of the lobster, crawfish, and wine was unchanged.

The conversation that evening among the five of us—including Christopher Dickey of the Washington *Post* and Gordon Mott of the Associated Press—said even more about the mood that prevailed in Nicaragua in those days than did the change in ownership of the restaurant. In the perfectly normal tones of chitchat, we talked about conspiracies and plots, agents and double agents, and other tactics of geopolitical warfare juxtaposed on the small, inbred world of a back-water capital.

Calero told us that in recent months leaders of his party had been approached by Edén Pastora, the Sandinista war hero now sitting unhappily on the sidelines, and that he had offered to be the Conservatives' "man" inside the FSLN. This was not entirely illogical. Pastora's family ties were to the Conservatives, and in 1967, before opting for the FSLN, he had been involved on the side of the Conservative Party in a shoot-out with the National Guard. But now the Conservatives were unsure about Pastora's purposes. It might be an attempt to entrap them in something. Calero said they ignored the proposition.

This led Dickey to reveal the plot for a novel that had been growing in his head since he began coming to Nicaragua. It involved a character not unlike Pastora who would become the CIA's "man" in the upper reaches of the Sandinista Front. What would happen with this alliance was not revealed to us that night (or perhaps I've forgotten it), but Dickey did say he envisioned a great chase scene through the earthquake ruins and weeds of old downtown Managua.

Gordon Mott then offered an interesting fact that he had picked up during the previous two weeks. This was not, he said, going to be Fidel Castro's first trip to Nicaragua. He had been here several times during the past year for secret meetings with the *comandantes*.* He had always landed at Montelimar, Somoza's former estate on the coast, where there was a jet-age runway. Soon after taking power, the Sandinistas had made a big thing of opening the hideaway one Sunday so "the people" could splash in the pool and inspect the remnants of the Somoza lifestyle, then had closed it behind a wall of military secrecy.

The prevailing atmosphere in which this conversation occurred,

---

*During the next few years, several people who resigned from the government told me they had heard reports of these secret Castro visits while in the government but had never seen him personally.

however, was that we were in an open city, grown politically sophisticated during the past year, a place where anything was permitted and anything could happen, where everybody still had a chance to win, and everybody played that way. Calero did not like the Sandinista Front and made no secret of the fact. He and María were planning to spend the weekend at the beach, away from the sights and sounds of the anniversary celebration. But he was upbeat and optimistic about the future. He still felt, as he had felt during the Somoza years, that all governments were transitory.

True, the vice president of the Supreme Soviet was already in town, and Fidel Castro was arriving the next day. But so was a United States delegation that included a Corn Belt senator, a Cabinet officer, a Citibank vice president, the archbishop of Miami, and the national commander of the Veterans of Foreign Wars. Less than three months earlier, the U.S. ambassador, not Fidel Castro, had seemed the pivotal person in Nicaragua as the Sandinistas and the non-Sandinistas tried to patch things up after the resignations from the junta and the stoppage at *La Prensa*. The reborn *La Prensa* was flourishing, and hitting the Sandinista Front over the head daily in front-page articles. It was also outselling the Sandinista newspaper *Barricada* and the pro-Sandinista *El Nuevo Diario* combined. Pedro Joaquín Chamorro Barrios, now unchallenged as the dominant voice at *La Prensa,* liked to say that the truth lay in the size of the press run.

After dinner we went to the Caleros' house for brandy, but as we drove away an hour later we were followed through the empty streets by two men in an unmarked car. Mott, who was driving, noticed it when he made a wrong turn into a short, dead-end street, and the other car did the same.

The next morning, Fidel Castro arrived to full honors at what was now called the Augusto César Sandino International Airport. He strode down the steps of his plane and began embracing almost everyone in sight. At first, he shook hands with Arturo Cruz and Rafael Córdova Rivas, the two Conservatives who had joined the junta in May, then he changed his mind and went back and embraced them, too. Managua was festooned with banners of Sandinista red and black and national blue and white, and the dusty, exhausted city was spiffed up to the extent possible. Attractive parks had been built in part of the earthquake ruins near Government House, and murals depicting Sandinista glories had been painted on some walls as long as a block. At the same time, security had been multiplied many times, aided by the arrival several days earlier of a group of crack Cuban agents who set up the security for Castro's visit. Street security was so overwhelming that news photographers shooting harmless street scenes often encountered security agents demanding the film from their cameras.

Nowhere was Castro's arrival in Managua of more interest than at General Omar Torrijos' house at Farallon, west of Panama City. Torrijos had been invited to the anniversary celebration, but he had not responded. He had become progressively more disillusioned with the Sandinistas in the year since he had played a key role in helping them reach power. He was particularly irritated that the Cubans were being allowed to play such an active, open role in the new Nicaragua. Now, Fidel Castro, whom he viewed as having one-upped him the previous year in the affair of Nicaragua, was going to dominate the anniversary scene, and he was not about to play backbencher to Castro.

A few days earlier he had told Ambler Moss, the U.S. ambassador, that he was not going to the anniversary observance if Castro went. Since Castro's participation had not yet been publicly confirmed, Moss asked Torrijos how he would be certain, before taking off himself, whether or not Castro was going to be in Managua. Simple, said Torrijos, he would wait in Farallon until the last minute, with his Falcon jet ready to take off. It could make the flight across Costa Rica to Nicaragua in less time than it would take Castro to come from Havana. But if Castro did go to Managua, Torrijos had decided to play the role of the *gran ausente* (the "big absentee"). And that is what he did. He gathered a group of his friends with him at Farallon, including former Venezuelan President Carlos Andrés Pérez, another key player in the rise of Sandinista fortunes, and when word came that Castro had landed in Managua, Torrijos' plane took off and carried Pérez and the other friends to Nicaragua. Torrijos stayed behind and sulked. But he would pick up all the gossip from the ceremonies when his plane brought Pérez and the others back from Managua.

In Costa Rica, another man who had played a major role in assisting the Sandinistas also stayed away. President Rodrigo Carazo faced a public that was beginning to sour on the rhetoric and excesses of the new Nicaraguan government at the same time it was learning the extent to which Carazo's government had aided the Sandinistas in reaching power. Many Costa Ricans were particularly nervous about the growing Cuban presence in the neighboring country. With none of Torrijos' behind-the-scenes maneuvering, Carazo simply said that he was not going because Castro would be there. "We did not help throw out one dictator to open the way to another," he told people who asked why he was staying home.

In Managua, the Sandinistas did not talk about who had turned down their invitation. They celebrated those who came, and announced long lists of delegations that had arrived or were coming. Besides Castro and former Venezuelan President Pérez, they included Yasir Arafat of the Palestine Liberation Organization, who was not scheduled to come until after the anniversary day; Prime Minister Maurice Bishop of Grenada, Premier George Price of Belize, former Costa Rican President José Figueres, Felipe González, leader of the Spanish Socialist Workers' Party, and delegations from most of Western and Eastern Europe, Vietnam, North Korea, and Kampuchea.

The U.S. delegation had been put together by Larry Pezzullo with great attention to balance and to his goal of presenting an empathetic view of Nicaragua to a broad segment of the United States through the eleven delegates. The leader of the delegation was Donald McHenry, the ambassador to the United Nations. Another prominent member was Senator Edward Zorinsky, the Nebraska Democrat who had played a crucial role in the aid battle as chairman of the Western Hemisphere Subcommittee of the Senate Foreign Relations Committee. Also in the delegation was William Bowdler, who had directed the ill-fated attempt in late 1978 to mediate a solution to the Nicaraguan crisis and avoid a Sandinista takeover. Bowdler had recently succeeded Viron P. Vaky as Assistant Secretary of State for Inter-American Affairs. The other delegates ran across a wide spectrum, representing church, labor, business, Hispanics, and more. One of the things the Americans were hoping to hear was the announcement setting a timetable for elections.

It irritated Pezzullo that during a news conference the day before Castro's arrival, junta member Moisés Hassan had downplayed the importance of U.S. aid to Nicaragua. Hassan had declared that Cuba had done the most for Nicaragua on the basis of its ability to pay. In dollar terms, he acknowledged, the most help had come from the United States and Venezuela. According to the embassy figures, the United States had disbursed loans, grants, and food aid worth $62.6 million during the previous year, and documents were ready to be signed for $60 million more. From all foreign aid sources, Nicaraguan officials said the country had received $580 million during the year.

Nicaragua under the rule of a variety of Marxist-Leninists in Cuban-made military uniforms was not a situation that Pezzullo had invented or that he may have desired—it was already well on the road to happening when he came into the picture—but he was determined that the United States not wash its hands of Nicaragua too soon. Despite having suffered a year of Sandinista Yankee-baiting, he felt that the United States might still be able to influence and moderate the path of Nicaragua. He continued to believe that most of the Sandinista leaders wanted to do the best thing for their country and to hope they would eventually outgrow their rhetoric and propaganda, which created a climate less than conducive to reason and common sense. Whatever they said and did for Fidel Castro this weekend, Pezzullo thought, on Monday it would still be Nicaragua. And Nicaragua lived in geographical circumstances and with internal issues that could not be swept away with revolutionary rhetoric.

That evening all the visiting dignitaries and the Sandinista and government leadership attended a reception, and Castro had an amiable conversation with McHenry, Bowdler, and Pezzullo. Castro had some friendly things to say about the way the Carter administration was dealing with Nicaragua and suggested the United States and Cuba could work together for the benefit of Nicaragua. He also assured the Americans that Cuba would do nothing that might work against President Carter in this election year. The possibility of a Reagan victory seemed to be of great concern to Castro.

On July 19 the Sandinista Defense Committees roused people before dawn in the poor neighborhoods of the capital and in surrounding towns. Those from outside were driven in to the city on trucks and buses, and those in the capital marched in formation from their neighborhoods to the recently finished Nineteenth of July Plaza, an immense sheet of asphalt straddling one of the highways circling Managua. Despite the heat, it was packed by ten in the morning. Officials claimed attendance was half a million, but 300,000 would have been a more realistic figure. People were not forced to attend, but in neighborhoods where houses were small or consisted of little more than shanties, it was difficult to pretend not to be at home when Sandinista activists came looking.

There was a review of Sandinista troops by Humberto Ortega, the army commander, and the visiting heads of government and former presidents all had something to say before the Nicaraguan speeches.

Most made only brief remarks. Castro, stepping out of the long row of Sandinista *comandantes* who wore uniforms almost identical to his, began by promising not to dominate the proceedings with a long polemic, then spoke for forty minutes. He recalled that when a group of Cuban exiles had sailed from Puerto Cabezas on Nicaragua's Caribbean Coast nineteen years earlier on what became the Bay of Pigs invasion, then-President Luis Somoza had asked the exiles to bring him back some hairs from Castro's beard. Now, Castro pointed out, he had come to Managua with his beard intact.

Then Castro proceeded to his main comments. After praising the reconstruction help that had come to Nicaragua from around the world, he said he understood the largest amount had come from the United States, but he suggested that the United States was still being stingy. "I only lament, sincerely, that it is little for the wealth of the United States. It is little for the richest country in the world. It is little for the country that spends one hundred and sixty billion dollars on military goods, or the country that, according to projections, is going to spend a trillion dollars on military items in the next five years." Castro also warned of the danger of new arms races, of cold war, and hot war. This, he said, became especially evident "after reading . . . the platform of the Republican Party of the United States. It is a terrible platform, threatening for peace, a terrible platform that threatens again to apply the club to Latin America." Castro said he had not come to Nicaragua to tell Nicaraguans how to carry out their revolution, but he added that he thought the promise of political pluralism was "one of the wisest things" the Sandinistas had done.

Daniel Ortega, the Sandinista *comandante* who was a member of both the National Directorate and the junta, delivered the main speech. He devoted a large part of it to a recounting of United States political and military interventions in the past, then noted that since the change of power in Nicaragua these relations had taken a sharp turn and were now based on mutual respect. As to the election question that many were hoping to hear answered, he touched it only halfway, saying the Sandinistas were committed to holding elections that were "appropriate with the spirit of this new democracy." But he said the anniversary was intended to honor the heroes and martyrs of the war against the Somozas, not to offer an opening to those who had not marched behind the Sandinista colors. By creating the Council of State two months earlier, Ortega said, the Sandinistas had already "ratified their decision to guarantee political pluralism, which is nothing more than a reflection of the policy of unity that our

[Sandinista] vanguard has pushed since its foundation." He said there had been no change in the decision to hold elections, but he said they would not be the kind of elections known in the past in Nicaragua.

When the ceremony closed with the singing of the Sandinista anthem, McHenry led the U.S. delegation in a walkout because of the line in the song denouncing Americans as "enemies of humanity." But the walkout was done in a low-key manner. Nobody wanted to create a fuss.

Within a few hours, the U.S. delegation went to the airport to fly home. I asked Senator Zorinsky if he had been disappointed by the lack of a clear-cut election announcement, and he said he was not greatly disturbed. "I spoke to Daniel afterwards," the senator said, "and he has some valid points concerning the inability of Nicaragua to hold federal elections at this point in history. Somoza destroyed all the records, all the registrations, and in order to accomplish a fair election, there needs to be done a great deal of work in addition to what has already been done . . . But he did indicate that it certainly was on the priority list to accomplish in the aftermath of the revolution." As for Castro, Zorinsky said that if he was concerned about the possibility of a Reagan victory, he should never have attacked the Republican platform because that would only serve to win sympathy for Reagan. Another member of the U.S. delegation, VFW national commander Howard E. Vander Clute, Jr., wrote Larry Pezzullo a letter when he returned to his office in Washington that praised Pezzullo's efforts and commented: "As for the future, the Good Lord only knows, but we have done our level best."

Without the red-carpet treatment that greeted the official visitors to Managua during those days, another group of foreigners was waiting quietly and secretly in the wings. They were Salvadorans, leaders of the four organizations then fighting a guerrilla war in El Salvador. Most of them had come in from Havana in June, others in July just a few days before the anniversary. In May, while Larry Pezzullo was helping to resurrect peace between the Marxists and non-Marxists in Nicaragua, Fidel Castro had been making peace among the four Salvadoran Marxist guerrilla groups, which had a history of bloody disputes. In Havana, they were convinced to unite under what was called the Unified Revolutionary Directorate, known as the DRU, its Spanish acronym. The DRU was made up of the top three commanders from the four guerrilla organizations. Castro, as he had done with the Sandinistas less than two years earlier, had conditioned his assistance on unification.

Now, the question they were waiting in Managua to have answered was how much "solidarity" could they count on from the Sandinistas. During the past year, at least in public, Sandinista *comandantes* had always insisted that while they could do nothing to prevent individual Nicaraguans from going to El Salvador to fight alongside the guerrilla forces, the only thing they could or would do as a government was to give the Salvadorans their moral support. A key part of that, Tomás Borge and other Sandinistas had said often, was for the Sandinista Front to "consolidate" its control in Nicaragua. The same things had been expressed to Larry Pezzullo during these very weeks in mid-1980 as he explained the implications of the rider in the U.S. aid bill providing for a cut-off in the funds if the Sandinistas were found to be assisting guerrilla movements elsewhere in Central America. Sandinista leaders told Pezzullo they differed with the United States on the question of El Salvador but had no intention of involving themselves there.

Regardless, during the days before and after the first anniversary, the Salvadoran guerrilla leaders were received privately at least twice by members of the Sandinista National Directorate, including a dinner at the home of Humberto Ortega, the army commander, and a meeting with Bayardo Arce, another of the nine *comandantes* in the FSLN leadership. The Salvadorans, in documents captured later, said they had discussed with Ortega the establishment of a military headquarters in Nicaragua and that during the subsequent talks with Arce he had promised them ammunition. Arce reportedly also said the Sandinista army would absorb some of the weapons the Salvadorans were expecting to receive from Communist countries and transfer to the Salvadorans some of the Western-made rifles then used in Nicaragua. On the Monday after the anniversary, Yasir Arafat arrived as expected, and the Salvadorans had a meeting with him. Castro remained in the country, and his program for the next several days was in large measure private, leaving space for discussions on the same questions.

But Monday also established, as Larry Pezzullo had predicted, that this was still Nicaragua. In the afternoon, the angry officers of COSEP, the private enterprise and professional organization, went to the bar of the Hotel Camino Real and held a news conference. Whatever place Castro, Arafat, and the Salvadoran guerrillas might have in the Sandinista heart, in the Nicaraguan reality of the moment the private sector still controlled 60 percent of the economy, including 80 percent of the agricultural production, and was crucial to recovery.

Jorge Salazar, the head of UPANIC, the farmers' organization, said the failure to announce an election timetable had broken a commitment made by the Sandinistas during the post-midnight discussion the two sides had held in May. "Our surprise was great on Saturday when we heard only a superficial allusion in that sense from our commander of the revolution," Salazar said. "That was not what was agreed on." Irritated by Ortega's suggestion that the demands for elections were coming from people who had played no role in the insurrection, Salazar recalled that it was the COSEP groups that had called the general strike that lasted for weeks after the murder of Pedro Joaquín Chamorro Cardenal in January 1978, that a similar strike had been called by the private sector in September 1978, and that it had supported the strike called by the FSLN in June 1979. The Nicaraguan private sector, he said, had participated actively in the overthrow of Somoza and had shown a "progressive mentality" in accepting the need for social and economic change in Nicaragua. This, he said, did not seem to be widely understood.

In May, he pointed out, the question of whether private farmers would plant cotton had loomed large in the minds of the Sandinistas as they made their election promise. Now, in July, with the cotton in the ground and sprouting—270,000 acres had been planted, a respectable though far from record-breaking amount, mostly on private farms—the Sandinistas were failing to keep their part of the bargain. If an election timetable were not forthcoming, Salazar hinted that COSEP would have to reconsider its participation in the Council of State.

Disputing the Sandinistas' claim to be the only representatives of the interests of the "people," the business leaders said they were looking out for the people's interests in demanding elections. That was one of the things Nicaraguans wanted when they threw out Somoza, said Ismael Reyes, president of the Chamber of Industry as well as the Red Cross. This was not just some bourgeois notion. Who, Reyes asked, would believe the FSLN in the future if it did not comply with its promise on elections?

12

JORGE SALAZAR AND ELECTIONS

AUGUST TO NOVEMBER 1980

On August 23, 1980, the FSLN finally addressed the question that concerned Jorge Salazar and other non-Marxist business and political leaders. No pretense was made of doing it through the junta; the National Directorate made and announced the decision. The occasion was the ceremonial closing of the Literacy Crusade, at which President Rodrigo Carazo of Costa Rica, whose country had sent teachers to Nicaragua, was the guest of honor. Carazo, who had stayed away from the July 19 anniversary ceremony because Castro was there, used this occasion to make an indirect plea for free elections in Nicaragua, backed by a suggestion that he had the right to make this plea because of the help Costa Rica had provided in the overthrow of Somoza. Costa Rica, he said, had learned the lesson of history, ". . . that popular power emanates from the people in the election booth."

Rebuffing Carazo, Humberto Ortega, in the ninety-minute main speech, said demands for elections were part of a growing counter-revolutionary threat. He said the opposition was attempting to confuse uneducated people about what was important and that it intended to use "false elections" to bring a return to the time of "exploiters and oppressors." He read an FSLN communiqué declaring that there would be no elections until 1985, no political campaigning until 1984, and implying that the elections when they came would be different from those usually seen in Western nations. In stronger terms than ever, the FSLN declared itself the head of the nation, the sole guardian of the people's interests ("authentic vanguard and leader of the Nicaraguan people") and the one to determine the future path of Nicaragua. The communiqué said democracy was much more than elections, that the economy had to be rebuilt and reordered first, and the people prepared for political participation. Even then, it said, there would be no turning back on the program of the FSLN and that those elected would be expected to carry out that program. Because of the backward state in which the FSLN had found the country in 1979, Ortega said, it would be necessary to wait until 1985 to hold those elections.

"As you can all understand, the elections of which we are talking are very distinct from the elections that are wanted by the oligarchs and traitors, Conservatives and Liberals, the reactionaries and imperialists . . . ," Ortega said when he finished reading the communiqué. "Keep in mind that [ours] are elections to advance revolutionary power, not to raffle off power, because the people [already] have power through their vanguard, the Sandinista Front of National Liberation and its National Directorate." He asked those in the crowd, mostly teenagers, if they were in agreement that the FSLN Directorate continue exercising power, and they shouted *Sí.* "Then," declared Ortega, "this is a vote, a popular election. This is Sandinista Democracy."

Larry Pezzullo and Larry Harrison, the U.S. Embassy aid director, walked out during the speech, which included an attack on U.S. electoral proceedings. Harrison, watching the young people in uniforms as they responded to Ortega's words, was reminded of films he had seen of Nuremberg during the 1930s.

Ortega's words threw the opposition groups into shock. They had come to view elections as the pivotal issue in whether Nicaragua would go a totalitarian route or accommodate itself to some form of Western democracy. Just three days before the speech, four of the opposition parties (the Democratic Conservatives, Alfonso Robelo's MDN, the Social Christians, and the Social Democrats) had issued a joint demand for elections, citing the junta's written commitment to the OAS in July 1979 to call elections. The four parties included a proposed timetable to begin the election process the following year, with municipal voting. Two days after Ortega's speech they published the pronouncement as a full-page newspaper advertisement.

The speech, the opposition leaders feared, marked the beginning of radicalization of the regime. Contributing to this fear was the adoption two weeks later of three decrees, numbers 511, 512, and 513, which prohibited "disinformation" about the economy and security matters, and also prohibited the naming of candidates for public office prior to 1984. The two decrees affecting the media forbade reporting on such things as shortages or price rises in basic food items, shootings or battles involving opponents of the regime, strikes, land takeovers, or breakdowns in public services—unless the information came from, or had been confirmed by, the junta, the army or the Interior Ministry. While the decree on politics officially stated only that there would be elections in 1985 and no nominations before 1984, the Sandinistas and their media talked of restrictions on "political proselytizing," which could be more broadly interpreted.

Particularly angry at these developments was Jorge Salazar, the president of UPANIC. He had played a major role in convincing others in the opposition to accept the Sandinistas' secret election commitment in May. Now the FSLN had reneged on its promise and, in his words, "shown its colors as Marxist-Leninist. There is no doubt. Our big question now is what kind of elections." The opposition interpreted Ortega's announcement to mean that the Sandinistas had no intention of carrying out Western-style elections in a multi-party framework, that the main electing bodies would turn out to be the "mass organizations" of the FSLN. Salazar, however, was not one to give up. He felt confident in his own power base among the nation's large and small farmers. Even before Ortega spoke, he had quietly begun to search for his own way of settling the issue.

Jorge Salazar, then forty-one, was the only son of Leo Salazar, who had once managed the immense farm in Matagalpa, then belonged to the National Guard in its infancy and served as Somoza García's personal assistant. But Jorge had been born when his father's connections to that era were coming to an end. Growing up on the family coffee farm at Santa María de Ostuma, then studying at a military school in the United States and a university in Brazil, he came into adulthood with traditional Conservative Party views in opposition to the Somozas. However, they were the ambivalent views of someone not politically involved, of someone who was neither helped nor hindered by the regime in power.

As for the Sandinistas, he had always felt they were Marxists, even before they came to power, and he had no use for Marxism. But there was also an element of tolerance in his attitude toward the Sandinistas. It was forced on him by family circumstances: Some of his in-laws and eventually his own children shared the widespread romantic view of the small guerrilla band, a view shaped by the Sandinistas' bravery and audacity in their confrontations with the National Guard. Sometime in 1977, while Sandinista co-founder Tomás Borge was serving a prison sentence, Salazar's four adolescent children asked him to go with them to a vigil being held in support of Borge, then on a hunger strike. Lucía Cardenal de Salazar remembered her husband's reaction:

"He had good, close relations with the children, so he agreed to accompany them. But he said, 'I want you to understand something. He for whom we are going to go on strike and conduct vigils is a Communist. It's true that they are mistreating him and have him incommunicado and that he is a human being and should be treated as such, but he is a Communist . . . That man is going to kill me. It is not Somoza or the National Guard that will do it. The day that the Communists come into power here I am going to be dead.'

"That was two years before they came to power. I was more enthusiastic for the Sandinistas than he was, and he would tell me if I wanted to wear red and black that was fine, but not in that house. He worried a lot about what would happen if Somoza were thrown out. But when everybody got very enthusiastic and thought the Sandinistas were part of a pluralistic, democratic movement, he thought there was a chance."

Lucía Salazar was one of ten children of one branch of the big Cardenal family from Granada. Her father, Julio Cardenal, was one of thirteen siblings, so there were a lot of cousins of one degree or another. Lucía and Jorge's third child was the one-hundredth descendant of her grandfather Cardenal, who had married twice. Among the first cousins of Lucía's father were Pedro Joaquín Chamorro Cardenal and Fernando and Ernesto Cardenal, the two priests so closely involved with the FSLN from the early 1970s. The priests, infected with a large dose of guilt, looked on their extended family as too privileged and too decadent. Nevertheless, they maintained close family ties, especially Fernando. As a teacher and youth leader during the 1960s and 1970s, he influenced two generations of young men, including various of the Cardenals.

Three of Lucía's younger brothers became guerrillas, two joining the Sandinista Front and one going to El Salvador to join a guerrilla group there. One of them, Gabriel, a talented artist who did light-hearted propaganda drawings for the FSLN, was arrested by the National Guard and executed in the last days of the insurrection. Jorge Jr., the second child and only son of Lucía and Jorge, had been interested in the Sandinista movement from the age of about twelve, but he was not yet sixteen when Gabriel joined the FSLN, and Jorge Sr. asked Gabriel to leave his son alone until he was an adult and could make his own choice. Among Lucía's sisters, two were married to men who became Sandinistas and joined the new government. Another sister, Indiana, was married to Alfonso Robelo. Politics would strain or end various of the marriages in the first years of Sandinista rule. The eldest Cardenal brother, Alejandro, was part of the MDN, the political party that Robelo organized in 1978, and when Robelo joined the new junta in 1979, Alejandro became minister of tourism.

In 1978, Jorge Salazar, who had been raising cotton, moved his family from Managua back to the coffee farm and resort hotel that his parents operated at Santa María de Ostuma in Matagalpa. He set out to replant and improve the trees, and during the time of near-anarchy before and after the fall of Somoza he emerged as the natural leader of the region. He secured food supplies and saw to the care of farms that the Sandinistas, in the last weeks of the fighting, took over from fearful Somoza associates or collaborators who fled. Even after Leo Salazar left the country in February 1979 for fear of reprisals for his ties to the early days of the National Guard, Jorge and Lucía provided meals for the Sandinista guerrillas who camped on their farm.

But Salazar also saw a power and influence vacuum developing in the coffee region as the result of the imminent downfall of Somoza, who, as the owner of La Fundadora, had dominated the coffee business there. Therefore, while people in Managua worried about the timing of Somoza's departure, the future of the National Guard, and the makeup of the junta, he had traveled the mountains of Matagalpa and neighboring northern Zelaya and convinced several thousand small coffee growers to join the Matagalpa growers' cooperative. The cooperative had existed for a long time, but it had previously been of little consequence because of Somoza's towering presence.

These activities served as Salazar's springboard to national agricultural leadership. He was one of the founders of UPANIC, and became its president soon after the change of government. Under Salazar, the farmers quickly became the most outspoken group in COSEP.

When the Sandinistas sent farm organizers into the Matagalpa-northern Zelaya area in late 1979, they discovered to their dismay that Salazar had already won the allegiance of most of the growers, with 7,000 members in the Matagalpa cooperative. The Sandinistas, wanting to break Salazar's hold on the small growers, who constituted the bulk of the cooperative's members, sent a government delegation led by Jaime Wheelock to Matagalpa for a meeting with them in October 1979. The Matagalpa cooperative, instead of opposing the visit, helped organize the gathering and invited all its members; the movie theater in which they met was packed. Salazar shared the stage with Wheelock and various Cabinet and junta people.

Without referring to Salazar by name, Wheelock began telling the growers that it was easy to be a revolutionary after the war, without having fired a shot, and suggested that Salazar was not the growers' true representative. With that, everybody in the audience stood up and started banging on the chairs and walls to protest. When they quieted down, a leathery-skinned man in a straw hat asked Wheelock for permission to speak. Then he said, "That gentleman there," indicating Salazar, "is my representative and the representative of all of us because we elected him. If I go to Managua to the door of the National Palace, no one pays attention to me, but that gentleman there knows what is happening with us." The meeting broke up with the growers carrying Salazar out of the theater on their shoulders.

Many Nicaraguans quickly realized that the handsome and determined Salazar had enough charisma to put him almost in the same league with Edén Pastora and that his charisma definitely exceeded that of the nine *comandantes* on the National Directorate. For his part, Jaime Wheelock appealed to foreigners because of his English rock-star looks, but he lost points with Nicaraguans when the story of the encounter in the Matagalpa movie theater got around.

Despite this, relations between Salazar and the Sandinistas were outwardly civil. He fought, on legal grounds, many of the confiscations of farms and coffee processing plants in Matagalpa and the surrounding area. But Salazar also recognized the need to work with the Sandinista Front in rebuilding Nicaragua. Wheelock often said that he, as the government's top agricultural official, and Salazar, as the leader of private farming, should work together to make Nicaraguan agriculture successful. They even made some attempts at camaraderie. In addition, Salazar was one of the group of business and farm leaders who made the rounds of Capitol Hill in late 1979 and early 1980 to help convince Congress to extend aid to Nicaragua.

But in mid-1980 Jorge Salazar began to lead two very different lives, one that was public and law-abiding, another that was private and conspiratorial. A few days after the installation of the Council of State on May 4, a cousin of his, Alejandro Salazar, who had a coffee and cattle farm in Matagalpa, was approached by Dora María Lau de Lacayo, whom he had known since childhood and who asked him to meet with a nephew of hers. The nephew, Nestor Moncada, was a member of the Sandinista army, serving as an immigration official. He was in his early twenties. Moncada told Alejandro Salazar that some people within the army were unhappy with the Sandinistas' deviations from the democratic program and were prepared to start an uprising. He said they thought Jorge Salazar was the right person to organize and lead it, including formation of a new government.

Alejandro carried the message to his cousin, who at first was reluctant to become involved in the plot. Until then, he had thought only of using peaceful methods to oppose the Sandinistas. But over the next few weeks, he became increasingly concerned about the problems private farmers were having with the Sandinistas and also concluded that he and the others who had made the secret election pact with the Sandinistas at the beginning of May had been tricked. He decided, in Alejandro's words, that the only way to get the Sandinista leaders out of power was "to shoot them out." Moncada told Jorge that among the army officers, who then numbered only a few hundred, about one fourth would join such an uprising, and that if it were a surprise situation, they could take control.

In late June or early July, the two cousins began to talk to a few trusted friends and associates about the scheme. The first person they sought out was Alfonso Robelo, the MDN leader and former junta member. Besides being brothers-in-law, he and Jorge Salazar had been friends since boyhood. Alejandro caught up with the frequently traveling Robelo by telephone while both were in the United States, but Robelo wanted no part of the plan. He still favored using only "civic" means to oppose the Sandinistas. Alejandro thought that was tantamount to hitting the Sandinistas over the head with a handkerchief.

The Salazars also sought out Leonardo Somarriba, a businessman and vice president of the Chamber of Commerce, who agreed in early September to join the plot. Somarriba saw it as an attempt to remove the most radical Marxist-Leninist aspects from *sandinismo*. Mario Hanon, a major rice grower, was another who joined.

While Salazar's contacts in the Sandinista army had access to the arsenal, they told him they would arouse suspicions if they removed large numbers of weapons, so Salazar was asked if he could acquire arms elsewhere. In addition, Salazar and his civilian collaborators planned to distribute weapons to some of Salazar's rural followers. The general idea was that the army people would begin the uprising, arrest as many members of the Sandinista Directorate and other FSLN leaders as possible, then seize a radio station and announce that a change of power was under way. The armed civilians, once they heard the radio broadcast, would come to the aid of the rebels. They did not plan to shoot any of the Sandinista leaders, just arrest them. In case of subsequent differences within the insurgent ranks, it would be useful to Salazar to have several hundred armed people of unquestioned loyalty to him. He had learned the bitter lesson of the insurrection against Somoza. All of this required hundreds, maybe thousands, of automatic weapons. Most would have to come from outside of Nicaragua.

Traveling abroad, Jorge Salazar met with various opponents of the Sandinistas in exile—"anyone who wanted to fight for the liberation of Nicaragua," in Alejandro's words. That included Enrique Bermúdez, a former National Guard colonel, and José Francisco Cardenal, the former president of the Chamber of Construction who had left the country in anger after the May pact between COSEP and the Sandinista Directorate.

Bermúdez, who was serving in the Nicaraguan Embassy in Washington at the time of the downfall of Somoza, had been one of those considered to take over leadership of the National Guard in the ill-fated attempt to merge it with the Sandinista guerrilla army in July 1979. He had then stayed on in Washington, and eventually, with some financial help from Luis Pallais Debayle, Somoza's cousin, had organized a group of former National Guardsmen into the Fifteenth of September Legion. Named for the date of Central American independence from Spain, it was making plans to initiate armed actions against the Sandinista regime, but most of the actions then being reported were conducted by former Guardsmen not affiliated with Bermúdez who were rustling cattle and robbing farmers along the border in order to sustain themselves and their families inside Honduras.

Cardenal, after leaving Nicaragua in May, had reached an agreement with Bermúdez to combine their efforts—military and political—into a group called the Nicaraguan Democratic Revolutionary Alliance, or ADRIN, its Spanish acronym. Little had been accomplished by this new group when Cardenal and Raúl Arana, another former Managua builder who was part of ADRIN, met with Jorge Salazar in Miami and offered to help in his undertaking. Cardenal had been ruthless in his denunciation of Salazar and the others who had made the election pact with the Sandinistas, but he was willing to forgive, and help, anyone who saw the error of his ways. Salazar feared the political consequences of connecting his operation with the National Guard or *somocismo* and apparently rejected any direct collaboration with the former Guardsmen. Though he had no serious differences with Cardenal and Arana, he was concerned about the possible implications of their new alliance with the former Guardsmen. He wanted all of the armed action to be conducted by people still inside Nicaragua.

Nevertheless, Cardenal and Arana went to El Salvador in September to assist the search for arms. Cardenal had become friendly with Fidel Chavez Mena, the Salvadoran foreign minister, a few years earlier when Cardenal's construction company built a suburban shopping center in Managua that was owned by a Salvadoran industrial family for which Chavez was the lawyer. Chavez put Cardenal and Arana in touch with Colonel Jaime Abdul Gutiérrez, then the Salvadoran army commander and a member of the ruling junta. Cardenal and Arana had breakfast with Gutiérrez and told him that El Salvador should help overthrow the Sandinistas because, otherwise, the Sandinistas would foment the growing guerrilla activity in El Salvador. Cardenal asked Gutiérrez to make available to the Salazar group about a thousand automatic rifles and other military equipment that Nicaraguan National Guardsmen had surrendered to Salvadoran authorities when they arrived in El Salvador seeking refuge after the fall of the Somoza government in July 1979. While El Salvador shared no border with Nicaragua, most National Guardsmen who fought on the Southern Front had taken boats up the coast to El Salvador, then had continued to Honduras or Miami. Cardenal also wanted training facilities in El Salvador for a select group of former National Guardsmen, whom he envisioned infiltrating Nicaragua as part of the uprising. Gutiérrez told Cardenal to return in a week for another meeting, but Cardenal and Arana thought Gutiérrez was already sympathetic to the proposal.

Internal difficulties in the Salvadoran army caused a delay in the second meeting, and before Cardenal and Arana returned to El Salvador, Leonardo Somarriba and Jorge Salazar went there on their own. Again, the meeting with Gutiérrez was arranged by Chavez Mena, who was also friendly with Somarriba, who managed the shopping center that Cardenal had built. What was decided between them and Gutiérrez is unclear. Somarriba told me that Gutiérrez made no commitments, but Cardenal and Arana understood that Gutiérrez was willing to proceed as proposed in the first meeting, but preferred to deal directly with Salazar instead of the exiles.

Besides the visit to El Salvador, Somarriba and Salazar went to Honduras, where they met with the foreign minister, and to Venezuela, where they made their case to President Luis Herrera Campíns. Somarriba said they encountered sympathy in both Honduras and Venezuela, but nothing else.

On September 17, 1980, Anastasio Somoza Debayle was blown to bits as he drove through Asunción, Paraguay, his exile home, but by then Nicaraguans were almost too busy worrying about the present to appreciate this last break with the past. For a few frantic hours, the members of the National Directorate raced around Managua in open vehicles and led the cheering, but an early evening rain stopped the celebration. The next morning, when I visited the Eastern Market, a fifty-square-block area populated by thousands of vendors, most people seemed unmoved one way or another by the death of the man who just a little more than a year earlier had seemed all powerful in Nicaragua. Said one man: "He was a human being, so I am not happy for his death." Seven members of an Argentine guerrilla organization were identified as the killers, but the Paraguayan government claimed the Sandinistas were behind it. Two members of the junta denied that the Nicaraguan government had had anything to do with the killing, but no such denial was made in the name of the Sandinista Front.

From September into November, Jorge Salazar's clandestine group held various meetings with people from the Sandinista army, all brought by Nestor Moncada. There was concern among the civilians that their army contacts were not old enough or of sufficient rank for such an undertaking. The Salazars and their friends were new to both politics and armed activities. At one meeting after the planning was well under way Nestor Moncada announced that a man of higher status would come to the next session. He said it was someone who had great regard for Jorge Salazar.

When Moncada identified the new man, Jorge Salazar immediately expressed his trust and confidence. Alvaro Baltodano was a military intelligence officer from a prominent family who had come into the FSLN through Church connections and had been one of the survivors of the suicidal Sandinista attack on the National Guard barracks in Masaya in October 1977. His father, Emilio Baltodano, was controller-general of the government, and a brother, Emilio Jr., was minister-secretary of the junta. The father had been a member of *Los Doce,* the business-professional alliance that had improved the Sandinista image during the insurrection. Salazar had known Baltodano for most of his life. Lucía Salazar's mother and Baltodano's father were first cousins. Most significantly, Salazar had saved Alvaro Baltodano from bankruptcy a few years earlier, when Baltodano, then a cotton grower, had a couple of bad crops in a row. Salazar trusted the man he thought was still grateful for that. Baltodano took part in the succeeding meetings.

Meanwhile, Alfonso Robelo and his party were stepping up public criticism of the regime, effectively challenging the new decree limiting political activity. After spending six weeks in August and September visiting Western European and Latin American countries to meet with political figures, Robelo gave a speech to MDN militants on October 10 in which he complained of totalitarianism and militarism in Nicaragua. He said many people were being watched, that the internal security system and bureaucracy were expanding their control and influence over people's lives, that the FSLN was twisting Sandino's nationalistic ideas into a Marxist-Leninist context, and that Nicaragua's army was not a national army, but the army of a political party. "I ask myself," he said, "why is it the privilege of the Sandinista Front to have an army all its own?"

Jaime Wheelock of the Sandinista Directorate responded that Robelo should not think that just because the FSLN had taken power that the MDN also had the right to take power. Robelo was wrong to say the FSLN was an armed party, Wheelock said, because what was armed was "the people of Nicaragua, led by a directorate."

Antagonism between FSLN forces and Robelo supporters flared up beginning on November 7, when the Interior Ministry prohibited the MDN from holding a rally planned two days hence in Nandaime, a town forty miles southeast of Managua. The ruling said the rally fell within the new rules against "political proselytizing." Robelo went to see Borge on the day the prohibition was announced and asked, with a degree of frustration, what kind of civic life was available in Nicaragua to people such as he. He remembered the exchange this way: "Borge said, 'I want to make clear that we have the arms and are never going to put them down. We will use them to maintain this revolution.' I said, 'I guess that means I either have to stay as a vegetable or leave.' He said, 'Continue doing what you're doing. Maybe someday we can see things differently.' "

Borge later said he had told Robelo that internal security officials had information indicating that the former National Guardsmen operating out of Honduras planned attacks to coincide with the MDN rally. The FSLN was increasingly expressing concern about what it said was the growing incidence of anti-Sandinista military actions. Sandinista leaders also said Nicaraguan "reactionaries" would find solace in Ronald Reagan's victory in the U.S. elections, held a few days before the blowup over the MDN rally. In line with what Humberto Ortega had indicated on August 23, pressures from the opposition for elections and political liberties were now characterized as acts in support of counterrevolution.

Not only was the Nandaime rally prohibited, but news media were ordered not to report on the prohibition. The Interior Ministry ruled that news coverage of the prohibition fell under one of the new decrees. *La Prensa* managed to convey a sense of crisis by reporting in banner headlines on November 8 that it had been blocked from publishing anything about "the political act of the MDN in Nandaime" because it fell within the "*et cetera*" in decree 511. It also published large photographs of the three men with whom it had done interviews on the decision: Alfonso Robelo and junta members Arturo Cruz and Rafael Córdova Rivas. The caption said the interviews had been ordered withheld from publication.

That same day, a group of MDN youth, protesting the prohibition of their rally, went to a school in Managua where Sandinista youth were holding a ceremony, and the two groups burned the other's flags and fought. The Sandinista group called in reinforcements and mounted a large demonstration, and police arrested four of the MDN youths. On Sunday a hundred or more Sandinista demonstrators, chanting "People's Power" and "Down with the bourgeoisie," broke into the MDN headquarters, burned files, and destroyed a car and other equipment.

News reports of the Sunday fighting were also censored, but *La Prensa* again conveyed a sense that something was happening by carrying a front-page NOTE TO THE NICARAGUAN PEOPLE that said the newspaper lamented the fact that it was unable, because of censorship, to provide information on "the important occurrences that the Nicaraguan people know have been developing . . ." There was also this heavy black banner headline: DR. ARTURO CRUZ SAYS: WE HAVE TO INVESTIGATE. The brief story told of the junta member's visit to the newspaper offices and his expressions of concern about circumstances that were not fully revealed.

Robelo responded to the Nandaime prohibition by making his criticism of the Sandinistas blunter in interviews with the foreign media. He complained about the large number of Cubans in Nicaragua, which he said had reached 4,000, including teachers, medical personnel, and military and security people. When he visited Tomás Borge, he had noted that the chief of Borge's personal bodyguard detachment was a Cuban. Robelo said Nicaragua had become "a satellite of a satellite of the Soviet Union." Referring to the often-rumored differences among the nine men on the Sandinista Directorate, Robelo said the force that bound them together was Fidel Castro. "Nothing of real import is done without at least checking what Fidel thinks. He's the best adviser they have."

On November 11, COSEP issued a lengthy criticism of the regime containing many points similar to those Robelo was making. Among their points were the following: that the FSLN, by its August 23 announcement, had decided to stay in power indefinitely; that it was destroying what political pluralism existed in Nicaragua with decrees 511 to 513; that the army and police were controlled by a political party; that the FSLN was confusing its own interests with those of the state; and that the FSLN had aligned Nicaragua's foreign policy with Cuba's.

On November 12, 1980, three of the opposition political parties, the six COSEP representatives, and two labor federations walked out of the Council of State. The walkout was precipitated by the refusal of the council leaders to allow Alvaro Jerez, the MDN representative, to respond to a report by Borge on the attack on the MDN headquarters three days earlier. Outside the hall, one of the COSEP representatives read a list of demands that opposition groups had been proposing in the council. They included revocation of decrees 511 to 513 and the calling of municipal elections in 1982.

. . .

Jorge Salazar, recently back from a trip abroad, went to Matagalpa the weekend of November 15 and November 16 to attend a coffee growers meeting. Alejandro Salazar stayed in Managua. Late on Sunday evening, Mrs. Lacayo called Alejandro and said things were going sour, but he thought she was just nervous. He decided it was too late to go to her house without arousing suspicions—he knew he had been followed previously. The next morning he stopped by Jorge's house and waited for him to arrive from Matagalpa. Once Jorge had showered, they talked about the planned meeting that evening of the conspirators. At midday Jorge had a meeting of the COSEP directors. He asked Alejandro to go to the headquarters of UPANIC to receive a delegation of coffee growers coming in from Matagalpa. The group was unhappy with the withdrawal from the Council of State. They drove together in Alejandro's Cherokee to the COSEP headquarters, with a driver following in Jorge's Cherokee, then Alejandro continued to the UPANIC building, about twenty blocks away.

Jorge Salazar presided over the COSEP meeting. Enrique Dreyfus, the president, was out of the country. One of the things they discussed was the walkout from the Council of State. Salazar was also pushing a plan to create a united front of opposition political parties that would allow COSEP to withdraw from purely political disputes. When the meeting ended, about two-fifty in the afternoon, Salazar got into his Cherokee and drove out the South Highway. He was going to meet Nestor Moncada, and they were going to inspect a farm of Salazar's to determine whether it might serve as a place to store arms. The driver lived along the South Highway and Salazar dropped him off before reaching his own destination.

At UPANIC, meanwhile, Alejandro Salazar learned that Mario Hanon, the rice grower in their group, had been arrested. He decided to drive over to COSEP to look for Jorge. But as he passed the Lacayo house he noticed various jeeps and other vehicles of the type that Nestor Moncada had been using. He thought people were already assembling for the meeting scheduled later. He parked and went up to the door and rang the bell. Suddenly he was surrounded by armed men. The leader of the squad motioned to him, in a friendly way, to run. Instead, he stood transfixed and, for reasons he couldn't explain, began to count to himself the number of men pointing guns at him. There were fourteen.

About the same time, Jorge Salazar was pulling into the abandoned Esso station at El Crucero, twelve miles south of Managua, where he was to meet Moncada. The farm they were going to visit was just across the road. Salazar parked and got out of his vehicle, the keys in his hand. He was unarmed. A few minutes later a white car carrying uniformed Sandinista security agents pulled into the gas station from the highway and opened fire. Salazar died with seven bullets in his body. Exactly what happened between the time Salazar stepped down from his vehicle and the arrival of the security police is subject to dispute. State security officials said at a news conference shortly after the killing that Salazar had been caught in crossfire. They claimed the man he was meeting, whom they did not name, opened fire on the agents as they tried to arrest the pair and the agents fired back. But in legal depositions taken later, one of the government's own witnesses, someone who had been standing beside the highway near the scene of the shooting, said the only firing came from the car carrying the *compas*—the Nicaraguan term for people in Sandinista military or police uniforms. Alejandro Salazar, whose wife and a grown son conducted their own investigation, said they found other witnesses who said someone first walked up to Jorge and shot him twice in the face at close range. According to that version, he fell wounded to the ground and was trying to crawl under his vehicle when the car drove in from the highway and two men in uniforms threw open the doors and began firing.

An hour later, with the body still on the pavement, security officials summoned people who lived or worked nearby and showed them a burlap bag containing six M-16 rifles that they supposedly found in the back of Salazar's vehicle. However, Alejandro Salazar said the witnesses interviewed by his wife and son said the security agents took the bag of rifles out of their own car with the intention of planting them.

Leonardo Somarriba, another member of the Salazar group, was picked up at his office about five o'clock the same afternoon of the killing and taken to the new internal security jail above the Bunker. Alejandro Salazar, Mario Hanon, Mrs. Lacayo, and her husband Gabriel, were also taken there and kept separately for interrogation.

Somarriba did not know yet what had happened to Salazar, whom he had last seen the previous Friday. He learned it the next day, when Tomás Borge came to see him and showed him a newspaper.

"They put me in an office, then Humberto Ortega and Tomás Borge and Lenín Cerna [chief of state security], and others came. They started shouting at me all at once. At first, I denied everything. Humberto Ortega asked if anyone knew I had been captured . . ." Somarriba took the remark as a threat.

"Borge told them all to leave. Then he seemed to go for his gun, but he took it off and gave it to an assistant to take outside, and he started talking, very friendly, a stick and carrot mix. He said he was very grateful to my father, who was a doctor in Matagalpa and had been kind to him and his mother as a child. His mother was of humble origins. He finally persuaded me they had all the pieces of the story, so I agreed to make a deposition."

Great cries of anguish erupted from both the Sandinista and opposition sides after the killing. Tomás Borge and other security officials said Salazar was a traitor who had been plotting to overthrow the regime. The Sandinista leaders acted the incensed, outraged potential victims of Salazar's plotting. However, Daniel Ortega, the Sandinista who sat on the junta, said the episode would not affect overall relations between the FSLN and the business community.

Salazar's friends and followers, most of them surprised by his double life, said he was a patriot and martyr who had been drawn into a trap laid by the expanding state security apparatus. COSEP called it "a political crime directed against a man of peace and work." His friends said he had been motivated only by a desire to return Nicaragua to the political commitments made at the time of the fall of Somoza. The Democratic Conservative Party asked why the Sandinista *comandantes* didn't give serious thought to why someone like Salazar had been driven to conspire against them.

One of the disturbing aspects of his killing to the opposition was that—like the killing of Pedro Joaquín Chamorro Cardenal during the Somoza era—it seemed to change the rules of the game. Did it mean that in a country without the death penalty opposition was to be dealt with by assassination? Why, it was asked, had he not been arrested and tried? The killing also shook the government itself. Salazar had friends and relatives there. Several of the political moderates, including Arturo Cruz on the junta, considered resigning, and Alejandro Cardenal, one of Salazar's brothers-in-law, did resign his ministerial post. There were allegations inside the government that Borge's security system had been allowed too much independence. At Salazar's crowded funeral, people chanted: "Who killed Jorge? Tomás Borge."

Within a month a total of seven civilians were found guilty of plotting to overthrow the government and were sentenced to prison terms ranging from eleven years for Mrs. Lacayo to two years for her husband, but the sentences were reduced by the appeals court. Then the Supreme Court, critical of the government's case, ordered everybody freed in less than a year.

Alvaro Baltodano, the man Salazar had once helped and whom he instinctively trusted, was the government's star informant. After testifying about the meetings in which he participated with Jorge Salazar and others, he returned to work. Nestor Moncada was tried by a military court on the conspiracy charges, but never imprisoned.

During the months in jail, including twenty-seven days in solitary confinement, Somarriba's mind was awash with theories about how the Sandinistas had laid the trap for them. Like other friends and relatives of Salazar's, he concluded that the Sandinistas created the plot in order to eliminate the most charismatic of the opposition figures, the one who might have most easily attracted a mass following. He could only wonder whether the dissident faction of the army had ever existed, whether Moncada had been sincere at the beginning, then been trapped himself, or whether he had been part of the trap all along.

"Jorge represented a real threat to them," Somarriba told me after he was freed and moved to Miami. "He would have made a great politician . . . If you ever saw him at farm meetings, it was incredible. He really had a following. Jorge was very outspoken. He had no respect for the FSLN. He shouted at them. He was not afraid of them. He said they were full of shit, and they resented him. They coldbloodedly eliminated him."

The killing of Salazar speeded up the hardening of lines between the Sandinista Front and the opposition that had been occurring since the previous April, when Violeta Chamorro and Alfonso Robelo resigned from the junta. Nobody gave up in the struggle over the future of Nicaragua, but both sides became tougher. Each side would have liked to bring the other to its knees, but each knew that was impossible. One of the things the Sandinista Front began doing in an attempt to overcome its problems with those involved in economic production was to meet with business and farm groups independent of the COSEP structure with the idea of winning them away from organized private enterprise.

About two weeks after Salazar's death, one such meeting with cotton growers and businessmen in León erupted into pandemonium. Three members of the junta, including Daniel Ortega, went to the meeting trailed by pro-government media representatives, including Sandinista Television, plus diverse security people. The farmers and businessmen refused to go into the meeting until the government press was excluded. After they went in, one of the government people recognized a *La Prensa* correspondent in the room and expelled him.

One of the participants in the meeting, however, kept a hidden tape recorder running, which provided a record of the meeting.

The session began with a speech by one of the businessmen, who said they wanted to cooperate in rebuilding the economy, but that the government was not listening to the productive sectors. He said the same attitude now prevailed toward the organized private sector that had prevailed in the time of Somoza, who had tried to split COSEP and had sometimes interfered in the business activities of those who did not support him. The remark infuriated Daniel Ortega, who responded by telling the hundred or so men in the meeting that they were "sons of bitches and cuckolds" whose only interest was in their pocketbooks. He said there was no sense talking to them and stormed out. Everybody started talking and yelling at once, and Lenín Cerna, the chief of state security, jumped up and said, "You're all under arrest!" One of the men in the room shouted, "Okay. Pick the cotton yourself!"

However, there was no massive flight of non-Marxists from the country. Small numbers of people were leaving regularly, but most did so because of the deteriorating economy rather than specifically political reasons. Salazar's killing was still taken to be an exception to the general understanding that the postinsurrection disputes would be handled without violence, and the two sides continued to talk to each other during occasional attempts at conciliation. Salazar had often made a point of saying after the Sandinistas came to power that the business and professional leadership had an obligation to remain in Nicaragua "at the side of the people," and after his death his friends distributed a poster with a photograph of him and a quotation from one of his speeches that began: "We are neither going to Miami, nor are we going to submit . . ."

Inadvertently, he had described the defiant mood that would prevail after his death. Those who thought as he did continued to insist that they had a right to remain in Nicaragua and a right to influence the political and economic future of the country. The Sandinista Front, by contrast, wanted them to work and produce according to the rules laid down by the Bulgarian economists who were advising the Planning Ministry, and to stay out of politics. None of that was acceptable to the opposition.

Ramiro Gurdian, a banana grower and cattleman from the department of Chinandega, was elected to replace Salazar as president of

UPANIC. He was no less confrontational toward the FSLN, but he did all he could to avoid any connection with subversive or potentially subversive activities. He was convinced that the Sandinistas needed private enterprise, especially the farmers, if Nicaragua were to avoid becoming a permanent basket case. Yet, whenever he had a nightmare, it was about his farm being confiscated. One day, driving toward the farm at the foot of a volcano, he told me that private enterprise and the Sandinista Front were like a frog and a scorpion trying to get across a river together.

"It's as if I'm the frog, and I've got the Sandinista Front on my back, and we're swimming across the river. The Sandinistas can kill me any time they want to. But if they kill me, they're going to drown. That's the way it is. If they kill private business in this country, they are going to sink themselves."

In that same conversation I asked Gurdian what he, as someone not politically involved at the time, had expected when the new government took power in mid-1979.

"I thought that we were going to have a free society, with a free press, with elections, with a very good legal system in which the Supreme Court was going to have power for the first time."

Why did he believe this?

"Because I saw so many other democratic countries supporting it, all the Andean Pact countries,* Costa Rica, the United States, also *La Prensa,* the archbishop, the Church, Alfonso Robelo, Edén Pastora. So I thought, if the United States and Carlos Andrés Pérez are backing this revolution, how can it be wrong? I mean, they are respectable people, and they must know, I thought, what is going on. But I learned my lesson. They didn't know what was going on."

---

*The Andean Pact countries are Venezuela, Colombia, Ecuador, Peru, and Bolivia.

13

THE VANGUARD

While such key practical considerations as the economy and Nicaragua's geographical location seemed to require that the Sandinistas respond to demands for political and economic pluralism, the Sandinistas had by the end of 1980 declared themselves the owners of the truth, and that truth told them something different. It told them that Nicaragua's correct path was one laid out by the nine *comandantes* —the Vanguard. They were the new elite, an elite based not on land and money and guns, but on ideological formation, party discipline, and guns. In setting goals and policies the Vanguard could do no wrong. Demands for, and questions about, such things as pluralism and living at peace in Central America were now brushed off. The Sandinista leaders learned to react to those questions with a tone of condescension. The person who asked them was to be pitied and treated with patience, for he or she had not had the same advantages, had not experienced the same kind of conversion or enlightenment as they. In polite conversation, such a challenger was likely to be dismissed with an admonishment to read more history.

There would no longer be debate over political legitimacy, over who was to hold power, or over who was to decide who held power. That was reserved for the Vanguard. Elections would not change that. Elections would only confirm "revolutionary power." The Vanguard ruled for "the people," and the Vanguard knew what was good for the people. *"Dirección Nacional: Ordene!"* became one of the FSLN's favorite slogans, a way of saying that one was at the orders of the National Directorate. It was another import from Cuba. It appeared on billboards and banners, on television and in *Barricada. La Prensa* belittled it. Individual opponents clicked their heels when they said it—in private. The "process" was declared the property of the FSLN and everyone who opposed it was an enemy, not just of the FSLN but also of the people.

The Sandinistas expected approval, especially from outsiders, not on the basis of what they did but on the basis of their claims to be the government of the people, to be helping the poor, curing the sick, educating the illiterate. They refused to be judged on how they reached their decisions or their refusal to share the right to make those decisions. To suggest that there was little, if any, difference between the methods the Sandinista Front used in governing Nicaragua and the methods that Somoza had used or that General Pinochet used in Chile was to be told that what mattered was that Somoza and Pinochet had only demogogic ends while the Sandinistas worked toward greater philosophical and social ends.

The nine members of the National Directorate, by retaining at least outward unity once in power, confounded the critics and analysts who had thought there was no way that nine men with their history of differences could share power on an indefinite basis. Despite their unified face, some were obviously more powerful than others. And despite the attitudes each held when they assumed power, the role that each carried out once in power would do much to shape his views. Figuring out all of this, along with the changing tides of power and influence, became an important pastime in Managua.

From the December 1979 purge of the Cabinet onward, the nine *comandantes* individually filled a broad range of jobs that gave them power over the major aspects of Nicaraguan life, either through what were traditional executive branch functions or through what were traditional party functions. Four of the nine held Cabinet posts in charge of ministries that operated autonomously of the junta, empires in themselves; another led the junta; one was a key deputy minister; and two exerted major influence in party positions.

Humberto Ortega, as minister of defense, controlled an armed force that already was, in 1981, the largest in Central America and growing quickly, that had the beginnings of a tank force and plans for modern warplanes. This, coupled with his background as the masterful but withdrawn strategist of the Sandinistas' alliance with the bourgeoisie that brought them to power, often made him appear the definitive voice among the nine. But Tomás Borge as interior minister controlled the police and internal security apparatus, including an elite army of several thousand men who had had the advantages of the best Cuban training for gathering information and interrogating people. The power to arrest and to use information, backed by his own military force, made Borge an imposing figure.

Though he held no formal government title, Bayardo Arce was the *comandante* whose power came closest to matching that of Humberto Ortega and Borge. Educated as a journalist, he was elected president of the Council of State when it was organized on May 4, 1980, but later that post was passed to Carlos Nuñez, who had a reputation as being the diplomat among the nine.* Arce, however, assumed direction of a broad range of activities having to do with propaganda and ideology. This covered two crucial areas: the media and the Sandinistas' mass support organizations, such as the block committees and the Sandinista Youth. In addition, Arce began to oversee foreign policy matters for the National Directorate. He was the man at the top in a shadow foreign ministry that superseded the regular ministry in crucial matters. In addition, Arce, like Humberto Ortega, played a major role in relations between the FSLN and the Salvadoran guerrillas— the Farabundo Martí National Liberation Front.

Jaime Wheelock, as minister of agriculture, had power, or potential power, over food and land, and this also encompassed prices paid to farmers and the size of export crops. To many, these were the most important elements in Nicaragua, but no guns went with the agriculture portfolio, a fact that limited his potential for wielding power. Henry Ruiz, the planning minister, became the economic czar, the man who held veto power over virtually all economic decisions. Contributing to his importance was the fact that he was the only one of

---

*Nuñez occasionally damaged this reputation, as when he labeled *La Prensa* the "newspaper of infamy."

the nine to have studied in the Soviet Union—though he had left Patrice Lumumba before graduating—and was seen, whether accurately or not, as the one with the most direct channel to the Kremlin.

Daniel Ortega, Humberto's older brother, as the dominant member of the junta was theoretically head of government. To the outside world he was the authority figure in Nicaragua. His power, however, was largely dependent upon the arms and strategies of his brother and the concurrence of the other *comandantes*. That Daniel should have been picked for the figurehead role instead of Humberto might be explained by various factors. He was marginally less shy and withdrawn than Humberto. He also had the distinction of having spent seven years in one of Somoza's prisons during the time Humberto was associated with some less noble undertakings in democratic Costa Rica—a shootout in which the Sandinistas killed one Costa Rican Civil Guardsman and wounded two.

Of the remaining two members of the National Directorate, Luis Carrión Cruz became deputy interior minister under Borge and was noted as the one most prepared to argue and expound upon social and political theory. He was also the member from the most privileged family background, which did nothing to soften his criticism of the bourgeoisie. Victor Tirado, born in Mexico but a part of the FSLN since its early days, was the least powerful of the group. He had no permanent government function but had cultivated a reputation as being accessible and able to get along with everybody.

On the basis of the old division of the FSLN into three factions, the Ortega brothers and Tirado represented the *terceristas,* the group that had forged the alliance with the non-Marxist opposition to Somoza; Borge, Ruiz, and Arce represented the Prolonged War Faction; and Wheelock, Carrión, and Nuñez were the Proletarian leadership. These factions had to do with strategies for reaching power, not methods of governing.

Once the Sandinistas had been in power for a while, observers and analysts detected new alignments, under which the nine *comandantes* were generally divided into two camps that went by various names, generally meaning "hard-line" and "pragmatic." The designations did not refer to greater or lesser degrees of Marxism-Leninism, but to how much accommodation they might make to non-Marxist Nicaraguans and to the United States in the interests of retaining power and reaching their long-term goals. These new divisions seemed in part the result of day-to-day experiences in their areas of responsibility.

In this division, Wheelock was generally identified as the most pragmatic, in part because his proletarian approach had convinced him that Nicaragua still had not passed through enough of the phases on the road to Marxism, but also because he wanted to adopt economic policies that would encourage private farmers to remain in Nicaragua and produce. The Ortega brothers were generally classified as pragmatists, too, as was Carlos Nuñez. On the so-called hard-line side fell Arce, Borge, Ruiz, and probably Carrión Cruz. They were less concerned about the effect of the flight of educated and trained people, less willing to concede ideological points in the interests of social peace. They were capable of saying there would be a Marxist revolutionary Nicaragua or no Nicaragua at all. Ruiz could describe himself to other members of the government as a "prisoner of ideology."

Some interpretations also put Humberto Ortega in the hard-line camp as the years passed. Despite his key role in the 1977 pact with the bourgeoisie, his preoccupation, once in power, was with military hardware and security, which put a different coloration on his views. These military concerns, and the frequent exposure to Cuba and the Soviet Union that went with them, led him to downplay the need to keep relative peace with the opposition. His Soviet bloc contacts did not condition their help on human rights protection and political pluralism, as did the United States and some other Western nations. What had seemed important and logical while sitting in a suburb of San José, Costa Rica, in the mid-1970s plotting against Somoza hardly seemed relevant once he had sat around a table at the Kremlin. Daniel, by contrast, traveled to Western countries as often as to Socialist bloc nations and received a steady stream of U.S. congressmen and officials from democratic Latin American governments and Western Europe. He had to listen to constant reminders of the rights of the opposition.

Only one person who was not on the Sandinista National Directorate proved capable of making a significant place for himself in the power structure. He was Sergio Ramírez, the writer and intellectual who had been a civilian member of the FSLN since the early 1970s and had collaborated with Humberto Ortega in creating the alliance with the bourgeoisie. When Ramírez was named to the junta during its creation in Costa Rica in June 1979, journalists labeled him a social democrat and some predicted that he would be the "swing vote" on the governing body, with Daniel Ortega and Moisés Hassan to the left of him and Robelo and Violeta Chamorro to the right. But the junta proved irrelevant in running the country, and Ramírez turned out to be totally loyal to the views and decisions that emerged from the Sandinista National Directorate. After the junta was reduced from five men to three in early 1981 and Daniel Ortega became its "coordinator," Ramírez was named "counselor" to Ortega. But it was not clear whether he exerted real influence on policy or merely tried to interpret National Directorate decisions and make them palatable. A man with a hulking frame, brooding eyes, and a soft voice, he was a talented enigma and perhaps the only real politician in the Sandinista leadership. Friends said that he went through periods of severe emotional crisis in the early years of the new government, some having to do with the education of his children under the new order. But his skill with words made Ramírez indispensable to the Sandinistas. He could make tough and totalitarian positions sound mild and logical. He could explain and justify radical policies in a framework of Western liberal theory. He could deflect criticism and turn it back against the questioner. But what he himself thought almost no one knew.

Many civilians other than Ramírez served in high-level government posts, Sandinistas and non-Sandinistas, but none appeared to exert real influence on policy. Most were useful for either their image, such as Arturo Cruz on the junta and the various priests in the Cabinet, or for specific expertise, such as banking and finance.

The Sandinista leaders, as they increased their control, did not formally reject the Plan of Government that had been drawn up in 1979 in collaboration with the moderate opponents of Somoza, but it was increasingly made clear that the FSLN would decide what constituted compliance. It would not concede on any point that violated its ideology in a substantive way. Little by little, references to the "Historic Program of the FSLN"—adopted in 1969 while the Sandinistas were a small, clandestine organization—slipped into declarations and decrees, supplanting the Plan of Government as the underlying logic of decisions. While there were some similarities, the Historic Program was focused more toward the formation of a "revolutionary state" than was the Plan of Government, promised more drastic measures for state control of the economy, and was less clear on civil and human rights issues.

Though the way they ruled was increasingly Marxist-Leninist, the Sandinistas said little in public to acknowledge it. But on June 23, 1981, Humberto Ortega set out the Vanguard's view in blunt terms in a speech to a gathering of Sandinista army and militia officers. It was not a public event, and when copies of the speech were circulated later by the government, the most controversial parts had been deleted. These quotes are from the original:

". . . our revolution has a profoundly anti-imperialist character, profoundly revolutionary, profoundly classist; we are anti-Yankee, we are against the bourgeoisie, we are inspired by the historic traditions of our people, we are inspired by *sandinismo,* which is the most beautiful tradition of this people, developed by Carlos Fonseca, we are guided by the scientific doctrine of the revolution, by Marxism-Leninism.

"We were saying that Marxism-Leninism is the scientific doctrine that guides our revolution, the instrument of analysis of our Vanguard for understanding [the revolution's] historic process and for carrying out the revolution; *sandinismo* is the concrete expression of the historical development of the fight in Nicaragua. Without *sandinismo* we cannot be Marxist-Leninists, and *sandinismo* without Marxism-Leninism cannot be revolutionary. For that reason they are indissolubly united and for that reason our moral force is *sandinismo,* our political force is *sandinismo,* and our doctrine is Marxism-Leninism."

Ortega repeated the assertion of the 72-hour Document that the FSLN had made the pact with the moderate opposition only for the purposes of getting rid of Somoza, holding off U.S. intervention, and keeping the economy in place. That pact having been made, he said, did not mean the FSLN was going to obey any bourgeois program for the country. The unity pact, in the view of the Sandinista Front, had been the way of least sacrifice for the Nicaraguan people on the road to inevitable Sandinista rule. All of the non-Marxists who had been allied with the FSLN against Somoza were now declared the enemy.

Those people and groups, he said, mentioning by name only Alfonso Robelo, wanted a political system for Nicaragua similar to that of Costa Rica. Ortega agreed that Costa Rica had a system superior to other countries of Central America in socioeconomic terms, but he said that while Costa Rica had reduced the exploitation of man by man, it had not eliminated it. He also acknowledged that the Left was allowed to participate in the political process in Costa Rica, but he said that whenever the Left appeared to threaten the existing system then the bourgeois power structure blocked its freedom of action.

"That is the democracy that Robelo asks, that is the democracy that Robelo wants; that they [the bourgeoisie] have the army, the power, and that we Sandinistas be what the Left is in Costa Rica, a sector, an organization that is free to move about, that publishes its newspaper, but that they, the bourgeoisie, be the ones to control power. Now it is the reverse. Here in Nicaragua power is held by *sandinismo*. The people have it. And they [the bourgeoisie] must be, insofar as we want them to be, a political force that moves within the limits that the revolution has imposed. That's the way it has to be.

"They do not want to conform, and they have spoken of elections from the beginning, but we have not compromised ourselves with the elections that they think we are going to promote. And we are never —we have already said it on other occasions through the National Directorate—going to discuss power, because the people took this power with arms. The power of the people will never be in play here."

14

THE *CONTRA*
AND RONALD REAGAN

FEBRUARY 1981 TO JULY 1982

One day in late February 1981, a few hours after I arrived in Managua from El Salvador, a taxi driver asked if I happened to know whether it was true that the Marines were preparing to land in Nicaragua. It was not so much that the possibility perturbed him; it was that he wanted to be able to plan ahead.

His question seemed prompted by the near-hysteria emanating from the Sandinista leadership, the result not of the attacks along the border with Honduras but of two major foreign events the previous month that had an overlapping impact in Nicaragua. Ronald Reagan had been inaugurated President of the United States, and guerrillas of the Farabundo Martí National Liberation Front had mounted a large-scale, but unsuccessful, offensive in El Salvador.

In recent days the State Department had issued a White Paper based on captured documents revealing that the Salvadoran guerrillas had been armed for the offensive with weapons shipped from various Soviet bloc and Arab countries through Nicaragua. United States economic assistance to Nicaragua had been suspended in reprisal, including concessionary wheat sales. The Sandinista press was now proclaiming in banner headlines that Ronald Reagan was taking bread from the mouths of Nicaraguans. If this had happened, could the Marines be far behind?

In fact, the issue had been quietly developing before Reagan's election. In October 1980 the State Department had told the Sandinistas that it had reports that they were assisting the Salvadoran guerrillas and had warned that such assistance violated one of the conditions Congress had placed on economic aid to Nicaragua. The aid agreement between the United States and Nicaragua had not been signed until October 17, 1980, even though much of the money had already been disbursed. Part of the reason for the delay was State Department concern about whether Nicaragua would live up to the condition of the agreement. A week before the signing, Ambassador Pezzullo and James Cheek, a deputy assistant secretary of state, spent many hours talking with top Sandinistas about the condition and the consequences of violating it. The Sandinistas indicated they had no difficulties with the condition and had signed. Not until late December or early January, Pezzullo said, did the United States get a fuller picture of how much Nicaragua was helping the Salvadoran guerrillas.

In the weeks and months following the aid cutoff, the *comandantes* made an indignant defense of their right to identify with what they viewed as just causes elsewhere, without admitting outright that they had shipped or forwarded arms to the Salvadoran guerrillas. Daniel Ortega declared that the right to "express solidarity with El Salvador" had been won by the Sandinistas in their victory over Somoza. The Sandinistas cast themselves as the weak, innocent victims of a tough, new administration in Washington. The United States, they charged, was committing an act of aggression by cutting off aid at a time when Nicaragua, by all admissions, was already heading into an economic crisis. They viewed the aid, especially the wheat, as a birthright, something that had always been available to Nicaragua, and always should be available regardless of other circumstances.

Behind this anguish lay the fact that the United States had been the major aid donor to Nicaragua in the first two years of the new government. Despite the greater praise and publicity the Sandinistas had given to the aid from Soviet bloc sources, it was the hard-currency help from the United States and other Western nations that kept their government afloat. When aid was suspended, the United States had already disbursed more than $118 million since the change of government in July 1979, and in the next few months it disbursed $10 million that had been in the pipeline to nongovernmental organizations. Immediately lost to Nicaragua by the cutoff was $15 million in undisbursed money from the 1980 funds and $35 million from the 1981 aid budget.

The State Department said this was not a formal termination of aid, that it did not yet consider Communist domination of Nicaragua to be a _fait accompli,_ and that it hoped the Sandinistas would see their error and halt assistance to the Salvadoran guerrillas. There was a hint that aid would be resumed after a "testing period."

Larry Pezzullo began to pressure the _comandantes_ to end their involvement with the Salvadorans but without demanding an outright confession of guilt. He thought it should be done without making them lose face. He also reasoned that the Sandinistas may have been drawn into the venture by a sense of obligation to Fidel Castro. While Castro had often said in public that he understood the need of the Sandinistas to maintain political pluralism and good relations with the United States, Pezzullo thought that in private Castro was leading the Sandinistas down another road. If so, Pezzullo still wanted to give them the chance to turn around. He also thought it was possible that Nicaraguan participation in the arms supply operation may have been limited to certain _comandantes_ rather than the entire group. If so, the Sandinista leadership might be able to straighten out the problem internally.

U.S. intelligence found that the arms traffic slowed or ceased by March, and some in the State Department wanted to resume aid. But the dominant argument in the Reagan administration was that the interruption in arms traffic resulted not so much from a change of heart by the Sandinistas as from the fact that the Salvadoran guerrillas probably did not need weaponry at that point because they had eased up operations after the offensive and had stock on hand. The administration also faced opposition from a few outspoken anti-Communists, such as Senator Jesse Helms, who wanted to call in the loans that had already been extended and demand immediate repayment, which was also possible as a condition of the aid. With a delay of several months in naming an assistant secretary for inter-American affairs to replace William Bowdler, who had been abruptly fired, the Reagan administration found it easier to devote its attention to El Salvador, which seemed a clear-cut situation to Secretary of State Alexander Haig, while Nicaragua presented endless complexities.

The mood between the United States and Nicaragua, however, was clear in a visit to Managua in late April by three Democratic members of Congress: Senators Thomas Eagleton of Missouri, Christopher Dodd of Connecticut, and Representative Michael Barnes of Maryland. The meeting between them and Daniel Ortega and other officials was tense and hostile, accompanied by name-calling and language problems. While Dodd and Barnes took it in a subdued manner, Eagleton dismissed Nicaragua as a dictatorship, "ninety-nine percent in the Cuban camp." He said that Daniel Ortega "wants the Cubans to run his army and educational system and wants the United States to finance it."

By May 1981, U.S. officials in Washington had concluded that the ties between Salvadoran guerrillas and the Sandinistas were as strong as ever. Indeed, Salvadoran guerrilla leaders were making public appearances in Managua, which was the headquarters of their high command. Among other Salvadoran guerrilla undertakings in Nicaragua was the tower and operations center for their clandestine radio station, on the side of Coseguïna Volcano, just across the Gulf of Fonseca from El Salvador.

At the same time, the Sandinistas were involved in several military and economic aid deals that softened the blow from Washington while, in some cases, adding to the friction. The Libyan government extended Nicaragua a loan of $100 million. Essentially a deposit in Nicaraguan banks at interest, it allowed Nicaragua use of the hard currency for an indefinite period. Mexico, in addition to oil sales at preferential prices, made the first payment on what would total $150 million in aid in the next year and a half.

Further, the FSLN secretly received about thirty Soviet-built, second-hand T55 tanks and stored them near Managua. The tanks probably arrived at the beginning of 1981, but their presence did not become known publicly until the Reagan administration complained about them in June. It was the beginning of a tank force that would reach one hundred and fifty by mid-1984. The Sandinista leadership declared its right to acquire arms wherever it could, citing the renewed U.S. military aid to El Salvador and the increase in the formerly minuscule military assistance to Honduras. Tomás Borge, talking about Nicaragua's arms buildup, said in a speech in mid-1981: "Whatever the brand might be, from whatever part of the world, we don't have to explain to anyone where those arms, those rifles, those cannons come from. They are going to defend the revolution and the people." The Sandinista Army was, by early 1981, estimated to number between 30,000 and 40,000, and was still growing. In addition, a part-time militia was being created that would substantially exceed the regular army in size.

Pezzullo discounted the Sandinistas' argument that they were arming themselves against implied U.S. threats that had been made since the installation of the Reagan administration. He said the deal for the tanks, which came from Algeria, probably had been made prior to January 1981, the month when U.S.-Sandinista differences became public. He thought the Sandinistas had, in fact, decided to acquire them by early 1980, when they were already beginning to feud with Honduras over questions that at that time only marginally involved the former National Guardsmen who had taken refuge in Honduras.

Into this atmosphere of mutual distrust, then, came Humberto Ortega's June 1981 speech declaring Marxism-Leninism the guide of the Nicaraguan revolution, and the antagonism began to compound.

There was still little impact inside Nicaragua from those conspiring against the Sandinista Front from outside. The attempted alliance between former National Guardsmen and José Francisco Cardenal, the former president of the Chamber of Construction who had tried to acquire arms for Jorge Salazar's ill-fated operation, had fallen apart about the time of Salazar's death in November 1980. The problems had to do with control, money, and political philosophy. Also, Cardenal and his civilian collaborators were bothered by the image question of associating with the former Guardsmen, which they feared hurt them internationally and inside Nicaragua. Their organization, ADRIN, had accomplished little in its short life-span except to begin some political organizations in various U.S. cities and Costa Rica.

After the split, the National Guardsmen, led by Enrique Bermúdez, resumed use of their old name, Fifteenth of September Legion, and made connections with the Argentine military, then in power. Some seventy or eighty former Guardsmen, including Bermúdez, went to Argentina in late 1980 for training and advice. The trip also produced some financial help, estimated to me by one source at $300,000.

Meanwhile, Cardenal and other civilians formed the Nicaraguan Democratic Union, or UDN, its Spanish acronym, with the motto *Sin comunismo, sin somocismo*—Without Communism or Somocism. In October and November 1980 a small group held meetings at Cardenal's Miami town house and wrote the statutes, then set out to find fighters and money. A military arm was created under the name Nicaraguan Revolutionary Armed Forces, which was not affiliated with the Guardsmen, though Cardenal said former Guardsmen could join if they accepted civilian leadership. Orlando Bolaños, a Nicaraguan who once served in the U.S. Air Force, was named chief of staff. Another key member of the military structure was Edmundo Chamorro, who with his brother Fernando, then still inside Nicaragua, had a long history of fighting the Somozas, beginning with their student days in the late 1950s. In November 1960 they and a few followers had captured the public's imagination when they briefly seized the National Guard barracks in Jinotepe and Diriamba, towns just south of Managua. They also organized independent actions against the Somozas through the next two decades. On July 20, 1978, Fernando took a seventh floor room at the Hotel Inter-Continental in Managua and fired two rockets out the window at the Bunker across the street as Anastasio Somoza was meeting with his staff. Only one exploded, and no one was hurt in the Bunker, but two pedestrians were killed when the National Guard opened fire on the hotel. Later, Fernando served in the Sandinistas' Southern Front with his old friend Edén Pastora. The Chamorro brothers, however, found little appeal in the FSLN from the time it took power. Edmundo chose exile, and Fernando returned to his job as a Chevrolet salesman in Managua.

The UDN leadership raised enough money among Nicaraguan exiles to buy some weapons and radio equipment. Raúl Arana had, meanwhile, cultivated friendships and contacts within the Honduran military and among former National Guardsmen not connected with Enrique Bermúdez. In early 1981, Arana arranged the purchase of two hundred weapons—hunting rifles, shotguns, submachine guns, and civilian versions of the M-16—from Miami gun shops. Lacking a permit to buy that quantity himself, he rounded up dozens of individuals willing to sign and present their driver's licenses as identification. Everything was packed up and, by prior arrangement, shipped to Honduras in the name of FUSEP, the Honduran armed forces. By February, Arana had established himself in a Tegucigalpa hotel as the "coordinator" of combat operations and was in radio contact with small bands carrying out operations in the name of the UDN. Actions were concentrated in the mountainous Jinotega region of Nicaragua on the Honduran border. They operated on the theory that an internal uprising would eventually occur and that those from outside, by their activities, would help set it off and then support it. Cardenal, meanwhile, with his wife supporting the family in Miami, set out in search of political and economic assistance from friendly governments and individuals. He reasoned that the foreign image of the Sandinistas would be as crucial in trying to defeat them as it had been in defeating Somoza.

Even after the anti-Sandinista forces had been launching attacks for several months, the Sandinistas complained only when it served them politically. If they wanted sympathy, they would complain that an attempted counterrevolution was under way. Otherwise, they dismissed the attacks as insignificant, a slight inconvenience in the affected rural areas. Most of the response was left to the local militia forces, formed in early 1980 under the national leadership of Edén Pastora.

Part of the reason for the low level of activity by the new guerrillas was that they lived a hand-to-mouth existence. But in May or June of 1981, Edmundo Chamorro and other members of the UDN high command made a trip to Argentina that improved their situation. In a meeting with army officers, the Nicaraguans were handed a plastic bag containing $50,000 in hundred-dollar bills. The group returned immediately to Honduras, where food was running short in the guerrilla camps. After laying in a food supply, the leaders continued to Miami to buy more weapons.

After that trip, the Argentine military passed a message to Enrique Bermúdez and Cardenal and other key exiles offering to provide more money and training and send advisers to Honduras if the feuding Nicaraguan groups would unite.

Meanwhile, in Washington, Thomas O. Enders, a career diplomat with a reputation for aloofness but superior intellect, had been named Assistant Secretary of State for Inter-American Affairs. Enders had no experience in Latin America but had varied Asian and European experience, including several years at the beginning of the 1970s as deputy chief of mission in Cambodia. He had also served as assistant secretary for economic and business affairs and as ambassador to Canada. Now he was part of an effort by the Reagan administration to put into the Latin American bureau of the State Department people with a fresh perspective, or people not under the influence of previous Latin American policies. Despite the newness of the subject to him, Enders proved himself a quick study in both the region and in Spanish.

By August, Enders was ready with proposals for the Sandinistas.

He flew to Managua on August 11 as Larry Pezzullo was retiring from the Foreign Service. Pezzullo had been in Managua slightly more than two years, a typical stay for such a country. But his departure also reflected the desire of the Reagan administration to put a different stamp on Central America, and Pezzullo suffered from identification with the policies of the Carter administration. Pezzullo insisted he had had no problems with Haig. It was a civilized departure.

Enders made four basic demands of the Sandinistas: that they withdraw from arms trafficking to El Salvador; that they slow or cease their own military buildup; that they take steps to comply with their promises of political and economic pluralism inside Nicaragua; and that they temper their association with Cuba and the Soviet bloc. In return, he told them, the United States would resume economic assistance and would commit itself not to help the exiles seeking to overthrow the regime.

The *sine qua non,* Enders said, was the halt in arms and logistical assistance to the Salvadoran guerrillas. If that activity were terminated, Enders said, the United States was willing to proceed to discuss the other points, including Nicaragua's fear of U.S. intervention.

These were tough demands. For committed Marxist-Leninists, compliance would mean an assault on their entire ideological base. It might mean an eventual departure from power. Even halting their assistance to the Salvadoran guerrillas was not a simple logistical or technical matter. Their faith required that they practice "internationalism"—assisting other Marxist groups.

Nevertheless, both sides displayed a positive attitude about the contacts. Among other things, the Sandinistas had found Enders more respectful toward them than they had expected from a representative of the Reagan administration.

But Enders was deadly serious about his demands. If the Sandinistas were taking Nicaragua "the way of another Cuba," he wanted to be certain everybody understood each other before it happened. If the Sandinistas were to come to the realization that getting caught in the East-West struggle was playing with fire, they could still put aside the matches.

On the day Enders arrived in Managua, there was another, unpublicized meeting of equal importance for the future of Nicaragua. A group of Nicaraguan exiles, including Raúl Arana, Orlando Bolaños, and Enrique Bermúdez, met in Guatemala with a group of Argentine military officers and signed a unity pact providing for Argentine military assistance. The new Nicaraguan group that emerged from the meeting as the partner of the Argentines was the Nicaraguan Democratic Force, or FDN, its Spanish acronym. Bolaños was named chief of the high command, with Bermúdez as the second man. The intention was to pair civilians with National Guardsmen for balance in the leadership. Edmundo Chamorro, not wanting to accept direction from the military men, chose to go his own way and retain the old UDN name.

Cardenal, who had not gone to Guatemala, met in the Miami airport a few days later with an Argentine colonel named Julio Villegas. The colonel, who told Cardenal he represented the government of Argentina, said a three-way agreement had been made among the governments of the United States, Argentina, and Honduras to assist the FDN with equipment, money, and military advice. Cardenal understood this to mean the money was coming from the United States.* Argentina was to provide direction and leadership, both military and political, through a group of Argentine officers to be assigned to Honduras. Villegas said he would return soon to Honduras and take charge of the military part. Another colonel, Oswaldo Ribeiro, was to be in charge of political activity. Villegas said the material help should begin to arrive in Honduras on a significant scale by January 1982.

Relations between Cardenal and the Argentines quickly became as testy as his relations with Bermúdez and the other National Guard officers. At first, the Argentines were not interested in creating a strong political arm for the FDN, which Cardenal thought was necessary to present the exiles' case to the world and also to give the movement political respectability and develop a framework for a future government. He did not wish to have to dodge questions from the press and others about whether the rebels simply wanted to restore

---

*Several months later, in early March 1982, the Washington *Post* reported that the CIA had proposed a plan for covert action against the Sandinistas to President Reagan on November 16, 1981, and the President had approved it at some later, unknown date. It was characterized within the U.S. government as an attempt to disrupt arms supply routes from Nicaragua to El Salvador. However, the information from Cardenal and Arana indicates the CIA was backing the anti-Sandinista activities several months earlier, and to them it was never anything less than an effort to topple the Sandinistas. Cardenal said Colonel Villegas told him the FDN had been selected as the next "vanguard" of Nicaragua.

the old Somoza system. But the Argentines, he found, were interested in getting rid of Communists and not particularly concerned about establishing political democracy in Nicaragua. Eventually, the Argentines agreed to the creation of a three-man political commission. Cardenal was named "coordinator" and Mariano Mendoza, a former trade union leader and close collaborator of Cardenal's in exile, was named to the commission as well. The third, selected by the former National Guardsmen, was Aristides Sánchez, the son of a man who had served in various civilian capacities for the Somoza government.

During the last months of 1981 and the first two months of 1982, the political commission organized support committees in various cities, including Los Angeles, San Francisco, Washington, New Orleans, Houston, and Miami. In Honduras, training and preparations were under way. Argentine accents—closer to Italian in tone than Spanish —had become common in the lobbies of one of Tegucigalpa's best hotels.

Still, no significant operations were being conducted.

Cardenal and others in Miami, including members of the local committee (made up of various people who had been prominent in business and politics in Nicaragua), began to pressure for the beginning of military activities. Reading the news reports of ongoing meetings and exchanges between U.S. and Nicaraguan representatives about the Enders proposals, and an offer by Mexican President José López Portillo to help bring about nonagression pacts between Nicaragua and the United States and between Nicaragua and its neighbors, the civilian group feared the United States was on the verge of abandoning the understanding with Argentina to help the exile force. They were concerned about the possibility that the U.S. and Nicaraguan governments would reach some kind of agreement that would leave the Sandinistas secure in power and the opposition with only unpleasant options. They thought something dramatic needed to be done to disrupt any progress that might be under way in the negotiations.

The first attempt to do something dramatic had failed when William Baltodano, a civilian member of the new FDN high command, went into Nicaragua on a mission to blow up a cement factory but was captured at a Managua house on January 2, 1982. Baltodano's confession included details of the trip to Buenos Aires in May or June 1981, when Argentine officers met with representatives of the old UDN and gave them $50,000.

Just before midnight on March 14, 1982—hours after Secretary of

State Haig handed a new proposal on Nicaragua to Mexican Foreign Secretary Jorge Castaneda—FDN saboteurs slipped into Nicaragua and planted explosives at two bridges over rivers near the Honduran border. The four-hundred-foot-long span over the Negro River in the department of Chinandega was totally destroyed, halting all vehicular traffic on the main highway between Honduras and Nicaragua. The bridge over the Coco River near the town of Ocotal in Nueva Segovia was damaged. The attacks served as an unofficial declaration of war. It made clear, finally, that the Sandinistas were no longer facing a challenge from mere cattle rustlers.

"It was that action that made us feel like an organization capable of accomplishing things," Enrique Bermúdez told me several years later. "All those other things, the ambushes and so forth, had no impact. We launched that action thinking that if it had an impact then we could enter into the struggle on firm footing."

In reaction, the Sandinistas declared a state of emergency, citing the U.S. news reports a few days earlier that President Reagan had approved plans to support covert action against the Sandinista regime. Under the state of emergency, radio newscasts and political party opinion programs were suspended and all radio stations had to link up with a government network at certain times of day for newscasts. Prior censorship was instituted for the print media, though in practice it applied almost exclusively to *La Prensa*. Previously, censorship had been selective.

On the day the bridges were blown and the state of emergency decreed, Anthony C. E. Quainton arrived in Managua to fill the post of U.S. ambassador, vacant since Larry Pezzullo's departure the previous August. Quainton, who had been director of the State Department's Office for Combating Terrorism and had served in Africa, Asia, and Europe, but never before in Latin America, picked up the threads of the on and off negotiations with the Sandinistas over the issues Enders had raised in August. At times there were signs of progress, but nothing resulted. Mainly, each side talked about what topics it wanted on the agenda, with almost no substantive exchange. Each side now seemed less interested in making progress in negotiations than in gaining time to reach other ends.

The rebel operations against the Sandinistas experienced a temporary setback when the United States sided with Britain in the two-and-a-half month war (April–June 1982) over the Malvinas-Falkland Islands, a U.S. policy that alienated most of Latin America. The

Argentines pulled out of Honduras in anger, but they soon sent a message to Cardenal saying they would return and continue to advise the Nicaraguans. By July, the insurgents were presenting a serious challenge to the Sandinista army and militiamen in the border area and launching small strikes deep into the department of Jinotega.

Thanks to the headline writers, the insurgency soon had a special name: *la Contra*—short for counterrevolution in Spanish. Though many of the anti-Sandinistas, including Cardenal, denied being counterrevolutionaries, the name was adopted almost universally both by people who supported the Sandinistas and those who hated the Sandinistas. It was a short, handy term reflecting the institutional status that the *Contra* acquired.

Fed by Sandinista policies and Yankee dollars, the *Contra* could only grow.

15

THE CHALLENGE TO THE CHURCH

Most Nicaraguans agree that they are a highly religious people, not in a pious way, but in the sense of finding a religious explanation or connection for almost anything that happens. This characteristic took on new meaning after the Sandinista Front became the supreme power in the land. For example, when some of the *comandantes* claimed that imperialism was at fault in a fatal military air crash because the United States had refused to provide spare parts for their plane, many other Nicaraguans were saying that the Lord had caused the crash in retribution for the Marxist godlessness of the Sandinistas. A hurricane, a drought, and a few other natural woes were similarly attributed to a vindictive God.

Those in positions of power or influence in Nicaragua also agreed that it was not fair to manipulate this religiosity, but they did so anyway. While the Sandinistas consulted Marx, Lenin, Castro, Guevara, and other worldly figures before coming to power in 1979, they soon seemed to be spending as much or more time analyzing the Bible and the Virgin Mary in their search for the means to consolidate themselves among people who insist on reassurance about a place in the Hereafter.

The Sandinistas found Christian supporters, some of them in Nicaragua and many more abroad, who said that what was occurring was an exciting experiment to bring about collaboration between the faith and Marxism-Leninism. But Nicaragua's Roman Catholic Church leadership interpreted the Sandinistas' religious talk as just a new and sophisticated means to an old end: the destruction of Christianity or its subjugation to Marxism. The religious hierarchy set out to defeat this strategy, even if it meant doing a bit of manipulation of its own. The result often appeared to be, in the words of one foreign diplomat, "the first good religious war since the seventeenth century."

Signs of this were plentiful. For a while, Tomás Borge took to referring to certain dead guerrillas as saints. The archbishop of Managua, Monsignor Miguel Obando y Bravo, responded in one of his Sunday masses by saying that people who die in the service of their country may be called heroes, but not saints. At another time, the FSLN had a slogan painted on the side of the only highway overpass in Managua claiming immortality for itself. When *La Prensa* tried to publish this revelation, the government censored the photograph. Subsequently, the Sandinista Front had the overpass painted with a more innocuous message.

The Roman Catholic bishops, for their part, did not discourage the various reports of appearances of the Virgin in Nicaragua in the first years after the Sandinistas came to power. One of the Sandinista leaders commented that the frequency of such sightings was truly remarkable when you considered that there had not been a single recorded appearance in all the years of Nicaraguan history prior to 1979. The most noted appearance of the Virgin occurred in the Valley of Cuapa in 1980, and the man who reported it said she was telling Nicaraguans not to worry, that she was with them in their time of trial. Then there was the plaster figure of Mary that appeared to be perspiring, which government opponents interpreted to mean that she was grieving for the sad state to which Nicaragua had fallen under the Sandinista Front. Government supporters, after asking questions around the neighborhood where this occurred, claimed that the "sweating" had been accomplished by soaking the statue in water, putting it in a deep freeze overnight, then bringing it out in the tropical heat and humidity the next morning.

The Church hierarchy took the step of consecrating the entire nation to the Virgin in late 1982 in a series of open-air masses that the Sandinistas feared would become the pretext for a call to mass insurrection, or, perhaps just as bad, the beginning of a crusade to convert the infidels, Nicaragua having only one significant group of infidels. Neither of these things happened, revealing not so much that the Sandinistas underestimated the potential power of the bishops as that they misunderstood the ways in which the Church was prepared to use that power. The hierarchy also made considerable use of a poster showing the archbishop astride a burro, Christ-like. The poster found its way onto the walls of many humble homes. In the Indian artisan community of Monimbó I came across a man who had that poster on his wall along with one of the late Che Guevara and one of Luis Herrera Campíns, who was at that time the democratically elected president of Venezuela. The man was protecting himself for most of the foreseeable possibilities.

Both sides demonstrated a special fondness for analogies between Nicaragua's situation and the circumstances and events surrounding the Last Supper. The archbishop once implied that the Sandinistas were the equivalent of Judas, and Tomás Borge said the archbishop aspired to be the anti-Christ. The Sandinistas suggested that they were really Christ in fatigues and that the guerrillas opposing them were trying to crucify the saviors of Nicaragua. Jaime Wheelock, another of the *comandantes* on the Sandinista National Directorate, advanced this theory before a group of Miskito Indians in the guerrilla-infested mountains of Jinotega in late 1982. He went on to equate the United States to the Romans who prosecuted Christ and the Nicaraguan church hierarchy to the priests who accused Christ of being a false representative of God. Tomás Borge hung several dozen crucifixes on a wall of one of his offices at the Interior Ministry, an impressive setting in which to receive the foreign religious delegations pouring into Nicaragua. Borge usually allowed people to draw their own conclusions about why he hung crucifixes on his wall, but when asked he said the collection began with one delegation, which presented him with a crucifix. He put it on the wall. Then, other foreign groups heard about it, and bestowing crucifixes on the *comandante* became quite the thing to do.

All of this added up to a heavy debate, one that seemed to delve always deeper into the religious subconscious of the population. Yet, as recently as 1979, the Roman Catholic Church and the FSLN had seemed united in their vision of the future of Nicaragua. Although Archbishop Obando y Bravo had helped in the unsuccessful attempt to put together a more moderate, non-Marxist succession to the Somoza dynasty, in the end he participated in the transfer of power to the new regime, in which Marxists and non-Marxists set out to share power. Regardless of the underlying nervousness, the perception existed that the new government in Nicaragua had the blessing of the Church.

Within a short time, however, a multisided conflict exploded that added new dimensions to the usual confrontations between church and state and between Marxism and Christianity. Aside from its outright differences with the Sandinista Front, the Church suffered a rebellion within its ranks that turned Nicaragua into the foremost testing ground in the world for liberation theology, which combines Marxism's promise of social justice with Christianity's promise of salvation. Liberation theology picked up many adherents during the 1960s and 1970s among priests and nuns working in Latin America. An offshoot is the Popular Church, which is more a way of thinking than a formal structure. It is generally taken to refer to those who embrace and practice liberation theology through "base communities," which serve for both Bible study and political action. In Nicaragua, a few proponents of liberation theology gave clandestine support to the Sandinista Front for many years before it reached power. Once the FSLN was in power, they created a form of the Popular Church in Nicaragua, or more precisely a pro-government branch of the Roman Catholic Church, though without formal rupture from the hierarchy.

One of the effects of this division was to confuse the faithful about whom to believe. This was obvious in a church dispute I watched at first hand during several days in mid-1982 in an area of Managua called Santa Rosa.

Like most other humble neighborhoods in Managua, Santa Rosa seems temporary, as if people came with the intention of just camping for a while. Earthquakes, hurricanes, and perpetual intense heat have taught Nicaraguans that unless one can afford a really substantial house, it is best not to put much bother into shelter. Children and adults alike came out of the wooden and metal shanties and occasional well-built house for the rare sight of a passing car, even though the one paved street in Santa Rosa is only a block south of the highway that comes into Managua from the north.

A banner hanging over the doors of the one-story wooden church proclaimed that it now belonged to the *Comunidades Cristianas de Base de Santa Rosa*—the Santa Rosa Christian Base Communities. The building was shut and locked, but a teenaged boy in blue jeans and a fatigue cap opened the door and showed me to the interior patio. The boy, Enrique Báez, said he and others from the neighborhood had "taken" the church after the archbishop had decided to remove the parish priest of the previous eight years, Monsignor José Arias Caldera, and replace him with a newly ordained priest. It was now Friday morning. On the previous Wednesday, about thirty people of the neighborhood had organized a march to the headquarters of the archdiocese, where they engaged in what Báez described as a "small ideological fight" with the Reverend Bismarck Carballo, spokesman for the archdiocese.

"He told us we were being manipulated and supported by yellow journalism," Báez said. "The people of Radio Sandino were there. We told him this was the work of a Christian Base Community. Monsignor Arias has been a progressive, revolutionary priest, and we want him to stay. We want a church that is at the side of the poor. We know that he [the new priest] is not going to help us to form a proletarian church."

The situation worsened that evening, when the delegation returned to Santa Rosa and rang the bells in the church patio to call the people of the neighborhood. About a hundred crowded into the narrow worship hall, and what happened next is subject to dispute. Báez said everybody had begun to sing when they suddenly saw Monsignor Bosco Vivas, the auxiliary bishop of Managua, striding up the aisle toward the altar. Monsignor Vivas told me later that he had arrived outside the church with some nuns who had an errand there and that what he heard coming over a loudspeaker from inside the sanctuary was not religious singing, but a political speech. "They were attacking Monsignor Obando very hard, and the one who was speaking was saying, 'I'm not a Christian, I don't believe in anything, but I come to support this priest because he is with the poor.' "

Monsignor Vivas decided the church was being profaned and that he should rescue the altar pieces used in the sacraments. "So I went in, without any problem, and when I took the *santísima,* they all said 'We want to talk,' and I said, 'First, I have to take out the *santísima,'* but they hardly let me finish. Immediately, one of them gave a signal 'that he not leave!' They closed the doors and threw themselves on top of me. They took the *sagraria* away from me, and when I resisted they hit me and broke my glasses and threw me on the ground before the whole church. Then, the nuns who were out front with some seminarists and other priests who had arrived, when they heard the noise, they came to the church and broke the doors, and took me out."

The archbishop declared the next day that anyone involved in the attack automatically fell into excommunication. This kept Margarita Fuentes in a state of tears off and on in the coming days. She was sixty-seven years old and had assisted the various priests who had served the Santa Rosa church for the thirty-four years she had lived in the neighborhood. She, along with the young Báez, was holding the church on the morning of my first visit. No one, she said, had struck the auxiliary bishop the night he visited the church. She said she was sitting near where he came down from the altar and saw him trip on the low step and fall.

Báez said he just happened to recover the altar pieces when the auxiliary bishop tripped. "Before God, we have not touched Monsignor Vivas," the youth said. He acknowledged, however, that people in the church fought with the seminarists and priests accompanying Monsignor Vivas, which he justified by saying that those accompanying Monsignor Vivas came as men, not as clergy.

"Why do they say such things?" Mrs. Fuentes asked, smoothing her gray hair with a shaking hand. "We have nothing against the archbishop. We are Christians and Catholics. We are not involved in politics. What we want is that they leave our priest here."

Mrs. Fuentes' forty-five-year-old daughter, minding her own child in the patio, interjected an assessment of the situation in the tone of an uninvolved observer. She said Father Arias had, from time to time, participated in government functions, giving benedictions and that sort of thing at the request of the Sandinista National Directorate. She believed the archbishop did not appreciate these activities. There was one other thing. Father Arias had been given the Order of Carlos Fonseca, the highest honor that *sandinismo* can bestow.

Her mother said she believed there was no way the Sandinista Front could be manipulating the people of Santa Rosa. It really began with her, Mrs. Fuentes said. She had gone to Father Arias when she heard the news of his transfer on Radio Sandino the previous Tuesday and told him she did not want to continue working at the church without him there. At first, the priest himself insisted it could not be true, but he went to the archbishop and confirmed it.

"Those who understand these things better than I do put the movement together," Mrs. Fuentes said. "But everyone involved is from this church. There is no one from outside. It just spread, like when you spill water on a table."

"The problem produced the spontaneous formation of a Christian Base Community, which is going to keep the church closed until we get our wishes," said Báez, who displayed an exceptional political vocabulary for a fifteen-year-old growing up in such a modest environment.

As usual, Nicaragua's three daily newspapers were doing little to clarify the situation. *La Prensa,* fiercely antigovernment and pro-church, reported SACRILEGIOUS ACTS IN SANTA ROSA, with banner headlines, basing its stories almost exclusively on the statements of the church hierarchy. *El Nuevo Diario,* pro-government and anti–*La Prensa,* took more than half its front page to tell of "Phariseeism" in the temple and "ire, hate, provocation" on the part of church authorities. The people were crying for Father Arias, it said, and devoted four inside columns to accounts of the affection for him in Santa Rosa. *Barricada,* the official organ of the Sandinista Front, shared the distinction of having broken the story along with Radio Sandino, but it maintained a certain bureaucratic straightness in its coverage. With its Marxist perspective, the Sandinista newspaper pretended to stand above the battle between two sets of believers in another faith, once it had helped set things in motion.

Father Arias was then sixty-five years old, with forty years as a priest, a soft-spoken man with light brown skin. Wearing a sport shirt and tan trousers, he came back for a visit with his former flock that Friday night. The crowd that had gathered in the church thought he had come to say mass, but he would not do that because he believed priests had to obey their bishops. He believed it, but he did not like it. Monsignor Arias was not left without a parish in this uproar. Before, he had had two. He remained with one, the Church of the Assumption in the middle-class Ciudad Jardín neighborhood. He had proposed that the new priest be sent to Ciudad Jardín, but the archbishop rejected that. Sitting on a stool in the patio surrounded by churchgoers, he read the newspaper accounts of the fighting in the church.

"The sacraments should not be the patrimony of any priest. Why do they want to take them away?" he said to no one in particular. "It's imprudent on the part of the archbishop."

Taking the stool beside him, I asked whether it was true, as people said, that he had once provided a hiding place for Carlos Fonseca, the most important founder of the Sandinista Front and, since his death in the northern mountains in 1976, its leading martyr. A soft smile crossed the priest's face. He remembered Carlos Fonseca as what he called a "marvel of a man." Sometime in the mid-1960s Fonseca had sought out Monsignor Arias, who was then serving the Church of Santa Faz, in another Managua neighborhood. Fonseca was suffering from an old wound and needed a secure place to rest. The priest built a *casita,* a small house, for Fonseca on the west side of the church grounds. There Fonseca healed and met with his followers and collaborators. Tomás Borge came frequently, as did Daniel Ortega, then still in his teens. Silvio Mayorga, who with Fonseca and Borge had founded the FSLN, gave classes in the primary and secondary school at the church. When a young man named Lenín Cerna was released from prison he too came to the Church of Santa Faz, and the priest offered what he remembered as a little party, with Coca-Cola.

Those exhilarating days at the Santa Faz church ended when Fonseca left for the mountains and the renewed guerrilla struggle that would not be victorious until three years after his death. By the time of our conversation, Borge and Ortega had become among the most powerful men in Nicaragua. Lenín Cerna worked under Borge as chief of the state security police, a feared man to those Nicaraguans not enchanted by the Sandinista government. Mayorga, like Fonseca, had died in combat.

A year later, in mid-1983, I returned to the church in Santa Rosa for a Thursday afternoon mass. The twenty-three-year-old priest whose assignment to replace Father Arias had set off the 1982 controversy conducted the mass before a medium-sized group that included women and children and older men from the neighborhood. There were no young men in fatigues, nor was Mrs. Fuentes there. One of the worshipers told me Mrs. Fuentes had left to work for Father Arias at his other church. During the intervening year, Archbishop Obando y Bravo himself had said two crowded Sunday masses at the dilapidated church, an unofficial declaration that he had won at least this one among the many battles in his effort to halt the insurrection in Nicaraguan Catholicism.

Monsignor Vivas, the auxiliary bishop, said the removal of Father Arias from Santa Rosa was not intended as punishment for his political beliefs. He pointed out that it was one of about ten changes of parish priests during the year and that none of the others produced opposition because the priests involved were of no political value to the FSLN. It was simple and logical, he said. There was a newly ordained priest who needed a church, and Monsignor Arias had two. It was the Sandinista Front, he said, that had turned the matter into a political confrontation.

However, when the archbishop ordered that Father Arias be replaced in Santa Rosa he had on his desk a lengthy letter from Pope John Paul II to the Nicaraguan bishops that was probably his strongest public attack to date on the Popular Church. In the letter, which the government censor blocked from newspaper publication until three weeks after the Santa Rosa episode, the Pope said, among other things: "A 'Popular Church' opposed to the Church presided over by the legitimate pastors is—from the point of view of the teaching of the Lord and of the Apostles in the New Testament and also in the old and recent teaching of the solemn magistery of the Church—a serious deviation from the will and the plan of salvation of Jesus Christ." The Pope also urged religious workers in Nicaragua to remember that it was "not in a political role but for their priestly ministry that the people want them nearby."

With the letter, and subsequent statements, the Pope seemed to have brought the Church full cycle in its debate over what means were acceptable to help the poor find social and economic justice. The evolution of this is generally dated from Vatican II, the 1962–1965 ecumenical conference, which, by its easing of institutional rules, increased the possibilities for the Church to participate in worldly concerns. But the watershed event in Latin America was the 1968 conference of Latin American bishops at Medellín, Colombia, from which emerged a consensus that the Church should show a "preferential option for the poor." The Medellín conference was preceded by several years of debate among those clergy and religious workers in Latin America who had lost faith in reformism as a means of improving the lives of the poor. Most of these were members of religious orders, either foreigners or Latin Americans educated in prestigious institutions abroad.

One of the foremost among them was Gustavo Gutiérrez, a Peruvian educated at the University of Louvain in Belgium, who is looked to as the father figure of liberation theology. Gutiérrez led the way in using Marxism to analyze the causes of social and economic underdevelopment in Latin America. With rare exceptions, these people did not embrace the idea of violence to bring about a Marxist revolution, at least in the early years. It was these generally young, intellectual churchmen of the Gutiérrez line who dominated the staff of experts that prepared the working papers and documents emerging from the Medellín conference.

Increased ferment within the church in Latin America followed Medellín as the more activist priests and nuns considered how best to carry out the option for the poor. This coincided with the election of

Salvador Allende, a Marxist, as president of Chile in 1970. During Allende's three years in office Chile became the setting for the first significant movement in which liberation priests took an overt political stance in favor of a particular kind of government. Pro-Allende priests founded a group called Christians for Socialism, which invited church people of like mind from around the region to a conference held in Chile in 1972, despite the opposition of Raúl Cardinal Silva, the archbishop of Santiago.

In January 1979 the Latin American bishops held another extraordinary meeting, this time in Puebla, Mexico. The bishops wanted to take a new look at their Medellín positions in light of emerging political ramifications that most of them had not foreseen: that the Medellín stand for social justice had become the justification for some in the Church to embrace Marxism and, beyond the theoretical significance, to become directly involved with partisan politics. Penny Lernoux, in *Cry of the People,* her 1980 book on the Church in Latin America, said conservative bishops around the region had pushed for the conference for several years with the idea of calling a complete retreat from the social justice stand. Some thought they had been misled or taken advantage of by Gutiérrez and other theologians who prepared the 1968 documents.

The new Pope, John Paul II, came to the opening of the conference. He expressed his disagreement with those who tried to depict Jesus Christ as a political and ideological figure and warned against a break in Church unity that would confuse Roman Catholics. "This idea of Christ as a political figure, a revolutionary, as the subversive man from Nazareth, does not tally with the church's catechesis," he said. "By confusing the insidious pretexts of Jesus' accusers with the very different attitude of Jesus himself, some people adduce as the cause of his death the outcome of a political conflict, and nothing is said of the Lord's will to deliver himself and of his consciousness of his redemptive mission." Under this influence, the bishops adopted a statement that spoke of a continued commitment to the poor while also opposing such concepts as "parallelism," their term for the liberation theologians' talk of a people's, or popular, church.

Several Nicaraguans from affluent families, educated abroad for the priesthood, were caught up in liberation theology from its early days. Among them were the two brothers from the influential Cardenal family of Granada, the old stronghold of the Conservative Party. Fernando Cardenal became a Jesuit, and Ernesto prepared first with Thomas Merton to become a Trappist, then abandoned the monastery and became a diocesan priest. He organized a peasant artisan and religious community on Solentiname, an archipelago near the southern shore of Lake Nicaragua, which also served as a center of anti-Somoza activities. Ernesto Cardenal also distinguished himself as a poet, with a substantial following outside of Nicaragua. Ernesto Cardenal told me he had declared himself a Marxist Christian in 1972 as a result of participating in the conference in Chile. Before going to Chile he went to Cuba, and was so impressed by the accomplishments of Fidel Castro's revolution that he decided it constituted the Gospel in practice. But it was not until he met the priests working in Chile that he concluded it was possible to combine Christianity and Marxism.

Another such Nicaraguan was Uriel Molina, a Franciscan priest, who came home from his studies in Italy in the late 1960s to build a church and school in an area of Managua just being urbanized. Influenced by Vatican II and the Medellín conference, Molina also sought contact with the broader world. He organized Bible study classes and taught theology at a university. One day in 1971 a group of university students, mostly from prosperous families, appeared at his parish and asked him to assist them in a communal living and study experiment. About a dozen moved into the rectory with their cots. They studied the Bible first thing every morning, then went to classes at the university, and in the evenings they returned to the parish for discussions in which they used Marxism to analyze Nicaragua's circumstances.

Molina said the Christians for Socialism conference in Chile had a great influence on the students living with him. Its final document as well as Gustavo Gutiérrez's 1971 book, *Teología de la Liberación,* published later in English as *A Theology of Liberation,* were the group's primary reference materials. Molina said that prior to the conference he was unable to accept the idea of armed struggle as the natural extension of the Christianity he was preaching, but implied that as a result of the experience in Chile some of his doubts were removed.

While he was in Chile, a leading *comandante* of the Sandinista Front, Victor Tirado, moved into the church and formed ties to the university group. The next year, in 1973, the students* left the parish to join the Sandinista Front. Throughout the seventies, Father Molina

---

*After the Sandinistas came to power, most of the members of Molina's university group took important posts in the new regime, one becoming a member of the National Directorate and another chief of staff of the army.

maintained clandestine contacts with the Sandinistas, and his church occasionally served as a gathering place for them.

While these Nicaraguan priests and a few others were following the radical path of opposition to the Somozas, the thrust of the traditional Church in Nicaragua also was to criticize Somoza rule, without resorting to liberation theology. Monsignor Miguel Obando y Bravo became archbishop of Managua in 1970 and set the tone of things to come by refusing Anastasio Somoza's offer of a Mercedes-Benz. The bishops soon began to speak out on the misdeeds of the regime. The perception of the Church being in opposition to Somoza was enhanced when the popular archbishop, a stocky man of humble birth and part-Indian ancestry, was called upon by the Sandinistas to act as mediator in their two major urban terrorist actions: the 1974 Christmas Party Raid, at which rich and influential hostages were exchanged for the freedom of imprisoned Sandinistas, and the 1978 takeover of the National Palace, which also produced a hostage-prisoner exchange.

At the beginning of 1977 the Nicaraguan bishops issued a pastoral letter accusing the government of killing more than two hundred peasants during the previous two years as part of its counterinsurgency campaign. The letter helped to focus international criticism on the Somoza regime. Later that year, Archbishop Obando y Bravo organized politically moderate opponents in an unsuccessful effort to convince Somoza to step aside before the expected violence could erupt. A year later, when the United States was beginning the mediation mission in Nicaragua, all of the bishops issued a call for Somoza to resign. Just six weeks before Somoza fled in mid-July 1979 the bishops declared that the Nicaraguan people had a right to carry out an insurrection.

During the first months after the fall of Somoza, the bishops issued a lengthy pastoral letter, dated November 17, 1979, that many interpreted as support for the Sandinista revolution but which also contained a number of reservations and warnings. The letter, addressed to all Christians in Nicaragua, said in one of its early passages:

> We believe that the present revolutionary moment is a propitious occasion to turn into reality the ecclesiastical option for the poor. Nevertheless, we must recall that no historical revolutionary undertaking has the ability to exhaust the infinite possibilities of justice and absolute solidarity of the Kingdom of God. In addition, we must affirm that our commitment to the revolutionary

process cannot signify naïveté or blind enthusiasm, much less the creation of a new idol before which one has to humble oneself unquestioningly. Dignity, responsibility, and Christian liberty cannot be renounced as part of active participation in the revolutionary process.

The bishops went on to say that they already had some concerns about abuses of prisoners and the unclear attitude of the Sandinistas toward the liberty of other political groups. But they said Nicaraguans should not fear a Socialist government if this meant the preeminence of the interests of the majority, including a "progressively participative" planned economy. They said they could not accept a Socialism that would interfere with religious liberty or the right of parents to educate their children according to their convictions or that would pretend "to submit the people blindly to the manipulations and dictates of those who would arbitrarily and unlawfully hold power . . ."

Temporal authority had many faces in Nicaragua in those early days of the new order, and this created uncertainty about where the power structure stood on religion. In the Plan of Government, issued by the junta shortly before it took office on July 19, 1979, there was a guarantee of "the full exercise of the freedom of worship." Nothing more had been said, particularly by the nine *comandantes* of the Sandinista National Directorate.

However, two key religious events approached to test the Sandinista Front in the last months of 1979. The first was *Purísima,* the feast of the Immaculate Conception of Mary on December 8, of major significance in Nicaragua, which has one of the most profound Marian traditions in the world. *Purísima* is celebrated in the streets on the evening of the seventh as a sort of Halloween in a religious context. Families compete to build the most beautiful and unusual altars in homage to Mary and also give "loot"—treats of candy, small toys, and trinkets—to the children and adults who roam the streets and stop in front of the altars to shout: "What causes so much happiness?" The response: "The Immaculate Conception of Mary." In 1979 many people were fearful that the Sandinistas would try to eliminate the festival, so, as if to challenge that possibility, they put forth more than usual effort in the quality of the altars and the loot. It was widely described as the "greatest *Purísima* ever." Instead of repressing the festival, however, the Sandinistas concluded that it had largely Nicaraguan roots and decided to adopt it. Two members of the National

Directorate, Tomás Borge and Daniel Ortega, joined in festivities arranged by liberation priests, establishing a pattern for the coming years, when employees of Government House began to stage a *Purísima* themselves.

The first Christmas was a more serious dilemma for the Sandinistas. The propaganda and political education section of the Sandinista Front prepared a brief, secret document to tell its local political leaders how to approach Christmas activities in their neighborhoods. The document seemed to reflect differences within the Front between conventional Marxist-Leninists and those who were either strongly nationalistic or Christian. After opening with a criticism of the commercial nature of the Christmas celebration, which the authors described as more pagan than religious, the document said:

> Now, after the triumph of the Popular Sandinista Revolution, we are orienting the celebration of Christmas specifically [toward] the children, and with a different, fundamentally political, content. In essence, this means to rescue for the revolution a tradition that, even though religious, is deeply rooted in our people. It is thanks to the Sandinista Revolution that our children can now celebrate Christmas in liberty and grow up in a country that assures them their future and their happiness. This is the central thinking of the celebration.
>
> This does not mean to reinforce a tradition, particularly a religious one, but, by contrast, to interpret the subjective reality of our people today; so as, in the process, to transform it. To confront a tradition of more than 1,979 years in a direct manner, in these moments, less than five months after the triumph, would carry us into political conflicts and we would lose influence among our people. At the same time, it would feed the campaign that our enemies abroad are launching against our revolution.

It concluded that since sixty-two years of revolution still had not "totally eradicated" the Christmas tradition in the Soviet Union, it would be foolish to attempt such a thing so soon in Nicaragua.

Most Nicaraguans were unaware of this exposition of Sandinista purpose as they went about their traditional Christmas observances that year. The document did not become public until September 1980, when it was leaked and published in *La Prensa*. It did not shock people as much as it might have the previous year because it came out at a time in which the conflict between the Church and the Sandinista

Front and between the bishops and the believers in liberation theology was clearly emerging. The bishops had begun to worry about Marxist thinking showing up in the educational process, about the government's dispatch of young Nicaraguans to Cuba for six years of study, and about the Cuban teachers and workers spreading out around the Nicaraguan countryside, some of them making fun of religion and appropriating village churches for activities they organized. The bishops had noted disunity and confusion within the Church itself and were particularly vexed at the priests who insisted on serving in the government or the Sandinista Front.

At first the bishops had taken a benign attitude toward the matter of priests serving in the government. But in May 1980 the Pope made known that he did not want priests involved in politics anywhere in the world. A short time later the Nicaraguan bishops issued a mild statement saying that it had been acceptable for priests to serve in the government during the emergency but that the emergency was now over and they should look for civilians to take over their jobs. The bishops indicated that the only way the priests could continue in the government was by obtaining individual permission from the Vatican.

In addition to the two priests then in the Cabinet—Foreign Minister d'Escoto and Culture Minister Ernesto Cardenal—the bishops' request was understood to cover Father Edgard Parrales, who was then director of the Social Security Institute, and Fernando Cardenal, then in the temporary post of director of the Literacy Crusade. However, no deadline was set for the priests to resign, and they gave no indication that they were even listening. Later in the year, Father Parrales joined the Cabinet as minister of social welfare, and when the Literacy Crusade ended, Fernando Cardenal became director of the Sandinista Youth, a part of the FSLN and a more obviously political post than running the literacy program. In addition, both Cardenals and d'Escoto were members of the Sandinista Assembly, the organization of eighty-one top members of the FSLN.

For supporters of liberation theology, 1980 was a year of great excitement, during which they set out to perfect and advance a revolutionary theology under the influence now of a country where their theories were finally being put into practice. The great thinkers of liberation theology, both Roman Catholic and Protestant, poured into Nicaragua to see and expound. Nicaragua had become a religious frontier, a laboratory where a major breakthrough was expected to be made. Although such visitors came regularly, the centerpiece in 1980 was the

Encounter of Theology, held September 8 to September 14 in Managua. It attracted about forty theologians from eight countries. Out of the gathering emerged a book of the latest thoughts and ideas of the liberation theologians.

In their working papers and speeches, the conference participants generally took it as a given that they were looking for ways to assist the Sandinista Front in carrying out its political programs. They used the term *Iglesia Popular* (Popular Church) to describe the movement that they were supporting but insisted it did not signify "ecclesiastical parallelism" or a rupture with the church hierarchy. They recognized, however, that there was "a growing tension between the Popular Church and the hierarchy." They took a critical attitude toward the hierarchy for not being more forthright in support of the "revolution" —used in this case to indicate the specific ideas and programs of the Sandinista Front. Like the Sandinistas, they spoke in terms of confronting the bourgeoisie now that Somoza and the National Guard had been removed from the scene.

Several conference participants accused the church hierarchy or the majority of the Nicaraguan clergy of being motivated by a fear of Marxism in their hesitation about supporting the Sandinistas. Jon Sobrino, a Spanish-born Jesuit theologian whose writings and speeches on Christology constitute the most serious effort to establish a connection between liberation theology and the experiences of Christ himself, suggested that Marxism, in the form of the Sandinistas, represented "a new Word of God." Sobrino, who had written that Marxism constituted the second phase of the Enlightenment, said that by an excessive fear of Marxism, the traditional church might be failing to hear "precisely that Word that God wants it to hear."

While there were no formal conclusions, a summary prepared by participants said they needed to concentrate on the following tasks: pushing theological growth among the faithful through such means as a rereading of the Bible in "revolutionary" terms; using the Christian base communities to promote Christian participation in FSLN activities; publishing reading material in simple language; winning the bishops over to a revolutionary line; and promoting research and study on the relationship between Marxism and Christianity. Finally, in subtle terms, there was a call for a campaign to convert the non-believers of the Sandinista Front.

On October 7, 1980, the Sandinista Front issued a formal communiqué on religion that tried to limit the damage from the recent publication of its 1979 Christmas document and also address some of the issues raised in the conference of liberation theologians. It began with an acknowledgment that the Sandinistas owed a debt to Christians, citing various fallen guerrillas, including Gaspar García Laviana, a Spanish priest who fought and died under the Sandinista banner, and also the bishops for having "valiantly denounced the crimes and abuses of the [Somoza] dictatorship."

The communiqué then made these main points, some of which were directed at Christians, while others seemed to respond to Marxist-Leninists impatient with religion:

- The "right to profess a religious faith is an inalienable right of the people . . ."
- While there is "historic value" to the argument that religion can be used to justify the exploitation of the poor, the experience of the Sandinistas "shows that when Christians, supported by their faith, are capable of responding to the needs of the community and of history, their same beliefs push them toward revolutionary militancy."
- "The FSLN has a profound respect for all of the religious celebrations and traditions of our people," and these may not be used for "political or commercial ends."
- While denying responsibility for any division among Christians, the FSLN acknowledged that it would "look favorably" upon a church that was more supportive of Sandinista undertakings. "Logically, the Sandinistas are good friends of the Christian revolutionaries, but not of the counterrevolutionaries, although they call themselves Christians."

Two weeks later, the bishops had something to say. They issued a call for church unity in which they spoke more bluntly than in their letter of the previous year. They criticized the liberation theologians for downplaying the importance of Mary in Catholicism and also said it was an error "to affirm that political, economic, and social liberation coincided with the salvation of Jesus Christ or that the Kingdom of God is identified with the kingdom of man." They repeated their views on Socialism of the year before, giving both the acceptable and unacceptable versions of it, but said Christians should understand that unjust social structures were not the only evil thing in the world, that the transformation of individuals was also necessary to eliminate injustice. They warned that a "parallel magistery" to that directed by the bishops was totally unacceptable and also cautioned against the exploitation or manipulation of church organizations by "fashionable ideologies."

The bishops said they intended to assert themselves more in directing the pastoral life of Nicaragua. They announced the reopening of the national seminary, and they laid down rules for the foreign religious workers pouring into Nicaragua. The foreigners who came with the intention of working in the evangelization were told to register with the archdiocese and to bring letters from their religious superiors.

About the same time, the bishops set a deadline for the priests to leave the government, quietly passing the word that they expected the priests to choose between politics and the Church by the end of the year. The deadline was not met, but during the last months of 1980 and the first half of 1981, all sides—the bishops, the government, the priests, and the Vatican—grappled with the question.

The government sent various delegations to the Vatican, generally civilians of bourgeois, Catholic backgrounds, to argue that the priests should remain in their posts because Nicaragua was short of qualified people. It was not clear whether the Vatican was pushing the bishops to raise the issue or whether the bishops were pushing the Vatican to back them. Archbishop Obando kept saying the priests could remain in government if they obtained special permission from the Vatican. On the other hand, a government official who took part in two of the missions to the Vatican told me that Vatican Secretary of State Cardinal Agostino Casaroli told them the bishops had authority in the matter. Pope John Paul did not appear to be concerning himself directly with the issue at that point, and the archbishop complained during an interview near the end of 1980 that the priests in the government seemed to have more friends and influence within the Vatican bureaucracy than he and the bishops.

In July 1981 the bishops met with the four key priests—the Cardenal brothers, d'Escoto, and Parrales—in Matagalpa, and the priests proposed a compromise whereby they would remain in government but take what amounted to a leave-of-absence from the priesthood. They would not wear their robes, say Mass, christen babies, or exercise any other priestly function as long as they remained in politics. Nor would they use their status as priests to justify actions of the government or the Sandinista Front. Daniel Ortega traveled to Matagalpa at the same time to plead the issue with the bishops from the standpoint of the FSLN. The bishops decided to accept the proposal, though they did not like it. Their written statement noted:

The bishops, for their part, though they feel profoundly that this situation of exception does not fill or satisfy the primary objectives of the priestly functions, will tolerate it temporarily; in addition, they insistently reiterate their requests that these priests, as is the express desire of the Holy See, and which the urgent needs of our people demand, return as soon as possible to the exercise of the priestly ministry.

Aside from those in the government, Sandinista supporters among church people developed their activities in about a half-dozen institutes and think tanks. Some existed in limited form before Somoza's fall, but the growth of such groups was largely a post-Somoza phenomenon. The bishops did not oppose their establishment, but frequently pointed out that the groups were not organs of the Church.

The Antonio Valdivieso Center, named in honor of an activist bishop from the colonial era, became the most active and notable. It was founded by Uriel Molina, the Franciscan priest whose church in the Riguero neighborhood served as an early Sandinista gathering place, for the purpose of "ecumenical reflection" on the changes occurring in Nicaragua. Other such groups included a historical research center directed by a Nicaraguan Jesuit; an agrarian reform study center directed by an American priest; and the Evangelical Committee for Development Assistance, known as CEPAD, a Protestant umbrella group that came into existence to dispense aid after the 1972 earthquake but that took on a broader function after 1979.

Protestantism was growing in Nicaragua at the beginning of the 1980s, as elsewhere in Central America, and CEPAD included thirty-eight denominations claiming the religious allegiance of approximately 12 percent of the population. While CEPAD quickly gave its support to the Sandinista regime, other Protestant groups, mostly sects, did not support it, and some of the denominations in CEPAD, especially those whose membership was mostly Miskito Indians, divided on political questions after the Sandinistas came to power.

The activities of the Valdivieso Center fit within the plan of action laid down at the 1980 Encounter of Theology. Operating out of a large house in Managua, the center began to hold conferences and publish and sell books, newsletters, and other literature. It became the intellectual headquarters for visiting priests, ministers, academics and others in the liberation theology camp. These visitors, returning home to the United States or Europe or elsewhere in Latin America, would write or speak in praise of the Sandinista Front and its Christian supporters. Most of what the center published or sold in its bookstore consisted of writings on liberation theology, the memoirs of Sandinista guerrillas, or the works of Marx, Lenin, and Engels.

After the Pope began to oppose the Popular Church concept, the Valdivieso Center and other groups in the same line began to deny that they were promoting such an idea, although the term had been widely used in their Encounter of Theology. They did not significantly change their policies, however. To all appearances, they changed only their vocabulary and began to say there was no such thing as the Popular Church in Nicaragua.

The Valdivieso Center, though dominated by Roman Catholics, received financial assistance from the World Council of Churches. Leaders of the center told me they received only start-up money from the World Council, and they denied that they continued to receive such assistance once the center was fully functioning. However, Monsignor Bosco Vivas, the auxiliary bishop, said Vatican officials had shown him documentation indicating that the WCC was providing continuing support to the center at the level of about $175,000 as late as 1983. The World Council, responding to my request to clear up the issue, provided a document indicating that the Valdivieso Center had received money from more than one fund of the WCC for several years, including $50,000 in 1983.

These *ecu-dolares,* as the archbishop called the Protestant assistance, were a sore point with the Roman Catholic hierarchy. Officials of the archdiocese said they did not criticize this out of opposition to ecumenism but felt that the money from the Protestant world body was advancing political ends in conflict with religion in Nicaragua. The archbishop also said that the Valdivieso Center, through its foreign sympathizers, served to manipulate public opinion in the United States and Europe on questions concerning Nicaragua. He viewed this as part of Sandinista strategy for the use of the Popular Church. As he explained:

"When the government wanted to attack the Church, what it did was to launch the Popular Church . . . They think that to be a Christian one has to be Marxist because only Marxism liberates. In their attitudes they are against the hierarchy, against the Pope, against the institutional church. They say they are the church of the poor, but that is only the mask they present to impress . . . We say we have an option for the poor, but neither can we neglect those who are not poor . . ."

An idea of the intensity of the debate between the two religious sides in Nicaragua comes from listening to some of the things other Nicaraguan church figures said about the issues between them and about the government during the first five years of Sandinista rule. The political and religious questions tended to overlap.

The Reverend Rafael Aragon, a Dominican priest from Spain who came to Nicaragua after the Sandinistas took power and became a prominent figure at the Valdivieso Center, defended liberation theology and Marxist Christianity as basically survival strategies for the Church in the face of inevitable Marxist revolutions. Said Aragon:

"In our preachings there is no difference between us and them. We respect the liturgical laws, we celebrate the Eucharist and the rest of the sacraments in accordance with the laws of the Church . . . The big difference is that we understand our Christian commitment not just in the celebration of the cult inside the Church but as an option of service to the brother, which signifies to us to involve ourselves in the history of the people, commit ourselves in the tasks of social transformation. Our clash with the hierarchy is nothing more than that. We do not reject our bishops. We don't want a church without bishops . . .

"One thing the more traditional Church does not want to accept is that the Church has a political potential . . . We are convinced that the Christian dimension has a political potential . . . [But] our problem is not ideology. Our problem is practical. We support a process of transformation in the practical, the Literacy Crusade, being with the sick, helping to build houses. The ideological will come later. So, we are supporting a revolutionary process, a revolutionary process that is made through a rationale that could be Marxism. We are going to see how far Marxism and the faith can go together . . .

"What we want is an evangelical and critical presence in the revolution, but inside the revolution. What we do not want is that all this political potential be a potential that goes against the [revolutionary] process . . . If the Church moves apart from the revolution and puts itself in the opposition, as the archbishop proposes, then it is seen as an opposition church, the enemy, not as the brother who is inside. So that when the revolution has to defend itself, it becomes authoritarian, dogmatic. The participation of church people inside the revolution can serve to prevent radicalization. It can be the most important aspect in assuring that it will be a self-critical, humanitarian, open, pluralistic process."

Monsignor Pablo Antonio Vega, the bishop of the region of Juigalpa, who succeeded the archbishop in 1983 as president of the Bishops' Conference, talked to me about what made the Sandinistas and the liberation priests different from conventional Marxists: "One of the tactics of these people has been not to present themselves, ever, as Communists, as atheists, nor as against religion, but wishing to be the interpreters of the Church. It is for this that they speak of the Popular Church . . . Thus, their slogan, 'Between Christianity and Revolution there is no contradiction.' But in fact there are many differences. We have the advantage in that the people don't analyze things for the image but according to the facts. For that, it is the people themselves who are the first to denounce the public relations idea that there is respect for religion [by the Sandinistas]. It's an old tactic. A Russian theologian denounced it in 1917. In Russia they [the Marxists] had an advantage because the church had already been declared a national church, so people already thought that religion was part of the state."

What was happening in Nicaragua, Vega said, "is not just [creation of] a state religion, but within the Communist philosophy, what enters is a substitute for religion. Since they [the Marxists] never go to the causes, but simply analyze the phenomenon, they look for a substitution, and the substitute is the absolute state. But not just the absolute state. There is also all the metaphysical in the sense that there is nothing, ever, behind or beyond mankind [in Marxism]. They merely want religion to give a religious mystique to 'the cause.' "

Vega, who was educated as a sociologist in Canada, said he strongly believed in the need for social change in Nicaragua and he had seen the fall of Somoza as a "special moment" to begin because everyone was willing. But he said that possibility was lost because the Sandinistas allowed themselves to become the tools of "a new imperialism, with the great inconvenience that this imperialism is not economic but ideological." Vega said the Marxist priests in Nicaragua were in the minority and overwhelmingly foreign, except for the few in the government and others who were highly visible, such as Father Molina:

"The popularity of Marxism comes more from foreign priests here. They see the necessity of social changes, but they have the bad habit of always thinking over the heads of the people, and taking the place of the people. They always think of people as an object to be saved by the others. It's the new generation of Latin American priests coming in here who see our people as the subject of the change. They need to understand it is the people themselves who must be considered as the owner of the change . . . Our revolution should be from the people and with the people, I always say. And not a scheme imposed from outside because it takes away all the human vitality from the process. In addition, they take away the economic incentives that are a necessary part of human realization."

Monsignor Bosco Vivas, the auxiliary bishop of Managua, called the Popular Church "a species of fifth column, or a column within the church that is at the same time an enemy of the church."

"Why? Because it is formed by groups of priests, by religious, and people who say they belong to the Church. But their authorization does not come from the authorities of the Church, but from the authorities of a political party. So, while they insist on remaining inside the Church, they do not live submitted to the authority of that church. For that [reason] the Popular Church is prejudicial. It has used its religious character or its religious motivations to develop or fortify a Marxist political ideology.

"The Popular Church in Nicaragua has certain characteristics. First, the Popular Church is in power here, and in other places of the world and Latin America they are talking and writing about it, but from below. Here, they do it with all the disposition of the media, and with all the open economic possibilities. Here, the Popular Church is not contemplating the rise to power, but is already in power. They, who so often accuse the hierarchical church of defending its power— in fact, it is they who are in power now . . .

"The problem is that they use the Marxist method, and [that means] they lie. For us, by saying lie we are expressing a serious judgment of moral fault. But for a Marxist, no. To tell a lie is valid because with it you can better implant the ideology. So, the Popular Church, by using the Marxist methodology and all that manner of behavior, also falls into the same error of seeing things from another ethic, from another moral angle. It is not the Christian angle."

Luz Beatriz Arellano, a Franciscan nun on the staff of the Valdivieso Center, said she came to support the Sandinista Front as a result of social activism that began in the early 1960s. She concluded that social assistance [by the Church] was not sufficient in the face of the structural problems in society that caused poverty. "It was evident that exploitation had deep roots, and it was evident that religious life played a role. It contributed to repression." She began to work in the "base communities," the Bible study groups that some priests used as centers for political activism, and she took part in Father Molina's university group with a number of people who became Sandinista leaders.

After the rise of the Sandinistas, according to Sister Luz, there was a lot of religious manipulation on behalf of "economic interests." She claimed that bourgeois and business people not previously noted for their religiosity used it to oppose the Sandinistas. "The Church must not be converted into a barricade behind which conservative elements can operate . . . The rich in this country did not get their riches honestly—unless they won the lottery. They made money paying unjust wages and using political power to get land." The only religious persecution in Nicaragua, she said, was by "conservatives" against "progressives." The archbishop, she said, "is used by the United States and the opposition. We respect him as a bishop, but as a human being he is subject to mistakes."

Edgard Parrales, a diocesan priest, who began to actively oppose Somoza in 1970 and served as a Cabinet minister and in other high-level government posts after the Sandinistas came to power, made these points: "One of the errors of the Church, in my judgment, is its authoritarianism . . . I think the bishops were only against Somoza, more than in favor of the revolution . . . For us the priestly mission is not just the sacraments. It should be an attitude toward life—a 'light for the world.' Evangelism encompasses all life, wherever I can spread light. The theology of many of the bishops is out of step with the times. The Catholicism now of many people is not a Catholicism of faith but of economic interests. They try to make of religion an antireligion because it serves their economic interests. The revolution has many Christian elements and a lot of coincidences with Christian values . . . The *comandantes* don't confess, but they have Christian values."

Miguel Angel Casco, a Protestant preacher working with the Valdivieso Center, told me that Christians ought to give what he termed critical support to the FSLN, particularly in its social programs, but without becoming fanatical Sandinistas. Although saying most Protestants in Nicaragua lacked the analytical capacity to determine whether the FSLN was trying to subvert religion to its own purposes, Casco said he did believe that counterrevolutionaries were trying to use religion for their ends. Part of the reason that was possible, he said, lay in the methods of Roman Catholicism. "It has taught them that theology comes from Heaven and cannot be made by the masses. It is a theology that does not deal with daily life. It has profound roots, however, that can't be broken overnight . . . Many people in the Church here are not disposed to renew their thinking. The enemies of the revolution know that."

. . .

In an effort to find out the degree of support enjoyed by the two church camps I visited a number of parishes. At first I had the idea I could just go out and get the votes of the parish priests on the question of whom they supported: traditional church or Popular Church? At the same time I thought I could get some kind of reading of public opinion, operating on the theory that where people went to church would indicate a sort of vote for something, or against something.

I started going to masses, three times on Sundays, two or three times during the week. Drawing conclusions turned out to be more complicated than I had anticipated, but both sides had accepted from the outset, as Bishop Vega said, that the majority of priests serving parishes generally supported the bishops. I saw nothing to dispute that claim. One parish priest said 90 percent of all the Nicaraguan priests serving parishes in the Managua archdiocese supported the bishops. However, at that time, late 1983, Nicaraguan priests comprised only about one third of the priests serving parishes in the archdiocese, a ratio that probably extended to most of Nicaragua. It was agreed, however, that the bishops also had the support of at least a significant number of the foreigners serving parishes, probably assuring them a majority of the total. Father Aragon, the Spanish Dominican, agreed that the bishops had the overt following of the majority, but claimed that many of those priests felt intimidated by the bishops.

However, a priest I met in one church told me the intimidation that he had experienced came from the Sandinistas, not the bishops. This young man, also a foreigner, who feared having his name published, said he had been in Nicaragua during the time of the 1979 war against Somoza and had been told by his order to leave for security reasons in the last weeks of the war. As soon as the fighting stopped, he got on the first plane he could to get back into Nicaragua, brimming with enthusiasm for the promises of the new government and eager to begin the social projects he thought could finally be carried out.

He began working on a housing program that had the support of an international Catholic agency. Under the program, he hoped to help about two hundred poor families obtain low-cost houses, which the agency would send to Nicaragua in prefabricated sections. But he quickly ran into difficulties with the Sandinista Defense Committees and other militant groups being established by the new rulers. They wanted to approve the families selected to take part in the housing program, presumably to give preference to Sandinista sympathizers. The priest resisted, and a *comandante* wrote a letter warning him not to compete with the "mass organizations." Eventually, the priest gave up on his program. "No *comandante* is going to tell me how to run my church," he told me with a tone of bitterness and a glance over his shoulder. He discovered, he said, that in the new Nicaragua one either had to be a Sandinista or was classified as a reactionary.

Generally, I found that the liberation priests did not attract big crowds to their masses. There were even a number of expressions of concern from these priests to the effect that their followers were now so involved in working in the numerous Sandinista support organizations that they had little time or energy left for church. At some of the crowded churches where the priests were "in communion with the bishops," the expression used to indicate agreement with the hierarchy, I noticed that someone had provided special buses to bring people to the church, but there were other such priests who had standing-room-only crowds and no buses outside. Later, however, in conversations with various people about where they went to mass, I discovered that while some followed their politics in choosing a priest, others might, for various reasons, be going to a church where the priest had opposing political views, as long as the priest didn't wave them like a red flag during mass.

One Sunday morning I went to masses conducted by the archbishop at two country churches. When he left the first village, San Marcos, for the second, La Concepción, the dusty road down which he traveled was lined with palm and banana trees for more than a mile. He rode into La Concepción standing on the flatbed of an old red truck, smiling and waving, as a dozen men on horseback cleared the path in front of him and crowds of people stood on both sides of the road. As he passed under an arch of palms and climbed the steps into the adobe church, peasants reached out to touch him and shouted praise to him and the Pope.

Even on a normal Sunday, in Las Sierritas de Santo Domingo, an affluent suburb whose modern white church became parish home for the archbishop after the downtown cathedral was gutted by the 1972 earthquake, people filled the pews an hour before the mass and all the standing room was taken. Some of those attending were opposition leaders, businessmen, and diplomats from other Latin American countries, but many more came out of the poor neighborhoods on public buses and in the backs of trucks, then hiked the two miles up the hill from the highway to hear Monsignor Obando.

During the first few years of the Sandinista regime, there was usually little politics in the archbishop's homilies. He might include an expression of concern about prisoners or a mildly stated warning to parents to be vigilant about the moral values being imparted to children in the new educational system. But most of the blunt talk was left for interviews in his office and statements abroad. After about three years of Sandinista rule, however, he became gradually more forthright on public affairs, even in church.

Regardless of what he said, his magnetism seemed, in large part, to be a combination of personal appeal and the trappings of his office. Even in the heat and dirt of Nicaragua, he favored white and gold robes. He continued to use incense in the mass after most Latin American priests had ceased doing so, which critics saw as part of an effort to add a certain mysticism to his image, though in other ways he accepted modernization. There was lively guitar music, and young people singing at the top of their voices.

The archbishop, as he confronted the regime and the liberation theologians, did not like to justify or explain himself or his actions, especially to critics. He behaved like a combination of movie star and religious *caudillo,* a man who expected to be loved, honored, respected, even sometimes feared. He was supremely confident that the great majority of the people were with him, that he read them better than others, and that he was, in every way, the pastor of the Nicaraguans.

These characteristics made it difficult for him to win over the visiting foreigners, who came expecting intellectual discourse on the religious and political issues in Nicaragua. They found that kind of exchange with the liberation priests and with Bishop Vega, the president of the Bishops' Conference, but not with the archbishop. He talked readily and pleasantly to foreigners, but had no use for those who would treat him as just another human being. Only the Pope or the Lord might challenge the correctness of his actions.

A primary part of Monsignor Obando's tactics in dealing with the Sandinistas and the revolutionary Christians was to keep himself constantly before the people. He tried to get around to each of the sixty parishes in the archdiocese at least once during the year, and his datebook of other public activities filled up a year in advance. He also prided himself on the number of people waiting in his outer office when he arrived each morning. At times the archbishop seemed to be challenging the faithful to show more love for him than for the *comandantes.* He even turned his twenty-fifth anniversary as a priest, in 1983, into a big celebration, inviting, among others, the ambassadors of Venezuela and the United States, who later suspected they had been somewhat used.

However right or wrong his methods, his dispute with the Sandinistas made him easily the most popular man in Nicaragua. This was acknowledged, at least privately, by his critics and opponents, though many would claim he was only more successful than others in manipulating people. Some in the government admitted it was a foolish tactic to try to portray him as the defender of outdated, bourgeois interests, but they saw it as the only way they had to oppose him, short of outright oppression, which they feared would make him more popular.

In obvious contrast to the archbishop were the pastoral methods of Father Uriel Molina, the director of the Valdivieso Center and parish priest with historic ties to the FSLN. He seemed to function as the unofficial archbishop of the pro-Sandinista priests, meeting frequently with government leaders and taking part in ceremonial occasions, such as receiving high-level visiting church groups sympathetic to the Sandinistas. The ambiance of his mass was so distinct from that of the archbishop as to make it seem that the two men were leading the worship of different gods.

Father Molina's church, a large, octagonal structure dominating the Riguero neighborhood in eastern Managua, was approached through dirt streets torn up by ditches and other work—Riguero was favored by the new government for much-needed public works. As the time for the Sunday evening mass approached, guitar music poured out of the church, and people of the neighborhood sat outside and watched the cars, buses, and jeeps make their way through the potholes to unload foreigners at the door. Those arriving were North Americans and Europeans, pale-skinned people wearing sandals and carrying cameras and tape recorders. Before the mass, they would mill about inside, studying life-size murals that glorified the Sandinista Front and its war against the National Guard. For a while, the door through which they entered the church was covered by a poster showing a U.S. military helicopter hovering over a peaceful peasant scene drawn in primitive style and carrying the caption: HEROD SEARCHES FOR THE CHILD TO KILL HIM.

By the time the mass began, there were usually thirty to forty foreigners in the pews and fewer Nicaraguans, but the Nicaraguans continued to arrive until they outnumbered the foreigners about four to one. There were plenty of places to sit. Father Molina nearly always had a foreign priest to assist him, perhaps someone from the University of Louvain or from the United States. He would run quickly through the Bible lesson and go into the homily, which he often devoted to a recitation of the latest misdeeds of Ronald Reagan, and he would thank the foreign delegations for coming to show their solidarity. Then he would take off his robe to reveal a polyester-blend leisure suit and come down from the altar with a small microphone on a long cord, and encourage the audience to participate. If the archbishop's style seemed to be that of a movie star, then Father Molina's was that of a television talk-show host. He urged worshipers to expound on political issues for benefit of the visitors. José Andrés Solís, who had earlier participated in the mass as a lay reader, came forward one evening.

"In Somoza's time," he began, "the government had the support of North American imperialism. Dollars came here to keep us oppressed. After the revolution, the government worries about the well-being of all Nicaraguans instead of just the capitalists, landowners, and bourgeoisie. The peasants and others were marginalized before. The Sandinista revolution has helped our development with education and health programs. Before, the peasants didn't know what sugar was, now they use it."

Solís continued at great length, for longer than Father Molina's homily. Many of his claims for the accomplishments of the regime might have been challenged outside the church, by peasants, for instance, on the sugar question, but everyone inside listened raptly. He finished by providing the latest production statistics from the milk plant where he worked, then shouted *Patria Libre o Morir* (Free Fatherland or Die) and sat down amidst applause.

Father Molina asked that a mother come forward and speak on the military draft law, which had been enacted the week before this mass and which the bishops had strongly criticized. A woman rose, and Father Molina introduced her as a "militant revolutionary" with one son in the Sandinista army and another in the Sandinista Youth. Her message was brief and simple: "I believe, as a revolutionary Christian, that we have to contribute what we love most, and that is our children."

The conflict surrounding the Nicaraguan Church did not, of course, grow in isolation. It developed simultaneously with the issues facing all Nicaraguans. The Sandinistas were gradually putting in place a

Leninist structure—the vast network of defense committees, youth and children's groups, militia, internal security police and army created as an extension of the Sandinista Front. As this happened, non-Marxists were splitting with the Sandinistas; many turned to violent opposition and eventually found CIA backing. The opposition that remained inside the country—business and farm groups, traditional political parties, media, labor federations—was repressed, broken, confiscated, censored, or otherwise lost ground. All of this served to thrust the Church hierarchy into a more visible and active role in opposing Sandinista measures, whether they touched directly on the Church or not.

The resulting growth in criticism from the Church hierarchy infuriated the Sandinista Front, which responded in various ways. When the differences first became heated, in the middle of 1981, Sandinista groups began to periodically send the *turbas* (mobs) to taunt the archbishop and attack other priests. Daniel Ortega, of the Sandinista National Directorate, once acknowledged the paternity of these organized militants by saying that he preferred to call them *turbas divinas*—"divine mobs." The most infamous series of such actions occurred in August and September 1982, beginning about three weeks after the dispute over the change of priests at the little church in the Santa Rosa neighborhood.

The Reverend Bismarck Carballo, the spokesman for the archbishop, was forced by four members of the Sandinista police to run naked out the door of a suburban house before a crowd that included a news photographer and a television crew. The circumstances leading up to this event were subject to dispute. Father Carballo said he was having lunch at the home of one of his female parishioners when the police broke in, forced both of them to undress and then dragged him outside. Later, however, the woman said in an interview with *El Nuevo Diario,* a pro-Sandinista newspaper, that her relations with the priest were not of a priestly nature. At any rate, Father Carballo was arrested on the spot, after the photographer and cameramen had recorded the event, and was taken to a police station. The papal nuncio, Monsignor Andrea Cordero Lanza di Montezemolo, was called to the police station, and he asked what crime, if any, Father Carballo had committed. The police finally decided there was nothing to charge him with, and Carballo was released to the Vatican envoy.

After a day of hesitation, the government censor allowed *El Nuevo Diario* to publish its photographs of the nude priest, graced by a large black X, and Sandinista television showed its tape of him being dragged out of the house. It was strictly coincidental, government authorities insisted, that the crowd and media happened to be present in that suburban neighborhood at midday.

Most Nicaraguans turned out to be less outraged by the possible relationship between the priest and the woman than about the lack of respect shown them. Roman Catholics serving in the government told the Sandinista Front it had gone too far with the episode, which was generally blamed on Interior Minister Borge and the Cubans serving as internal security advisers. It was privately acknowledged that no Cuban from Cuba under the age of thirty-five had any recollection of, or respect for, religion. But before the cooler heads could find a way to appease the Church and the public in the Carballo matter, the crisis had grown into something bigger.

On the following Saturday—August 14, 1982—the archbishop went to say mass in the town of Masaya, about twenty miles outside Managua, and there was a clash between a Sandinista *turba* and the seminary students accompanying the archbishop. On Monday the Roman Catholic schools in Managua decided to strike, and the school in Masaya run by the Salesian Brothers, the archbishop's order, did the same. The school in Masaya was then visited by *turbas*. When the mob appeared, a priest rang the church bells and neighborhood people came pouring out of their homes to confront the intruders. Some people sacked the local police station, set the prisoners free, and took the weapons. That afternoon there was shooting at the school. At least two people died, both members of the pro-government group. The next day, the government trucked more supporters into the outskirts of Masaya, and Interior Minister Borge gave a speech in which he said the uprising of the day before had been part of an attempt to stage a counterrevolution. The government took over the school and arrested nearly a hundred people, though most were soon released without charges.

The Sandinista Front leadership, once it had had a chance to reflect on what had happened, was collectively chagrined. It put the question of the school in the hands of Carlos Tünnermann, the minister of education and a practicing Catholic. Tünnermann negotiated with a delegation sent from the Vatican and in two weeks the school was returned to the Salesians. The government prevailed only in the expulsion of one Spanish priest. Tomás Borge was sent on a long tour of the Soviet Union and Bulgaria.

Aside from these occasional major blowups, the *turbas* were active in late-night attacks on the humble meeting places of many religious sects, groups distinguished from Protestant denominations by their refusal to recognize any temporal government. This attitude created particular problems between the sects and the Sandinistas because the sects often told their members not to send their children to the government's vaccination or literacy programs. The proliferation of sects had begun in Nicaragua only as recently as 1980, and since the sects were alleged to be receiving financial help from religious groups in the United States, Sandinista leaders charged that foreign missionaries were actually CIA agents sent to destabilize the regime. Leaders of the Sandinista Defense Committees in the neighborhoods usually used the CIA accusation to justify *turba* attacks on the meeting places of the sects.

One such attack occurred in late 1982 at the Mormon Church in the San Judas neighborhood of Managua. The morning I arrived, a black and red Sandinista flag was flying in the front yard, and a poster with the likeness of Che Guevara was pasted on the outside of what had now become the Roberto Vargas Batres Pre-School. Enrollment was to begin soon. Sixto Ulloa, a Protestant pastor who was one of the leaders of CEPAD, the evangelical committee, had told me the Mormons were considered a sect. They further complicated things, he said, by sending young American men in dark trousers, white shirts, and neckties to organize and run their churches. Neckties had gone out of style in Nicaragua with the departure of the last Somoza. Whereas most of the sect meeting places being attacked by *turbas* were little more than shanties, this was a new, one-story building built of concrete block. Missionaries had just finished painting it the day before the attack and had not yet begun holding services.

I asked a man and woman waiting for a bus nearby who had taken over the church. "They did it, the Sandinistas," the woman said. *"Las turbas divinas,"* said the man.

Then I went to a house across the street that had a soft-drink sign hanging over the door. The woman gave me a Coke and pulled up a rocking chair for me. She was not at home the night the church was occupied, she said. She had returned from mass about ten in the evening, and the deed had been done. The next day, she bought *La Prensa* hoping to find out what had happened, but there was not a word in the paper. She had not been aware of a large number of Mormons in San Judas, but she said there did seem to be a lot of people passing by the house selling Bibles lately. "One is Catholic, so one believes that God is Catholic," she said with a small laugh and a shrug.

But she said there were no problems over religion among the people of San Judas and that usually she did not know whether one of her neighbors was Catholic or something else. She and her family had gotten through the war against Somoza without any problems, except for the two bullet holes in her Coca-Cola sign. Now, she said as she rocked, there were so many strange things happening.

The Nicaraguan church issues boiled over into Pope John Paul II's visit during his Central American tour in March of 1983. Things began on the wrong note when the news of his planned visit was initially censored out of the newspapers in Nicaragua, then government leaders and Archbishop Obando y Bravo sparred over who would receive him and how. The Sandinistas, after considering the political benefit, wanted to receive the Pope like a chief of state. The Vatican would not agree to this, but when John Paul landed at the Managua airport, Daniel Ortega departed from protocol and delivered a fifteen-minute political speech attacking U.S. policies in Central America. Then, when the Pope greeted the waiting Cabinet ministers and came to Culture Minister Ernesto Cardenal, he reacted with visible displeasure. Cardenal, wearing his usual blue jeans, loose white shirt and black beret, went down on his knees to kiss the Pope's ring, but the pontiff shook his finger in the priest's face and told him to straighten out his relations with the Church.

The Pope's public homily, which he devoted to a call for Catholics to unify behind him and the bishops, was interrupted repeatedly by Sandinista militants who had packed the front rows in the plaza and grew angry that he did not condemn attacks by anti-Sandinista guerrillas. Between shouts of *"Silencio!"* to the crowd, the Pope repeated his previous criticism of the Popular Church concept, terming it "absurd and dangerous." He said no Christian, much less a priest or nun, could take it upon himself or herself to break church unity by acting independently or against the will of the bishops. "That [rule] is valid in any situation or country, without any process of development of social elevation that is undertaken being able to legitimately compromise the identity and religious liberty of a people . . ."

Later, those in the front, including Culture Minister Cardenal, chanted *"Poder popular"* (people's power) as they jabbed their fists in the air. Back at the airport for the Pope's departure, Daniel Ortega said the Nicaraguan people demanded solidarity from the Pope, implying that they had not gotten it.

Pro-Sandinista Christians acted as if they were personally offended after the Pope was gone. They felt he had merely taken the side of

Archbishop Obando and had contributed to dissension in the church. Some claimed the archbishop had misled the Pope into thinking Nicaragua was like Poland, where the church faced persecution, and as a result the Pope came in with a tough line. But his comments did not allude to persecution. The Vatican's representative in Nicaragua, Monsignor Lanza di Montezemolo, had made known beforehand that he thought Nicaragua's main problem was the attempt to divide the Church and that persecution had occurred only in a few cases, such as that of Father Carballo. The Sandinista Front said that while the Pope had wanted to remove the Church from politics, his call for unity and obedience to the bishops was really a political statement because church people had all assumed political positions in Central America. The FSLN expressed the hope the Pope might reflect on what he had said and change his attitude.

A few months later, the Sandinistas indicated they had not greatly altered their view of how to deal with the Church. The Sandinista-backed *Semana Cómica (Comics Weekly)* devoted most of its twelve-page August 1983 issue to what it headlined as the FIRST ANNIVERSARY OF THE CARBALLO CASE. The cover drawing was a caricature of Father Carballo, nude, strumming a guitar and singing beneath the balcony of a house. The rest of the issue was sprinkled with cartoon drawings that varied between risqué and obscene. There were also simulated advertisements from the likes of the U.S. and Spanish embassies congratulating Father Carballo.

The church leadership reacted with a cry of anger, and the government responded in a tone of surprised innocence, saying the whole thing had slipped by the censor. The issue was ordered withdrawn from circulation, but by then there were so many copies in circulation that anyone in Managua who wanted a copy could get one. The papal nuncio protested to the Foreign Ministry, saying he was unconvinced by the argument that the publication had been missed by the censor in a regime of "strict state control." Many people were further unconvinced because of the fact that one of the artistic talents behind *Comics Weekly* was Rosario Murillo, longtime companion of Daniel Ortega.

As the Sandinistas played tough, the bishops, and the archbishop in particular, also became tougher and more political, presumably indicating that they enjoyed the full support of the Pope. During 1983 and 1984, the nine bishops making up the hierarchy took the offensive. They opposed universal military draft on the grounds that the Sandinista army was run by a quasi-political party instead of a national government; they questioned Sandinista intentions to carry out free elections as planned in late 1984; and—the most controversial of all —they called on the government to open "reconciliation" talks with the anti-Sandinista guerrillas attacking from north and south.

Also, the archbishop spoke out on his own. One of the things he regularly criticized was press censorship. When asked by pro-Sandinista journalists why they did not condemn the guerrilla attacks, he and Bishop Vega would say censorship impeded their knowledge of such matters. When the Sandinistas tried to link Monsignor Obando to corruption of the Somoza era, such as a *Barricada* story claiming he had once accepted thirty-six cases of whisky from Somoza, he would remind people that some of the Sandinistas owed him their lives and that the whole movement was in his debt. "I also put my grain of sand for the revolution," he said. At one point, he said, he talked Somoza out of killing imprisoned Sandinistas. "If that had happened," he said, "some of them would not be here today to tell the story."

The Sandinistas continued to look for a way to handle the Church without a head-on confrontation. This was evident in one of the most ambitious undertakings of the Valdivieso Center, a four-week seminar in the second half of 1983 that attempted to establish that Marx, Christ, and Sandino were of the same mind. Dr. Giulio Girardi, a Marxist philosophy professor at the University of Cagliari in Italy and a former member of the Salesian Brothers, came to Managua to research the question and lead the seminar sessions. In essence, he used liberation theology to make the connection between Marx and Christ, but he had to break new ground where Sandino was concerned.

Sandino left behind a substantial record of documents and interviews making clear he did not like Marxism. However, Girardi argued that there were many coincidences in the ideas of Sandino and Marx and only two basic contradictions. For one thing, Sandino did not like the concept of class struggle, but Girardi claimed this was because Sandino knew he had to "use" the bourgeoisie for tactical reasons to help him achieve his nationalistic goal of expelling the U.S. Marines from Nicaragua. The other conflict with Marxism was Sandino's Roman Catholic faith, but Girardi concluded that this would not have been a problem had Sandino lived into the 1980s because he would have seen the union of Marxism and Christianity in liberation theology.

This was an immensely useful thesis to the Sandinistas if the Nicaraguan people could be made to believe it. But if this happened—in effect, rendering the hierarchy impotent—how long would the Christians in the liberation theology line survive with the FSLN? Would the FSLN still need its Christian friends? Could one—the FSLN or the Marxist Christians—subvert or convert the other? Occasionally, *comandantes* hinted that they might be susceptible to embracing the faith. Borge once said publicly that he "aspired" to be a Christian but would not proclaim himself one until he was perfect. It was difficult not to view this as an audacious tactical move, the kind the Sandinista leaders had shown themselves capable of in the past. Was it any different from the appeal they once made to non-Marxist opponents of Somoza claiming that the FSLN was prepared to set aside its Marxism in the interests of forming a broad alliance?

However, the archbishop and the bishops were gambling that Nicaraguans would not accept an official religion. They thought the people were more inclined to believe the Roman Catholic hierarchy than the Sandinistas if the price was not beyond their capacity to pay.

It was an uphill battle for several reasons. One was the difficulty in holding on to youth in a country where ideology increasingly intruded into education and where by 1984 half the population was under sixteen and could not remember a time when newspaper headlines did not declare Marx and Christ to be partners. Also, as government took over more and more of the economy, the political and religious views of those entering the job market became crucial to a person's economic well-being. In addition, the government had control or influence over most of the media, and the Marxist Christian groups had more money and international support for propaganda purposes than the hierarchy.

One of the Church's frustrations was its difficulty in finding international financial support and general sympathy among foreign church organizations. It received $324,000 in U.S. government aid between mid-1979 and early 1981, when the aid was terminated because of Sandinista support for the Salvadoran guerrillas. The Reagan administration wanted to continue extending aid to nongovernmental groups, such as the Church, but the Sandinista government would not permit it. Some financial support for the programs of the Roman Catholic hierarchy in Nicaragua also came from the Venezuelan government or other sympathizers in Venezuela.

Despite these problems, what was a backwater Catholic hierarchy when the Sandinistas came to power was learning to defend itself against the sophisticates. The Pope's growing involvement in the

Nicaraguan dispute was, to all appearances, of benefit to the archbishop. The archbishop came home from a private, ninety-minute meeting with the Pope in May 1984 and seemed invigorated and ready for battle. Even before that, the bishops were working on youth questions and creating their own "base communities"—Bible study groups for adults that, unlike those of the liberation priests, stressed obedience to the bishops. Catechism classes also received special attention, and some of the busiest priests in the country took time to conduct them. Monsignor Vega, the Juigalpa bishop, said he knew this attention to youth was paying off when boys and girls from his parishes won election to school offices, despite the influence of the Sandinista youth movement. The only young people he considered lost to church influence were those sent to Cuba for secondary education.

The bishops set out to increase Nicaraguan control of the parishes, though saying they had nothing against foreigners; three of the nine bishops were foreigners in 1984. Aside from the obvious reason, that Nicaraguans might be less susceptible to the currents of fashionable ideologies, another reason for this became apparent in July 1984 when the government expelled ten foreign priests who supported the bishops, accusing them of playing politics. Among them was a Canadian priest who had pioneered the establishment of non-Marxist "base communities" in the Carazo region south of the capital. The work of the priest, the Reverend Benito Laplante, had often been singled out for praise by the archbishop.

By 1984, three or four young priests were graduating each year from the revived national seminary in Managua. Preparatory seminaries in other dioceses had much larger enrollments, creating the possibility of larger classes in the upper-level seminary in coming years. Monsignor Vivas said there was an awakening of interest in the priesthood among Nicaraguan boys and their families as a result of the difficult times. Each new Nicaraguan priest was a small victory for the bishops.

16

THE
MARKET VENDORS

The queen of commerce in Nicaragua since the early 1950s has been
Managua's *Mercado Oriental* (Eastern Market), a collection of some
twelve thousand vendors selling from carts and stalls spread over fifty
square blocks just east of the old downtown area. It is a dirty and
seemingly disorganized place, but those who sell there and those who
shop regularly understand its order and believe a certain basic standard is maintained. The vendors are organized by what they sell: basic
grains and dry foodstuffs in one area, fruit and vegetables in another,
meat and cheese, electronics, hardware, clothes in others. Pickup
trucks inch their way through the maze of potholes and human madness to unload or load, men and boys pull wooden carts. Shoppers
range from poor to rich. Most of the sellers are women with brown
skin; some with plump upper arms and soft young faces, others bone
thin and weathered. All of them are strong enough to lift a day's stock
and balance it on their heads when necessary. Men also sell in the

markets, but the women dominate the scene. They have powerful lungs and an invincible manner. To the visitor, the market crowd looks exactly like what the Sandinistas would describe as *puro pueblo* —real people, the bedrock of Nicaragua.

However, the Eastern Market was transformed into enemy territory for the Sandinistas in the early years of their regime. Police and inspectors learned to take care on entering the market area and to protect their flanks. Sandinista *comandantes,* respected or feared by most Nicaraguans by the time they had been in power a short time, found that the market women invariably dared to talk back, and even fight back.

The Eastern Market is the most visible and vocal part of a traditional marketing system that numbers at least 60,000 vendors throughout Nicaragua—a formidable force in a country of fewer than 3 million and a labor force of 900,000. Although air-conditioned supermarkets and a few shopping malls exist in Nicaragua, open-air markets have always sold most of the food and a significant share of clothing, hardware, small household items, and even some furniture. Government officials estimated that as of the end of 1983 there were about thirty thousand licensed open-air vendors in the department of Managua alone, which includes the capital city and some small towns in the surrounding rural area. Most operated their stalls or carts in one of the eight large marketplaces, though some of the fruit and vegetable sellers operated at the entrances to residential areas. The remaining thirty thousand vendors sell in the rest of the country, primarily in the central markets of sizeable towns.

It was sugar that ignited the dispute between the Sandinistas and the market vendors. To understand how the issue of sugar could be so explosive, one has to understand its importance to Nicaraguans. Aside from drinking rum, Nicaraguans put as much sugar as coffee in a cup and many spoonfuls in a glass of iced tea, and they sweeten fruit juices. Most desserts feature primarily sugar. Some Nicaraguans claim, with a decree of pride, that they consume more sugar per capita than any other nation. But in early 1982 the government instituted sugar rationing. The amount of the ration was sufficient for the sugar appetite of most people, but consumers faced the inconvenience of obtaining a ration card from their local CDS (Sandinista Defense Committee). They were also assigned specific stores in which to buy sugar, according to their neighborhood, and specific days on which to buy it. In the interests of an efficient bureaucracy and control of sales, only the government's new People's Stores and the supermarkets—all or partially owned by the government—were designated to sell sugar. The open-air vendors were legally excluded from being supplied with sugar to sell.

The sugar action was followed during the next three years by similar measures for many other products basic to human existence in Nicaragua. In some cases it was outright rationing. In others the government was establishing controls over how each item could be acquired and sold by the retailer, creating state middlemen who decided which retailers would be supplied. The effect was to cut out more and more of the traditional sellers. By 1982 private middlemen and nongovernmental cooperatives had been officially eliminated from the wholesale distribution system, and by mid-1984, market vendors and most other private retailers had been legally excluded from selling nearly twenty items, including rice, sugar, milk, bananas, cooking oil, soap, sorghum, and toilet paper.

The government justified the distribution controls and rationing on various grounds. The primary reasons cited at the beginning were falling production and the need to export more of products such as sugar and import less of such things as bottles and paper. For a while, the government said consumption had risen after the fall of Somoza, which for the first year or so may have been true, but after the shortages began it was obvious that people were no longer able to consume at a higher level, even if they could afford it. The shortages, of course, brought higher prices, and the government said one of the reasons it needed distribution controls was to prevent hoarding and speculation. After anti-Sandinista guerrillas began to increase their actions in mid-1981, the warfare was increasingly cited as the reason for declining production. Private farmers were also accused of not producing enough, and they responded that they needed income incentives and guarantees against confiscations. The private farmers also said they were producing as well as the state farms, even though the state farms had the best land because the biggest of them were former Somoza-owned farms. As guerrilla warfare grew through 1982, 1983, and 1984, the government was also diverting more food to the army and was stockpiling certain items.

The dispute between the vendors and the Sandinistas, however, extended to the deeper questions of how people had a right to earn their living and the FSLN's desire that no important group of people be outside its political control. It was a clash of basic concepts between those whose natural instinct was to control and those whose natural instinct was to resist and overcome, whose first objective was to assure their supply line and then to do anything to keep it open.

The market vendors formed the grass roots of private enterprise and as a group were possibly the most independent people in Nicaragua, the ultimate entrepreneurs and problem solvers. Streetwise and unwilling to concede defeat, they had learned to do business out of an apron pocket, with little or no education, but with heads like calculators. The market vendors tended to look on selling as one of their basic human rights. Most had been doing it since the age of five or six when they had begun helping their mothers or fathers. They thought the public had an obligation to buy and the government an obligation to leave them alone.

But the Sandinistas were not the kind to leave things alone. They wanted everyone to belong to their revolution. That meant to join the CDS's, fly the red and black flag, turn out for demonstrations, and read *Barricada.* Also, the Sandinista leaders, from their first days in power, had been keenly aware of the opposition tactics that had been used in Chile against the Socialist government of Salvador Allende between 1970 and 1973. As a result, they feared the consequences of allowing people outside of their political camp to control food distribution in Nicaragua.

The conflict over marketing rules began in the first months after the new government took power. The Ministry of Interior Commerce decided to create the *Empresa Nicaraguense de Alimentos Básicos*— Nicaraguan Enterprise of Basic Foods, known as ENABAS—a state middleman. Farmers would sell corn, rice, beans, and other foods basic to the Nicaraguan diet to ENABAS, which would sell them to the market women, supermarkets, and other retailers. ENABAS also began to subsidize about ten basic food items, paying more to the farmer than it sold them for to the retailer.* Government advertising on television and in newspapers described ENABAS as "the granary of the people."

The Chamber of Commerce took part in early discussions with the ministry at the end of 1979 and beginning of 1980 when ENABAS was being formed. But with the private wholesalers a part of the Chamber

---

*But in June 1984, under the pressures of a collapsed economy, the government eliminated all subsidies except those on sugar and milk.

of Commerce, it opposed state involvement in wholesaling and abandoned the discussions. It then helped the wholesalers and some of the market vendors to form their own buying cooperative for basic grains, which bought directly from farmers and processors.

At first there was no rationing. There were price controls over wholesale and retail prices of basic food items, but with a more or less adequate supply the controls did not disrupt the market. However, distrust developed between the market vendors and the *comandantes* over a variety of political questions before the economic issues became significant.

I saw an example of this in early 1981 while Jaime Wheelock, the minister of agriculture, was giving a news conference in Government House about his latest plan to "guarantee" an adequate food supply. Suddenly, people were shouting and banging on doors outside the sealed, air-conditioned building. Wheelock winced when the noise began and brought the news conference to a quick close, then left in a hurry, going out a back door into a guarded, fenced parking area. I went out the front and found a couple of hundred vendors from the Eastern Market. Most of them were women wearing dresses and aprons. A few carried placards, and a few carried babies.

The demonstrators began to talk, all at once, about a multitude of things over which they were unhappy. One of their complaints was of having been denied stalls in three new markets on what the women charged were political grounds. The new markets—clean and spacious facilities with tile counters, refrigeration, and bathrooms under high roofs—had been built with U.S. aid money under the reconstruction program that followed the 1972 earthquake. For various reasons they had been finished long after the fall of Somoza, and the Sandinista media had made a big point of saying the new markets were an example of how the FSLN treated the people and the dilapidated Eastern Market an example of how Somoza had treated the people. There was no reference in this propaganda to who paid for the new markets. The second major complaint of the vendors was that the government now was trying to drive them out of business at the old market by cutting off the bus routes. The demonstrators also complained of being called *somocistas* and thieves by government functionaries and of being pressured to join the CDS's.

"We are not *somocistas and thieves,* said one woman. "We are hardworking people just trying to earn a living for our children from the sweat of our brow."

Some showed me the CDS cards they said they had bought under duress. They said they had paid one hundred córdobas to join and were paying five córdobas a month dues and that it was a worthless investment; the CDS did nothing for them.

There were also complaints that the FSLN wanted to "proletarianize" them. This was a word one was beginning to hear a lot in Nicaragua from critics of the Sandinistas. I assumed it meant an effort to turn them into time-card punching assembly-line workers, with the political acquiescence that might come through state control of the factory and/or trade union. Considering the declining number of assembly lines in Nicaragua, this seemed an unrealistic goal.

After a few hours a delegation was admitted to Government House, and Daniel Ortega came downstairs to talk to the group. It was not a friendly exchange. The women repeated their complaints about the new markets and the bus routes. Finally, they said, word had reached them that Ortega had referred to them as "scum." Before any of these issues could be discussed, a dispute erupted over whether a photographer from *La Prensa* should be allowed to take photos, and Ortega stormed off after saying, "If you like *La Prensa,* then take your problems to *La Prensa* to resolve." Ortega did talk to the women twice again, but in the more controlled environment of the FSLN's *Face the People* television program. He denied that political considerations had been used in assigning stalls for the new markets and, after indicating there had been some thought of closing the Eastern Market, committed the government to keeping it open. As for the "scum" charge, he first denied using it, then said maybe he had, and that if he had, he was now taking it back.

Later came the sugar rationing and the disputes over access to products and over prices. Vendors did not accept any of this willingly. At dusk one evening in June 1982, when the issue was developing, I drove to the earthquake-damaged building that served as headquarters of ACOPROBAMA, the private buying cooperative that had been established with the help of the Chamber of Commerce when the government created ENABAS. ACOPROBAMA now claimed to represent eighteen hundred vendors of basic foodstuffs in the Eastern Market. Eight members of the board of directors, all vendors themselves, were waiting to tell me in angry words how the government was trying to exclude them from commerce. The reasons, they said, were as much political as economical: ENABAS was the means to exercise political control over the market vendors, and the rationing cards, which had then recently appeared, were a means to exercising political control over the entire population. One threatened the vendors' livelihood, the other threatened the people with hunger. They pounded the table and swore to fight by whatever means they could find. It was a choice of fighting or leaving, one said, and leaving would be to create an empty seat for a Cuban.

Within the government, the vendors told me, a debate was under way about whether to nationalize all of commerce. They showed me a photocopy of a twenty-year-old news story about the nationalization of small commerce in Cuba and a more recent story about Cuba's attempts to revive private sales of fresh foods in hopes of making consumers happier. Could not the *comandantes* learn anything from Cuba's mistakes, they wondered.

"We are outside the political line that they advocate. In it, commerce has no place," said Milisia Blanco, the president of the cooperative. "They are trying to take away our livelihood, and that is against human rights. They try to say that here in Nicaragua there is liberty, but we are certain that they are even going to take away the air that we breathe. People don't matter to them. Their objective is their political line: Communism."

Another of the board members said, "People who come to the market believe the reason for the shortages is that the *comandantes* send the grains to the Socialist countries to pay for arms. They are playing with the stomachs of the people, and that is very dangerous."

In part, the vendors told me, the problem was that the private farmers were now being told that they could sell certain items only to ENABAS, the government's central supply agency, which meant the buying cooperative no longer had access to most of the products it had been handling. In turn, they said, ENABAS was refusing to sell to the vendors in the Eastern Market because the government wanted to force them into line politically. The market vendors said they were resisting Sandinista efforts to get them to buy and sell *Barricada*, to join the CDS's in the marketplace and the Sandinista militia, and to take part in pro-government demonstrations and other activities. They said they did not want to be involved in political questions, that their only interest was to be free to practice commerce, into which they thought religion and politics should not enter.

"Do you know what we call Nicaragua?" one asked. "We call it the country of decrees—one per day."

"I could have a stall in one of the new markets," another of the directors of ACOPROBAMA said, "but I would have to close one day a week to train for the militia. I am not going to kneel before anyone for a hundred pounds of rice."

. . .

To decree that products would be sold only in a certain way was one thing, but to force the market vendors to comply was another. Walking through the Eastern Market one morning when the government had recently begun to control rice distribution, for example, I found heaping mounds of rice in dishpans on many of the small counters. I asked Ramona Brenes, a tiny woman with gray hair pulled back in a tight bun, how she got the rice she was selling.

"It's contraband," she said without hesitation.

Mrs. Brenes regularly bought from men who passed through the market at daybreak and sold it for the equivalent of somewhere between $40 and $48 a hundred pounds, compared to to what was then the authorized wholesale price of $23 a hundred. She passed the higher cost on to the customers, who paid willingly because they were unable to find rice elsewhere at that time. She and nearby vendors claimed they could only guess who these mysterious men might be. Perhaps they were farmers circumventing the government's middleman role. More likely, in the opinion of several women, they were government employees with access to the storage areas of ENABAS who were trying to make extra income. Some of the rice, in fact, arrived in bags stamped ENABAS.

Mrs. Brenes dismissed any notion that there were legitimate shortages of basic foods. Nicaragua had always been self-sufficient in rice, and there had always been sugar to burn. There would be enough now, she thought, if people would stop playing politics with food.

"The government—those *comandantes*—are keeping it all to themselves," she said, crossing her arms against her chest to emphasize what she meant.

That same morning at La Fuente, one of the new markets built with U.S. aid money, things were orderly and inviting, but there was a distinct shortage of customers. While there was contraband rice at the Eastern Market, La Fuente had none, and there had been none for about a week. Unless customers could expect to find everything they needed, they would not come to La Fuente to buy the attractive fruits and vegetables and the refrigerated meats. People who dealt in contraband could not enter the new market because there were only a few entrances, and the market management could keep an eye on everything that came in.

Violeta Flores Lazo, a young mother with two toddlers playing on a pallet behind the counter of her new stall, was one of the vendors suffering for lack of rice. So she was in no mood to be receptive when a man came by selling *Barricada*. "I don't know how to read," she snapped, and he retreated. She did know how to read. She had already read *La Prensa*, which lay on a shelf under her counter.

From mid-1982 the Ministry of Interior Commerce and its various organs, such as ENABAS, gradually spread their control and influence. Food, like everything else in Nicaragua, was becoming not a matter of the farmer and the marketplace but of government agencies, studies by foreign analysts and the like. A research institute attached to the Agrarian Reform agency, for example, drew up an extensive chart under the heading THE PROBLEM OF SHORTAGES and, among other things, characterized one of the major reasons for shortages as *coyuntural*, which might be translated as "arising from the situation." The government leaders talked a lot about the need for "secure channels of distribution," which seemed to reflect a lack of trust in traditional sellers.

There were also disputes between the government and the private sector about how much power the government legally had to fix prices. When the ministry published lists of approved retail prices for a number of items, *La Prensa* checked the decrees and found that only certain of those items could be controlled under existing laws. In late 1982 the ministry ran a newspaper advertisement stating that it had the right to fix the price of any item, food or otherwise, sold for internal consumption, and the Chamber of Commerce complained that this was contrary to the Plan of Government drawn up just before the change of power in 1979, which had said only that basic food items would be price controlled. The tactics used by both sides—government and vendors—varied according to what the other did. When one side did something tough, the other side responded with something tougher.

The Ministry of Interior Commerce created a body of civilian inspectors to make the rounds of each market every few weeks to check prices and find out whether vendors had products they were not supposed to have. The inspectors would confiscate rice, sugar, and other items, depending upon the regulation of the moment, and issue citations. But the vendors, faced with the loss of what probably represented their income for the week, would fight back. Many slugfests resulted. Sources on both sides claimed that government agents had been killed in such encounters, but I found no official government acknowledgement of that.

In mid-1982, when government inspectors backed by uniformed police went into the central market in Masaya, twenty miles south of the capital, and took away rice and other grains, the fighting disrupted the entire market. After it was over, the Masaya vendors and those in the nearby town of Granada closed for two days in protest.

One of those caught in another such raid, in the Eastern Market in late 1983, was Milisia Blanco. A few days after it occurred, when she and eight other vendors were fighting a government order to vacate their stalls, I asked her what she was accused of and how such things occurred.

"They accuse us of scandalous conduct. That's what they call it when those individuals [the inspectors] arrive at our businesses and we say we are not going to let them pass unless they have an eviction order. Second, they accuse us of hoarding, but it's not possible to hoard in an area two yards by two yards square. Third comes speculation . . . There are cases when the person cannot obey the law because there is not an adequate supply and therefore has to buy from higher priced sources . . . Also, they accuse us of putting in danger the lives of the inspectors. Since the precedent is that they take away all the products, what usually happens when they arrive is that the people [vendors] are afraid they are going to rob them of their products, without even a receipt, so they get up on their hind legs. In the moment that they are carrying away things, one looks for a way of defending oneself. Then you get a bunch of people crowding around . . ."

Before rationing became so extensive, one tactic used by vendors to get supplies was to buy from the supermarkets, which were more adequately supplied by ENABAS. When the stores opened in the morning, the vendors would be waiting in line to buy all they could find of a particular product. Sometimes, the women would send children or relatives to buy for them if the store was limiting the size of purchases. The Sandinista media, writing about these tactics, concluded that the only solution was to expand rationing.

Barricada and *El Nuevo Diario* regularly criticized the market women, especially those of the Eastern Market. The vendors soon learned that whatever item the two Sandinista papers were complaining about would be the next product covered by a decree. For example, in June 1982 *El Nuevo Diario* did a long story headlined, CONSUMERS ASK PRICE CONTROLS, claiming the vendors were routinely making 100 percent profit on fresh foods and sometimes more. The newspaper said the poor were suffering because of these prices and called for fruits and vegetables to be sold in People's Stores.

Later the government did begin to assume control over fresh food. In early 1984 it created the Distributor of Perishable Products—a new middleman. It was set up initially to handle bananas, but other fresh fruits were added in the same way that ENABAS's control over basic dry foods had expanded step by step. The government also continued to open new People's Stores to sell the controlled or rationed products.

High chain-link fencing was installed along the street curbs in the area of the Eastern Market. Ostensibly, and logically, it was intended to prevent shoppers from crossing back and forth across the street in the middle of the block, a custom that had made the market area a nightmare for drivers. But vendors pointed out that the fences also made it more difficult for sellers of contraband to get into the market. Instead of simply pulling up to a group of stalls to unload, they had to carry the merchandise to the end of the block and enter on foot, which made it easier for inspectors to catch them.

The CDS's were also used to watch for those with surplus or illegal products. Vendors with a few bags of rice or other items stored in small metal sheds were occasionally detected by a CDS representative, exposed and publicized as criminals, with such headlines in the Sandinista press as HOARDER TRAPPED and a photograph of the offending person.

The CDS's set up headquarters in the administration building of each market and played a leading role in policing the markets. Olga Orozco, the twenty-five-year-old daughter of a market vendor, presided over the central committee for the CDS's in the Eastern Market from a small desk beneath photographs of Lenin, Che Guevara, and Cayetano Carpio. She said the CDS's had been set up in the market "to further the tasks of the revolution." This was made difficult, she said, by the fact that many of the vendors had a "mercantilist attitude" and did not respect the prices set by the state. She claimed that relatives of many former National Guardsmen were selling in the Eastern Market, which compounded the problem. Also, she said, the "rightist" political parties and the private enterprise organizations had influence there.

Though Orozco claimed that three fourths of the vendors in the Eastern Market belonged to the CDS's, which were organized by square block and numbered more than fifty, the leader of one CDS told me many people did not come to CDS meetings. Discussions and activities at the meetings, she said, ranged from planning parties to encouraging people to sign up for militia training.

"Before the triumph [of the Sandinistas] I was apolitical," said María Elena Guerrero, a used-clothing seller and leader of the CDS for her area of the market. "We could be Liberal or Conservative or nothing. Now, we need to define ourselves. It's true that we have to defend our livelihood, but it is more important to defend the 'revolution' since it protects our livelihood."

Milisia Blanco, the president of ACOPROBAMA, said most of the people who took an active role in the CDS's did it under force, a fear of losing their products or their stall. "As Pedro Joaquín Chamorro always said, 'Each person has his own fear,' " she said, quoting the late publisher of *La Prensa*. "So I say that I'm not going to join in order to continue working, but other people have to face their own fears. They may go into the CDS's in order not to be called a *contra* or a reactionary, but they are there under force."

When it became risky for sellers of contraband to enter the markets, the Managua vendors began to travel to outlying areas in the middle of night, where they found farmers and others still willing to circumvent ENABAS. They would return to the market after four in the morning, when the CDS militants assigned to "revolutionary vigilance" had gone home, or during suppertime, when the vigilantes were at home, eating.

In response to the out-of-town buying trips, the government set up police control points on the roads and highways to prevent vendors and others from moving products from one department to another. Even a person driving down the highway with one new consumer item in the car, such as a pair of shoes, might be stopped and asked to show a purchase receipt. But the actions of the police fell hardest on women struggling with bags of rice and men carrying cages of chickens. While the government did battle with bigger businessmen and other opposition groups across the conference table from time to time, these small merchants had their confrontation with the Sandinistas beside the highways in the middle of the night.

Newspapers began to carry such reports as that of a man being stopped on the highway and found to be in possession of forty chickens and 3,000 bananas, all of which were confiscated. From a woman, the police took a hundred pounds of rice, a hundred pounds of sugar, and a bag of toilet paper. Another man was caught with seven chickens and another with sixty-five pounds of "hot meat."

Milisia Blanco, faced with a fight that was becoming more and more difficult for her and other independent vendors, summed up where she thought the government policy was leading. "Before, we had the traditional system of commerce. There was supply and demand. The producer or the importer sold to the wholesaler, and the wholesaler sold to the retailer, who sold to the consumer. But not now. Now a machinery has been created, a dreadful state machinery. They created it parallel to the existing system to eliminate the other part. Now they are trying to mix two functions: the distribution and commercialization of the product. Now the distributors and importers have no place in Nicaragua. The state is the only importer, the only distributor, the only producer, the only seller, and eventually, I think, the only buyer."

17

WORKERS
AND PEASANTS

About two years into the Sandinista regime, the evening newscast on
the Sandinista Television System began to use as its regular opening
a professionally done film montage that showed the Sandinistas overwhelming the National Guard, then setting out to make their mark
on glittering world capitals. Scenes of the *comandantes* in starched
uniforms expounding at international forums were juxtaposed with
films of Reagan and Castro and other world leaders. The montage,
accompanied by catchy, upbeat music, ended by focusing on a Nicaraguan peasant, a small, bony man with stubble on his chin, wearing
a torn straw hat, standing beside a barbed-wire fence. With a toothless
smile, he declared: "I'm a free man, as free as the light of day." All
of the things that the Sandinistas had done and were doing, the
montage suggested, were for this man.

Except that Orlando Ney Dávila would have preferred they had not
done it, had not put him in that film like some clown and made him

the laughingstock of his rural relatives and neighbors, who immediately began to address him mockingly as *el hombre libre*—the free man. Indeed, when I went looking for him along the dirt roads off the old highway to León, a young woman at the first house I came to laughed and said, "Mr. Ney Dávila? The free man? He's my husband's uncle." When I reached the farm where he and his family worked as caretakers, Ney Dávila told me it had been like that for two and a half years, since the Sandinista Television crew filmed him in May 1981. He was fifty-one years old and had eight children and felt that he should be treated with more respect. "You know, it's not fair for them to put a clown there [on television] to amuse people. When I come on the screen every night I look ugly—my hat is torn—and I'm for the amusement of people."

If the television people had wanted to show him once, as in a news story, he might have understood. But they had used his face now hundreds of times. They ought to take him off the air or pay him as an actor. That was why he had a lawyer in the capital searching through Nicaraguan laws to try to find grounds to sue Sandinista Television. All those reruns of the film ought to be worth several hundred thousand córdobas.

But just as bad, Ney Dávila said, was the fact that what he said to the interviewer had been used out of context. The way it came about, he said, was that the crew had stopped beside the road in front of the farm and called him over to the fence. "He asked my name. Then he said I had been denounced as a *contrario*—someone against the Sandinista Front. I said, 'How can I be a *contrario* when, in my whole life, I've never given my vote to anyone? Never in my life have I chosen a party. A poor man like me, how can I be partisan? No, what interests me is to work in order to eat. That's the way it is.' Then he asked how life was in the countryside. He asked about farming. I said that I had started following behind my father planting yucca when I was seven years old, that we planted it every sixteen inches. '*Qué lindo*'—lovely—he said. I asked if he knew how to plant watermelon, and I told him that you did it thus and thus. '*Qué lindo.*' To everything I said, he said, '*Qué lindo.*' I told him how to protect the earth from erosion. I said corn should be planted in a circle toward the ocean. '*Qué lindo.*' He asked if I had a television set, and I said no. 'You are going to have it, *compañero*,' he says. Then he asked if I had any problem about being on the air, and that was when I realized that they were going to put me on television.

"And I said, 'No sir, I'm a free man, as free as the light of day.'
" 'Cut, cut,' he says. *'Qué lindo.'* "

The experience of the Sandinista Television System with Ney Dávila, while a special situation, reflects the challenge the Sandinistas faced in finding common ground with the segments of the Nicaraguan population that were supposed to form its base. The difficulties began during the guerrilla years when the needs of peasants were, in theory, much of the reason the Sandinistas were trying to overthrow the Somoza regime. But during those long years in the mountains, which the Sandinistas thought would forge bonds between them and the peasants, the guerrillas had encountered mostly rejection or indifference. The peasants were conservative people, distrustful of those from cities, loyal or acquiescent to the landowners who assured their tenuous existence and to the local National Guard commanders.

The Sandinistas had encountered similar difficulties in their more limited attempts to win over urban workers before reaching power. They infiltrated some unions and placed a few organizers and propagandists in working-class neighborhoods of Managua, but the effort was hindered by the workers' loyalty to employers and existing unions, including the federation controlled by Somoza. When workers struck against Somoza in the last year of his regime, it was because their employers wanted them to do it, or because their employers and union leaders had reached agreement on the strike. Further limiting the Sandinistas' efforts to make inroads with the proletariat was the small size of the industrial worker class in Nicaragua. People who would be working in factories in more developed countries were, in Nicaragua, making their livings as small entrepreneurs. They were the market vendors, the taxi drivers, people with a horse or vehicle to hire out to transport things. They survived by their own sweat and ingenuity, and they found little time in their dawn-to-dusk work days for politics.

As a result, as has been discussed in earlier chapters, it was not the masses, but the economic and political elites who made it possible for the Sandinistas to march triumphantly into Managua in July 1979. It was a revolution facilitated by the Conservative and libertarian opponents of Somoza, by priests, by business competitors and landowners, and by people who had risen out of the urban poor. The struggle over the political and economic structures of Nicaragua that followed the fall of Somoza was among these people, not between rich and poor.

Nevertheless, the Sandinista Front needed the workers and peasants on its side in that struggle, as the means to justify and retain power. The Leninist structure that it created to spread its influence would work only if the workers and peasants formed its rank and file. This was most true of the peasants and small farmers, representing more than one fourth of the population.

Though land ownership in Nicaragua was heavily concentrated in the hands of people who owned large farms when the FSLN reached power, there had always been a significant number of small landowners, plus many tenant farmers who planted their subsistence plots on rented land. The need for broader land distribution had been tacitly recognized by the Nicaraguan government for years before the fall of the Somoza, in part because of pressure from U.S. aid programs. The U.S. Embassy, in a report prepared in the mid-1970s, before the insurrection against Somoza began, cited the pressing need to provide land to more people and said that land ownership was becoming more concentrated, not less so. But unlike some countries in the region, particularly El Salvador, Nicaragua had a surplus of arable land that was either unused or underutilized. With roads and other infrastructure, there could be land for everybody who wanted it. At the time of Somoza's downfall there was a program to assist tenant farmers to buy the land they farmed and also an effort to make reclaimed or virgin land available for farming. But the project was not funded adequately enough to make an impact.

When the Sandinista Front and the junta took over the government in 1979 they immediately confiscated all farms belonging to Somoza and anyone remotely connected to him. After three months in office, the new regime claimed to have taken 1.8 million acres of such land, though not all of it was arable. Eventually, it took a total of 2.75 million acres on the grounds that the owners were *somocistas.* In addition, a new agrarian reform law permitted the confiscation of large farms that were judged by the government to be inefficiently operated, even if the owners had not been *somocistas.* Large was defined as more than 860 acres on the Pacific side of the country and more than 1,720 acres on the Atlantic side. Anything smaller than that, even if inefficient, was not supposed to be confiscated. Under that law, 1.1 million acres were confiscated between 1980 and 1984. In addition, the government periodically confiscated other farms for political reasons, such as criticism of the government by the owners. The takeovers represented more than a third of all farmland. It is impossible to be more precise because of conflicting figures on the amount of arable land in Nicaragua. The Sandinistas made clear they would have liked to have taken all of the land, but they were held back by their 1979 commitment to retain private ownership and by the fear that production would be adversely affected by more extensive state control.

Jaime Wheelock favored the state farm concept, which he had studied in its theoretical form and considered to be potentially more efficient and productive than private or cooperative holdings. Thus, the large farms taken from the *somocistas* were simply converted into state farms with workers and managers, a system not very different from that of the Somoza days. Now, the people on the farms worked directly for the state, having previously worked for the man who was the state. But, under the pressure of peasant expectations to control their own land and, later, the fear that peasants would be attracted to the *Contra,* Wheelock began to distribute other confiscated lands —those that had not belonged to Somoza people—to peasants in cooperative societies or as individuals. By mid-1984, about one third of the rural population had benefited from this program, either being assigned an individual piece of land or becoming part of a cooperative that held title to a farm. Workers on state farms were not counted in this estimate because their status was essentially unchanged from the Somoza days. As the *Contra* movement grew through 1983 and 1984, it drew its rank and file from two sources in the northern mountains: peasants attracted by promises of land in their own names and small independent farmers who feared that their land would be confiscated or that they would be brought under state control in some other way, such as being forced into a state-run cooperative. The nervous government reacted to the lure of the *Contra* by putting more and more emphasis on individual ownership rather than setting up new state farms and cooperatives, but agrarian reform officials made clear that the trend toward granting individual ownership was a temporary measure to be terminated once the insurgency had ended.

One of the people who benefited under the land programs of the FSLN was Leonardo Calero, a member of a cooperative that received title in mid-1983 to a farm of several hundred acres on the outskirts of León. Three months later, after being elected president of the cooperative, Calero stood in a cotton field while a fumigation plane circled overhead and explained to visitors that the members had wanted to plant corn on the land but that the government had told them to plant cotton because it could be exported for dollars. Calero was barefoot, wearing tattered trousers rolled to the knees, and a straw hat, and he kept both hands on a hoe. He was new to making decisions about what to plant. Before the Sandinistas came to power, he had worked on coffee farms owned by people affiliated with the Somoza family; when those lands came into state hands under the Sandinistas he had simply transferred his work loyalties to the state. Later, the government moved him to this cotton land and issued to him and the other cooperative members a restricted title giving them the right to the income from the land and to someday pass along their shares to descendants. The cooperative members could not sell their land or break it up into smaller holdings.

Five years earlier, in 1978, as a worker on a private coffee farm, Calero said he had been paid ten córdobas a day. Now, he was receiving a credit of forty-four córdobas a day from the bank until the crop came in and the cooperative members tallied up the gain or loss. The distinction between wages and credit against future profit was not clear to him. He had always had a *patrón,* and he believed that he had simply exchanged a *somocista* one for a Sandinista one. At legal exchange rates prevailing in the two periods, each sum of money represented about $1.50. But because of the vagaries of the black market, inflation, price controls, and subsidies, it was impossible to make a meaningful comparison of what the two sums meant in purchasing power in Nicaragua. Perhaps a more meaningful conclusion could be drawn from asking what he and his family of seven children ate regularly. Beans, rice, bananas, and corn. They no longer knew what meat was, he said. Then the government representative standing nearby spoke up and said that Mr. Calero did not mean to say he could not afford meat or that there was no meat to buy; the problem was that this farm was so far from the nearest town that a person traveling on foot could not return with meat before it had spoiled.

In addition to land redistribution, the FSLN attempt to win over the peasantry included education and health care programs, whose results were impossible to measure in the early years of Sandinista rule. It was also difficult to determine to what extent the programs exceeded what had existed before and to what extent they were promises or plans. The airways and Sandinista newspapers were filled with claims of what the FSLN had done to improve the peasants' lot, while the rumor circuit was equally rife with jokes, frequently obscene, that punctured such claims. The most visible accomplishment was the Literacy Crusade, which sent thousands of middle-class teenagers from the towns and cities into rural areas to live among peasants and conduct classes in reading and writing during several months in the middle of 1980. The FSLN claimed that the crusade almost wiped out illiteracy, which had previously been more than 50 percent, but most of those completing the course acquired skills equivalent to only the first year or two of primary school, such as signing their names and reading a primer with a limited vocabulary.

However, as much or more than social justice and land distribution, the Sandinista agricultural program concentrated on the ideological formation of peasants and small landowners and their acceptance of the FSLN view of things. To this end, agricultural associations and farm-worker unions were created to compete with existing nongovernmental groups, or to move into areas where none existed. In the process the FSLN barred a private enterprise group—the Nicaraguan Development Foundation—from continuing to advise twenty cooperatives established prior to 1979. The members of these groups were small farmers who worked their land individually but went together to seek credit and make purchases of equipment and seed. A major part of the function of the Sandinista-created groups was to educate peasants and small farmers about the sins of imperialism and the bourgeoisie and to convince them of the necessity to produce hard currency for the country, and at the same time, defend the Sandinista regime. They were urged to sign up for the militia and offer their able-bodied sons for the army. It was in their own best interests, they were told, to keep the FSLN in power. In addition to teaching basic reading skills the 1980 Literacy Crusade had served as a vehicle to teach Sandinista political thought. Political influence and control were also part of the motivation behind FSLN programs to move dispersed rural families into settlements in 1983 and 1984, especially those closest to the borders. While this helped to prevent peasants from coming under *Contra* attacks, it also made it more difficult for them to assist the *Contra* and easier for FSLN organizations to reach them politically.

As for urban labor, the Sandinistas came to power advocating a single labor federation under their control to which all trade-union groups would belong, but they did not force the issue immediately. They created the Sandinista Workers Federation, using as leaders their own small group of labor activists from underground days, but the rank and file of the new federation was the membership of the old Somoza federation. What had been the old *oficialista* federation became the new *oficialista* federation. However, the other federations continued to function, and a Maoist group came into being. By mid-1981, however, the Ministry of Labor could report that total trade-union membership was only 70,000, of which about half were thought to belong to the Sandinista federation and most of the others to two non-Marxist federations. The largest of these was the Nicaraguan Workers

Federation, affiliated with the international Christian Democratic movement, followed by the Labor Unity Federation, with indirect connections to the AFL-CIO. The figure for total trade-union membership probably did not rise significantly over the next few years because industrial jobs were being lost to the failing economy.

As with people in the countryside, the political formation and loyalty of urban workers was the FSLN's priority in its relations with them. The Sandinista labor group sought recruits for the army, sent its share to the militia, and pressured other labor federations to collaborate. Strikes were forbidden by the FSLN, as were, for the most part, wage increases.

An indication of the FSLN view of traditional trade-union activity came in the early months of the new regime. Workers at the Pellas family's Nicaragua Sugar Estates, accustomed to being the best-paid laborers in Nicaragua, were preparing to strike, but the Sandinistas changed the workers' minds by threatening to send in the army. Later, in mid-1984, workers at the same plantation and refinery did strike—going against the dictate of their Sandinista-affiliated union—after the government blocked a wage increase that the owners were willing to give. The strike was quietly settled with a small wage increase, but news coverage of it was censored from Nicaraguan newspapers, probably for fear that other unions would decide to follow suit. Paradoxically, it had been among the Nicaragua Sugar Estates workers that the Sandinistas, during their guerrilla days, had sought to find combatants and collaborators by promising that when the revolution triumphed the workers would become the owners of the company. The former Sandinista guerrilla leader who told me, years later, about his organizing work among the sugar workers justified his intentional lie on the grounds that he had had the greater good in mind.

Though the non-Sandinista union groups encountered no legal impediment to their existence, they ran into growing Sandinista antagonism toward their activities and violent attempts to prevent their organizing among nonunion workers, as well as efforts by the Sandinista federation to break some key union locals (such as the port workers) away from the other federations. Various tactics were used. Taxi drivers, for example, were told they needed to be affiliated with the Sandinista federation to obtain their licenses. There were frequent roundups and jailings of local union leaders affiliated with the non-Sandinista federations. Tomás Borge once remarked that he planned to crush one of the other federations "like cockroaches." The *turbas* (mobs of Sandinista militants) were periodically turned loose on the headquarters of the non-Sandinista federations and homes of the leaders.

Some of the differences were over labor matters—such as the right to strike and negotiate improved contracts. But other, more political, issues also divided the FSLN and its federation from the two non-Marxist groups. The Nicaraguan Workers Federation, in a document issued at its national congress in late 1982, complained that "the military group in power has been gradually and systematically eliminating the rights and liberties of the workers and the people . . ." It cited not only labor matters but most of the political issues, such as press censorship, that concerned the opposition political parties and private enterprise. The labor group said the Sandinista Front spent its time finding ways to eliminate liberties while the social and economic problems inherited from the Somoza era were growing worse and making the lives of workers more difficult.

Lucio Jiménez, a former tailor who was a labor organizer for the FSLN during the insurrection against Somoza and then became secretary-general of the Sandinista Workers Federation, said his organization placed the defense of the Sandinista regime first on its list of priorities—which meant keeping up production and supporting the militias and other Sandinista groups. He defended the decision of the FSLN to prohibit strikes on the grounds that Nicaragua was threatened by a possible "intervention" on the part of the United States. "The workers don't need to go on strike," he told me. "Why go on strike if it will only destroy the little that we have? The worker who goes on strike is seen by the others as crazy . . . It means the factory will probably close for bankruptcy, lack of materials, and so forth. It causes unemployment, which means we couldn't accomplish anything."

Luis Orlando Valverde, the general secretary of the Rural Workers Association (the Sandinista-controlled union that had opposed the 1984 strike at Nicaragua Sugar Estates) said that there was no need to consider striking under the new government because it was committed to protecting workers' rights and there was no reason to doubt this commitment. "We used strikes to weaken Somoza," he said. "Now the demands of the workers are being dealt with to the extent necessary and possible. So there is no reason to strike. To strike would be to do damage to oneself."

The idea that striking was a right or a necessity, Valverde said, was a misguided notion being spread by the bourgeoisie and the Trotskyites.

18

THE MISKITOS

While Mayan-descended Indians on the Pacific side of what is now Nicaragua were being conquered by the Spanish in the sixteenth and seventeenth centuries, and some of them exported to South America, the non-Mayan Indians on the Atlantic side were making love, peace, and business deals with those who washed up on their shores. Christopher Columbus had sailed up against the jutting, northeast coast of Central America in 1502 and named it *Cabo Gracias a Dios*—Cape Thank God. The Spanish, however, did not follow his exploration with attempts at conquest of the area. French buccaneers were the first Europeans to have contact with the Indians there, in about 1612, then English pirates appeared around 1630 and other Englishmen soon established a trading post. In 1641 a Portuguese vessel carrying African slaves sank offshore, and most of the survivors were captured by the Indians. Out of these various unions emerged what came to be called the Miskitos, a new race. Through the centuries there were further additions to the blend, including Germans, Spanish, and Chinese. The area they inhabit is usually referred to as the Atlantic Coast or Miskito Coast, even though much of it is inland. It is also called Miskitia.

In the eighteenth century, the Miskitos became strong allies of Britain in its wars with Spain. They were given arms by the British and used them to subjugate about twenty other Indian tribes in Honduras, Nicaragua, Costa Rica, and Panama, collecting tribute from some of the other groups. The Miskito Coast was a British protectorate from 1678 until 1894 and did not take part in the independence movement from Spain and the early nation-building struggles that engaged the Spanish-dominated society on the Pacific side. After British pirates gave up the area, British business interests grew, to be joined later by other Europeans, and in this century by American interests. None of this led to a high level of development. Most of the foreign economic activities were centered on fishing, mining, and lumbering.

Today, no more than 200,000 people live in the Atlantic Coast area, which contains about half of Nicaragua's national territory. Besides the Miskitos, numbering between 120,000 and 170,000, there are 20,-000 to 30,000 English-speaking blacks, primarily descended from people who migrated from the West Indies at the turn of the century, and a few thousand from the Sumo and Rama Indian groups. Among the Miskitos, it is common to hear names that are English, Spanish, German, Chinese, and Indian, while most of the blacks have English names. The Miskitos speak their own tongue as the first language, but many of them also speak Spanish or English, or both. The blacks tend to consider English their first language, but most also speak Spanish. Miskitia also extends into Honduras; the Miskitos have generally paid no attention to the political frontier formed by the Coco River. Some have traditionally lived in villages on the Nicaraguan side but farmed on the less populous Honduran side.

The area is low-lying, hot and swampy, isolated from the Pacific side by mountains. Coves and inlets made the coast appealing to pirates. Much of the inland area is covered by pine forests, and there are some gold mines. Few food crops grow there. Until recently, there were no road connections to the western side of Nicaragua from the Atlantic Coast. There are only two towns of any size. Puerto Cabezas, in the northern part of the coast, is a largely Miskito community of 12,000 to 15,000 people. Bluefields, in the southern part of the coast, is predominately black, with 22,000 to 25,000 inhabitants. Most of the

Miskitos and the other Indians live in river-fishing villages or in the pine forests.

The religious life of the area has been determined and led by missionaries, both Protestant and Catholic. Most of the blacks are Moravians, while the Miskitos and other Indians are divided between Catholic and Protestant, including not only Moravians but numerous other denominations. German missionaries brought the pietism of the Moravian church to the area in 1849, and in this century, U.S. Moravians took on much of the missionary work, eventually passing church leadership to Nicaraguans. The Catholic Church remains a missionary outpost, in the hands of Capuchin priests, most of them Americans from the upper Midwest, but many with several decades of service in Nicaragua. Whether Catholic, Moravian, or one of the numerous other Protestant denominations, people of the region routinely claim to be "more Christian" than people in Managua.

This history, coupled with cultural and geographical distinctiveness, has made Nicaragua's Atlantic Coast a very different place from the more populous Pacific side. There is something of an anti-Spanish tradition in the area, and this has translated in modern times into poor relations with the Pacific side of Nicaragua. Despite its isolation, the area has occasionally played an important role in the machinations and policies of Spanish Nicaragua. It served as the launching area for various uprisings led by Spanish Nicaraguans and as a landing place for the U.S. Marines in this century. The northern part of Miskitia, along the Coco River, which forms the frontier with Honduras, was the area that Sandino claimed for his communal farming venture after making peace with President Sacasa in 1933. During World War II, the U.S. military built a landing strip at Puerto Cabezas and developed the port, both of which were turned over to the Nicaraguan government after the war. Puerto Cabezas was also the takeoff point for the Bay of Pigs flotilla that attempted to invade Cuba in 1961 with the Somozas' blessings and CIA direction.

Basically, though, the Atlantic Coast was left to slumber in isolation, rain, underdevelopment and easygoing tolerance. But in 1973 a group of Miskitos led by Wycliffe Diego, a Moravian pastor, organized to seek redress from the Somoza regime for a number of long-simmering complaints. They formed ALPROMISU—Alliance for the Progress of the Miskitos and Sumos. Their goals included restoration of control over communal lands, primarily the forests; teaching of the Miskito language, which had been put into written form by Moravian missionaries; Indian representation in the Managua government; and an arrangement whereby a portion of the money made by the government in Miskitia would be returned to the region in public works. The government at first refused to listen to AL-PROMISU, calling it separatist and subversive, but the leaders continued to press their goals and were beginning to be heard just before the insurrection developed against Somoza.

Most Miskitos and others on the Atlantic did not participate in the 1978–1979 uprising, and there was no fighting in their region, though the radio brought news of what was happening elsewhere in the country. Part of the Atlantic Coast's ambivalence resulted from the generally good relations between the people of the area and the local National Guard commanders of the Somoza years. The change of power came peacefully along the Atlantic. In Bluefields, about eighty National Guardsmen turned over their weapons to the Roman Catholic bishop and a priest while the Sandinistas were still miles away by river. The National Guard commander in Puerto Cabezas surrendered his command to the FSLN in a public ceremony, and local people demanded assurances about his security. Later, when he died in prison in mysterious circumstances, many of the Miskitos protested.

However, several young Miskitos were studying at the national university in Managua during the insurrection, and they had opened contacts with the Sandinista Front in 1978 in the name of AL-PROMISU. This effort was led by two Miskitos who had roomed together as students, Steadman Fagoth Müller and Brooklyn Rivera. The FSLN wanted them to formally join forces, but the Miskitos created their own organization, converting ALPROMISU into MISURASATA—an acronym for Miskito, Sumo, Rama, and Sandinista. The Indian leaders believed that the Sandinistas were promising their region a degree of autonomy in exchange for this support. Toward the end of the war, and as a result of the agreement between the Sandinistas and MISURASATA, a platoon of Miskitos joined the Sandinistas in combat.

So, even though the Atlantic side had not played an active part in the war, there was good feeling toward the Sandinistas as the result of the word spread by MISURASATA, which enjoyed widespread allegiance. When the new government organized the Literacy Crusade in early 1980, Fagoth and Rivera demanded classes in Miskito for their people, and they found educated Miskitos to conduct them. MISURASATA joined the Council of State, with Fagoth as its principal representative.

Within a few months some tensions surfaced between the Miskitos and the Sandinistas. People on the Atlantic Coast who had joined CDS's (the Sandinista Defense Committees) were quickly turned off by the rhetoric of CDS leaders and the posters of Ho Chi Minh and Lenin that appeared on public buildings. Also, in September 1979, just two months after the change of power, about thirty young Miskito men were rounded up by Sandinista troops in Puerto Cabezas and accused of antigovernment activities. After a mass gathering in the park, at which other local people successfully demanded that they be set free, most of them ran off to Honduras. There was no public note of this in Managua.

Three issues would combine to make things explode in a serious way during the following year, two of them having to do with Sandinista plans, the other rooted in Miskito culture and expectations. First was the military importance that the Sandinistas saw in the region. The Sandinistas, despite their talk of improving the lot of those on the Atlantic Coast, gave first priority to the area's potential strategic value: it was the region of Nicaragua closest to Cuba. Daniel Ortega visited Puerto Cabezas in the first few weeks, made a public appearance on the steps of the large house beside the ocean, and asked to whom the house belonged. Learning it was the property of the vicariate of Bluefields, the Roman Catholic authority for the region, he commented to an aide that the FSLN would need the site in the future.

By the end of 1979, large numbers of Sandinista troops had begun to arrive on the Atlantic side, growing to an estimated seven thousand by the beginning of 1981. About a fourth were stationed at two bases on the edge of Puerto Cabezas, creating a uniformed presence in the town that was many times the size of the force maintained by the National Guard under Somoza. The number seemed excessively large to people in the region because of the low population and small communities. At first, the troops were poorly equipped, but that gradually changed. Dozens of East German troop trucks called IFAs soon dominated the dirt roads around Puerto Cabezas. Jeeps also appeared, along with modern weapons.

The second issue, developing at the same time, was Cubans. Doctors, nurses, and teachers sent by the Castro regime were saturating the region from the beginning of 1980. There were soon a thousand teachers in the department of Zelaya, which encompassed most of Miskitia. Most were assigned to remote interior hamlets. Again, this seemed to be a large number for the small population. There were not many more Cuban teachers in the rest of the country, which had more than ten times the population of the Atlantic region. The government in Managua said the Cubans were primarily filling rural teaching posts that Nicaraguans did not want, but in some cases they replaced teachers who had been trained and placed in schools by the Protestant denominations and the Roman Catholic vicariate and who were willing to stay. The medical teams worked in the larger communities, such as Puerto Cabezas and Bluefields. In the Miskito areas the Cubans often worked in clinics and hospitals that had formerly been staffed on a rotating basis by medical teams from the University of Wisconsin.

At the end of September of 1980 a demonstration against the presence of the Cubans erupted in Bluefields, primarily among the black population. The uprising began after the government announced that additional Cuban teachers and medical personnel would arrive in Bluefields to join an estimated three hundred already working in the vicinity. It continued for three days and at times, according to the government, the demonstrators numbered five thousand.

Various acts inflamed them. A delegation was rejected when it tried to petition local Sandinista authorities to expel the Cubans. Then police confiscated film from Venezuelan journalists covering the demonstration. Some demonstrators were arrested. A group went to the military command to protest and was turned away with gunfire, causing injuries. The demonstrators went to a house occupied by Cubans and tore down a Cuban flag. Demonstrators also stole arms from a government office. The authorities eventually promised to open a "dialogue," but when the local people sent a delegation to talk they were attacked, beaten, and arrested by internal security police sent from Managua.

The government in Managua, which censored news reports from Bluefields after the first day, claimed the coastal people were mounting a separatist movement. Bayardo Arce, one of the *comandantes* on the Sandinista National Directorate, said they sought to install a "new Guantánamo," a reference to the U.S. military base on the Cuban coast.

A couple of weeks later, the Permanent Commission for Human Rights sent a delegation to Bluefields to investigate. It reported that the local people resented foreigners attempting to raise their political consciousness and also that the local people said the Cubans and

Sandinista representatives made fun of blacks as being ignorant and stupid. There were also complaints that the Cubans were taking jobs that ought to be filled by Bluefields residents, who had a relatively high level of literacy. The rights group said the net effect of the uprising and the way it had been handled was to strengthen the negative opinion the coastal people already held toward the rest of Nicaragua.

To the north, in the predominantly Miskito area, the same issue was developing. Miskitos boycotted the Cuban-run classrooms, particularly in the inland rural areas. Miskito parents decided the Cubans were putting too much partisan politics into their teachings. They also decided the Cubans were godless and antireligious. Another presumption by the Miskitos was that the Cubans were intelligence or security operatives as well as teachers. The Miskitos kept their children out of school, and when officials went looking for them, entire families disappeared into the bush. The Miskitos also beat some of the Cubans and threatened others.

Most of the teachers in Puerto Cabezas itself continued to be Nicaraguans or missionaries, but absenteeism also occurred there because parents became upset about the army and militia training being conducted around school grounds. The firing of weapons frightened everybody. People in the area had been unaccustomed to weapons, except for hunting. The Sandinistas told them they were firing blanks, but no one believed them.

The Miskitos also boycotted the Cuban-run clinics, after convincing themselves that the Cuban doctors were not qualified or did not care about their health. They claimed there were cases of ailments being seriously misdiagnosed or ignored. So they stopped going to the doctors, going instead to medical practitioners or traveling elsewhere in the country to see Nicaraguan doctors. Whether these accusations against the Cuban doctors were true or not, the tendency of Miskitos to share both property and opinions meant that when one Miskito developed a certain opinion of the Cubans, then the opinion was soon universal.

In January 1981, Sandinista troops shot a nineteen-year-old Miskito in the town park in Puerto Cabezas, and an angry demonstration followed. Townspeople took the youth to a clinic, where they said Cuban doctors refused to treat him. They took him to one of their houses and decided he was dead, then put the body in the car of a taxi driver and followed it all over town demanding justice.

. . .

Meanwhile, Fagoth's efforts in Managua to obtain Sandinista commitments on the key Miskito demands, such as communal control of the forest lands, were going nowhere. In January 1981 the MISURASATA leaders decided, in Fagoth's words, "to declare open political war on *sandinismo.*" He had concluded, he said later, that the Sandinistas were not willing to consider the interests of any group but themselves. "The fundamental problem is that one's own identity and organization don't matter [to the Sandinistas]. They brought state corporations. Communal life doesn't belong to an individual, and it doesn't belong to the state. We made our claims, and every time they told us: 'We can't give you autonomy because it's a very unstable time, we have a bad economic situation, there are *somocistas* in Honduras.' They said we didn't have the administrative capacity to handle our own community, and I asked them if they had gone to some kind of university to learn how to administer Nicaragua."

Luis Carrión Cruz of the Sandinista National Directorate, who during that time was put in charge of Miskito affairs, said the Sandinistas, on taking power, had found the Miskitos to be suffering "a very large ideological backwardness."

"We found communities that live in a very primitive state of development, that have not divided except in small degree into social classes, that have communal property forms, and that do not identify with the rest of the nation," he said.

In other words, the Sandinistas, for whom class struggle was a necessary element, theoretically leading to a proletarian state, could not effectively mount their program among people who acknowledged no class differences at the outset. And while the Sandinistas themselves were restricting private ownership on the Pacific side of Nicaragua, they could not accept the communal ownership advocated by the Miskitos. In both cases, it was something outside the control of the state.

MISURASATA quit the Council of State and planned to announce its total break with the FSLN at a meeting in Puerto Cabezas to celebrate the end of the Miskito-language Literacy Crusade, which had been conducted later than the Spanish-language campaign. Instead, Fagoth was arrested in Managua in mid-February of 1981 while trying to arrange the ceremony. More than thirty other prominent Miskitos were picked up around the region, setting off days of demonstrations.

A few days after Fagoth's arrest, eleven Sandinista army troops walked into a Moravian church in Prinzapolka, south of Puerto Cabezas on the coast, looking for Elmer Prado, another MISURASATA leader. Prado was one of nearly ninety Miskitos in the church, where services were being held. The Miskitos asked the soldiers to wait until the service had finished. The soldiers refused, and everybody started yelling and threatening. Then the troops began shooting. The Miskitos, unarmed but more numerous, grabbed some of the rifles and began firing at the soldiers. Most of the Miskitos fled and began to make their way toward the Honduran border. Four soldiers and four Miskitos were left dead in the church.

Fagoth, meanwhile, remained under house arrest in Managua, accused of having once been a Somoza informant, a common charge against those who had differences with the FSLN. People on the Atlantic Coast, for whom Fagoth now could do no wrong, dismissed the accusation with the explanation that if Fagoth had been a Somoza agent, then it must have been a good thing to be. He was released May 6 with the understanding that he would go to the Atlantic Coast and quiet people down, then accept a "scholarship" to one of the Soviet bloc countries. Fagoth flew to Puerto Cabezas and continued immediately to Honduras.

The arrests and the shootings during the first half of 1981 set off a massive flight of Miskitos to Honduras, mostly by young men who feared being arrested or shot. At the same time, the Sandinistas unleashed reprisals and toughened up their treatment of the Miskitos who stayed behind. People were dislodged from meetings in several Moravian churches after the Prinzapolka episode, some MISURASATA offices were sacked, and any Miskito who identified with MISURASATA feared arrest or death. Between fifteen hundred and three thousand fled in the first months of 1981.

In Honduras, the refugees camped along the river and in swampy areas at Mocoron and Mistruck, outside Puerto Lempira, an army outpost. They lacked food, clothes, and bedding. Fagoth, Diego and some other leaders moved into a hideout near Tegucigalpa, the Honduran capital, and set out trying to collect supplies for the refugees. Fagoth also began to broadcast into the Miskito area of Nicaragua on Radio Fifteenth of September, operated clandestinely by what were then small bands of anti-Sandinista guerrillas attacking from Honduras. For a while there was talk about efforts to bring him and Nicaraguan authorities together in Honduras to negotiate over the differences, but nothing occurred.

· · ·

When I visited Puerto Cabezas in August 1981 I found people who felt that they were under occupation because of the strong Sandinista army presence and people still upset over the Cuban issue. However, the Cuban teachers had been withdrawn after the arrest of Fagoth, and people in Puerto Cabezas were convinced in August that the Cubans would not return.* Everybody was talking about who was fleeing and listening to the radio for any message from Fagoth. Brooklyn Rivera, who had succeeded Fagoth as head of MISURASATA inside Nicaragua, at first said Fagoth had been mistaken, but within a few months Rivera made the same decision and left for exile.

Puerto Cabezas was also crowded with state security people in civilian dress, who stopped and questioned all strangers, including nuns, priests, and ministers. The airstrip was surrounded by field artillery, and the runway was being lengthened to a size that could handle most fighter planes and other jets. Older townspeople said that the U.S. military had built it originally at a length of three kilometers, about nine thousand feet, and that it was being lengthened by more than a kilometer. IFA trucks rumbled through the gravel streets, stirring up dust and overwhelming the simple wood-frame houses.

People talked about how roads leading out of the airport were occasionally closed for two or three days, during which time they presumed something mysterious was being unloaded. Boxes of guns and ammunition also had been unloaded from a ship. When local people protested, troops claimed the bullets were all blanks. Teachers and church people told me many young people were dropping out of school, even those without Cuban teachers, presumably to go to Honduras. Foxholes had been dug every ten feet or so along the coast beside the big house still occupied by the Sisters of Saint Agnes. Townspeople also claimed about twenty Miskitos had been killed in the area around Puerto Cabezas since the Sandinistas came to power, some taken out of jail and shot.

To those who had any sense of politics the reason for being opposed to the Sandinistas was very simple: they had turned out to be Communists. The Miskitos had made the mistake of believing the Sandinistas were democratic. There was also the matter of their being perceived as antireligious and the fact that they had brought in the Cubans. Much of the population identified with English-speaking nations,

---

*The Cubans did, in fact, return within a short time, and in October two Cuban teachers were killed by what the government described as "counter-revolutionaries" at a settlement near the mining district of Siuna.

especially the older residents. One man who had been an adult during World War II told me that the gringos had built and paid for Puerto Cabezas—meaning the airport and the port, the only significant infra-structure—and therefore the place should belong to them. "The presence of the soldiers makes it worse," he told me. "Everywhere you turn, you see them. They are not rude to us, but they are here. People hardly sleep. We get up in the morning and start worrying first thing."

The Sandinistas did show they were not oblivious to Miskito issues when the FSLN and the junta issued a joint declaration promising, among other things, to legalize the ownership of the lands on the Atlantic Coast and grant land titles to each community. While saying the "revolutionary state" was the only entity empowered to determine the utilization of natural resources, a reference to forests and minerals in the area, the FSLN and the junta said they recognized the right of the indigenous communities to receive a portion of the benefits from the exploitation of those resources.

But for those in Honduras, as well as many of the Miskitos still inside Nicaragua, the issue had gone beyond that. Before Fagoth's arrival in Honduras, along with the several thousand young men who preceded or followed him, the insurgency was small, only a few hundred men, mostly former National Guardsmen. But it began to grow almost immediately, with the arrival of Fagoth and the young Miskitos. What had been sporadic attacks across the Coco River in the Miskito area increased dramatically in late 1981, but there was only limited coordination between the Miskito insurgents and the other exiles.

On December 14, 1981, insurgents ambushed a twelve-man Sandinista border patrol in the river community of San Carlos, Fagoth's hometown, took all of them across to Honduras, and killed them. On December 18, three more soldiers were killed as they approached San Carlos in a boat. Three days later, a Sandinista helicopter carrying eight soldiers tried to land in the area and was attacked by waiting rebels, who killed all eight soldiers. The army later implicated twenty-one people in the San Carlos attack, including thirteen former National Guardsmen and a Moravian pastor. The army said that in the two-month period from early November 1981 to early January 1982 a total of forty-five soldiers and fifteen civilians were killed in the attacks from across the Coco as part of what was dubbed "Operation Red Christmas."

Authorities subsequently jailed about a hundred people in Puerto

Cabezas and tried more than sixty of them for crimes connected to the attacks, which the government said were intended to set off a mass uprising. Some of the Miskitos who escaped to Honduras charged that many other Miskitos had been summarily executed in Sandinista custody during those days. One man, Vidal Poveda, said he had seen Sandinista forces execute several dozen prisoners at Leimus on the bank of the Coco River in the days just before Christmas 1981. Poveda said he and a few others decided to risk running away when they were taken out to be shot. One of his brothers was killed as he tried to flee and some of the others were wounded; only seven escapees lived.

The Sandinistas also responded with the forced relocation of Miskitos away from villages along the river, where they might provide food and refuge for *contras*. Beginning on January 14, about 8,500 Miskitos were resettled, their homes, churches, crops, and livestock burned and destroyed by soldiers. Restrictions were placed on access to Miskitia by outsiders, whether foreigners or people from the other side of Nicaragua. Those wishing to travel there needed a permit from the Interior Ministry. The uprooted Miskitos were placed in five camps created by the government about forty miles from the border. The government gave the resettlement area the name Tasba Pri, a Miskito word meaning promised land or free land. To most, it meant something less appealing.

During 1982 the insurgency grew, with direct CIA support replacing the Argentine connection, and in November and December 1982 the Sandinista regime responded with another massive relocation. About seven thousand Miskitos and Sumos were uprooted from eight villages on the Coco River, where it ran through the department of Jinotega to the southwest of the area that had been evacuated at the beginning of the year. They were moved south into central Jinotega and even farther south into Matagalpa to work on state coffee farms. Everybody older than eight, except the elderly and sick, made most of the trip on foot, walking through the mountains for several days under the guidance of soldiers, until they reached roads and could be picked up by trucks. The others were moved on transport helicopters.

Officially, the second resettlement was attributed to the fact that it had become almost impossible to get food and other necessities to the communities after anti-Sandinista guerrillas took control of large sections of the river, the traditional supply route. The army said it had lost sixteen *pipantes,* small river boats. But there were also allusions to the sympathies that the villagers felt for the guerrillas, some of whom were presumably relatives. From Miskitos outside of Nicaragua came the charge that the government would not have to supply food if it had allowed the Miskitos their usual free movement to hunt, fish, and plant.

In the midst of the late 1982 relocation, a helicopter carrying seventy-five Miskito children and seventeen women who had recently given birth crashed and burned, killing all of the children and nine of the mothers. Denying that the helicopter was overloaded, the Sandinistas blamed the crash on U.S. "imperialism" and the remnants of the Somoza National Guard. At first, nonmilitary sources in the FSLN claimed that insurgent forces had fired on the helicopter, which was denied by the other side. Then the Sandinistas dropped that suggestion and argued that the crash was still the fault of the United States because it had caused the insurgency. "Yankee imperialism imposes all of this on us only because we have said we are revolutionaries," declared Humberto Ortega, the defense minister and Sandinista army commander. When the children were buried in a common grave in the mountain village of San José de Bocay, near where the crash occurred, Jaime Wheelock gave a lengthy funeral oration before some six hundred grieving Indian families in which he claimed that the crash was the result of a plot by "imperialism" and *somocismo* to take over Miskito and Sumo lands.

In October 1983, exiled Miskitos said a third large resettlement had occurred, in which about 5,000 Miskitos were forced out of villages along the seventy-mile road linking Puerto Cabezas to the gold-mining area at La Rosita. They were reported resettled in a camp a few miles outside Puerto Cabezas.

Each of these relocations produced the simultaneous flight of more Miskitos, especially the young men, to Honduras. Some also made their way to Costa Rica. In those two countries, led by Fagoth in Honduras and Brooklyn Rivera in Costa Rica, many continued to join the insurgent ranks, by some estimates becoming the largest portion of the armed opposition to the Sandinistas.

The clergy and other religious workers in the area were divided in their attitudes toward the Sandinista government and how the Miskitos ought to deal with it. Only a few of the clergy serving the Atlantic Coast practiced liberation theology and sought to influence Miskitos toward Sandinista ideas. A larger number sought to maintain good or at least civil relations with the FSLN, without embracing Sandinista politics, on the theory that they could best serve their people that way. Others believed they had an obligation to go where their people needed them. They followed, and even led, their flocks into exile. The most notable example of this occurred in December 1983, when the Roman Catholic bishop for the region accompanied about a thousand Miskitos on a flight to Honduras that seemed to have been scripted by the authors of the Old Testament.

On December 19, Bishop Salvador Schlaefer, a Wisconsin-born Capuchin with nearly forty years in Nicaragua, had arrived in Francia Serpe, one of the Sandinista-created resettlement camps, on his pastoral rounds. He was accompanied by another American priest, the Reverend Wendelin Schafer. They conducted mass and spent the day doing other religious chores. Late that night a group of Miskito guerrillas came into camp and overpowered the policemen, then told the bishop everyone was leaving for Honduras. The guerrilla leader, whom the bishop had known for ten years, invited the priests to accompany them.

The people of Francia Serpe had been expecting the guerrillas and the call to leave for various days. They had already packed a few possessions. One woman had baked unleavened "journey bread" four times, but each time the departure had been postponed. Before daylight the people lined up single file, many of the women with babies on their backs. Then the two bridges outside the camp were blown up. The sixty-five-year-old bishop and Father Schafer, sixty-four, deciding that they had an obligation to be with their people in difficult times, drove their jeep up to the column and abandoned it, then set out with the others on the thirty-mile march to the border. On the second day, Sandinista troops caught up with the rear of the column, and Miskito guerrillas, armed with explosives and automatic weapons, fought them off. In Managua, the government was saying that the anti-Sandinista forces had kidnapped and killed the bishop. Late on the third day, however, the group reached the Coco River, then crossed into Honduras in large canoes the next morning. It was two days before Christmas. The bishop wanted to kiss the soil but was afraid he would be unable to get up.

The two priests flew to Miami on Christmas Eve, then went home to Wisconsin. On the flight north, the bishop told the story to George Stein, a reporter for the Miami *Herald*. "There wasn't enough time in this new revolution for religion . . . Communism has one goal and that goal is to have everybody sacrifice themselves for what they call collectivism," he said. "We told the Sandinista government from the beginning that they would have to respect the religious values of the people, the spiritual values, that if they tried to crush them or eliminate them, they would have trouble." After his Christmas vacation, the bishop went back to Nicaragua.

By 1984, estimates of the number of Miskitos, Sumos, and Ramas in exile ranged upward from 25,000. In addition, at least 20,000 had been resettled in camps inside the country that those outside described as "concentration camps," though security, in fact, was light, as shown by how easily the group left Francia Serpa. Every new group coming out of Nicaragua carried stories of widespread killing of noncombatants by Sandinista forces. Bernard Nietschmann, a Miskito-speaking geographer from the University of California at Berkeley, spent eight weeks in Miskitia in late 1983 and early 1984 and said he heard many such stories and believed them to be true. In some cases they came from people he had come to know well during previous extended trips through the area.

Miskitia had become an area of extensive and continuous warfare, not only between Sandinista troops and insurgents crossing from Honduras and Costa Rica, but also involving large groups of Miskitos who had taken up clandestine activities directly from within their country. Nietschmann, in testimony for the Inter-American Human Rights Commission in October 1983, said he was convinced, as the result of his travels in the area, that many of the armed Miskito warriers were operating out of semipermanent camps inside Nicaragua, at considerable distance from the frontiers. Hugo Spadafora, a Panamanian adventurer-idealist who spent months at a time fighting alongside the Miskitos, made similar claims on his trips out of Nicaragua. Occasional communiqués of the Sandinista army substantiated this view and indicated the whole region was a war zone. Despite the nominal alliances the Miskito insurgents had with the various Spanish Nicaraguan groups opposing the Sandinistas, the fighting in Miskitia was, in Nietschmann's words, "a real nineteenth-century Indian war."

Both sides, the Miskitos and the Sandinistas, were fighting for their own set of priorities. For the Sandinistas, the priorities were military security and political control. Past promises aside, these things were not negotiable. For the Miskitos, the priorities were communal rights and religion. These also were not negotiable.

19

AMONG
THOSE WHO LEFT

Edén Pastora, Leonel Poveda, Haroldo Montealegre, Arturo Cruz, Alfonso Robelo, José Esteban González, Edgard Macías, Adolfo Calero . . .

One day near the end of April 1981, about a half-dozen Sandinista leaders filed onto the speaker's platform of a meeting room in a former country club for a news conference with several hundred "progressive" journalists, members of a Prague-based organization that had convened in Nicaragua to express solidarity with the Sandinista Front. Among the *comandantes* and other FSLN stars on the platform was Edén Pastora, the Commander Zero of the 1978 National Palace takeover. As Humberto Ortega, the defense minister and army commander, began to read a list of every *Contra* incursion from Honduras since the first of the year, several dozen photographers went to work in the space between the audience seats and the platform.

Most of them focused on Pastora, who displayed a wide smile across his darkly handsome face.

With the click of camera shutters providing continuous background noise to Ortega's words, Pastora picked out one of the photographers for the focus of his own attention. She was tall and lithe and Nordic-looking, wearing faded blue jeans and a knit tank top. She was bra-less and well endowed. Pastora seemed to pose for her camera alone. He would stretch his legs out in front of him and cross them, Marlboro Man-style, then he would suddenly sit up and lean forward intently. He talked to her through the lens with his eyes until she broke up in embarassed laughter.

To most appearances, it was this crowd-pleaser role that Pastora fulfilled—and was happy fulfilling—after nearly two years of Sandinista rule. Passed over for the National Directorate, his loyalty to Marxism-Leninism and the nine members of the directorate always in doubt, he had served as deputy interior minister in the first months of the regime, then had become deputy defense minister and commander of the militia. If he was unhappy with his situation or the way the country was going, he showed no sign of dissidence in public.

Yet, on July 7, 1981, slightly more than two months after his carefree appearance before the journalists, Pastora and about a dozen men who had fought under him on the Southern Front in the war to oust Somoza drove to Costa Rica in a caravan and continued to Panama. Pastora left behind a letter dated June 26 and addressed to Humberto Ortega that was interpreted as meaning he was going off Guevara-style to join leftist guerrillas in Guatemala or El Salvador. "I am going to discharge my revolutionary gunpowder against the oppressor in whatever part of the world in which he is found, without it mattering whether they call me Quixote or Sancho," he wrote. This, theoretically, would not have clashed with the goals of the FSLN, but the worried reaction of the National Directorate made it obvious that something more was behind Pastora's departure. In a matter of days the National Directorate dismissed him from the army and ordered Nicaraguan newspapers to publish nothing about him without first submitting it to the Interior Ministry for clearance.

For the next nine months mystery surrounded Pastora's movements and his thinking, but it was possible to piece together part of the story in subsequent conversations with him and various people who had contact with him, or were otherwise involved.

Before his decision to leave, Pastora had been trying to force a realignment of power within the Sandinista Army. Many of the

Southern Front veterans felt they had been denied their just share of power while people who had risked less had been given the best positions. On July 2, just five days before departing Managua, Pastora talked about these efforts with a group of followers at the house of Leonel Poveda, the man who had hidden Pastora before the 1978 Palace Raid and was now vice-minister of internal commerce. Pastora told the group, in the words of another participant, that "all was lost, there was nothing more he could do."

When he reached Panama, Pastora moved into the Panama City apartment of Hugo Spadafora, a physician and adventurer who had led the Panamanian brigade that fought alongside Pastora's forces against Somoza. Spadafora, like Pastora, was close to General Omar Torrijos, the Panamanian National Guard director. One of Torrijos' sons, Martín, had served under Spadafora in the brigade at the age of fifteen.

Within a week or so of his arrival in Panama, Pastora held a strategy session with some trusted people, including two men who were still Nicaraguan government officials: Leonel Poveda and Carlos Coronel Kautz, the fisheries minister. Coronel, like Poveda, had been one of Pastora's closest collaborators during the Southern Front days. Many people viewed him as the brains behind Pastora, his key adviser. He had served as an intermediary with Fidel Castro and with the other top members of the FSLN, at one time arguing in favor of making Pastora a member of the National Directorate. Coronel did not return to Nicaragua after the Panama meeting, but Poveda returned to carry out the plan they had drawn up for keeping Pastora alive in the public mind.

Before anything could be done, however, an airplane crash on July 31 took the life of Omar Torrijos, Pastora's benefactor and idol. Pastora, who had been invited to accompany Torrijos on the tragic flight, immediately concluded that the Sandinista National Directorate was behind the killing. He and Spadafora thought their own lives were now in danger, so they grabbed pistols and raced out to Farallon, the Torrijos hideaway and airstrip west of Panama City. There they were contacted by Colonel Noriega, the National Guard intelligence chief, who said Carlos Andrés Pérez, the former Venezuelan president, had come to Panama and wanted to see Pastora at one of Torrijos' houses in the city. A small plane was sent to pick up Pastora, but Spadafora was not allowed to accompany him.

Back in the city, the man waiting for Pastora was not Pérez. He was Tomás Borge. Despite the surprise, everybody played a great scene.

Pastora laughed and said it had not been necessary to trick him into coming to talk with his dear friend Tomás Borge, that he would have come willingly. They embraced and slapped each other on the back. Borge said he had come because their dear friend Fidel wanted Pastora to come to Cuba and talk to him. This presented Pastora with a dilemma, but he could not afford to display his concern. Since he thought the Sandinista Front was responsible for the death of Torrijos and since he did not know who now held the reins of power in Panama, refusal might mean quick death. Pastora went to Cuba on the plane that was sent for him.

In Cuba, Pastora was part prisoner, part guest. He and José Valdivia, the former chief of telecommunications, who had left Nicaragua with Pastora, were installed in one of the Cuban government's "protocol houses," a group of 1950s-era residences once owned by the affluent of Havana. They were treated well, but they could not leave. Meanwhile, Torrijos' death was soon established to the satisfaction of most people in Panama to have been an accident. It is not clear why Noriega and the other Panamanian National Guard leaders had agreed so readily to the request that Pastora be dispatched to Cuba. One explanation I was given was that the Panamanians, with their own succession struggle facing them, did not want the added problem of the security of someone as controversial as Pastora.

In Nicaragua, there was great confusion about what had become of Pastora. Leonel Poveda heard rumors that Castro intended to hold him for months. He decided to proceed with the Panama plan. Poveda rounded up a dozen Southern Front veterans, most now in the Sandinista army or civilian government jobs, and supplied them with a large quantity of spray-paint cans. Overnight, at the end of August, Managua was decorated with slogans announcing the imminent return of Edén Pastora: "EDÉN IS COMING," "PASTORA RETURNS," and similar statements. Among those Nicaraguans wanting deliverance from the Sandinista Front, the messages stirred exactly the reaction Poveda had hoped for. The idea that Pastora had some kind of mystical power to resolve their problems was appealing to many Nicaraguans, who thought that he had earned the right to lead the country by his previous displays of daring. For the Sandinista leadership, uncertain about how much power Pastora might wield, the slogans were unnerving.

Two days after the appearance of the slogans, Poveda was called to the home of Victor Tirado, the Mexican-born member of the Sandinisța National Directorate. Like many others in the government, Poveda found Tirado the most accessible of the nine directorate members. He listened with sympathy to the complaints about policies, but seemed to do little to resolve them. When the call came Poveda sensed that something was wrong. In a moment of candor he had once told Tirado that if he were ever to be arrested, not to do it in his own home in front of his family. This might be Tirado's way of honoring that request. Poveda took his machine gun.

Tirado began to question him immediately about the slogan-painting, for which Poveda acknowledged responsibility. Poveda defended his actions by pointing out that he had been writing memo after memo to Tirado and others about errors being made by the government, particularly unjustified confiscations and other repressive economic measures that were hurting the nation's productive capacity. But Tirado had not responded, Poveda said, adding that a number of other Southern Front veterans shared his concerns.

At that moment, doors on either side of the room opened and out stepped Lenín Cerna, the chief of state security, and another security agent, both with machine guns trained on Poveda. He surrendered without a struggle, and his collaborators were picked up the following day.

What happened next is a matter of conjecture, but the outcome is known. In Cuba, Edén Pastora was somehow persuaded to tape a videocassette in which he condemned the action of Poveda's group and declared himself to be a "Sandinista revolutionary." On September 10, a week after Poveda's arrest, the leaders of the "Spray Conspiracy" were presented at a news conference. Poveda and others confessed their role in the affair. Said Poveda, "I arranged, manufactured, financed, structured, and directed a campaign using the name of the brother Edén Pastora Gómez, in order to create a fissure in the FSLN." Borge, after playing the videotape of Pastora and José Valdivia dissociating themselves from the undertaking, said it was a grave crime but that it had been the result of Poveda's "ideological debilities," so he sentenced him—at that moment, before the press and the television cameras—"to work the rest of your days for this revolution." Then Borge dismissed Poveda and everybody else.

Poveda decided that the way he would work for the revolution was to raise beans, a Nicaraguan staple in increasingly short supply. There was a piece of family land south of Managua not far off the highway to Costa Rica. Every day he would leave his house in Managua and go to the farm to oversee the planting and growing of the beans. It also gave him justification to drive on south to Costa Rica from time to time to buy things he needed for his farming venture, then return.

When Poveda and the others were arrested, Daniel Ortega was in Libya trying to obtain a new loan from Muammar Qaddafi ($100 million had been received from Libya earlier in the year). One of the Nicaraguan officials traveling with Ortega was Haroldo Montealegre, the minister of reconstruction finance, who was in charge of obtaining international aid. Montealegre, then about thirty, was a member of a family prominent in private enterprise. One of his brothers, Jaime, represented the Superior Council of Private Enterprise—COSEP—in the Council of State and was a frequent spokesman for opposition views. Haroldo, educated in economics at the University of Chicago and at Columbia, had joined the new government after being an anti-Somoza activist during the 1978 strikes and helping to organize the MDN, Alfonso Robelo's political party. First named vice minister of industry and commerce, he had become minister of reconstruction finance after Alfredo César, another young U.S.-educated business-man, was moved from that portfolio to head of the national banking system.

When Daniel Ortega told Montealegre, in Libya, about the arrests in Managua, the cabinet minister's stomach did flipflops. He had helped finance the slogan-painting operation and had attended the July 2 gathering with Pastora at Poveda's house. While trying to maintain a calm façade, he wondered if Ortega suspected him.

Since the beginning of the year Montealegre had been trying, without success, to win Ortega's backing for changes in economic policies. In January, Montealegre had appeared before the junta and warned that Nicaragua would run out of hard currency by August if it did not make some major economic changes. Some of the changes he proposed included proceeding with a long-promised law to attract foreign investment; negotiations with the International Monetary Fund; and incentives to promote exports. Though carefully expressed so as not to offend Socialist sensibilities, Montealegre's proposals, if adopted, would have turned Nicaragua's economic policies more toward the West internationally and would have supported private enterprise within Nicaragua. Daniel Ortega had asked Montealegre for a written copy of the proposals, then had carried it in his briefcase for several months. Montealegre received occasional assurances that consideration was being given to his ideas, which were in line with policies favored by various other civilians in the government.

Montealegre had also discussed the ideas with Victor Tirado, from whom he received the impression that the only opposition within the National Directorate came from Henry Ruiz and Tomás Borge. Tirado depicted them as hardliners and ideologues unable to accept economic policies not in line with those advocated by the Bulgarian advisers in the Planning Ministry. The Bulgarian approach, according to Montealegre, was to put political consolidation of the regime ahead of economic health. That meant reducing the "political space" of the non-Marxists and private enterprise. But Tirado led Montealegre to believe that Ruiz and Borge would not be allowed to prevail. In addition to what Tirado said, there was a current of opinion within the government at the time that a quasi coup d'état was under way against Ruiz and Borge to reduce their influence.

But in early 1981, after the dispute had begun between the Sandinistas and the Reagan administration, Humberto Ortega traveled to Moscow in search of military assistance. Though he and most of the Sandinista leadership had been to Moscow on previous occasions and were already receiving Soviet military help, Montealegre sensed that that particular trip had a watershed effect on Nicaragua's internal policies. It was on June 23, soon after his return, that Ortega made his speech declaring Marxism-Leninism to be the model of the Nicaraguan revolution. Then, on July 19, the second anniversary of the victory over Somoza, Daniel Ortega announced new confiscations and a new law allowing the confiscation of the property, including personal houses, of anyone who stayed outside the country more than six months. Montealegre, who had not been informed in advance of the economic changes to be announced, went to Tirado the next day and complained. Tirado told him that Humberto now felt that Henry Ruiz was right in accepting the centralized, Bulgarian view of economic policy.

Montealegre had begun to feel that he was "a suspect, an enemy" in the government. This feeling was enhanced when he made application for a regular passport soon after July 19 and it was denied. He had an official passport, but it could be used only for government-approved trips, such as when he accompanied Daniel Ortega to Libya at the beginning of September.

When the Nicaraguans left Libya, they were going to Cuba before returning home, but, traveling on a plane supplied by Qaddafi and flown by British pilots, they first made an overnight stop in London. There Montealegre told Ortega he needed to go to Washington to sign some papers at an international lending agency. From Washington, however, he flew to Costa Rica and sent his resignation to Ortega. Then Montealegre flew to Miami, where he told me that Pastora was being held a virtual prisoner in Cuba. He also told me not to believe the story that Pastora was going to join guerrilla forces in other countries. Pastora's real war, he said, was with the Sandinista National Directorate.

Pastora was allowed to leave Cuba in late September or early October 1981, after Martín Torrijos, the teenaged son of the late general, flew to Havana on a plane supplied by Mexico's ruling Institutional Revolutionary Party (the PRI) and picked him up. Pastora later told me that young Torrijos had been sent by the high command of the Panamanian National Guard. Presumably, the mission was also preceded by some kind of understanding between the PRI and Castro. After leaving Cuba, Pastora spent several months in Panama, and some time in Costa Rica, where his wife and younger children lived. He also made a brief attempt to assist a Guatemalan group called the Revolutionary Organization of the People in Arms, which Pastora considered to be the only guerrilla band in Central America not under the influence of Havana or Moscow. In November, José Valdivia broke with Pastora and returned to Nicaragua, drawn by the Sandinistas' appeal to his Marxist ideological purity and concern over family matters. Eventually, Pastora went to Cuernavaca, Mexico, to contemplate strategy for confronting the nine *comandantes* in Managua.

In November, another leading non-Marxist resigned from the Sandinista regime. Arturo Cruz, the one-time member of *Los Doce*, had served in various government posts, beginning as president of the Central Bank. He had moved to the junta in May 1980, following the resignations of Violeta Chamorro and Alfonso Robelo. In March 1981, feeling frustrated by his lack of influence in the government and under pressures to return to his family in Washington, he had resigned from the junta but had agreed to continue in the government as ambassador to the United States.

As ambassador, Cruz was in the middle of the feud between the Reagan administration and the Sandinistas. He put great hope in the contacts begun by Assistant Secretary of State Enders in August 1981, but as the matter dragged out with little progress he found himself in a difficult position with both sides. In dealing with the United States, he had to confront questions about the Cuban presence in Nicaragua and Sandinista aid to the Salvadoran guerrillas. But as a non-Sandinista (he was still a member of the Democratic Conservative Party), he was not privy to the kind of information that allowed him to deal intelligently with those questions. Further, while the Sandinista Front wanted him in Washington because it was a visible position from which to maintain a "moderate" image internationally, the FSLN still felt that he was, as was often said privately, "the State Department's card" within the Nicaraguan government.

At the same time, Cruz's colleagues in the Nicaraguan opposition were caught up in a new confrontation with the Sandinistas after Humberto Ortega charged in early October 1981 that some businessmen were working for "imperialism" and said that if Nicaragua should be invaded, they would be "the first to be hanged by the people along the roads and highways . . ." COSEP responded with an angry letter accusing the Sandinistas of bringing Nicaragua to the verge of economic collapse and of contemplating "genocide" against dissenters. It said private enterprise supported revolutionary change in Nicaragua but not a "Marxist-Leninist adventure." The Sandinista Front reacted by charging the six signers (the president and five vice presidents of COSEP) with violating the economic emergency law. Three were arrested, including COSEP president Enrique Dreyfus, a lifelong friend of Cruz's. One of the signers slipped into the Venezuelan Embassy ahead of the security agents, and two had left the country for a meeting the day after signing and stayed abroad when they learned of the charges.

In the weeks after the arrests, Cruz shuttled between Washington and Managua almost weekly, trying to launch a dialogue between the Sandinistas and the opposition that would, among other things, lead to freedom for the imprisoned businessmen and for several Communist trade union leaders who had been jailed about the same time. In addition, Cruz was trying to work on the issues between the Reagan administration and the Sandinista Front. On November 14, however, he effectively admitted defeat. He called a news conference on one of his trips to Managua and, in diplomatic language that skirted most of the issues, announced his resignation. Given the tensions that existed, he said, the job of ambassador to the United States "ought not be carried out by someone like me—loyal to the revolution but, after all, a dissident. Someone should carry it out, instead, who has all the credibility necessary that when he speaks to the United States does it with all the weight of the real power in this country, of the FSLN."

Cruz, after being replaced as ambassador, remained in Washington and returned to work at the Inter-American Development Bank as assistant treasurer. In theory, he had left Nicaraguan politics behind him when, in early 1982, Edén Pastora began to telephone periodically. Pastora wanted to emerge from his shell. In early March, Cruz went to Cuernavaca, Mexico, and, during an all-night session, he and Pastora drafted a statement of principles in which Pastora would make his first public attack on the Sandinista National Directorate. Pastora did not wish to condemn the entire Sandinista movement. He looked on *sandinismo* as basically an expression of Nicaraguan nationalism and still considered himself one of its adherents. In his mind, it was the National Directorate (the nine *comandantes,* plus a few others) who had led the whole thing astray, had subverted the movement. When the statement had been written, Cruz went back to Washington, and Pastora and his collaborators moved to Costa Rica.

Pastora also sent a message to Leonel Poveda that it was time to abandon his bean-farming operation for a return to politics. Poveda and his wife and children drove to Costa Rica on the pretense that it was just another fertilizer-buying mission, but this time they did not go back.

At the same time, another significant group of Nicaraguans was filtering out of Nicaragua and into Costa Rica. Most were members of the Nicaraguan Democratic Movement (the MDN), the political party of Alfonso Robelo, former junta member and prominent opponent of the Sandinista Front. On March 15, 1982, the day a state of emergency was decreed in Nicaragua in reaction to the FDN attacks on two bridges near the border with Honduras, Robelo was sitting in the Managua airport waiting to fly to San José, the Costa Rican capital. There was seemingly nothing unusual about this trip. Robelo had business interests in Costa Rica, and he traveled there regularly. He had already cleared immigration and was in the international departures area when Sandinista army officials came to him and said he could not leave. A few days later, after telling the media that the declaration of the state of emergency had been justifiable under the circumstances, Robelo was allowed to leave with the help of an invitation arranged by three U.S. congressmen to give a speech in the United States.

Once in Costa Rica, Robelo read the declaration drafted by Pastora and Cruz and tried unsuccessfully to convince Pastora to remove some of the passing words of praise for Cuban leaders. Otherwise, it was an almost classic statement of centrist democratic theory with extra touches of social and economic justice. But it was to be Pastora's declaration. Cruz and Robelo were not ready to say anything.

On April 15 Pastora convened a news conference in a San José suburb, inviting journalists from all over the hemisphere. Reading the carefully drafted statement,* he combined a call for political and economic pluralism with charges that the National Directorate was running a regime of terror, that it had made Nicaragua a pawn in the East-West struggle, and that it was copying the Cuban model. While expressing respect for the Cuban leadership, Pastora said Nicaragua must carve its own path. He said he had realized the Nicaraguan revolution was losing its originality when, just fifteen days after the triumph, Sandinista commanders returned from trips to Havana wearing Cuban uniforms. He called for foreigners in Nicaragua who were engaged in work other than health or education to return to their own countries, basically a reference to Cuban military and security personnel.

Once he had finished reading, Pastora exploded into verbal attacks on the nine members of the Directorate, saying they were living in ostentatious luxury and that he was going to take them out of their Mercedes-Benzes and mansions at gunpoint. He demanded that Humberto Ortega rectify the political, social, and economic errors. This was a recognition of the power of Ortega and the fact that it was he who had convinced Pastora to rejoin the Sandinistas in 1977.

To emphasize the point that he was still a Sandinista, Pastora spoke beside the banner of the old Sandino Revolutionary Front, a short-lived anti-Somoza group formed in 1959 in which the young Pastora participated. It had, as Pastora pointed out, predated the Sandinista National Liberation Front, formed in 1961.

Two days later Pastora told me, "If it weren't for the national Literacy Crusade, I would dare say to you that it is almost like the time of Somoza. We have more poor people, no less corruption, more foreign debt, less infrastructure, fewer liberties. At least in the time of Somoza we had the liberty to fight. The only thing they have not done is begin to kill massively . . . But they are repressing the peasants, and when the people realize that and when the [Sandinista] army realizes that, the army is going to open fire."

It was difficult to tell whether Pastora was more upset over the totalitarian drift of the regime or over his being excluded from power.

---

*The text of the declaration appears in the Appendix.

One of the things that emerged was his conviction that most of the power rested in the hands of people who had done little actual fighting against Somoza. He ran down a list of the National Directorate members and their experiences. Daniel Ortega and Victor Tirado, he said, had each participated in just two combat operations in their guerrilla careers. Humberto Ortega had, according to Pastora, seen action only once—the less-than-valiant shootout with Costa Rican Civil Guardsmen in 1969. Jaime Wheelock, Pastora said, didn't know how to load a pistol, and he labeled Henry Ruiz the "virgin *comandante,*" apparently a reference to Ruiz's limited combat exposure during the years he had spent in the northern mountains. Tomás Borge, Pastora conceded, had gone through some rough times but had been saved by him—Pastora—three times. The last was in August 1978, when Borge and various other Sandinistas were freed from prison as a result of the Palace Raid.

Pastora said he had never fully enjoyed the confidence of the nine *comandantes.* They had dismissed him as a Social Democrat, a Christian Democrat, or a *reformista,* and as someone lacking the intellectual capacity to understand the concept of class struggle. Yet, he did not want to put an anti-Marxist brand on his own actions. He wanted a movement without ideological labels that would eventually resolve Nicaragua's conflicts through elections. Pastora said he fully expected the Sandinista Directorate to call him a traitor and ally of the bourgeoisie and U.S. "imperialism," to send mobs into the streets to burn him in effigy, and to try to kill him. "But I'm going to bury them."

Despite the fiery language, Pastora did not say how he would accomplish his goals. He announced no combat plans, and the combat veterans around him were engaged more in politics and public relations than guerrilla planning.

Alfonso Robelo told me at the time that Pastora's hope was that the numerous supporters he still had in the Sandinista army would force the National Directorate to change its path, making armed action unnecessary. The intended audience for Pastora's declarations was the middle and upper levels of the army, a group of no more than three hundred men and a few women, mostly Southern Front veterans. Of that group, Pastora thought he had the sympathies of 70 or 80 percent. What this was, said Robelo, was a call to insurrection within the FSLN.

Robelo's own departure marked the end of his efforts to oppose the Sandinistas by internal, civic means. The entire MDN structure left Nicaragua, with most of the leaders moving to Costa Rica, some to

Honduras. The decision to leave had been preceded by a series of confrontations between the MDN and Sandinista *turbas* and between Robelo and the Sandinista leadership. His own home had been attacked by *turbas*. Since the death of his friend Jorge Salazar in November 1980 he had found it increasingly distasteful to be at the mercy of the Sandinista Front. He had led the opposition into a conference with the FSLN called the "Forum of Discussion of National Problems" in the second quarter of 1981, only to feel that the Sandinistas promptly violated some of the understandings reached. At the same time, the Reagan administration was sounding as if it intended to settle the Nicaraguan question in its own manner, and Robelo was frustrated at the lack of support and cooperation from "Liberal Democrats" in Washington, among whom he thought Nicaraguans such as he should have found natural allies in their efforts to force political and economic pluralism on the Sandinistas.

On June 16, 1982, in Panama, Robelo made his public announcement that he had joined Pastora in a "political-military alliance" to oppose the Sandinistas. He said he had taken the decision because the National Directorate was trying to consolidate a totalitarian regime based on Marxism-Leninism. It was totalitarian, he said, because it censored the press, because it had set off a campaign of hatred and class warfare among Nicaraguans, because it had created a politically partisan army and police force, because it had proclaimed itself the "eternal vanguard" of the people, because it had created a "machinery of terror," because it jailed independent trade unionists, because it had created its own, politicized branch of the church, and more. Nicaragua, he said, lived under a wave of terror in which Somoza had been multiplied by nine. It lived under intervention from Cuba and the Soviet Union, he said, with more foreigners giving orders to Nicaraguans than in the days of the U.S. Marines.

Arturo Cruz, because of his position at the Inter-American Development Bank in Washington, did not make his support for Pastora so public, but he felt that Pastora's action now freed a lot of other Nicaraguans to express their disagreement with National Directorate policies without having to appear to be counterrevolutionaries. During a long conversation in Washington a month after Pastora's announcement, Cruz told me that if he could do it over, could return to 1977, he would have ignored the entreaties to join the Group of Twelve. He had learned a bitter lesson, "that broad alliances do not function." Now, he was "eating a lot of crow" among friends and relatives for having involved himself with the Sandinista regime in the first place. He had been reading the writings of Carlos Franqui on the early days inside the Castro regime in Cuba and found that the stories matched—"chapter by chapter"—what was happening twenty years later in Nicaragua. In addition to implanting a totalitarian dictatorship, he said, the Sandinista Front had failed in its goal of improving the quality of life of most Nicaraguans.

"I explained to the revolutionary leadership that we—I assume part of the blame, since I served the government for almost three years—had failed to create the conditions for economic growth. On the contrary, not only had we failed to create those conditions, but the harassment, plus hatred, slogans, and unjustified seizures of factories, prevented that economic growth and therefore made the country more dependent. And if one of the objectives of the revolution is to liberate Nicaragua from this excessive dependence—because there will always be interdependence, that's unavoidable—that's where the revolution failed. The revolutionary leadership has also failed in raising the real standard of living of the people, though a lot has been done in the literacy campaign, and a lot of health centers have been opened. Some efforts have been made. But there has been a lack of determination to define a model acceptable to the mainstream of Nicaraguan society."

I asked him why the non-Marxists, who had looked so strong at the beginning of the new government, had so quickly lost influence.

"At the beginning, when there was a will, apparently, on the part of those who hold the real power in Nicaragua to give appearances of a pluralistic society . . . the moderates were very useful. In addition, at the beginning, there was a lot of jockeying, about how the [political] model would be, about where we were really going. Then the moderates were very useful. They were useful to those who wanted to influence the process to be an open system. And the moderates were also very useful for tactical reasons to those who already had the intention of making it a totalitarian system. You're useful at the time, but when polarization begins to grow, then the moderate is not only unnecessary, but he is always an obstacle. That's precisely why I felt that I should withdraw from the government . . .

"When polarization set in and the counterrevolution felt that it could someday overthrow the Sandinistas and the Sandinistas were becoming more and more radicalized, then the moderate became an obstacle to either side. To the counterrevolutionaries because they felt that the moderates were only legitimizing, somehow, a totalitarian system, and to the others because they felt the moderates were an obstacle and nuisance."

Cruz frequently became angry as his mind roamed over the recent years of his life, angry at himself for what he had tolerated for so long, angry at the Sandinistas for their trickery, their insistence that ideology would solve any problem, their attempts to destroy his reputation for honesty after he left the government. "I ask you," he said, suddenly pounding the table, "do you think a single one of them—the nine *comandantes*—could get a job and earn a living?" No answer was expected.

Edén Pastora's appeal to the upper ranks of the Sandinista Army bore little fruit. The ideological education program within the army had, instead, borne fruit for the National Directorate in the form of loyalty. However, large numbers of army rank and file began to show up in Costa Rica offering to fight under Pastora's banner, if he should ever unfurl it.

Soon after Pastora's April announcement, José Francisco Cardenal and Mariano Mendoza, representing the Honduras-based FDN, flew to Costa Rica and spent a week talking to Pastora and Robelo about a possible alliance. Pastora, Robelo, and Cardenal had all been high-school classmates, but their search for common ground went through a minefield of bitterness. Their meetings in mid-1982 were the beginnings of a search that would continue for the next several years in an effort to find a successful way to confront the Sandinistas. It would go in many directions, be torn by conflicting strategies, ideologies, and, most of all, personalities. When each of them, individually, gave his vision of the Nicaraguan future, it did not differ greatly from that of the others. Yet each felt betrayed by the role that the others had played in the past, and each felt the tug of ambitions in an uncertain future.

Specifically, Pastora saw Cardenal as the tool of the former National Guardsmen and the Argentine military. Cardenal complained of Pastora's egocentricity and his fuzzy position on Marxism. Cardenal also thought Robelo had made mistake after mistake in strategy over the past several years, first in opposing Somoza, then in dealing with the Sandinistas. Robelo, not given to the public explosiveness of Cardenal and Pastora, seemed the cool-headed technocrat, but the sudden shifts in opinion or strategy of his ally Pastora often caught him unawares and tested his control.

Not the least of the differences among them was the question of financing their operations. This meant finding international backing, which, in turn, required understanding the vagaries of public opinion and government policies in Western Europe and the United States. These questions came to occupy them more than the beans and rice and repression issues that dominated the lives of most Nicaraguans inside the country. In that, they were not unlike the Sandinistas themselves.

Unable then to reach agreement with Cardenal and the FDN, Pastora's resurrected Sandino Revolutionary Front, Robelo's MDN, and a Miskito Indian faction led by Brooklyn Rivera, came together under the name Democratic Revolutionary Alliance—ARDE. The unified group continued to seek political backing in Western Europe and among democratic Latin American governments, particularly Venezuela. Pastora wanted, in his words, "to disabuse" European Social Democrats of the idea that the Sandinista Front was a democratic body deserving their continued support. He hoped that pressures from the Mitterrand government in France, Spanish leader Felipe Gonzalez, and Willy Brandt, the power broker of the Socialist International, might force moderation on the Sandinistas.

Pastora encountered little success in the political crusade. At the same time, he was resisting the entreaties of the CIA to join forces with the Honduran-based FDN, and implying that he wanted nothing to do with either the former National Guard or the CIA. In fact, he was quietly receiving some CIA assistance, coming through "the Venezuelan route," according to a Nicaraguan involved as a go-between. In April 1983, a year after his public condemnation of the National Directorate, Pastora launched military actions into Nicaragua from Costa Rica.

In late March 1982 I ran into José Esteban González on a flight from Washington to Miami. González had been the national coordinator of the Nicaraguan Permanent Commission for Human Rights until September 1981, when he had joined the exile ranks. Now he was trying to educate foreigners about what was going on inside Nicaragua. He was talking not only about human rights abuses—about the uprooting of Miskito Indians, disappearances, and restrictions on political and press freedom—but also about the battle for existence that the human rights commission itself had gone through with the former guerrillas it had once defended.

Founded in 1977 by people affiliated with several political parties, including the Social Christian, the Conservative, and, secretly at the time, the FSLN, the commission had played a major role in drawing the world's attention to the human rights abuses of the Somoza regime. It represented a broad spectrum of Nicaraguan society, and its work was respected inside and outside the country. But after July 1979, when González and the staff and board of the commission began to apply the same critical judgment to the new regime, they quickly encountered the wrath of the Sandinista leadership, particularly that of Tomás Borge, who, as interior minister, had charge of the police and jails that González was criticizing.

Borge decided that what was needed in the human rights business was a little competition. In mid-1980 the government set up its own human rights commission, operating as an arm of the Foreign Ministry. The two human rights groups essentially represented distinct attitudes toward human rights. The Permanent Commission generally advocated the protection of the rights of the individual and believed that it should have an adversary relationship with government, while the Sandinista-created National Commission of Human Rights was an internal watchdog within what it saw as an essentially generous regime. One of its functions was to counsel political prisoners on how to adapt themselves to a system in which individual rights were not a priority. Another of its functions was to remind the government when prisoners had completed their sentences and then, ever so gently, to nudge Borge into releasing them.

At the same time, the Permanent Commission was beginning to lose support from some of its international backers, who found less need to monitor the Sandinistas' human rights performance than that of Somoza. In April 1979, before the fall of Somoza, González had gone to Geneva to the headquarters of the World Council of Churches and been received "with smiles and *abrazos*" by the Reverend Charles R. Harper, Jr., head of the Human Rights Resources Office on Latin America. González left with $15,000 in assistance, part of what he understood to be a commitment for $43,000. In May 1980, after ten months of Sandinista rule, González went back to Geneva and was told that there would be no further payment to the Permanent Commission. The reason he was given, González said, was that human rights were now guaranteed by the government in Nicaragua. Reverend Harper confirmed to me several years later that the member churches had decided there was no compelling reason to continue support for the Permanent Commission after the fall of Somoza, but said there had never been a formal pledge for additional financial aid.

The problems between the Permanent Commission and the Sandinistas worsened after González, during a trip to Europe in early 1981, met with Pope John Paul II and told him that Nicaragua had eight thousand political prisoners, mostly former National Guardsmen, and that about eight hundred people had disappeared or been killed for political reasons since the Sandinistas came to power, most in the first few months of the regime. The FSLN reacted with indignation and said González was lying. Before he returned home, security agents and Justice Ministry officials occupied the offices of the Permanent Commission for several days and photocopied the files, mostly consisting of complaints filed by relatives of prisoners and the missing. When González got back to Managua on February 13, several hundred supporters, including leaders of opposition political parties and various trade unions, went to the airport to meet him. But several hundred members of Sandinista Youth and other pro-Sandinista elements rode onto the airport grounds in army troop trucks, and a slugfest resulted.

Six days later, on February 19, González was arrested. He was charged with violating the public security law in making the accusations in Rome. Two weeks later, however, after friends of González's negotiated privately with the court, he was acquitted. But on September 8, he was stopped at the Managua airport as he was leaving for Switzerland to attend a United Nations conference on missing people. Documents and photographs were taken from him and his luggage was searched. Two days later, with the help of the Venezuelan Embassy, González fled the country for good. He moved to Caracas, from which he could freely criticize the Sandinistas. The Permanent Commission, however, continued to function in Managua under the direction of Marta Baltodano, a fearless young lawyer who had worked with González.

When I saw González on the flight out of Washington, he expressed his amazement at the change in attitude he had found among American church people since he had traveled to Washington in early 1979 to reveal the sins of Somoza. Then, he said, he had received a warm reception from Washington representatives of Catholic and Protestant church groups, who were prepared to believe what he had to say. But now that he was talking about the sins of the Sandinistas, the reception was very cool, even hostile.

"My impression is that among these organizations there exists a very simple attitude, even naïve, not very professional or responsible, over what constitutes a revolutionary process. I said that the FSLN has not complied with democratic processes, and a nun said that democracy has nothing to do with a revolution . . . And she said Monsignor Obando y Bravo is the most divisive person in the country.

"Among Protestants, I found that there was little real interest in humanitarian affairs. One of them said what worried him was the possibility that the Reagan administration was only concerned about the situation of the Miskito Indians for political reasons. I replied with a phrase from Saint Paul that it didn't matter for what reason you defend them. In general, I found an exaggerated desire to find something in what I was saying to use to criticize the present policies of the Reagan administration . . . The U.S. church sectors that are active in Latin America seem to act more for interests of a domestic political character than for evangelical reasons that are of universal validity."

In June 1982 a magazine called *Soberania* (Sovereignty), published by the Nicaraguan Interior Ministry, carried an article purporting to reveal scandalous information about Nicaraguan organizations and individuals being financed by the CIA. Those accused were not exiles aligned with the *Contra* but people and groups functioning inside Nicaragua. Predictably, they were the leading opposition political, economic, and labor groups. But it was difficult to take seriously the charge that the money in question came from the CIA because the sums were, in large measure, those that had been publicly revealed by the U.S. State Department as official aid to the various groups prior to the aid cutoff at the beginning of 1981.

One name was somewhat surprising. Edgard Macías Gómez, until a few months earlier the vice minister of labor, was accused of accepting $250,000 from the CIA for "diversionist" work in communications. ("Diversionism" was a common charge that the FSLN made against the opposition media, primarily *La Prensa.*) In addition, Macías' wife, Geraldine O'Leary, an American and former Maryknoll nun who worked with a private child welfare organization, was accused of receiving a smaller sum from the CIA.

Macías had founded the Popular Social Christian Party in 1976 as a small, radical offshoot of the Social Christian Party. It was an early advocate of armed action to oust the Somoza dynasty, and Macías and other party members formed a closer alliance with the FSLN than most of the groups opposing Somoza. They did not, for example, take part in the efforts of COSEP and various other political and labor groups to moderate the planned composition of the new government and to save part of the National Guard. After the victory, Macías joined the government as deputy minister of labor. In its public positions during the next two years his party seemed indistinguishable from the FSLN.

But in late 1981, Macías had taken the initiative in organizing a seminar called the Encounter of National Reflection and Convergence in an effort to resolve some of the disputes over national policies. The invitation to participate in the Encounter was accepted by the Social Christians, the Social Democrats, the Independent Liberals, and two non-Sandinista labor federations, in addition to Macías' own party. What emerged from six weeks of talks was a diplomatically worded call for a "democratic opening" within the framework of the Plan of Government written in June 1979.

A short time after the Encounter, Macías was fired from his government post. Then he was forced out of the party leadership by party members who wanted to continue to follow FSLN policies. Macías had decided the party should take a more independent and critical position. A few months later came the accusing article in *Soberania*.

The Macíases immediately filed suit against the editor of the magazine for "grave calumnies and injuries." Among other things, they demanded that the magazine produce proof of the CIA financing. Though the court accepted their suit, a news story on it was censored from *La Prensa*.

Macías told me shortly after filing the suit that he was being victimized by the "internationalists"—the foreigners who had poured into Nicaragua since 1979 to work for the government or the FSLN, or otherwise influence policies. They were "opportunists," Macias said. Freddy Balzan, the editor of *Soberania*, was a Venezuelan internationalist who had come to Nicaragua after the fall of Somoza and struck up a friendship with Tomás Borge. Now, according to Macías and various other people, he operated out of an office of the Interior Ministry.

"They are trying to create a dangerous situation," Macías said. "If you say in Nicaragua that someone is of the CIA, it puts that person in danger. At the very least they will attack you with rocks . . . They are trying to discredit people from political movements that can represent an alternative to the FSLN. And they are trying to mix me up in the question of the counterrevolutionaries."

A social worker by profession, Macías had become executive secretary of the 4-S Clubs, which worked among rural youth, when he left the Labor Ministry. The 4-S organization was in line to receive $402,-000 from the Inter-American Development Bank, an international lending agency that receives a significant portion of its capital from the United States, but processing of the loan was tied up in Nicaraguan government red tape. Macías said the idea that he was receiving CIA money was "garbage."

After the article appeared, Sandinista authorities, particularly internal security agents working under Borge, played a game with Macías that seemed calculated to make him nervous. He was frequently followed or under observance by people who could have been government agents. He was called to internal security headquarters. When he arrived he was told that the director, Commander Lenín Cerna, who was not there at the moment, wanted to see him. He was allowed to go home with the admonishment to expect another summons. During this period, Geraldine Macías left for the United States to try to find information to clear their names. A few days later, on July 9, her husband sought asylum in the Venezuelan Embassy. Lenín Cerna told journalists he could not understand why Macías had taken that step, since "no persecution existed against him." Cerna went on to suggest that by seeking asylum, Macías was admitting a CIA connection. On July 11, Macías went to the airport accompanied by two Venezuelan diplomats and took a flight to Costa Rica; he then continued to the United States to join his wife in exile.

As many of his friends and business and political collaborators and competitors soured on the FSLN and gradually left Nicaragua, Adolfo Calero Portocarrero seemed to maintain eternal optimism that somehow Nicaragua would get off the totalitarian path before it was too late. As political secretary of the Democratic Conservative Party, he was highly visible. He went to lots of parties and all the embassy receptions, invited people to his beach house regularly, had an opinion on everything, was always available to journalists, and traveled abroad frequently. He could be counted on to have the latest government or FSLN document embarassing to the Sandinistas. He also knew such important things as whose ancestors were Liberals and whose were Conservatives, and who didn't keep up his dues at the country club, when Nicaragua still had country clubs.

The plant he managed, which bottled Coca-Cola and various other soft drinks, had to struggle against sugar rationing and bottle shortages. But it was doing well financially for the manager and the owner, Manuel Lacayo, a Nicaraguan who lived in Costa Rica. The plant could sell all it produced and then some, and was just completing an expansion costing several million dollars. The Sandinistas, in fact, liked to point to Adolfo Calero as one of the few businessmen who showed his faith in Nicaragua by investing and expanding.

But as the Sandinistas moved into their third and fourth years of rule, Calero became more outspoken. In August 1981, on behalf of his political party, Calero had written a letter to the foreign ministers of most Western Hemisphere nations asking that they convene a meeting of the Organization of American States to consider the FSLN's non-compliance with the commitments on political pluralism made to the OAS in 1979. In large measure it was a futile exercise. Even though the OAS had, in a June 1979 resolution, reserved for itself the right to reopen the question of Nicaragua's future, there was no consensus then for reopening the Nicaraguan question, which involved the touchy intervention issue. But Calero's letter had served to remind the OAS nations that they carried some responsibility in Nicaragua.

Slightly more than a year later, in September 1982, Calero and José Castillo, the national coordinator of the Democratic Conservatives, addressed a long letter to the nine members of the Sandinista National Directorate rejecting their invitation to a political dialogue on the grounds that there was nothing to talk about until the FSLN complied with the 1979 commitments. Calero and Castillo said that what the FSLN wanted to accomplish in a dialogue with the opposition was the renegotiation of those commitments in its favor, but they were not renegotiable.

Two months later Calero and Castillo proposed that the FSLN open negotiations with the armed exiles. In response to Sandinista demands for national unity against the threats of the Reagan administration, the Conservative leaders said the primary cause of Nicaragua's problems was not international, but differences among Nicaraguans. So the way to resolve the problems, they said, was negotiations between the Sandinistas and their opponents, both inside and outside the country. Noting that various foreign governments were proposing such a dialogue for the warring elements in El Salvador, they said such a proposition was equally valid for Nicaragua.

The proposal angered the FSLN. Daniel Ortega said the Democratic Conservatives were committing a crime in proposing that the Sandinistas talk to the armed opposition. But Ortega told a crowd of supporters that the way to deal with the letter was not to jail the signers but for Nicaraguans to demonstrate their support for the Sandinista Front.

At the same time, as worried as he was about the doors closing inside Nicaragua, Calero was also worried about the lineup that was shaping up to challenge the Sandinistas from outside—Pastora,

Robelo, Cardenal, Cruz, Bermúdez, and, most of all, Ronald Reagan. In the struggle against Somoza, Calero had played his hand publicly, peacefully, inside the country. But, in the end, power had been defined from outside, and he had not especially liked the result. Now, if the Reagan administration was going to back the exiles in a big way, he wondered if power would again be defined from outside. Did he want to be inside, and left out, again?

The FDN was going through an internal power struggle after Cardenal's negotiations with Pastora and Robelo had failed to produce an alliance of the two exile camps. Cardenal continued to have political differences with both the Argentine advisers and the former National Guardsmen. In addition, he was experiencing personality and political differences with members of the Miami committee of the FDN. This group of well-heeled and influential Nicaraguan exiles thought Cardenal was the wrong man to lead the FDN politically.

Cardenal thought the one ally he had was the CIA. Although the Argentine advisers had initially been his only contact with the source of funding, he had by mid-1982 established his own CIA contact in Washington. That man seemed to agree with Cardenal, at least in assessing the Argentines as reactionary hardliners with no great desire to bring democracy to Nicaragua, and with his attempts to broaden and improve the political bases of the FDN.

But the CIA did nothing to protect Cardenal from the Miami committee. In early December 1982 a new leadership was announced for the FDN. Cardenal and Mariano Mendoza, the former trade union leader, were out.* The new directorate had eight members, including Lucía Cardenal de Salazar, the widow of Jorge Salazar; Edgar Chamorro, a cousin of the Pellas family, which owned Nicaragua Sugar Estates; Alfonso Callejas, who had once served as vice president under Somoza; Steadman Fagoth, the Miskito Indian leader; and Enrique Bermúdez, the former National Guard colonel. One of the eight was not identified. He was still inside Nicaragua.

After the new FDN leadership was announced, rumors spread

---

*At the time, Cardenal thought he had a commitment from the CIA to finance an "internal front," a network he had already developed among people still living in Nicaragua who were willing to organize sabotage and other actions against the Sandinista Front. But at the beginning of 1983, he said, the CIA withdrew from the plan, citing congressional criticism and unfavorable publicity about its funding of the *Contra.* So Cardenal quit politics and went to work selling insurance in Miami.

through Managua about the eighth person. Speculation centered on Adolfo Calero, who said nothing. The *comandantes,* of course, heard the same rumors that everyone else heard. Calero and his wife flew to Miami to spend Christmas with their daughter and other relatives. Then they went to Costa Rica to spend New Year's with Manuel Lacayo, the owner of the bottling plant. While they were in Costa Rica, another high-level member of the Democratic Conservative Party was turned back at the border when she tried to return to Nicaragua. Calero decided he would not go until he could get a safe-conduct guarantee. He delayed his return well into January. Meanwhile, friends and relatives were driving him crazy with advice, telling him not to go back, that he might be jailed, even killed. While Calero was still debating what to do, Tomás Borge's State Security agents pulled up to his house in Managua on January 27 and helped him to make the decision. The security operatives forced María Calero's sister and brother-in-law out of the house and occupied it.

Calero went to Honduras to tour the FDN camps and talk to combat leaders, then to Washington, where he called a news conference to announce that he had joined the FDN leadership. After meeting with State Department officials, he continued to Western Europe to lobby political leaders who had been supporting the Sandinista regime. Within a few months he had been named political and military leader of the FDN and was engaged in another attempt to overcome the differences between the FDN and the forces of Alfonso Robelo and Edén Pastora.

One morning in October 1983, Calero tended a Spanish omelet on the electric range of his Miami town house while he cradled the telephone on his shoulder and heard a report of a *Contra* action the night before. Three of five fuel tanks had been blown up in the port of Corinto, he told me when he hung up the phone. Then he talked for several hours about his eight months as a *Contra* leader. He feared that Central America was becoming one big free-for-all, like the Spanish Civil War. But that was the last thing he wanted.

"My idea would be to take the nine *comandantes,* plus the next nine down, and the next and the next, about sixty people or so of the Sandinista power structure, bind them up and put them on an airplane and drop them off in Havana. That would solve our problems—just as we once thought we could get rid of only Somoza and his top men and save thousands of lives. That is what I want."

20

TWO WHO STAYED

VIOLETA CHAMORRO AND OMAR CABEZAS

Anyone ringing the doorbell at the home of Violeta Barrios de Chamorro could not miss seeing the words *vende patria* scrawled in black letters on the wall above the bell. The expression, bedded deep in Nicaraguan history, translates literally as "country seller," a fanciful way of saying traitor. It was coined in 1914 by the old Liberal Party to denigrate the then ruling Conservative Party for signing a treaty giving the United States the right to build an isthmian canal across Nicaragua. Augusto César Sandino once said that it was this epithet being thrown at him by a drunken Mexican in 1926 that brought him home to join the Liberal armies in battle against the Conservatives. The FSLN resurrected the expression and made it part of the repertory of the *turbas* that it dispatched to attack the homes, offices, and vehicles of Sandinista critics.

"I guess they are telling me that whoever comes through my door is a *vende patria*," Violeta Chamorro mused. She also guessed that the term included her youngest child, Carlos Fernando Chamorro, the editor of *Barricada,* the official newspaper of the Sandinista Front. She said this with just the right tone of innuendo.

The widow of Pedro Joaquín Chamorro Cardenal and once the honored lady of the revolution who had accepted the call to join the new government and then resigned in April 1980 with diplomatic reference to health problems, she had become one of those vilified as "traitorous bourgeoisie." The first of several attacks on her home, an inviting white stucco house on a corner facing Las Palmas Park, occurred in March 1981. The walls were splashed with slogans and caricatures of her older son, Pedro Joaquín Chamorro Barrios, the co-editor of the family newspaper *La Prensa,* and of Alfonso Robelo, the friend and opposition leader who had served with her on the junta. The slogans called Pedro Joaquín an imperialist and traitor to his father's memory. *La Prensa* was described as the voice of the CIA. Death was threatened to Robelo—this a full year before he went into exile.

As *turba* attacks went, this was one of the milder examples. Most of those elsewhere were more destructive. Doña Violeta had to be treated gently, with respect. There could be no frontal assault on her integrity. Her status in the public mind—and that of her husband— meant the Sandinistas could not stand up and condemn her, but they could let a few things just happen. Violeta's nocturnal visitors came and went silently, without disturbing those sleeping inside. There was even a certain stylistic quality to the drawings left on the walls of the house, indicating, as she noted, that they had not been done by some poor illiterate. She decided not to paint over the work, but to let time clean it off. "I'm leaving it there for honor. It makes me a martyr," she told me.

It was typical of the gesture that she could make, such as letting her hair go gray—"for Nicaragua." No other woman in Nicaragua with enough money for hair coloring would dream of such a thing.

She could also, after the *turba* decorations had been on her house walls for eight months, invite a hundred or so people to a buffet dinner in honor of a delegation of foreign newspaper publishers and editors and include various Sandinista *comandantes* on the guest list, among them Tomás Borge. She would challenge them to walk through that door beside the hated slogan and listen politely, drink in hand, to the newspapermen's plea for press freedom in Nicaragua. But the *coman-*

dantes, who had crowded into Violeta's house to toast her when she left the junta the previous year, did not come this time. None of them even bothered to send a note declining the invitation. The day after the party she was properly miffed at the display of bad manners.

Despite all this grief from the Sandinistas, Violeta Chamorro was one Nicaraguan who did not go into exile. She would not entertain the thought. When I visited her in late 1983, about two years after the party for the visiting newspapermen, she said she would abandon Nicaragua only when she was buried. She would stay to guard the past's truths and deflate Sandinista egos. She was newly outraged over another *turba* attack a month earlier. There had been more than one since the original paint job, and insulting telephone calls came almost daily.

This time she had been in Pedro's study with her brother-in-law and sister-in-law when they heard rocks hitting the roof. Some of the barrel tiles broke. Later the same evening another rock was heaved over the seven-foot chain-link fence that had been installed after the attacks began. A white truck sped away. She went to authorities and filed a complaint, but when *La Prensa* tried to publish an article on it, the Interior Ministry censored it. Violeta then insisted to Pedro Joaquín that the censor's communiqué be published. "I said we had to be firm and maintain our position. They close the paper or they don't close it, but this is too much. We have to put it [the communiqué] out. Investigation? Hah. Here, the investigations are not to be believed. The same thing is happening that happened in the time of Somoza. Anyway, over these rocks, since *La Prensa* went ahead and published the communiqué, they called us in the middle of the night—to Pedro or Jaime or Pablo Antonio [Cuadra], I don't know which—and said they had to present themselves. So Pedro said I had said it had to be published. My mother, *etcétera.* But Tomás Borge suddenly said that the whole thing—the attack—had been a barbarity. You see, he wanted to wash his hands of it in some way. He is a hypocritical man. So he says, 'I'll give orders,' and the order was to call someone to stop all the trucks in the country to find out who it was, and not just the white trucks, but all colors. So in five minutes he says the truck has already been found. But it is they themselves who do it."

Did I notice, she asked, what I was drinking from? It was the bottom half of a green wine bottle that had been expertly cut in two, the edge smoothed and polished. "During one period you couldn't buy glasses here, but there was wine. Now, we get glasses from Bulgaria. They [the Sandinistas] blame all of these shortages on Reagan. If you can't get a pair of shoes, they blame it on that gentleman. Everybody complains all the time about shortages. And who is it who suffers more if it is not the poor? This revolution is against the poor."

At the time of this conversation, Violeta Chamorro was fifty-four years old—tall, slim, elegant, and still pretty, even with gray hair. Her life's work had been to accompany her husband and rear their children, but it was impossible to have done those things in the Chamorro family in Nicaragua without being center stage in politics. And now politics had divided her family. She characterized two of her children as Sandinistas—Carlos Fernando and Claudia, who formerly worked in press relations for the junta and then became head of a section in the Culture Ministry. The other two were not Sandinistas—Pedro Joaquín* and Cristiana. Violeta and the children tried to maintain some closeness and not to talk politics when two family members of opposing views met. Carlos Fernando and Pedro Joaquín could still occupy the same fishing boat. Claudia could still call her mother when she wrecked a car and needed money. But the passage of time was making tolerance more and more difficult. The nation was becoming polarized, and for most Nicaraguans politics had become the main topic of conversation. When Carlos Fernando came to visit Violeta now there was not a lot to talk about.

"He drinks a glass of ice water with me, asks about my health. I say he looks skinny, and so on. We have correct relations."

She had not wanted to join the junta in the first place, but she had owed it to Pedro's memory and to Nicaragua. Unfortunately, that had been the beginning of her problems. Now she wished she could just erase the whole experience from her mind, not have to remember.

From the beginning of the new government, she found, the junta had had little to do with running the country. "Daniel [Ortega] and Sergio [Ramírez] always said, 'We have to consult,' before a decision was taken. When there was a Cabinet meeting, if there wasn't a representative of the National Directorate present, if he were busy or something, they sent whatever guy in olive green. Someone in olive green always had to figure into things."

It disturbed her no end that she and the other junta members were

---

*Pedro Joaquín Chamorro Barrios moved to Costa Rica at the end of 1984 to protest press censorship in Nicaragua and restrictions on his travel rights, but *La Prensa* continued to be published under the direction of his uncle, Jaime Chamorro.

not, in her view, complying with the written government plan that they had sworn themselves to uphold. When she resigned, matters had reached the point where she had to ask permission to sign a paper; she thought that if she had to have a kid telling her that because she was a bourgeoise she could not govern the country, then she might as well resign. Then she broke her foot as she left home for the office one morning, and that gave her a pretext for resigning without having to reveal her true feelings. She had also hoped the Sandinistas might repent and change their ways, but they did not, so now she would say what was on her mind. "I left the junta because they are traitors, and those that they sent to paint my house are traitors, too. For things to change in this country, they [the Sandinista *comandantes*] have to go. In Costa Rica they are preparing for the next elections and in the United States, even though the Democrats hate Reagan, they know he is going to leave power at a certain time. That's called liberty. With liberty things can be said."

Omar Cabezas was one of the people in Nicaragua with more than a passing acquaintance with the policies and actions that so angered Doña Violeta. He was a *comandante guerrillero,* the second highest honorary political title extended by the Sandinista Front, and also a *comandante de brigada,* the highest military rank of the Sandinista army. He was not one of the nine members of the Sandinista National Directorate, but he probably fit within the unofficial next nine in the Sandinista hierarchy. He was a deputy minister of interior, working under Tomás Borge.

His real work, however, was writing and talking. In this former guerrilla the FSLN had found a talented and entertaining spinner of revolutionary tales, a born creator of Sandinista mythology. His first book, *La Montaña es Algo Mas que una Inmensa Estepa Verde* (The Mountain Is Something More than an Immense Green Steppe),* was a runaway best seller about guerrilla life. It laid claim to be the biggest selling book ever in Nicaragua, with 50,000 copies in print. One of the things that people enjoyed about the book, even some who were not fond of the Sandinistas, was that it seemed to be the first ever written "in Nicaraguan"—that is, using the colloquialisms of Nicaraguans instead of the rules of the Spanish Academy. A second volume was to come.

---

*The book was published in the United States by Crown in 1985 as *Fire from the Mountain.*

The other part of his specialty consisted of receiving delegations of foreigners who came to Nicaragua to see a revolution in action. Like his boss, Tomás Borge, Cabezas had honed a skill for dealing with church delegations. It was considered very important to make a good impression on them. He had expected our group to be a church delegation, too, but it was not. I had joined six or seven visiting Americans, most of them academics, for the chance to talk with Cabezas. He kept us waiting several hours and when he arrived he said he had been to León to visit his mother.

Cabezas—then thirty-two years-old, with a thick black mustache and slim hips, wearing blue jeans and a knit shirt—was cordial. He came across as a charming rogue, as picaresque as his book. He had a reputation for not letting the truth stand in the way of a good story or a good line. He had heard all the questions before. And had given all the answers before. Such as the rundown on every indiscretion committed by the United States in the history of Nicaragua. There had been fourteen U.S. invasions, he claimed, beginning with William Walker's adventure in 1855. It does no good to suggest to a Sandinista *comandante* that Walker did not come to Nicaragua at the instigation of the United States government.

Cabezas said he came from a poor family in León, but his father was a sharp-witted survival artist. "One day he was walking down the street and came across a tin can and began kicking it along in front of him. After a block, he picked it up to see what it said, and it had instructions for making soap. Have you read García Marquez? My father could have been one of his characters. He became a small industrialist and made soap. He came to have three vehicles to deliver soap, had advertisements in newspapers and on radio, and called it Omar Soap, my name. But he went bankrupt as a result of the creation of the Central American Common Market, when soap companies from the United States set up factories in Central America. So he began inventing other things to do. He began making household decorations—ashtrays and other things to put in the living room— because he said the bourgeoisie was very strange—that they liked things that were ugly. So he would take these things to the houses and say, 'Look, have you ever seen anything so beautiful?' He was a bandit. He had a great desire to improve his lot in life. Like a good, underdeveloped person of the decades of the fifties and sixties, he began to read *Reader's Digest* and *Life,* and he was an admirer of the technology of the United States, *etcétera, etcétera.*"

When things were going well for his father, Omar had attended the best church-run school in León; when things soured, Omar went to public school. Then he went to the National Autonomous University, which was in León. He studied law and became a political activist, joining the student group affiliated with the Sandinista Front. It was the end of the 1960s and beginning of the 1970s.

Cabezas told us he knew almost nothing about Marxism-Leninism, but in his book he talks about teaching the *Communist Manifesto* to people in an Indian neighborhood of León and telling them it was what Sandino had believed in. What seems to have drawn him to the FSLN was a sort of mystique, part *machismo,* part spiritual. He becomes rather literary, for example, in describing the allure of the bonfires that FSLN student activists set on León street corners during demonstrations. Perhaps even more than the long-term goals of the Sandinista Front, the opportunity to test himself was what had attracted him. In that sense, going up to the mountain, as he did after he graduated from the university, was the supreme test. He was one of the students and recent graduates who joined Henry Ruiz in the northern mountains between 1972 and 1974 to try to breathe life into the nearly dead movement.

Even as he and a few others climbed with a peasant guide, Cabezas discovered that although he was only twenty-two and healthy, he was not prepared for life in the mountains. The most trying aspect was not the prospect of engaging in combat with the National Guard—there was almost none of that in the early years—but finding the means for physical survival. One of the first things that Cabezas learned to do was to shoot and skin a monkey and cook it. But the most important survival skill was winning the confidence of peasants. Before Cabezas could try to liberate the peasants he had to convince them not to turn him in to the Guard. It was not easy. Progress was slow and sporadic. He tried to convince them the world was round, that people in the cities had cars, bicycles, and ice for their drinks, and that when the revolution triumphed the same things would come to the mountains. What, asked the peasants, were cars, bicycles, and ice?

"If I were a Christian," Cabezas told us, "more correctly, if I were a bishop or priest—we could say that what we want to do is build the kingdom of God here on Earth." Later, after he learned we did not represent a religious organization, he expanded: "The revolution comes as a solution to the problems of survival. It is life insurance for the future generations. We want to make hospitals, we want to make schools and land reform and movie theaters, parks for the kids. We want everybody to have television like you. We want everybody to have electric shavers, *etcétera, etcétera.* We want the people in the countryside to have the same sort of things that they have in the cities, *etcétera, etcétera.*"

Noting that Sandinista plans gave little thought to such things as freedom of the mind, of choice, or how the rules should be decided, I asked him about the polarization in Nicaragua between the Sandinistas and those who wanted more political and economic pluralism, That whole problem, he said, developed this way:

"The big millionaires, who were always allied with Somoza and who always hated us, six months before the triumph, the big millionaires became anti-*somocista,* some actually became Sandinistas because they saw that we were going to triumph and they were afraid that this would be a conventional revolution in which we would wipe them out. So they began to bet on the horse that was going to win. And with the triumph of the revolution, it was one big honeymoon. Everybody was running around in olive green. The *lumpen* [proletariat], housewives, everybody looked like a leaf. And Robelo let his beard grow in the last six months so he would look like a guerrilla . . .

"Even before the triumph they had been showing discontent with Somoza, beginning in about 1972, but they did not become anti-*somocista.* They only began to *worry* about Somoza. Why? Because there was an earthquake. It destroyed Managua. Managua has no downtown because the earthquake destroyed it, somewhere between five hundred and seven hundred square blocks. After the earthquake there was a great demand for housing, so the capitalists, who smell money with a frightening capacity, realized that the thing to do was to invest in building houses. But for that you have to have land, so they began forming companies for selling real estate, mostly outside the city limits, but in order to buy land and build houses money was necessary, plus someone to build the houses.

"So the capitalists began to organize construction companies, loan companies, and companies to sell land. Somoza—let's say the bourgeoisie that surrounded Somoza—had never been into financial businesses like this. They [Somoza's circle] were fundamentally large landowners and in other kinds of businesses. But Somoza, very intelligently, began to create a bank, a new bank, and began to compete with the banks of the other two large economic groups [conglomerates] that existed in the country. He ordered the *somocistas* to withdraw their money from the other banks and put it in his bank. At the same time, he created mortgage loan companies and a construction company and companies to sell land. He also was the one who handled the foreign assistance money that came to rebuild Managua. "What Somoza was doing was putting himself into areas where he had traditionally not been involved. Logically, this produced a lot of disordered subdivisions around Managua. They built all these residential areas around the city, then had to build this weird highway system to connect them. From that point, Somoza slowly—and with an infinite hunger for wealth—began using his political power to compete in the marketplace with the other millionaires. In 1977, it occurred to the millionaires to organize a political party to compete with Somoza because he was becoming a danger to the increase of their capital. Not just that he was competing, but that he was not allowing them to get the profit margins that they wanted. This group of millionaires was led by Alfonso Robelo.

"With the victory of the revolution, we launched our project for a mixed economy and political pluralism, and we put Robelo on the junta. Naturally, we put three Sandinistas with the two millionaires. Why three Sandinistas? Because we were the ones who made the revolution . . . We first took everything that belonged to Somoza and then we became aware that if we wanted to have social justice, we would have to redistribute the wealth of this country . . . When we made this clear, the spell was broken, because they were thinking that with the triumph of the revolution, we—the guerrillas, the young men, enthusiastic, brave, valiant, good-hearted—were going to convert ourselves into the new National Guard and that they would be the ones who would rule the country."

In Cabezas' view (at least in late 1983) Somoza comes across as no more, or even less, of a villain than Robelo and others who opposed him from a non-Marxist perspective. The Sandinistas, he said, had always intended to overthrow both Somoza and the bourgeoisie, but when the bourgeoisie proved willing to join them against Somoza, it seemed to the FSLN an intelligent tactic to accept the help.

I asked Cabezas whether, given the small size of the FSLN in the mid-1970s and the fact that it had judged itself near extinction at the beginning of 1977, the Sandinistas could have possibly won on their own. Was not the common front approach decisive? And without the murder of Pedro Joaquín Chamorro, would there have been a common front? "Pedro Joaquín Chamorro was a patriot," he said, "incorruptible. They were never able to buy him, a man who at the beginning said we were boys of good faith but that we were mistaken, that he admired our courage but not the road we had selected, a man who little by little began to evolve politically and in this process his children evolved. So that even though he was not Sandinista he deserved and deserves all our respect. But fundamentally, we supplied the deaths for twenty years. We organized for twenty years. Pedro Joaquín Chamorro, logically, collaborated and put in his grain of sand. I am not ignoring that the bourgeoisie, at the last moment, put in its grain of sand. What I want to say is that the historical weight of the struggle was the Sandinista Front. It was the fundamental vanguard."

Grain of sand? This kind of argument incenses Violeta Chamorro. Her husband was opposing the Somozas before the FSLN was born. Everybody in Nicaragua had looked to him as the leader of the opposition. Of that she had no doubt. Few of the Sandinistas had done as much time in jail as he. It was his murder that shocked the world and changed the fortunes of Somoza, not the plotting of a few guerrillas. "The detonating spark was my husband, the detonator that created unity in this country. Then everybody began to work together and everybody gave their support to these children who betrayed us. If he had not died, there would have been no war—and no victory."

It was beyond her comprehension—beyond logic in her mind—to suggest that her husband served the purely financial interests of the bourgeoisie. She knew exactly what Pedro Joaquín Chamorro was about. He was fighting for a principle, the freedom for the mind and spirit that Cabezas ignored in all his expositions of Sandinista purpose. She believed that a large segment of the population obeyed that same principle, in some form, financial considerations aside.

In late 1982, in an open letter to Nicaraguans that had to be published in Costa Rica to avoid the censor at home, she had written that liberty of expression, written and spoken, was the indispensable element in her husband's vision of Nicaragua's future. "Nevertheless, after barely three years of having the Sandinista government in power, this same government, guided by totalitarian ideologies imported from other countries and foreign to our history and culture, maintains the concept that liberty of conscience is 'diversionism' and 'ideological war.'" Her husband, she said, had devoted his life to fighting the Somozas and now she felt that she was living through the same kind of nightmare because she shared her husband's sensitivity to all acts of those in power that work at destroying freedom.

"At the beginning," she wrote, "and when only freedom of the press is suppressed, the only thing apparently lost is the privilege of being informed, the right to complain and protest. But, before long, due to the lack of liberty of expression, public power increases,

becomes distorted . . . Now comes the second phase, in which abuse
is multiplied, violent acts are repeated and injustices occur in abundance."

To listen to Omar Cabezas and Violeta Chamorro was to hear two
people who did not inhabit the same mental landscape. Theirs was a
debate that could not be resolved. He believed Nicaragua's future
would be secure only if people who thought as she did either gave up
or left the country. She wanted the *comandantes* to leave. He believed
that declarations in favor of social justice justified the holding of
absolute power; she believed the mind and spirit were important as
well.

21

NOVEMBER 1984

On November 4, 1984, Daniel Ortega was elected president of Nicaragua. The elections were intended to solve some of the country's external problems, but made no pretense of dealing with its internal conflicts. Ortega, who turned thirty-nine a week after the voting, was the Sandinista *comandante* who until the elections had been the head of the government junta. Sergio Ramírez, the writer and intellectual who had worked with Daniel's brother, Humberto, in drafting the strategy that brought the Sandinistas to power in 1979, was elected vice president. The FSLN ticket of Ortega and Ramírez received 67 percent of the votes cast, with about three fourths of the eligible voters going to the polls. There was no immediate indication, however, that Ortega's assumption of the presidency would diminish the importance of the nine men who made up the Sandinista National Directorate. The *comandantes'* role as the insular and powerful Vanguard seemed destined to continue.

The elections that Humberto Ortega had declared in 1980 would not be held before 1985 were moved up a few months in an attempt to lessen international pressure and criticism, especially that from the Reagan administration. As he left the polling place on election day, Sergio Ramírez said the elections meant "we're going to have the legitimacy that the government of the United States has been trying to deny us."

Nicaraguans voted amidst claims from the Sandinistas that the United States was preparing to invade, and within a few days of the elections the Reagan administration began to issue ominous warnings against Nicaragua's military buildup, saying it was a menace to the region. For nearly four years the Reagan administration had demonstrated the capacity to tighten the screws and make the Sandinistas scream whenever it was deemed useful. Pressure tactics that had begun in early 1981 with the cutoff of concessionary wheat sales had progressed to battleships off the Gulf of Fonseca and the Atlantic Coast, troop maneuvers in Honduras, the mining of harbors, and overflights by spy planes emitting sonic booms. After the Nicaraguan voting, the United States alleged that Soviet ships arriving in the port of Corinto might be carrying MiGs, the Soviet jet fighters that the United States, for at least two years, had been privately telling the Sandinistas would constitute the straw it would not tolerate. Although those particular crates did not turn out to contain MiG pieces, the Sandinistas made no secret of their desire for high-performance fighter aircraft. Sandinista pilots had been training in Bulgaria to fly MiGs since late 1979 or early 1980.

The Sandinistas hoped to deflect this kind of pressure with the elections. As far as domestic policy was concerned, the *comandantes* had often said that the elections would serve only to "confirm revolutionary power" and that they simply could not imagine a situation in which they would be faced with handing over power. Even in calling the elections, Daniel Ortega had proclaimed the Sandinista revolution to be "already an irreversible process." This and stronger statements by Humberto Ortega convinced most people in Nicaragua the Sandinistas would not give up power even if they lost. Bayardo Arce, the *comandante* most concerned with matters of ideology and creation of the Leninist structure in Nicaragua, said a few months before the elections that they were a bother and did nothing to further the Sandinista cause.

"What a revolution needs is the power to enforce," Arce said. "This power to enforce is precisely what constitutes the defense of the dictatorship of the proletariat—the ability of the class to impose its will using the instruments at hand, without going into formal or bourgeois details. From that point of view, the elections are bothersome to us, as bothersome as are a series of other things."

Among those bothersome other things, he said, was the continued existence of private enterprise. He added: "It is convenient to be able to call elections now and remove one of the U.S. policy justifications for aggression against Nicaragua, because the others are impossible for us to concede. Imperialism asks three things of us: to abandon our internationalism [aid to the Salvadoran guerrillas], abandon our strategic links with the Soviet Union and the Socialist community, and democracy. We cannot stop being internationalists unless we also stop being revolutionaries. We cannot abandon our strategic links unless we also stop being revolutionaries. This is not subject to any consideration. But the superstructure, the democracy, as they call it, the bourgeois democracy, is indeed an element where we can make some positive headway in the construction of Socialism in Nicaragua."

But he also said it was time to begin to think about "eliminating all this, let's call it façade of pluralism . . ." Its usefulness, he said, had reached an end.

In theory, Arce's words reflected the hard-line, and minority, view within the FSLN National Directorate, a view shared primarily by Tomás Borge. But more than five years of Sandinista rule had demonstrated that the adherents of this view held at the very least a veto on public policy in Nicaragua and more probably reflected what most of the *comandantes* wanted for their country, though others might express it in milder language.

The traditional political parties were free to participate in the elections, and nearly half of the eligible voters denied their support to the FSLN—by either voting for one of the six other parties on the ballot, abstaining, or defacing ballots—but many things that had come to pass in the years since 1979 served to cripple the opposition.

For one thing, the FSLN controlled the election machinery, a situation not substantially different from that existing in late 1978 when the opposition to Somoza feared going into a plebiscite in which he controlled the election machinery. The electoral law in force in 1984 had been written in the Council of State, which had been packed by the FSLN over Alfonso Robelo's opposition in 1980. The understanding in 1979 had been that the first round of elections to be held in post-Somoza Nicaragua would be for a constituent assembly and municipal authorities. This would have meant two things important to the opposition in any nation on the road to democratization: (1) the rules for the next round of elections, for president, would have been drawn up by the popularly elected assembly, and (2) opposition groups would, theoretically, have had some representation among local authorities involved in the conduct of the presidential elections. Instead, when Nicaragua's electoral law was being drafted in early 1984, by the nonelective Council of State, the ample Sandinista majority was able to override the efforts of opposition delegates to have the first round of voting limited to election of a constituent assembly as originally envisioned.

In the weeks leading up to election day, representatives of the Sandinista Youth and the CDS's (Sandinista Defense Committees) went house-to-house giving lessons in how to mark and cast ballots. *Comandantes* said in speeches that those who refused to vote would be branded counterrevolutionaries. Though press censorship was eased substantially during the campaign, *La Prensa* had to continue submitting all its stories for prior review. One of the things that was still censored out of the paper was coverage of *turba* attacks on opposition rallies. The nation remained under the state of emergency decreed on March 15, 1982, the day after *Contra* forces blew up two bridges near the Honduran border. Also, the voting age was lowered from eighteen to sixteen, which brought onto the rolls a substantial number of youths who had been under the influence of the heavily politicized educational changes of the previous five years.

Perhaps more important, access to several basic food items depended upon being in good standing with one's CDS leaders. Daniel Ortega once said there would be no *nacatamale* elections under the Sandinistas—a reference to Somoza's custom of paying for votes with helpings of a popular corn-and-pork dish and the local equivalent of corn liquor. The Sandinistas did it differently. Instead of stooping to bribe or reward with something special, they exercised control over the food that went on every table in Nicaragua for every meal.

The opposition was further handicapped by the fact that some of the best known political leaders—including Adolfo Calero and Alfonso Robelo—were in exile, allied with armed guerrilla groups. Jorge Salazar was dead, his death in late 1980 having deprived the opposition of perhaps its most appealing leadership figure, just as the murder of Pedro Joaquín Chamorro in 1978 had denied the same groups their most unifying figure against Somoza.

However, Arturo Cruz, the former junta member, ambassador, and member of *Los Doce,* came home from Washington to head an opposition coalition (the Democratic Coordinating Alliance) made up of four non-Marxist parties, two labor federations, and all the business and professional organizations that belonged to COSEP. He also had some degree of support from the various armed anti-Sandinista groups that made up the *Contra.*

Like the Sandinistas themselves, Cruz's efforts addressed international perceptions more than domestic issues. He alluded to the importance assigned to the foreign perception of the events in Nicaragua by saying as he set out on the electoral venture: "When the Sandinistas win, there's going to be applause at Yale and Harvard, but it will be a Pyrrhic victory because it will not resolve any of the country's conflicts." His message, though directed to the outside world, was that political pluralism inside Nicaragua was the only way to resolve those conflicts, that trying to negotiate away the Sandinistas' weaponry and their ties to Marxist guerrilla groups elsewhere would not address the crisis at its core. A graduate of the Georgetown School of Foreign Service, he used diplomatic finesse to frame his arguments in ways that appealed to his listeners or readers. He would say it one way for Nicaraguan exiles in Miami, another for liberal Democrats in the northeast, and yet another for the Reagan administration and European or Latin American leaders. Since leaving the government in November 1981, he had been playing this balancing act, first as the ghost writer for Edén Pastora in speeches and the editorial pages of major newspapers, then as behind-the-scenes negotiator with various governments, as go-between with the guerrilla groups, and, finally, as public candidate.

Cruz and his vice-presidential candidate, Adán Fletes of the Social Christian Party, began to campaign in Nicaragua in August 1984, but they delayed the formal declaration of their participation in the elections and tried to negotiate better electoral conditions with the FSLN. Still, they drew enthusiastic crowds, and the worried FSLN sent *turbas* to attack all of their rallies. Backed by the social democratic parties of many countries that formed the Socialist International, by former Venezuelan President Carlos Andrés Pérez, and by the State Department, Cruz demanded that the FSLN agree to establishment in Nicaragua of a process of political democratization similar to that of other Western democracies, that it open up the media to allow opposition candidates more time and space, guarantee not to harass opposition rallies, make no political use of state transport by the FSLN on election day, lift the state of emergency, and, finally, postpone the voting until early 1985 to allow the opposition time to take advantage of the improved campaign conditions. After various stops and starts, the two sides were brought together in Rio de Janeiro at the beginning of October 1984 during a meeting of the Socialist International. With Carlos Andrés Pérez sitting in on the sessions, agreement was reached on a number of points—including postponement of the elections until early January 1985 and allowing Cruz to try to arrange an election cease-fire by all elements of the *Contra*—before the negotiations fell apart, with each side blaming the other. With that, Cruz and all the candidates of the Democratic Coordinating Alliance withdrew from the race.

Two opposition groups not affiliated with the Democratic Coordinating Alliance also had misgivings about participating in the elections but voiced them after it was too late to formally withdraw. They were one faction of the Democratic Conservative Party, which had split again after Adolfo Calero left to join the *Contra* leadership, and the Independent Liberals, a splinter from the old Somoza party. The Democratic Conservative faction that participated in the elections received the second largest number of votes, though well behind the FSLN, with 13 percent, and the Independent Liberals followed with 9 percent.

Ortega and other Sandinista candidates ran on a platform that legitimized the program the FSLN had been putting in place over the previous five years. It backed away from many of the commitments to political and economic pluralism made in the Plan of Government adopted by the junta in San José, Costa Rica, in June 1979 during the final days of the insurrection. It offered, for example, no commitment to press freedom or free speech. It spoke of continuing religious freedom but encouraged church groups and individual Christians to align themselves with the FSLN. There was no mention of the shape of the political system that the FSLN envisioned for the future, though that was officially to be decided by the new constituent assembly. It said "U.S. imperialism has been the greatest violator of the Nicaraguan people's human rights and public liberties." It said the FSLN was committed to support the activities of artisans and small business people, but they were encouraged to organize into cooperatives and affiliate with the FSLN. One of the overall themes of the platform, in fact, was to encourage all Nicaraguans to join or organize groups under the umbrella of the FSLN, all in furtherance of "people's power."

. . .

The nation of which Daniel Ortega became president could no longer feed itself. There were chronic shortages of nearly everything, even the most basic food items normally produced in abundance inside Nicaragua. One of the generally accepted explanations for basic food shortages was that the FSLN was stockpiling to feed the military in case of a larger war. This view was substantiated when large quantities of a few, but not all, basic items suddenly appeared on supermarket shelves just before the elections at decontrolled prices. It had become increasingly common for people to stand in lines all night to buy a number of items, including tires. The FSLN regularly pointed out, correctly, that it had eradicated several diseases in Nicaragua with vaccination campaigns, but medicines for most illness were no longer to be found in the country. Exports were not paying for half of the bare-bones imports. The government had stopped paying the interest on most of its $3.8 billion foreign debt, an amount that on a per capita basis put Nicaragua in the company of the most indebted nations in the world. Small industries and even artisans were halting work because of the absence of such things as black dye, cotton yarn, and nuts and bolts. Venezuela and Mexico, which once supplied oil to Nicaragua at reduced prices and on credit, had cut off supplies and demanded full payment of old debts, leaving Nicaragua dependent on the Soviet Union for fuel. In addition, the country's only oil port had suffered various attacks by *contra* saboteurs. The FSLN blamed the shortages and most of the other problems in the country on U.S. pressures, and many Nicaraguans accepted that logic. The Sandinista press dismissed the absence of toothpaste and toilet paper by saying that they were just bourgeois luxuries anyway. But there was also prevalent another form of Nicaraguan logic, which held that the Sandinistas were deliberately provoking the United States so as not to have to deal with such mundane matters as beans, rice, and toilet paper.

While the economy was shattered, the military was flourishing. There were 60,000 men in the regular army and ready reserves, six times the maximum size of the former National Guard, and another 60,000 in the active militia, plus tens of thousands of other people who had been given some degree of military training. Equipment poured into the country from Soviet-bloc and Arab sources. By late 1984 the Sandinista Army had an estimated 150 Soviet T54 and T55 tanks, 200 other armored vehicles, multiple rocket launchers, long-range artillery, early-warning radar, antiaircraft rockets, high-speed helicopter gunships, and several airfields capable of handling military jets.*

By Pentagon estimate, there were 10,000 Cubans in Nicaragua—substantially more, as the opposition liked to point out, than there ever were Marines during the 1920s and 1930s. The Cuban and Nicaraguan governments, while not confirming the 10,000 figure, said more than half of the Cubans in Nicaragua were engaged in nonmilitary work, such as health and education. In addition, there were several hundred other advisers of various kinds from the Soviet Union, Libya, and Eastern Europe.

While most of the weaponry could correctly be described as defensive in terms of national security, it also had an offensive effect internally because it was intimidating and overwhelming to those who would oppose peacefully. The size of the military also served that end. While one group of active militiamen might be sent into the mountains to protect coffee harvesters from the *contras,* others were available in the capital and other sizeable towns to form the *turbas* that attacked opposition rallies and the homes and workplaces of people, rich and poor, who did not openly support the FSLN. The number of people in uniform and the level of the weaponry demonstrated the invincibility of the regime to any who might waiver in its support.

For the Sandinistas, everything else was secondary to defending the regime. The FSLN was determined to match the Reagan administration tactically, to go to the wire, to test Washington at every turn. It refused to acknowledge that any of its problems originated in Nicaragua. Were it not for Ronald Reagan, the Sandinistas contended, there would be no *Contra.* They worked relentlessly to influence U.S. public opinion, hiring a public relations man in New York who directed a propaganda blitz in an attempt to ignite the U.S. public into coming to the support of the FSLN, primarily by pressuring Congress and the White House against continued assistance to the *Contra.* In the midst of the election campaign, Daniel Ortega took time away from running for president to tour the United States, attending dinners and parties arranged by sympathizers. Various attractive Sandinista women who held middle-level government or party posts were suddenly available for numerous interviews, in Los Angeles, Atlanta, and New York.

---

*This summary of Sandinista weaponry comes from an article written by Nestor D. Sanchez, deputy assistant secretary of defense, for the *Miami Herald,* published on December 9, 1984. Examples of the weaponry could be seen by almost anyone who visited Nicaragua in 1983 or 1984; only the numbers could not be independently confirmed.

Despite congressional restrictions on their CIA funding, and internal power struggles, the 15,000 anti-Sandinista guerrillas operating from Honduras and Costa Rica continued to make an impact inside Nicaragua. In the midst of the election campaign, visitors to rural towns in the center of the country stumbled across fire fights between the army and guerrillas. Substantial portions of the country were safer for the *contras* than for the army, though the rebels controlled no major towns. The always tenuous alliances of complicated personalities involved in the armed rebel groups fractured further in 1984, but new alignments came into being and some disputes were overcome. However, some of the Miskito leaders, fearing the cultural death of their dispersed people, considered abandoning the fight and going home in exchange for Sandinista recognition of Indian sovereignty over the Atlantic Coast region. After Congress cut off CIA financial assistance to the *Contra* in May 1984, Adolfo Calero and other leaders scrambled to find help from what they said were interested individuals and government-related groups outside the United States. Edén Pastora, whose fighters in the southern border area had lost CIA help earlier, because of his refusal to align himself with those operating out of Honduras, pleaded for help from the Nicaraguan and Cuban exile communities in Miami, and swore never to give up the fight. But while the insurgents' military presence on the ground was significant, they stood little chance of maintaining their momentum if the Sandinista army developed its desired air combat capability. It was clear that the FSLN's first priority in seeking air power was not to invade nearby countries but to defeat the *contras*.

As for the feelings of the people, both the Sandinistas and the *contras* obviously had considerable popular support. Neither group was capable of wiping the other out as long as both continued to be supplied. Whether the mass of people, such as workers and peasants, would fight loyally for the FSLN in the event of an invasion or other large-scale operation or whether they would someday rise massively in favor of the insurgents was impossible to predict. My theory was that the majority would go with the wind; whenever they detected that one side or the other was on the ascent they would go in that direction, just as they had in 1979 when they saw the underpinnings come out from under Somoza. When the shooting was over, they wanted to be able to proclaim loudly that they had supported the winner. While many of them had ideas and principles, their first priority was survival. If they could have all of those things, they would be delighted; otherwise, they would take survival. A taxi driver I knew for several years once explained that principle to me with a great tone of frustration at Yankee naïveté. Discussing the political squabbles that took place in the modest area of Managua where he lived, he said I had to understand that the same people in his neighborhood who had previously been the most vocal and loyal *somocistas* were now the most vocal and loyal Sandinistas.

22

THE STRANGEST OF WARS

DECEMBER 1985

No one described Enrique Bermúdez as a hero. No one said he was charismatic. This small man in his early fifties, with black hair, wearing blue jeans and a plaid shirt, had launched no daring assaults on Somoza, had made no principled departure from Sandinista-ruled Nicaragua. Now, pacing the floor in a rambling safe house on the outskirts of Tegucigalpa, he was a survivor, an example of low-keyed tenaciousness, a man who thought it was no crime to have been what he had been: an officer in the Nicaraguan National Guard in the days of the Somozas. Inside, he felt like Christopher Columbus, a man little regarded in his own time who would someday be vindicated. "They said Columbus was crazy. But for undertakings of that type, you need some fools, some crazy, irresponsible people."

People had thought Enrique Bermúdez was a little crazy when he set out to build the exile organization that had become the Nicaraguan Democratic Force, which was, like him, a survivor. It now claimed to have 18,000 men and women under arms, 10,000 of them fighting inside Nicaragua to bring down the Sandinista Front. Even the detractors of the Democratic Force thought his figures were reasonably accurate—if inflated, not greatly so. His people had just shot down a Sandinista Army helicopter deep inside Nicaragua using one of the Soviet-built surface-to-air missiles that their mysterious foreign backers had made it possible to buy. He had reason to feel optimistic.

After all the ringing threats and promises by all the determined, but feuding exile groups, this one had come to dominate the war against the Sandinista Front. It had passed through many forms, from the Fifteenth of September Legion, to union with José Francisco Cardenal and other civilians of the Nicaraguan Democratic Union, then evolving into the Nicaraguan Democratic Force, or FDN, which eventually formed a broad civilian directorate. Finally, Adolfo Calero, the former Conservative Party leader, had left Nicaragua to take the most visible role in the FDN as commander in chief, theoretically in authority over both political and military aspects. Calero and Bermúdez and everyone else in the FDN said it was a collegial arrangement. There had been many failed attempts to form working alliances with the Miskitos and Edén Pastora and the splinter groups that periodically surfaced in Costa Rica. The Argentine colonels had come and gone. The CIA had come and gone. There had been ups and downs in the rebels' relations with their reluctant hosts, the Honduran military and government. The money had frequently dried up, then had begun to come in again.

The FDN's existence was still precarious. For the last two dry seasons—during the Northern Hemisphere winter—it had managed to mount significant offensives. The 1985 offensive had come late, as the rainy season approached, but had posed a tough challenge to the Sandinistas. They had saved the situation by putting their new MI-24 helicopter gunships into action, forcing the rebels to retreat from ambitious goals of moving into the population centers on the Pacific side of Nicaragua. Now, a new dry season was beginning, and the Sandinista Army was threatening a major offensive that it claimed would wipe out the rebels. Bermúdez was trying to counter with a strategy for cutting the highway between Managua and Rama, the unloading point on the Escondido River for ships that picked up Sandinista military supplies in Cuba.

Unlike so many others performing in the Nicaraguan drama, Bermúdez did not like public relations or politics. He claimed to go months without reading newspapers. He felt maligned, misunderstood. So much had been said and alleged about him and his organization. He had accumulated documents, notes, and letters in a security box in Miami. Someday, if he had to defend himself for something or other, he would dig them out. He was not trying to create a political party here, but to run a military organization. Nor was he the type to lead lightning raids inside Nicaragua, to make exhausting treks through the mountains, to grow a beard and play the part of dashing guerrilla leader. He left that to his task force commanders and gave them full credit when they had a success. He didn't like to speak in the first person.

At the end of the Somoza regime, Bermúdez had been a colonel in the National Guard. While the rest of the National Guard was trying to put down the insurrection, he was serving as military attache at the Nicaraguan embassy in Washington, a suburbanite commuting from Bethesda, Maryland. When Larry Pezzullo, in June and July 1979, was trying to find a new commander for the Nicaraguan National Guard, somebody at the State Department or the Pentagon who thought well of Colonel Bermúdez had put his name on the list, another of the names that would be passed over by Somoza. When everything collapsed, Bermúdez had found a job driving a truck for a magazine distributor in Maryland. It paid $5.25 an hour. Then, the telephone calls began to come in.

"There were friends of mine who lived in Nicaragua, and they contacted me and told me that there were many people in Nicaragua among whom I had a certain degree of credibility and prestige and that I ought to be one of the organizers of a movement to throw out the Communists. They said that the arrival of communism in Nicaragua was nothing more than a matter of the passage of time."

He began to travel to Miami in January and February 1980 for meetings with people who came out of Nicaragua on visits. Even now, more than six years later, he did not want to reveal most of their names. Some, at that time, were in, or had only recently left, the new government. Later that year, he met with Jorge Salazar, the farm leader who would soon die in a trap laid by Sandinista state security agents. The telephone calls to his home in Bethesda and the trips to Miami were becoming so numerous that he and his wife decided to move to Miami. In a U-Haul truck, pulling a trailer, they drove straight through in twenty-four hours.

"With Aristides Sánchez, I went around looking for people. We were looking primarily for people who had been opposed to Somoza. In my case I could not come out openly because I had been a functionary of the government. Credibility required the participation of all those who had been in opposition to Somoza and were now opposing the Sandinistas. But at that time it was viewed as madness, folly. There had been a triumphant revolution, supposedly of the people, with worldwide sympathy. Anyone who went around trying to do something against them was viewed as a bum, an idiot, very irresponsible, like an opportunist who was trying to live by asking for money for a lost cause."

By the end of 1980, Bermúdez had moved on to Guatemala, where another former National Guard colonel, Ricardo Lau, was already trying to organize something. A small group of former officers soon began to gather around Bermúdez. They had no troops, no resources, few prospects. "At times we did not have anything to eat," Bermúdez recalled. "There were people who cooperated, with $50 here and there. Or someone would give us a plane ticket. For example, in Guatemala, there was a shrimp company that gave us the fish that was brought in with the shrimp."

Over on the Honduran-Nicaraguan border, another small group of former National Guardsmen, primarily noncommissioned officers and enlisted men, was already mounting small military actions aimed at the Sandinistas, but that group was not yet connected to the former officers who were gathering in Guatemala. At the time, the Sandinistas usually dismissed the border activities as banditry. The group in Guatemala took the name Fifteenth of September Legion and initially concentrated their efforts on forming alliances with others in the already simmering alphabet soup of exile groups and on finding money and political sympathy.

"There was always a desire to unify the distinct groups that were trying to do something against the Sandinistas. But each chief of a group thought that he had the winning number, so he didn't want unification. The most out of favor was the group of former military men because we were viewed as 'assassins, the genocidal National Guard, and so forth.' "

Meanwhile, the Argentine military government, concerned about the presence in Nicaragua of members of the Montoneros and other South American guerrilla groups, had sent intelligence operatives to Central America. Sharing many of the same concerns, the Argentines and the Fifteenth of September Legion eventually made contact and began to collaborate. Even before the Legion formed its alliance with

Cardenal and other civilians, the Argentines had provided some training and money for the former National Guardsmen. Later, after the union that created the FDN, the Argentines sent advisers and trainers to Honduras, where the FDN set up its headquarters. One of the first things the FDN leadership did with its new-found affluence was to buy uniforms for the troops—dark blue, cotton twill mechanics' work clothes from Sears.

In the aftermath of Argentina's defeat by Britain in the war over the Malvinas-Falklands Islands in the first half of 1982, the Argentines withdrew from Honduras, but by then CIA advisers were on the scene, a development made possible by decisions taken during 1981 in Washington. The emergence in late 1982 of a new FDN leadership had been partly the result of the CIA's desire for broad-based unity and partly the result of differences between Cardenal and Bermúdez and between Cardenal and influential Nicaraguans in Miami. Adolfo Calero, who would assume the overall leadership a few months later, had begun to talk secretly with Bermúdez on trips away while he was still living in Nicaragua. He was a man who did not look down on former Guardsmen, who thought they were Nicaraguans like everyone else. At the same time, he had a respectable political image. He had favorably impressed officials of the Carter Administration in 1978 and early 1979 during the efforts to mediate the crisis over Somoza.

Another issue facing the FDN was Ricardo Lau. There were allegations linking him to political killings in the region, particularly in El Salvador. His reputation had been a bone of contention in the failed talks among Cardenal, Pastora and Alfonso Robelo in Costa Rica. Finally, Bermúdez had broken the news to Lau that he had to go. "Lau left the movement because he was becoming the object of attacks and calumnies. It was decided that his reputation damaged the movement—this was at the beginning of 1983. I spoke with him before Adolfo Calero arrived. I told him he had to make a patriotic sacrifice —even though the attacks came from the Sandinistas and the groups in Costa Rica. The situation was very delicate then. It seemed that the presence of Lau had damaged the movement a great deal."

From the time that the CIA's role had gradually become public, during 1982, there had been an obvious contradiction between the reason the Nicaraguans thought they were fighting and the reason the United States government said they were fighting. In the meeting rooms of Congress and in the growing number of public acknowledgments of the American role in the war, the Reagan Administration said that the rebels had been armed and trained so as to interdict arms being sent from Nicaragua to the guerrillas of the Farabundo Martí National Liberation Front in El Salvador. But critics began to ask how many arms shipments the rebels had captured and to charge that their operations seemed directed primarily at overthrowing the Sandinistas. Bermúdez told me that the CIA had never directly stated to him its reason for supporting the operation. Before the end of 1982, United States support for the rebels ran into difficulties when some members of the House of Representatives became upset about news stories indicating that the Nicaraguan rebels' priority was to overthrow the Sandinistas. In December 1982, what became known as the Boland Amendment was adopted by Congress. It prohibited the CIA and the Pentagon from furnishing "military equipment, military training or advice, or other support for military activities, to any group or individual, not part of a country's armed forces, for the purpose of overthrowing the Government of Nicaragua or provoking a military exchange between Nicaragua and Honduras."

During the summer of 1983 there was active discussion of this issue within the Administration. There were many who had not favored the arms interdiction argument in the first place. They lobbied to change the policy from one of interdiction to one linking military, diplomatic and political strategies. The idea was advanced of creating what was called the "Core Four," meaning that the United States would seek to isolate the Sandinistas by establishing common Central American goals with Costa Rica, El Salvador, Honduras and Guatemala. Support for political democracy and economic recovery in those four countries was part of the strategy.

On September 20, 1983, President Reagan signed a new "finding," after consultation with the intelligence committees, which said that the CIA was going beyond its program of arms interdiction until the Sandinistas stopped their subversion in neighboring countries. The full Congress, in approving aid to the rebels for the 1984 fiscal year, declared that Nicaragua was violating the Charter of the Organization of American States by providing military assistance to the Salvadoran guerrillas and other groups trying to overthrow Central American governments.

As the covert operation came into the public domain, it acquired a comic opera dimension, with occasional glimpses of the tragedy behind it all. Adolfo Calero remarked to me in early 1983 that Edén Pastora, despite all his declarations about wanting nothing to do with the CIA, was getting his money and supplies "from the same place we get ours—Santa Claus." In Honduras, at first, Ambassador John Negroponte would deny knowing anything about anything called the *Contra,* claiming that the only Nicaraguan he knew there was the ambassador from the Sandinista government. The statement, according to members of his staff, was literally true throughout 1982.

But a different attitude evolved during 1983, when it came to seem artificial to deny knowledge in Honduras of what was being publicly debated in Washington. In addition, visitors from Capitol Hill and sympathetic columnists began to show up in Tegucigalpa and demand help in meeting the rebels. By the latter part of 1983, when there was a large number of congressional delegations visiting Honduras, the embassy was organizing weekend tours to give them a quick, intensive view of the *Contras,* including an FDN hospital, where they listened to wrenching stories from the wounded about why they were fighting. Some congressmen and staffers who had been very hostile to the rebels were touched by the conviction they heard from hospital beds. Squeezed into the tour schedule might also be "Cocktails with the *Contras,* " a social meeting with rebel leaders. Touring congressmen and their staff members sometimes requested, as well, a visit to the bar in the Tequendama Hotel, a place of *Contra* lore.

But the mining of Nicaragua's harbors in 1984 and the claim of the intelligence oversight committees of Congress that they had not been adequately notified in advance by the CIA precipitated a new crisis over aid to the rebels. In early October 1984, Congress voted to terminate all aid to the rebels but promised to reconsider it after February 28, 1985, with the condition that it could be resumed only upon enactment of a Joint Resolution of Congress. But after that came news that the CIA had produced a psychological warfare manual for the rebels that could be interpreted as condoning assassination, which seemed to make the possibility of a positive vote after February 28 less likely. The last of the appropriated money had already been spent some six months before the vote to terminate aid.

Critics of the Nicaraguan rebels and defenders of the Sandinistas had long predicted that without CIA support, the FDN would dry up, that it would lose its manpower and would not find the money for munitions and equipment. The opposite happened. Despite its beginnings as a group of National Guardsmen, it had, during the years of feuding over unity with other exile groups and the attacks on its image, begun to draw the nameless masses. For a multitude of reasons, they had left their lands in the northern mountains, especially during the year after Congress terminated CIA funding. This influx doubled the number of available FDN combatants from about 9,000 at the time of the CIA cutoff to the 18,000 that Bermúdez claimed by the end of 1985.

These Nicaraguans seemed to have been spurred on in their offer to take up arms by two basic motives. First, they had some reason to dislike, distrust or oppose the Sandinistas. That often had something to do with land and how they were allowed, or forced, to work it. These were mountain people who had been accustomed to being left relatively alone by the Somozas. Some came from communities that had been centers of recruitment for the old National Guard and so had antagonistic feelings toward the Sandinistas from the beginning of the new regime. Most called themselves peasants, although many, perhaps most, were not landless, as that word usually implied. They were generally farming independently in some way. Some owned, or came from families that had claims to, vast tracts in the isolated stillness of upper Jinotega, Matagalpa and Nueva Segovia. Much of their land was in wooded areas lacking roads and other infrastructure. Others had small coffee farms of maybe a dozen acres. Theirs was a frontier existence. They viewed themselves as a class very different from the affluent men who controlled the labor-intensive sugar and cotton farms on the rich Pacific coastal plain. For those who had not lost land or who were not trying to protect land they still held, there was the hope of getting some if the rebellion succeeded.

Many of the combatants had stories similar to that of Hubert Rodríguez, an FDN soldier who talked to me when he went to Dallas in September 1985 to receive an award from American backers of the FDN. His father owned a farm at San Juan de Rio Coco in Madriz, the small department just below Nueva Segovia. He had about 200 acres of arable land. The three elder sons in the family had helped the Sandinistas in the insurrection, Hubert said, "although some of them just went into the street and shouted." But during the early days of the Sandinista regime their father was taken prisoner, even though, Hubert said, the three elder boys were all in the Sandinista Army at the time. Freed six months later, the father returned to the farm to find it vandalized. Later, Hubert said, the Sandinistas took away the father's land and tortured him. During that same period, the forerunners of the FDN had begun to come by the farm, and eventually all four boys took to the mountains to join them. Hubert had been sixteen years old then. He was now twenty-one. He had lost a leg when gangrene set in during a long march after he had suffered an injury.

Bermúdez urged me not to think in "intellectual terms" about why people had joined the FDN. "Those people do not know how to tell you what communism is. What they say is that people from the Sandinista Front come and tell them to do things they don't want to do. 'They mistreat us,' they say, 'and want us to do what they say, want us to work in a certain way.' For them, that is communism, the form in which communism manifests itself. But many journalists come and say, 'Do you know what communism is?' 'Yes,' the people say. 'Then, what is communism?' asks the journalist. What is a peasant going to say to that? Even I wouldn't know how to say what communism is. But their motivation is this: There are those who are religious, and their community has been prohibited from practicing religion. They have seen their ministers assassinated, principally evangelicals and mainly those who are Mormons. There are people who are Catholic and have seen how the Sandinistas repress the believers, how they mistreat priests, burn churches, and so forth. For others, it is because their relatives have been assassinated, or they have been taken prisoner. So, they have motivations against a repressive regime. Others had their property confiscated. Others don't want to go into the [Sandinista] militia. Others don't want to join cooperatives or the state farms or go to the settlements where the Sandinistas take them."

The second reason the Nicaraguans in the north rallied to the FDN was that after several years of tenuous existence the FDN had come to be, in their eyes, the only alternative to the Sandinistas with any possibility of success. Bermúdez explained how he thought this evolution in thinking had occurred. "When this movement started we didn't have resources. We didn't have money to pay for food. Our forces were badly dressed. We had no military weapons. When we started to receive some funds, we decided to buy first-class clothes, jungle boots and backpacks. The effect on the population was very positive, so people started to join us. At the beginning they had seen us as a force that had no chance to defeat the Sandinistas. Later, when they saw us very well dressed and with weapons, people started to join because they saw us as potential winners. . . . The success of recruitment is directly related to military actions. When the action is more intense, people get more enthusiastic. If we go through a period of inactivity, then the people cool off a bit. When the rhythm of our action is more intense in the military zones, more people join."

Finding the means to continue to wage the war and maintain the growing combat force after the CIA cutoff challenged the abilities of the *Contra* leadership and its sympathizers in the United States and elsewhere. There had always been an element of support from wealthy or committed foreigners—before, during and after the CIA involvement. Guatemalan and Honduran businessmen and landowners helped, just as farmers and others in Costa Rica had helped the forces of Pastora. Humanitarian and charity groups in the United States with an anticommunist bent had provided medical care and other things. But the CIA, during its nearly three years of support, had made all the decisions about the bulk of supplies—had bought them, distributed them, and otherwise served as war tactician, administrator and purchasing agent. All of that had to be replaced.

Adolfo Calero became the most visible fundraiser. He traveled the United States, Latin America and Europe speaking and meeting with backers and potential backers. He sought to maintain the private support that had long existed while reaching out to create a vast, new network. He worked the right-wing cocktail circuit and anticommunist groups. Sometimes, Calero—who had once commented to me while he was still living in Nicaragua that his Conservative Party was more liberal than most Democrats in the United States—would try to explain that, while the Sandinista Front was Marxist-Leninist, Nicaragua's problems could not be solved merely with anticommunism. The solutions, he would say, had to be internal Nicaraguan solutions. Hardly anyone wanted to listen to that. Generally, smiling politely, drink in hand, he listened to almost anyone who came along with a fundraising scheme or promise. His efforts were facilitated by several key men who put out the word to others who might help him. Among them were two of the super-rich Hunt brothers of Texas, Herbert and Nelson Bunker. The Hunts would not specify how much help they had provided, but they turned out for fundraisers, and one of their organizations arranged speaking appearances for Calero. With an eye on the Neutrality Act, the money that Calero raised was deposited in bank accounts abroad. Much of it, he said, came through European or Latin American corporate connections, or from individuals living in those areas.

Perhaps the most important connection that Calero made was with retired Major General John K. Singlaub, who had won a following among ardent anticommunists when he engaged in a public feud with President Carter in 1977 over the level of American troops in Korea. A hero of World War II, he had been in every American war since then and had vowed to devote his retirement to preventing the advance of communism. From his post at the head of the United States

Council for World Freedom, he garnered support for anticommunist guerrilla groups around the world. But it was the Nicaraguan rebels who received most of his attention. He grew close to Calero and Bermúdez while reaching out to those in the United States and elsewhere who shared his ideals. Recalling the alliances between the rich and the brave forged in the time of the American War of Independence, he sought to bring together people willing to risk part of their fortunes with those willing to risk their lives. Whatever they lost, he would say, their honors would be secure. Singlaub's organization raised money and collected contributions in kind, but, also conscious of the Neutrality Act, he declared that everything contributed in the United States was to be used for nonlethal things, which could range from medicine to boots to helicopters for transporting the wounded.

Subtle word also went out from the White House encouraging supporters of Ronald Reagan to provide help in time or money. Working from a small office on the third floor of the Old Executive Office Building adjacent to the White House, an outgoing Marine Corps lieutenant colonel named Oliver L. North spoke to everything from conservative women's groups to gatherings of establishment lawyers and wealthy individuals. As a member of the National Security Council staff, he would show videotapes of the FDN at war and still photographs of the combatants that he took during his frequent visits to the FDN camps. Tears often welled in his eyes as he spoke of the determination of the fighters and their suffering for lack of boots, medical transport and other things. If someone offered money when Colonel North was appearing before some group in the United States, he would say that he couldn't take it but that there were places abroad where they could send it.

With the money raised, Singlaub advised Calero and Bermúdez on weapons and munitions purchases, guiding them through the intricacies of the international arms market, which was dominated by weapons of Soviet Bloc origin. Among other things, they bought AK-47 automatic rifles and Soviet-designed surface-to-air missiles to use against the Sandinistas' fleet of Soviet-built attack helicopters. The exact amount they raised during 1984 and 1985 was uncertain, in part, they said, because some of it came "in kind." Singlaub estimated the total of money and goods at as high as $25 million, while Calero said that it might have been no more than $15 million.

In addition to money and goods, all of this activity generated grassroots enthusiasm in the United States and, to a lesser extent, elsewhere. These rebel supporters countered the network that had developed earlier of activists who worked in some way for the good of the Sandinista Front. They were people who had fought and lost in other causes against communism, who were bitter about the American withdrawal from Vietnam. Many of them made pilgrimages to the rebel camps to deliver contributions, perform services or bring back images to share with others.

One such supporter was Larry Duyck, a former medical student who sold his BMW and his house in Dallas to devote his time and money to setting up field hospitals for the FDN and helping Miskito refugees. Duyck, who said that his fencing company was failing for lack of attention, traced his interest in Central America to a visit he made to two orphanages in the western part of El Salvador in January 1980. "I came back after 30 days," he said, "but I couldn't get the place off my mind." Later, he traveled to Honduras, talked to relief workers and visited the camps for both Salvadoran and Nicaraguan refugees. He decided to help the Nicaraguans, who he concluded were not receiving fair treatment from the United Nations High Commission for Refugees. Now, he told me, he had two Miskitos staying at his home in Dallas while they underwent medical treatment. One, he said, had been hit in the neck by three bullets, and the other had lost half of one of his feet to a mine.

Another man who embraced the Nicaraguan rebel cause as his own was William J. Murray, an unordained evangelical minister in Dallas with a surprising background for a man who said he was "determined to share our revolution with nations that are oppressed." In 1963, at the age of fourteen, he was the plaintiff of record in the Supreme Court decision that banned prayer in public schools. The case was brought by his mother, Madalyn Murray O'Hair, who had reared him as an atheist and a Marxist. After dropping out of the University of Hawaii, Bill Murray found success in the business world and abandoned his mother's political and religious views. In 1980, he became a Christian and set up an independent ministry to get involved, as he told me, in whatever happened to interest him, Nicaragua for one thing. He rented a small warehouse, marked off spaces with yellow paint, and assigned them to organizations that wanted to collect supplies for the rebels. By the time I talked with him, in late 1985, he had twice flown to Honduras on an elderly DC-4 loaded with 20,000 pounds of medical supplies, boots, and hospital and communications equipment.

"I watched the stuff being sorted, watched it go into the jeeps, watched it go to the base camps, and then I followed it out by foot into Nicaragua and I saw the material going where I said it was going."

He stayed at a rebel military camp, attended a strategy session, and had his photograph taken examining an AK-47. Then he preached to the troops and passed out Bibles. On his return to Dallas, Murray wrote and distributed a newsletter about his trip, illustrating it with photos that he had taken. He also made himself available for a variety of duties at fundraising events, ranging from giving the opening prayer to moderating panels about guerrilla goals and strategies.

There was also Ellen Garwood, an Austin, Texas, woman in her eighties, wife of a retired justice of the Texas Supreme Court and mother of a federal judge. Dismissing Congress as a bunch of bubbleheads for its hesitation in supporting the rebels, she provided $65,000 to buy a used helicopter, wrote out another check for the price of thousands of pairs of boots, and exhorted her friends to give up a few trips to Europe and a few new outfits to do the same. Her contributions came from a cotton fortune made in other times by her father, William L. Clayton, who as undersecretary of state in the Truman Administration was credited with being the idea man behind the Marshall Plan. It was because of him that she helped the Nicaraguan rebels. "I could not let all the work that Dad did to keep the free world free from communism go under," she told me. "And we're about to go under unless we keep those freedom fighters going."

Some supporters, including General Singlaub, would claim that the aid cutoff had been the best thing that could have happened to the Nicaraguan rebels. It had forced them to find real friends and to build their own support, albeit with considerable sympathy and advice from the White House. And the fact that they had continued to attract combatants while support was so uncertain seemed to prove the appeal of the opposition movement. Long criticized as the creature of the CIA, the FDN had now established that the opposition to the Sandinistas had a dynamic, a reason, of its own. Those who had once claimed that the FDN would not exist were it not for CIA money and advice were now complaining that the *Contra* was driving American policy in the region rather than following it. Among the solidarity and church groups and others who defended the Sandinistas, many claimed that the money still came from the CIA, but they offered no credible evidence. Officials in various government agencies privately complained that the congressional ban had been so well worded as to legally exclude sophisticated circumvention tactics.

In mid-1985, Congress voted to resume aid to the Nicaraguan rebels but limited it to "humanitarian"—or nonlethal—uses. This meant it could be used to pay for food, medical care, clothing and transport.

Two developments had influenced Congress in reaching this decision. For one thing, it was impressed by the growth and apparent appeal of the armed opposition. It had concluded that the *Contra* had become a force that would not just go away, that had to be dealt with as a major phenomenon on the scene. However the *Contra* got there, it had become—by all assessments—the largest guerrilla force ever assembled in Central America. On the other hand, there was the behavior of the Sandinista Front. Daniel Ortega had offended many members of Congress by traveling to Moscow just days after Congress voted down lethal aid in April 1985. This anger helped to produce overwhelming support for some kind of assistance to the rebels when the Administration made the request for nonlethal aid two months later. Congress was also dismayed by the Sandinistas' increasingly repressive domestic policies, particularly toward the press and the Church. By the middle of 1985, the FSLN had lost virtually every defender it ever had in Congress. But Congress was still reluctant to say that the United States should seek the overthrow of the Sandinista Front. It approved the new aid only after President Reagan made a written commitment to negotiations, toward which many members of Congress hoped that the rebel force might provide leverage on the Sandinistas, and to working for an improved human rights performance by the rebels.

By then, this had become the strangest of wars, one in which the rank and file fought for the most fundamental of human desires—to think for oneself, to work as one wanted, to live where one wanted—but whose management seemed to be dominated by questions of public relations. Selling the *Contra* to public opinion in the United States and abroad became a primary consideration of the rebel leadership and the Reagan Administration.

Under American pressure on the image question, Adolfo Calero joined with Arturo Cruz and Alfonso Robelo to create the Unified Nicaraguan Opposition, or UNO. The new umbrella group's first function was to be the spending and disbursing of the $27 million in nonmilitary aid, but it also represented a new attempt to expand exile unity. Cruz had returned to his longtime home near Washington after dropping out of the 1984 presidential race in Nicaragua. A familiar figure in Washington, he enjoyed wide respect in Congress and among American intellectuals and editorial writers. Robelo, who continued to live in Costa Rica, signed on with UNO after numerous disputes with Pastora over money and alliances. A number of other Nicaraguan exile groups and prominent individuals also joined, including part of the divided Miskito movement, in return for a commitment to share in the $27 million. Pastora refused to join, complaining about FDN control but also demanding a more dominant role. This left his dwindling force in a near-destitute state. Throughout 1985 his operations appeared to decline, until he was left with only a few hundred combatants. Within and without UNO, the external opposition to the Sandinista Front remained an alphabet soup of groups, goals and personalities, among which the United States was always seeking greater unity. Nicaraguan strategists in the Reagan Administration cited Fidel Castro as their model in this regard; because he insisted on unity among guerrilla movements that Cuba assisted, the United States should do the same.

Although the three UNO leaders shared many goals, history and ambition made it difficult, as in previous attempts, to maintain a facade of union. They had old differences over many things, and each worried about how he might be positioning himself for future roles. Human rights brought forth one such dispute, after allegations of abuses became part of the international debate over the rebel cause. Various human rights groups accused the FDN of executing prisoners and killing and torturing civilians in the battle zone.

Assessing the extent of these human rights transgressions was complicated by the usual Central American problem of finding reliable figures on casualties in general. Nothing seemed to add up. As in the 1978-79 insurrection, the casualty figures appeared to be manipulated, by both sides. For example, when journalists and diplomats in Managua tried to total up the periodic casualty counts issued by the Sandinista government, the figure usually ran to about 15,000 in four or five years of combat. Yet, Nicaragua's American lawyers, when they went to the World Court in 1985 to accuse the United States of violating international law by supporting the rebels, said that the figure they could credibly argue for reparations purposes was about 3,000 deaths among Sandinista military forces and civilians in the three-year period from the end of 1981 to the end of 1984. The government had names and hometowns for that many victims, the lawyers said. If one added to these the numbers that Nicaraguan Defense Minister Humberto Ortega issued at the beginning of 1986 for the year 1985—1,143 Sandinista soldiers and 281 civilians dead—then the total for government and civilian deaths since the war had begun in seriousness came to fewer than 4,500 people. The government, however, made claims of killing at least four times as many rebels as it lost in manpower—supposedly 4,608 rebel dead in 1985 alone. But the rebel leadership said its combat deaths totaled only about 500 and claimed, in turn, that rebel troops had killed more than 5,600 government troops. Accepting either side's claims about the other's losses could obviously lead to wild extrapolations over several years. My inclination was to accept each side's claim for its own losses as a ballpark figure and to discount what it said about the other's losses. For one thing, losses at that level for the rebels would have represented almost a 50 percent death rate for FDN forces said to have been inside Nicaragua during 1985. Had there been as many injuries as deaths, which would have been likely, then the rebels would have had to replenish their entire force, which clearly was not the case. Trying to make sense of these figures brought to mind something said to me by a Nicaraguan who was an important Sandinista combat leader against Somoza in 1978 and 1979, but who sat out the second war in Costa Rica. "Everybody is doing the same thing we did in '79," he said, "adding a zero."

The greatest potential for human rights abuse charges lay in the civilian casualty toll. But Humberto Ortega's figure of 281 civilian deaths at rebel hands during 1985 was the only figure available upon which to base a discussion of this issue, and it was much lower than would have been expected, given the intensity of accusations against the FDN. If he were wrong, it seems likely he would have erred on the side of exaggeration, making it possible that the real toll was less. At the same time, a few of the civilian deaths he was attributing to the rebels may have been people killed by the Sandinista Army's own actions, such as the MI-24 strafings. In addition, some of those listed as civilians may have been people the rebels considered to have a combat significance. Each side made claims against the other about the way it treated civilians. Rebel leaders, for example, claimed that the Sandinistas put rebel uniforms on civilians they killed or on their own casualties and then claimed they were rebels. The Sandinistas claimed the rebels routinely killed anyone identified with the regime, including teachers, when they came into town.

It was over the degree to which the rebels ought to respond to the accusations against them that Cruz and Calero had one of their most serious disagreements, which led Cruz to consider resigning during the second half of 1985. Under the pressure of the human rights promise that President Reagan had made to Congress to obtain the renewal of aid, the three UNO leaders finally agreed to set up a human rights commission under the supervision of Cruz. But he and Calero disagreed on the degree of access and power that the commission would have in investigating and punishing acts of abuse by rebel combatants. Cruz insisted on naming Alvaro José Baldizon Avilés, a recent defector from the Sandinista government, as a human rights investigator. This irritated Calero because it meant allowing into the innermost *Contra* ranks someone who had relatives still in FSLN hands and whose loyalties were untested. Already in this war, various people had "turned" and then been turned back again. Also, as the military and political commander of the FDN, Calero felt the obligation to defend his troops, whatever international opinion thought. He eventually agreed to Baldizon's role as well as to other human rights measures after he, Cruz and Robelo signed a "coincidence" document in late 1985 that balanced the two sides of the human rights debate. It claimed that there was no disagreement over the substance of the question, adding: "Our commitment to respect human rights applies even while we are fighting against those who systematically violate the rights of other, innocent Nicaraguans. We agree across the board about the need for systematic procedures to insure that this commitment is implemented by our troops and that violations are punished. Such procedures have been in place for some time. They are continually tested and will continually be improved." It went on to add that only very naive people could imagine "that we could fight a guerrilla war with no misconduct by our troops."

There were also external pressures on the rebel leaders and their organizations to create a common political platform that would answer questions about the kind of future the rebels envisioned for Nicaragua. Much of the logic behind this lay in making the opposition more appealing to Congress, Western Europeans, intellectuals and the media. Again, there were differences based on issues from the past that many outsiders could not understand, or did not care to understand. Calero, for example, wanted no promises of a "mixed" economy or international "nonalignment," which had been among the basic tenets of the Plan of Government drawn up in San Jose, Costa Rica, in June 1979 as the Somoza regime was crumbling. Calero wanted to forget all about that, never again hear the words mixed economy and nonalignment. Mixed economy had, in his eyes, come to mean confiscation; nonalignment meant thousands of Cubans in Nicaragua. Others, however, stood by parts of the 1979 document and felt the need to defend it, depending upon their degree of responsibility for it. Some of those who had served in the Sandinista-dominated government in its early years felt that those who wanted to reject the old Plan of Government were primarily interested in recovering lost property, particularly those who had been connected to the Somoza regime. Cruz and Robelo, while neither was directly involved in writing the 1979 document, had based their positions since leaving Nicaragua upon demands that the FSLN comply with the commitments made in the Plan of Government, especially those for political pluralism and freedom of press and religion. Enrique Bermúdez's argument against creating a specific government plan was that it would, in effect, turn the FDN into a political party. Creating a political party with a plan for governing would look to many Nicaraguans, he said, like an effort to set up another one-party state. Matters of public policy, he argued, had to be decided by an electoral process once the Sandinistas were gone.

Part of the dispute between Cruz and Calero resulted from the fact that, even though they were products of the same Conservative Party political traditions inside Nicaragua, they had been thrust into different roles in exile politics. Cruz listened to liberals and intellectuals, who talked about human rights and economic and social reform. Calero listened to people who had money to contribute and talked about the need to defeat communism. Each had his journalist and columnist defenders who tried to cast the two men in good guy-bad guy roles. Cruz's advocates saw Calero as a power-hungry man with the potential to become another Somoza. Calero's advocates charged that Cruz could never make up his mind and had been involved in some of the Sandinistas' unpopular policies.

The "coincidence" document written at the end of 1985 acknowledged the existence of differences of opinion within the rebel leadership on economic and social questions but said that there was agreement on basic political procedures. "We recognize that the only legitimate source of power is a free electoral process," it said. "We agree completely on the need to overturn the Sandinistas' totalitarian control of Nicaragua. We prefer to do so by negotiation, but we recognize the need now to fight for this objective. We are determined to respect human rights even at the height of the struggle, and we hope to establish a genuinely democratic system under which every Nicaraguan has the right to participate in the political process."

EPILOGUE

There seemed, at the beginning of 1986, to be no satisfactory exit from the Nicaraguan situation. On the one hand, there was a well-armed Marxist regime unacceptable to the United States and many other countries of the region for its external policies and unacceptable for its internal policies to those Nicaraguans seeking political pluralism. On the other hand, the large anti-Sandinista armed force raised moral and ethical questions for the United States, and its actions lacked the international emotional support that had helped justify the armed opposition to Somoza in 1978–1979.

The Sandinista Front probably would have become a footnote to history had a moderate regime been able to assume power in Nicaragua before the end of 1978. But the Carter administration could not make the decision to do what was necessary to bring this about, nor could it make the decision to resume military and political backing of Somoza, which would likewise have prevented the rise of the Sandinistas, though probably with other undesirable consequences. The United States ignored its own significance in Nicaraguan history in refusing to use its power to help Nicaragua evolve into a politically open society. The Carter administration would neither back Somoza nor tell him to go. Somoza himself was determined to stay, and faced with the indecisiveness in the White House, he thought he could win the United States back to his side in time to defeat the guerrillas militarily.

The rise of the Somozas and their permanence in power for nearly half a century is a shared burden of U.S. and Nicaraguan history, and the Sandinista quest for power was, in turn, aided by the refusal of the Somozas to open the political system to all who wanted to participate. But the thesis that dictatorship of the right begets dictatorship of the left is not fully applicable here. The Somoza dynasty, in fact, permitted a greater degree of political, social, and economic liberty than most such regimes, and in that ambience, moderate political alternatives to Somoza developed. Part of this came out of Nicaragua's own political history. In addition, the United States contributed to the development of those alternatives over two decades by directing its aid programs to nongovernmental institutions as well as the government, by its support of the Central American Common Market and independent labor groups, and by maintaining contact with opposition politicians. What was missing when the whole thing came to a head was the determination of Somoza or the Carter administration that a peaceful transition should occur. Because of its desire to adhere to the nonintervention principle, the Carter administration could not make Somoza go at a time when a moderate succession could have occurred.

The leaders of the Sandinista Front intended to establish a Leninist system from the day they marched into Managua, whether they called it that or not. Their goal was to assure themselves the means to control nearly every aspect of Nicaraguan life, from beans and rice to religion. This was demonstrated by such things as creation of the block committees and other organizations under the FSLN banner, the pressure for the media to support the FSLN program, the importance attached to making the Church sympathetic to the FSLN, the political use of the army, the rapid development and expansion of the state security apparatus, and various statements and documents about future FSLN plans. All of this was under way before the end of 1979, at a time when the Carter administration's main operating premise toward the Sandinistas was to do nothing that would make the United States appear to have been responsible if Nicaragua took the path of Cuba. Also, it was before the Republicans had nominated Ronald Reagan the first time. This tends to negate the arguments that antagonism from the United States nudged Nicaragua along a totalitarian path. Any indication the Sandinista leaders gave of wanting something other than a Leninist system in Nicaragua was, as they admitted several times, for tactical or strategic purposes, not for reasons of substance.

It cannot be argued that the Sandinista Front was created by Moscow or Havana, but it is certain that the Sandinistas, from the day in 1961 when they created the FSLN, anticipated close ties to those countries. The Cuban connection was established through military training, advice, and supplies that the Cubans provided to the Sandinistas during and before the insurrection. That support carried with it the obligation to assist other guerrilla organizations. Once in power the Sandinistas turned quickly and willingly to Moscow, first accepting Bulgarian economic advisers, then seeking arms ties with the Soviets, and eventually offering themselves meekly to the Soviets in exchange for more and more weaponry. In a sense, they sold themselves for the means to stay in power in the face of failed policies and widespread unhappiness. But these ties were also the result of the Sandinistas' belief in their own principles, the ideological convictions that they themselves held, and for which they were willing to risk the wrath of the United States.

While a valid point may be raised about whether this military dependency on the Soviet bloc might have been avoided if the United States, in the first months of the new regime, had been willing to provide military equipment to the Sandinista Army, it is very likely that any such arrangement would have been hampered by the Sandinista leadership's ideological loyalty to Marxism-Leninism and by the fact that the United States would never have been willing to provide arms at the levels the Sandinistas thought necessary to consolidate their power internally.

Sandinista internal policies planted the seeds for the rise of the *Contra*. It was the broken commitments and the exercise of total power on the part of the FSLN that sent many of those who had earlier led the opposition to Somoza into subsequent armed opposition to the Sandinistas, finding common cause with the National Guardsmen of the old regime. It is also true that the Reagan administration, particularly by making CIA money available, encouraged some of those people to give up peaceful internal opposition and go into exile. Given all that happened inside Nicaragua in the first year or so after the fall of Somoza, armed opposition to the FSLN was inevitable, though the dimensions it reached were the result of U.S. support.

Two basic objections were raised to the *Contra,* even by many U.S. and foreign critics of the Sandinistas. One questioned the morality of the decision by the United States to fund and advise a paramilitary force, mine harbors and sanction—in a *Contra* training manual—the assassination of rural Sandinista officials. There was good reason for these objections, at least to some of the specific actions, but it was not as easy to argue against the general principle of backing the *Contra.* This had to be viewed in the light of the validity of the cause and the size of the military force the anti-Sandinista forces faced, and whether there were other means available.

The second objection held that the *contras* accomplished nothing except to contribute to death and destruction, including the killing of noncombatants, and that they gave the Sandinistas reason to institute repressive policies. This presumed they would not have adopted the policies they did if there had been no *contras* and ignored the sequence of events in 1979 and 1980. Had there been no *contras,* the Sandinistas might have had no justification to stockpile food, to institute the military draft, and to pressure people to join the militia. But the absence of the *contras* and other external pressures would also have made it easier for the Sandinista Front to crack down on the press, the Church, and opposition groups without attracting international criticism. It is true, for example, that the state of emergency was instituted in March 1982 in reaction to the first significant *Contra* attack, but it is also true that the state of emergency decree basically formalized the restrictions already being applied on a de facto basis. It may be true that the *Contra* operations reduced the size of the coffee harvests in 1983 and 1984, but the *contras* also forced the FSLN to orient its agrarian policies away from state farms and toward individual ownership.

In essense, while it is true that, without the *Contra,* circumstances in Nicaragua may have been marginally better in economic terms, its existence—along with all of the other external and internal pressures —represented what little hope there was to force the Sandinista Front into accepting major structural changes toward an open political system.

Among those who debated and analyzed Central America on the fringes of American policymaking—academicians, think tank scholars, writers of Op-Ed pieces, members of former administrations, and dissenters within the Reagan administration—it was often argued that a negotiated settlement was possible between the United States and the FSLN. Such a settlement, it was said, could involve an exchange: the Sandinistas' retention of power in exchange for an end to their assisting of Marxist guerrilla groups elsewhere. It was a version of the proposal that the former Assistant Secretary of State, Thomas O. Enders, had put to the FSLN in August 1981. The way the argument went, in early 1986, was that the Sandinistas, after years of guerrilla warfare, might be more inclined to satisfy the security concerns of the United States.

However, the likely price to the United States for such an agreement was the end of the *Contra*. That, in turn, would have amounted to consolidation of the Sandinista regime internally, and tacit U.S. approval for policies that would never lead to the political pluralism that was the goal of so many Nicaraguans, first when they opposed Somoza, and later when they turned against the Sandinista Front. It would have been a peace without real solutions, one that did not resolve most of the outstanding issues.

This matter of internal political pluralism, and the extent to which the United States can or should intervene to bring it about, is the real dilemma for the United States in much of its foreign relations and particularly in the Central American and Caribbean area. Intervention refers not only to direct military action but also to broader attempts to influence the internal politics of a country through all the methods at the command of the United States. Should we threaten to invade Nicaragua only if it introduces MiGs, or could we justify intervention or other forms of pressure in the interests of internal changes? Even if the tactics in question did not include invasion, could they be justified?

Just as the intervention issue had dogged the Carter administration, it also dogged the Reagan administration, which, while using different language, came no closer to resolving it. Much of the confusion about the goals and the function of the *Contra* was linked to this debate.

Reluctant to pursue an overtly interventionist policy, the Reagan administration at first refused to address directly the most legitimate part of the Nicaraguan question: the internal policies of the FSLN. Instead, the White House invented other reasons for training and financing the *Contra*. It publicly claimed the *Contra* forces existed to interrupt arms supplies from Nicaragua to guerrillas of the Farabundo Martí National Liberation Front in El Salvador, though CIA officials were allowing *Contra* militants to think that they were fighting to rescue their own country. While the evidence of logistical and advisory connections between the Sandinistas and the Salvadorans was strong, including the presence in Managua of the Salvadoran guerrilla high command, relatively few actual arms shipments were captured, and those were captured by Honduran or Costa Rican authorities, not the Nicaraguan rebels. As a result, critics of Reagan policies attacked the support for the *Contra* on these grounds, which tended to invalidate the *Contra's* own cause, and that of the entire Nicaraguan opposition, in the eyes of the outside world. Not the least of the ethical questions about the U.S. role in creating the *Contra* was whether the United States should have manipulated people who only sought for their country the things the United States had long encouraged them to seek in opposing Somoza, a chance to test political pluralism as the means of addressing its problems. The opponents of the Sandinistas, whatever their own differences and personality clashes, always had internal change in Nicaragua as their goal. Yet, they were sometimes perceived as mercenaries because of the way they were used. In September 1983, the justification for supporting the *Contra* was broadened, but it was still based on Sandinista external policies. Only after the CIA support was terminated by Congress, in 1984, did the Reagan administration begin to justify the existence of the *Contra* on the grounds of Sandinista domestic policies.

Even then, it was not fully clear whether the real purpose of the *Contra,* in the mind of the Reagan administration, was to bring down the Sandinistas (or force a major structural change in the regime) or simply to put a piece on the gameboard that could be taken off to gain something else, such as concessions on the Salvadoran guerrilla question or the departure of Nicaragua's Soviet Bloc advisers. If the Reagan administration, for example, had been serious about trying to bring down the FSLN, it would have supported *Contra* efforts to set off insurrection activities in urban areas, as the FSLN itself did in 1978–79. Instead, this proposal was dropped in early 1983 because, according to the CIA, of media suggestions that the *Contra* was trying to do something other than stop the Salvadoran guerrilla arms supply.

Gradually, however, views in Congress changed, which permitted the administration to focus its policy more directly on internal Nicaraguan issues. By mid-1985, the majority of Congress had come to accept the State Department's arguments on two major points: the basically repressive nature of the FSLN regime and that it was providing munitions and other support for the Salvadoran guerrillas. While strong voices remained in the public arena, mainly belonging to church-related and solidarity groups and academicians, that either defended the Sandinistas' internal policies or dismissed the importance of the arms issue, those involved in policymaking had sharply narrowed their differences. Congress and the administration came to share common concerns about the Sandinistas and common goals in Central America, though there were still differences over specific steps and methods. This shift led to the congressional vote in favor of resuming aid to the rebels. In turn, Congress demanded that everything be done publicly, and it forced the administration to shape and justify its policies on human rights and political grounds. Congress itself was drawn into sharing the responsibility for creating a viable force, politically and militarily, to counter the Sandinistas. Yet, there were many who continued to doubt that the *Contra* could ever defeat the Sandinista Front, or whether any degree of pressure would produce concessions from the FSLN. Those who believed strongly in supporting the rebels argued that it was necessary to persevere for the long term, as Castro did for the groups he supported, and look for breaks as time passed.

A proposed Central American peace treaty, known as Contadora for the Panamanian island where the drafting began in January 1983, attempted to deal with all of the Central American issues by committing the signatory nations to internal democratization as well as reductions in armaments and the departure of foreign military advisers. The FSLN indicated its willingness to sign the first draft of the treaty when it was produced in mid-1984, but, after a year of negotiations to satisfy the concerns of the four other Central American countries and the United States, the Sandinista government withdrew when a new draft was finished, saying that the real dispute was between it and the United States, not among the Central American nations. The issue, the Sandinista Front declared, was that the United States was supporting the anti-Sandinista rebels, and this had to be negotiated on a bilateral basis. The United States continued to insist that it would not reopen bilateral talks with Nicaragua until the Sandinistas opened a "dialogue" with representatives of the armed rebels and other opposition groups.

At the end of 1985, the Contadora effort looked dead, but in early 1986, the four countries that had undertaken to sponsor the treaty drafting, Venezuela, Mexico, Colombia, and Panama, made an effort to revive it. Both the Sandinistas and the United States expressed support. Still, the main sticking point, the argument over political principle, remained. It was not over guns, really, but over politics. The Sandinistas, on one side, and, on the other, the four other Central American governments, along with the Nicaraguan rebels and the United States, held diametrically opposing views on the kinds of political systems that were desirable. It came down to a dispute over whether it was possible to find accommodation between those who believed in a basically Leninist government structure and those trying to create, in some cases with great difficulty, basically liberal systems. While there were some differences between and among the four other Central American countries and the United States over approaches to the issue, there was general agreement that the major problems of the region were linked to the existence of the Sandinista regime in Nicaragua. Even if the Sandinistas were eventually to sign a treaty, experience had demonstrated that it was unlikely they would alter their policies in any substantial way except in the face of real or implied military force or some other insurmountable pressure.

There has been a tendency in the United States and the developed Western world in general to view Central America's crises as the result of either Cuban and Soviet support for insurgencies or internal economic and social shortcomings. Those elements were all present in Nicaragua in the insurrection against Somoza, but the roots of the dispute had been how and by whom public policy would be shaped, about the philosophical bases for decision making, which the Nicaraguans, after a century and a half of independence, were still trying to determine. That set off the insurrection against Somoza, though the other elements—outside support for insurgencies and economic and social questions—eventually contributed to it. Likewise, it was foolish to try to assess the worth of the Sandinista government on the basis of its economic and social policies when the questions of who had a right to govern and how the government should be selected had not been resolved. Putting the political issue first, whether in dealing with Somoza or later with the Sandinistas, would have allowed the United States to address its other concerns—national security and the whole range of human and civil rights issues. A political democracy along U.S. or European lines is not likely to forge military alliances and stockpile weapons contrary to U.S. interests. At the same time, it offers the possibility of ending political repression, dealing with social and economic injustice, and establishing a rule of law in which courts function as a check on the excesses of the military and the executive power.

But bringing this about implies more intervention than the United

States has been willing to tackle in its recent history, except when things have reached the point of outright military operations. Even when President Hoover withdrew the Marines at the beginning of 1933, he did so largely in reaction to the public outcry against intervention. Part of the problem is the pejorative connotation of the word intervention. The basic tenets of international relations since World War II have been nonintervention and self-determination, though most Third World governments have been more concerned with advocating nonintervention from the podiums of international forums than with practicing self-determination at home. Cuba and the Soviet Union get around the connotation associated with intervention by using another term, internationalism, to describe their attempts to guide the development of other countries along statist, totalitarian lines. Internationalism has a more positive ring to it than intervention.

It is valid to argue that the United States cannot intervene wherever in the world there is a government it does not like, that the United States cannot be a global policeman. But foreign policy must be formulated in response to the dynamics of specific situations, taking into account a country's internal situation, its location, and the history of its relationship with the United States. Only by promoting democratic political development on a long-term basis can the United States hope to avoid the hard choices between sending troops and living with untenable situations.

The bitter lesson for the United States is that a democracy, especially one that allows broad participation in the formulation and conduct of foreign policy, cannot let a situation reach a point that demands a black and white choice between national security and national conscience. The United States should not allow itself to be trapped into having to accept, in an area as closely tied to it as Central America, either a repressive right-wing dictatorship because it is not threatening to U.S. national security or a repressive left-wing dictatorship in exchange for commitments not to overthrow a neighboring government or acquire MiGs.

The hour was late for this lesson to be applied in Nicaragua. Those who wanted democracy there were left in a vise, forced to accept that their goals were hostage to other people's priorities. The establishment of a totalitarian regime, tragically, was seen as secondary. As so often in the past, Nicaraguans faced the bitter realization that their own needs, and dreams, were subjugated to matters beyond their borders.

SOURCE NOTES

To a large extent, the sources used in this book, both individuals and documents, are apparent in the text. I have generally identified people who gave me information in interviews or have indicated when something came from a public speech or news conference. Many of the episodes in the book were events that I witnessed. In addition, I have made use of news accounts from three Nicaraguan newspapers, *Barricada, El Nuevo Diario,* and *La Prensa,* the reports of the Foreign Broadcast Information Service, and four U.S. newspapers, the Miami *Herald,* the Los Angeles *Times,* the New York *Times,* and the Washington *Post.*

What follows is an indication of the major interviews for various chapters, plus printed material that was used in addition to the media cited above, and explanations about some specific pieces of information. Not every chapter is mentioned because in some chapters all of the sources are cited directly or the information comes from the news media cited above.

1 THE BAGGAGE OF THE PAST

INTERVIEWS:
Leopoldo Salazar Amador.

BOOKS:
Carr, Albert Z., *The World and William Walker* (New York: Harper, 1963).

Millett, Richard, *The Guardians of the Dynasty* (Maryknoll, N.Y.: Orbis, 1977).

Macaulay, Neill, *The Sandino Affair* (Chicago: Quadrangle, 1967).

Selser, Gregorio, *Sandino, General de Hombres Libres* (Editorial Universitaria Centroamericana: San José, Costa Rica, 1980).

Román, José, *Maldito País* (Managua: Editorial Union, 1983).

Beals, Carleton, *Banana Gold* (Philadelphia: Lippincott, 1932).

2 THE YEARS OF THE DYNASTY

BOOKS:
Borge, Tomás, et al., *Sandinistas Speak* (New York: Pathfinder, 1982).

Chamorro, Pedro Joaquín, *La Patria de Pedro* (Managua: La Prensa, 1981).

Diederich, Bernard, *Somoza* (New York: Dutton, 1981).

Hernández Sancho, Plutarco, *El FSLN por Dentro* (Self-published: San José, Costa Rica, 1982).

Nolan, David, *FSLN: The Ideology of the Sandinistas and the Nicaraguan Revolution* (Coral Gables, Fla.: University of Miami, 1984).

Wheelock Román, Jaime, *Frente Sandinista: Hacia la Ofensiva Final* (Havana: Editorial de Ciencias Sociales, 1980).

Wheelock Román, Jaime, *Imperialismo y Dictadura* (Mexico: Siglo Vientiuno, 1975).

DOCUMENTS, SPECIAL ARTICLES, AND SPEECHES:
Fonseca, Carlos, *"Pensamientos,"* published by Instituto de Estudio de Sandinismo, November 4, 1982.

Molina, Uriel, *"El Sendero de una Experiencia,"* published in *Nicarauac,* quarterly magazine of the Nicaraguan Ministry of Culture, April 1981.

Ortega, Humberto, *"Carlos; el eslabón vital de nuestra historia,"* text published in *El Nuevo Diario,* November 12, 1981.

Permanent Commission of Human Rights of Nicaragua: various documents and reports.

Ruiz, Henry, *"La Montaña era como un Crisol donde se forjaban los mejores Cuadros,"* *Nicarauac,* May 1980.

The material on the business community and its relations with Somoza after the 1972 earthquake comes from interviews with various businessmen and news accounts at the time. The background on Nicaragua Sugar Estates Ltd. comes from Julio Vivas Benard, a descendant of one of the early owners.

3–7 THE DYNASTY WEAKENED, THE CATALYSTS, THE MEDIATION, THE INSURRECTION BEGINS, DEFEAT AND TRIUMPH

INTERVIEWS:

Jerry Apodaca, Zbigniew Brzezinski, Adolfo Calero Portocarrero, Rodrigo Carazo, Ernesto Cardenal, Alfredo César, Violeta Barrios de Chamorro, Arturo J. Cruz, Joaquín Cuadra Chamorro, Juan José (Johnny) Echeverría Brealey, Elio Espinar, Plutarco Hernández Sancho, Gabriel Lewis Galindo, Felipe Mántica, (Ret.) Lt. Col. James L. McCoy, Haroldo Montealegre, Ambler H. Moss, Jr., John Murphy, Luis Pallais Debayle, Robert Pastor, Carl Perian, Lawrence Pezzullo, Leonel Poveda, Ismael Reyes, Alfonso Robelo Callejas, Mauricio Solaun, Carlos Tünnermann Bernheim, and various sources who requested anonymity, including former members of the U.S. Embassy staff in Managua and San José, Costa Rica, other current and former State Department officials, a CIA source, some Nicaraguan sources, and one Colombian intimately involved in these events.

BOOKS:

Diederich, Bernard, *Somoza* (New York: Dutton, 1981).

Hernández Sancho, Plutarco, *El FSLN por Dentro* (San José, Costa Rica: Self-published, 1982).

Peña, Alfredo, *Conversaciones con Carlos Andrés Pérez* (Caracas: Editorial Ateneo, 1979).

Somoza Debayle, Anastasio, and Cox, Jack, *Nicaragua Betrayed* (Belmont, Mass.: Western Islands, 1980).

Urcuyo Maliaño, Francisco, *Solos* (Guatemala: Editorial Academica Centro Americana, 1979).

DOCUMENTS AND SPECIAL ARTICLES:

"Cuban Support for Central American Guerrilla Groups," CIA Memorandum dated May 2, 1979, published in the Congressional Record for May 19, 1980.

Documents of the Group of Twelve for 1978, compiled and made available by Carlos Tünnermann Bernheim.

Documents of the Broad Opposition Front for 1978 and 1979, compiled by the Instituto Nicaraguense de Desarrollo.

"Informe Sobre el Trafico de Armas," report of investigation into arms trafficking by the Comision de Asuntos Especiales of the Costa Rican Legislative Assembly, dated May 14, 1981.

"Implications of an Orthodox Communist Political System in Nicaragua," by Arturo J. Cruz, Occasional Papers, Institute of Interamerican Studies, Graduate School of International Studies, University of Miami, Coral Gables, Fla.

"La Estrategia de la Victoria," pamphlet containing two interviews with Humberto Ortega Saavedra, published March 1980, by the Junta of National Reconstruction.

Letter dated July 12, 1979, in San José, Costa Rica, from the Nicaraguan junta to Alejandro Orfila, secretary-general of the Organization of American States.

Program of Government of the Junta of Government of National Reconstruction, issued in San José, Costa Rica, June 1979.

"Report to the Secretary of State on the Work of the International Commission of Friendly Cooperation and Conciliation for Achieving a Peaceful Solution to the Grave Crisis of the Republic of Nicaragua," prepared by special envoy William Bowdler in early 1979.

Series of communiqués of the Sandinista National Liberation Front (FSLN) published in the newspaper *Novedades,* Augusto 26, 1978.

"Testimonio del Comandante Edén Pastora," Pastora's account of the Palace Raid, published in *El Nuevo Diario,* July 12, 1981.

8 THE TROUBLED HONEYMOON

INTERVIEWS:

Tomás Borge, Adolfo Calero, Arturo Cruz, Lucio Jiménez (national director of the Sandinista labor federation), Leonel Poveda, Alfonso Robelo.

DOCUMENTS:

"Analisis de la Coyuntura y Tareas de la Revolucion Popular Sandinista," report issued by FSLN National Directorate of meeting held September 21–23, 1979.

"Un Nuevo Marco Socio-Economico dentro de la Revolucion," annual report of the president of the Nicaraguan Development Institute, issued February 29, 1980.

Permanent Commission of Human Rights of Nicaragua: Various documents and reports.

9 CUBANS, GRINGOS, PANAMANIANS, AND "REVOLUTIONARY INTERNATIONALISM"

INTERVIEWS:

Arturo Cruz, Lawrence E. Harrison, Ambler H. Moss, Jr., Lawrence Pezzullo.

10 THE RUPTURE

INTERVIEWS:

José Francisco Cardenal, Pedro Joaquín Chamorro Barrios, Violeta Barrios de Chamorro, Xavier Chamorro Cardenal, Lawrence Pezzullo, Sergio Ramírez, Alfonso Robelo, and numerous other sources in Nicaragua during and after the events who requested anonymity.

12 JORGE SALAZAR AND ELECTIONS

INTERVIEWS:

Raúl Arana, José Francisco Cardenal, Lucía Cardenal de Salazar, Ramiro Gurdian, Alejandro Salazar, Leonardo Somarriba.

DOCUMENTS:

Documents of the First District Criminal Court of Managua.

13 THE VANGUARD

The analysis of the nine *comandantes* is the result of conclusions I drew over a five-year period of reporting in Nicaragua, based on information and interpretations from numerous Nicaraguan sources, inside and outside the government, and foreign diplomats.

14 THE *CONTRA* AND RONALD REAGAN

INTERVIEWS:
Raúl Arana, José Francisco Cardenal, Lawrence Pezzullo, and various State Department sources who requested anonymity.

15 THE CHALLENGE TO THE CHURCH

INTERVIEWS:
The Reverend Rafael Aragon, Sister Luz Beatriz Arellano, Monsignor José Arias Caldera, Emilio Baltodano Cantarero (as secretary to the junta), the Reverend Ernesto Cardenal, the Reverend Miguel Angel Casco, Archbishop Miguel Obando y Bravo, the Reverend Edgard Parrales, the Reverend Sixto Ulloa, Bishop Pablo Antonio Vega, Monsignor Bosco Vivas.

BOOKS:
Gutiérrez, Gustavo, *Frontiers of Theology in Latin America* (Maryknoll, N.Y.: Orbis Books, 1979).
Gutiérrez, Gustavo, *Liberation and Change* (Atlanta, Ga.: John Knox Press, 1977).
Gutiérrez, Gustavo, *A Theology of Liberation* (Maryknoll, N.Y.: Orbis Books, 1971).
Lernoux, Penny, *Cry of the People* (New York: Doubleday, 1980).
Pico, Juan, et al., *Apuntes para una Theología Nicaraguense* (Managua: Centro Antonio Valdivieso and the Instituto Historico Centroamericano 1980).

DOCUMENTS AND SPECIAL ARTICLES:
Belli, Humberto, editor, *Una Iglesia en Peligro,* pamphlet containing documents about the Nicaraguan church conflict published by *Confederacion de Laicos para la Fe* in Bogota, Colombia, February 1983.

FSLN Communiqué on Religion, issued October 7, 1980.

Molina, Uriel, *"El Sendero de una Experiencia,"* published in *Nicarauac,* April 1981.

Pastoral letters and statements made public by the Nicaraguan bishops' conference or the Managua archdiocese.

Various issues of *Amanecer,* the newsletter of the Valdivieso Center.

Vatican letters and statements made public by the Managua archdiocese or at the Vatican.

19 AMONG THOSE WHO LEFT

INTERVIEWS:
Edén Pastora, Leonel Poveda, Haroldo Montealegre, Arturo Cruz, Alfonso Robelo, José Esteban González, Edgard Macías, Adolfo Calero.

20 TWO WHO STAYED

INTERVIEWS:
Omar Cabezas and Violeta Barrios de Chamorro.

21 NOVEMBER 1984

For the factual information in the final chapter about the period before and during the election campaign in Nicaragua I am particularly indebted to Juan O. Tamayo of the Miami *Herald* for his superior reporting and other details that he provided me.

22 THE STRANGEST OF WARS

INTERVIEWS:
Alvaro José Baldizon Avilés, Enrique Bermúdez, Adolfo Calero, Arturo Cruz, Larry Duych, Ellen Garwood, Hubert Rodríguez, Aristides Sánchez, (Ret.) Maj. Gen. John K. Singlaub, William J. Murray, and various United States government officials who requested anonymity.

DOCUMENTS AND SPECIAL ARTICLES:

Report of the Select Committee on Intelligence, United States Senate, January 1, 1983, to December 31, 1984.

Calero, Adolfo; Cruz, Arturo José; and Robelo Callejas, Alfonso, " 'Contras' are on the Right Track," statement published on Op-Ed Page of *The New York Times*, December 13, 1985.

APPENDIX

Following is the text of the statement that Edén Pastora read in San José, Costa Rica, on April 15, 1982, announcing his break with the FSLN. The translation is the author's.

I will be the watchful eye to see that the revolution is never subverted or betrayed. This is what I declared on July 20, 1979, in the Plaza of the Revolution in Managua, Nicaragua. Historic circumstances assign responsibilities to men. Those circumstances oblige me to comply with my obligation as a Nicaraguan Sandinista. I was born in the obscurity with which *somocismo* dishonored and degraded my homeland, Nicaragua. At the age of seven I suffered the loss of my father, when he was assassinated by the oppressors of my people. When I grew up, I realized that many other Nicaraguan families were suffering the same grief. Later, thanks to the opportunities for education that my mother offered me, I discovered the sad reality that U.S. imperialism had violated the sovereignty of my country many times and that the great majority of my fellow citizens were victims of the most degrading social injustice.

In the course of my education I also learned that there had been a patriot who loved Nicaragua immensely and that he gave his life in his fight for the liberation of us Nicaraguans. That man, Augusto César Sandino, is the fundamental inspiration of my civic life.

When I was very young I made the decision to be a revolutionary. I learned that it was necessary to take up arms to overthrow the tyrant and I abandoned my medical studies in Guadalajara, Mexico.

With the maturity brought by years of fighting, I became convinced that the only way to find real peace was through the establishment of democracy and the elimination of exploitation and all kinds of injustice.

Since I come from a family of working people, I alternated my periods of armed struggle in the mountains with periods of work in cattle raising, farming, commerce, and fishing. It may be to that experience that I owe my firm belief in the need for guarantees and incentives for production and investment as bases for economic development.

The despotism of the system that prevailed for more than forty years awakened in me the abhorrence of arbitrary rule and the love of individual liberty. Those principles form the bases of my revolutionary ideas, and I want to make clear once and for all that I have never concerned myself with doctrinaire labels. Guided by those principles, I was one of the founders of the Sandino Revolutionary Front in 1959, the first revolutionary movement that vindicated General Sandino as the immortal leader of our resurgence as a sovereign people.

Later, in 1961, I reaffirmed my Sandinista ideals—anti-imperialist, democratic, and popular—as one of those who forged the Sandinista Front of National Liberation, to which I have the honor of having given twenty-one years of discipline and loyal militancy. In 1976 I ended a period of tranquility and work at the side of my beloved wife and children in order to begin another chapter of struggle, responding to a call from my Sandinista companions. On that occasion I kept an appointment on the field of battle for what was the beginning of a transcendental crusade in the history of my people: the unification of all the national sectors in order to expel the dynastic tyrant from our homeland forever and establish a system of social revolution. An eminently just revolution, with the help of everyone, with hate for no one, motivated by justice and ready to defend the national sovereignty.

I must say with pride that the Sandinista Front of National Liberation, by taking up the glorious red and black flag of General Sandino as the historic vanguard in the war of liberation, has created the greatest epic in the national history. The Sandinista Front of National Liberation gave many martyrs and heroes to the nation. Many other citizens made sacrifices to support the fight for the liberation of our people. The biggest was that of Sandino, then his glorious generals and other companions, heroes whose names have been left in oblivion because of ingratitude and injustice. . . .

Together with other companions, I gave my contribution to the war of liberation, commanding the various missions that the revolutionary high command assigned to me, among them the taking of Rivas, the National Palace, and the political-military campaign of the Southern Front. I render respectful homage to the martyrs and heroes who made that glorious gesture possible, including the illustrious guerrilla priest Gaspar Garcia Laviana.

After the triumph I gave my services enthusiastically for the consolidation of the revolution, fulfilling whatever job the National Directorate of the Sandinista Front of National Liberation ordered me to do. Nevertheless, from the moment of the triumph I noted political and even moral deviations that endangered the revolutionary process and the very security of the Nicaraguan state.

I pointed out to my superiors the risk to which those imprudent acts and errors could expose the country. I did it in the interest of rectification and with revolutionary loyalty. After getting no response, I decided that the most appropriate thing was for me to separate myself from the government, channeling my revolutionary ideals into internationalism as a continuation of *sandinismo.* I made this decision with profound regret and without rancor. My dissidence and my cooperation have been, are, and will always be within the revolution.

I have kept silent, confident that patriotism would prevail among the leaders of the revolution. But my exhortations were never heard and, in response, I was attacked politically by those who considered themselves my brothers. Today, after ten months of prudent silence, I find myself obliged to break that silence and make public my attitude. At the same time I want to make clear my categorical repudiation of any aggressive action against my people and that I am disposed and prepared to combat from my trench any violation of the national soil.

Those Nicaraguans who truly love Nicaragua and who desire success for a just revolutionary process note with satisfaction the peace initiative of the president of Mexico, José López Portillo. I include myself among such Nicaraguans. The peace of our people is aided by the extent to which we are truly nonaligned. Contradictions and ambiguities have no place in *sandinismo.* Just as the invasion of Vietnam was imperialistic, so the invasion of Afghanistan is imperialistic. Just as a [country] that supports a fascist junta in El Salvador is imperialistic, so is that which supports a totalitarian regime in Poland. Our *sandinismo* cannot permit that we be caught up in the East-West conflict, since that is contrary to the national interests.

We know that injustice and class exploitation are the roots of the tragedy that Central America is living through and we must attack those roots with zeal. Today, just as yesterday, people have the obligation to liberate themselves from oppression and exploitation.

We must promote Central American fraternity, allowing each brother nation to seek social transformation by the way most suitable to its own reality and interests. In that connection, we must aspire for our revolution to be truly Nicaraguan, as the Mexican revolution is Mexican and the Cuban revolution is Cuban—to which I render homage of admiration. Both have positive aspects that could enrich our revolution, but we must preserve [our revolution's] genuine, Nicaraguan character.

I am an internationalist because I am a free man and I want to contribute to the liberation of all men. The total unselfishness of Commander Ernesto "Che" Guevara is, for me, a motive of inspiration. I am grateful . . . for the support that the internationalists of Panama, Costa Rica, Cuba, and other brother nations gave us during the war and are giving us now during the endangered peace. [But] in this moment, I express the sentiments of the majority of Nicaraguans when I say that the hour has arrived when they [the internationalists] should leave us alone—those who are not involved in activities that contribute to health and education. As someone who loves my people I take honor, like Sandino, in calling for all Nicaraguans to put themselves on a war footing as long as there is a foreign soldier on the native soil.

I know that the ranks of the Sandinista Popular Army and the Sandinista Popular Militia are filled by men and women of honor and love and that they constitute the only guarantee that the revolution is irreversible. Today I appeal to that honor and that love. The national economy, vital for the revolution, will recover only if we create a political climate that stimulates production and investment within a mixed economic system. A political system that generates internal and external peace can only be that in which democracy enjoys the status to which it is entitled, without omitting party pluralism, free elections, strict respect for individual rights, and the restoration of the rights of the worker.

The freedom of worship is not a simple declaration. It must be a reality that receives the most profound respect.

The revolution has no need to limit the freedom of press, since if it does, then the walls and fences, even in the prisons, will become newspapers.

The fundamental statute of the republic, the statute on rights and guarantees of Nicaraguans, is not complied with when, in the light of day or under cover of night, the seizures, confiscations, and expropriations overwhelm *somocistas* and anti-*somocistas,* counterrevolutionaries and revolutionaries, guilty and innocent. In the jails counterrevolutionaries rub elbows with Marxist revolutionaries, the latter being castigated for the serious crime of interpreting Marx differently than their comrades in power. With sorrow I have seen that intranquility reigns among my people, also anguish, fear, bitter frustration, personal insecurity. Our Miskito, Sumo, and Rama Indians are persecuted, jailed, or assassinated. And the press and radio are unable to denounce to the world this regime of terror that the feared State Security creates on the Atlantic Coast and in all of Nicaragua.

For all the reasons I have stated here I wish to make clear my disagreement with the conduct of the National Directorate, since to continue otherwise would force the people to pay a very high cost, even a return to the past, unless an armed people expels from power those whom the accusing and condemning finger of Sandino points to as traitors and assassins.

Index

ABOUT THE AUTHOR

SHIRLEY CHRISTIAN was born in a farmhouse in western Missouri and grew up in Kansas City. She earned degrees from Pittsburg (Kansas) State University and Ohio State and was a Nieman Fellow at Harvard. As a journalist, she has worked in many Latin American countries, first for the Associated Press, later for the Miami *Herald* and the New York *Times*. Her coverage of Central America for the *Herald* won the Pulitzer Prize for international reporting in 1981 and the George Polk Award for foreign reporting in perilous circumstances. She has also written about Central America for the *Atlantic Monthly* and the *New Republic*. She is now a bureau chief for the New York *Times* in Buenos Aires.